NON SANS DROICT.

THE MOST LA-
mentable Romaine
Tragedie of Titus Andronicus:

As it was Plaide by the Right Ho-
nourable the Earle of *Darbie*, Earle of *Pembrooke*,
and Earle of *Sussex* their Seruants.

LONDON,

Printed by Iohn Danter, and are
to be sold by *Edward White* & *Thomas Millington*,
at the little North doore of Paules at the
signe of the Gunne.
1594.

William Shakespeare

The Tragedy of Titus Andronicus

Edited by Sylvan Barnet

The Life of Timon of Athens

Edited by Maurice Charney

With New and Updated Critical Essays and a Revised Bibliography

THE SIGNET CLASSICS SHAKESPEARE
General Editor: Sylvan Barnet

SIGNET CLASSICS

SIGNET CLASSICS
Published by New American Library, a division of
Penguin Group (USA) Inc., 375 Hudson Street,
New York, New York 10014, USA
Penguin Group (Canada), 90 Eglinton Avenue East, Suite 700, Toronto,
Ontario M4P 2Y3, Canada (a division of Pearson Penguin Canada Inc.)
Penguin Books Ltd., 80 Strand, London WC2R 0RL, England
Penguin Ireland, 25 St. Stephen's Green, Dublin 2,
Ireland (a division of Penguin Books Ltd.)
Penguin Group (Australia), 250 Camberwell Road, Camberwell, Victoria 3124,
Australia (a division of Pearson Australia Group Pty. Ltd.)
Penguin Books India Pvt. Ltd., 11 Community Centre, Panchsheel Park,
New Delhi - 110 017, India
Penguin Group (NZ), 67 Apollo Drive, Rosedale, North Shore 0632,
New Zealand (a division of Pearson New Zealand Ltd.)
Penguin Books (South Africa) (Pty.) Ltd., 24 Sturdee Avenue,
Rosebank, Johannesburg 2196, South Africa

Penguin Books Ltd., Registered Offices:
80 Strand, London WC2R 0RL, England

Published by Signet Classics, an imprint of New American Library,
a division of Penguin Group (USA) Inc.

First Signet Classics Printing (Second Revised Edition), January 2005

Contents

Shakespeare: An Overview

Biographical Sketch

Between the record of his baptism in Stratford on 26 April 1564 and the record of his burial in Stratford on 25 April 1616, some forty official documents name Shakespeare, and many others name his parents, his children, and his grandchildren. Further, there are at least fifty literary references to him in the works of his contemporaries. More facts are known about William Shakespeare than about any other playwright of the period except Ben Jonson. The facts should, however, be distinguished from the legends. The latter, inevitably more engaging and better known, tell us that the Stratford boy killed a calf in high style, poached deer and rabbits, and was forced to flee to London, where he held horses outside a playhouse. These traditions are only traditions; they may be true, but no evidence supports them, and it is well to stick to the facts.

Mary Arden, the dramatist's mother, was the daughter of a substantial landowner; about 1557 she married John Shakespeare, a tanner, glove-maker, and trader in wool, grain, and other farm commodities. In 1557 John Shakespeare was a member of the council (the governing body of Stratford), in 1558 a constable of the borough, in 1561 one of the two town chamberlains, in 1565 an alderman (entitling him to the appellation of "Mr."), in 1568 high bailiff—the town's highest political office, equivalent to mayor. After 1577, for an unknown reason he drops out of local politics. What *is* known is that he had to mortgage his wife's property, and that he was involved in serious litigation.

The birthday of William Shakespeare, the third child and the eldest son of this locally prominent man, is unrecorded, but the Stratford parish register records that the infant was baptized on 26 April 1564. (It is quite possible that he was born on 23 April, but this date has probably been assigned by tradition because it is the date on which, fifty-two years later, he died, and perhaps because it is the feast day of St. George, patron saint of England.) The attendance records of the Stratford grammar school of the period are not extant, but it is reasonable to assume that the son of a prominent local official attended the free school—it had been established for the purpose of educating males precisely of his class—and received substantial training in Latin. The masters of the school from Shakespeare's seventh to fifteenth years held Oxford degrees; the Elizabethan curriculum excluded mathematics and the natural sciences but taught a good deal of Latin rhetoric, logic, and literature, including plays by Plautus, Terence, and Seneca.

On 27 November 1582 a marriage license was issued for the marriage of Shakespeare and Anne Hathaway, eight years his senior. The couple had a daughter, Susanna, in May 1583. Perhaps the marriage was necessary, but perhaps the couple had earlier engaged, in the presence of witnesses, in a formal "troth plight" which would render their children legitimate even if no further ceremony were performed. In February 1585, Anne Hathaway bore Shakespeare twins, Hamnet and Judith.

That Shakespeare was born is excellent; that he married and had children is pleasant; but that we know nothing about his departure from Stratford to London or about the beginning of his theatrical career is lamentable and must be admitted. We would gladly sacrifice details about his children's baptism for details about his earliest days in the theater. Perhaps the poaching episode is true (but it is first reported almost a century after Shakespeare's death), or perhaps he left Stratford to be a schoolmaster, as another tradition holds; perhaps he was moved (like Petruchio in *The Taming of the Shrew*) by

> Such wind as scatters young men through the world,
> To seek their fortunes farther than at home
> Where small experience grows.   (1.2.49–51)

In 1592, thanks to the cantankerousness of Robert Greene, we have our first reference, a snarling one, to Shakespeare as an actor and playwright. Greene, a graduate of St. John's College, Cambridge, had become a playwright and a pamphleteer in London, and in one of his pamphlets he warns three university-educated playwrights against an actor who has presumed to turn playwright:

> There is an upstart crow, beautified with our feathers, that with his *tiger's heart wrapped in a player's hide* supposes he is as well able to bombast out a blank verse as the best of you, and being an absolute Johannes-factotum [i.e., jack-of-all-trades] is in his own conceit the only Shake-scene in a country.

The reference to the player, as well as the allusion to Aesop's crow (who strutted in borrowed plumage, as an actor struts in fine words not his own), makes it clear that by this date Shakespeare had both acted and written. That Shakespeare is meant is indicated not only by *Shake-scene* but also by the parody of a line from one of Shakespeare's plays, *3 Henry VI*: "O, tiger's heart wrapped in a woman's hide" (1.4.137). If in 1592 Shakespeare was prominent enough to be attacked by an envious dramatist, he probably had served an apprenticeship in the theater for at least a few years.

In any case, although there are no extant references to Shakespeare between the record of the baptism of his twins in 1585 and Greene's hostile comment about "Shake-scene" in 1592, it is evident that during some of these "dark years" or "lost years" Shakespeare had acted and written. There are a number of subsequent references to him as an actor. Documents indicate that in 1598 he is a "principal comedian," in 1603 a "principal tragedian," in 1608 he is one of the "men players." (We do not have, however, any solid information about which roles he may have played; later traditions say he played Adam in *As You Like It* and the ghost in *Hamlet*, but nothing supports the assertions. Probably his role as dramatist came to supersede his role as actor.) The profession of actor was not for a gentleman, and it occasionally drew the scorn of university men like Greene who resented writing speeches for persons less educated than themselves, but it was respectable enough; players, if prosperous, were in effect members of the bourgeoisie, and there is nothing to suggest that Stratford considered William Shakespeare less than a solid citizen. When, in 1596, the Shakespeares were granted a coat of arms—i.e., the right to be considered gentlemen—the grant was made to Shakespeare's father, but probably William Shakespeare had arranged the matter on his own behalf. In subsequent transactions he is occasionally styled a gentleman.

Although in 1593 and 1594 Shakespeare published two narrative poems dedicated to the Earl of Southampton, *Venus and Adonis* and *The Rape of Lucrece*, and may well have written most or all of his sonnets in the middle nineties, Shakespeare's literary activity seems to have been almost entirely devoted to the theater. (It may be significant that the two narrative poems were written in years when the plague closed the theaters for several months.) In 1594 he was a charter member of a theatrical company called the Chamberlain's Men, which in 1603 became the royal company, the King's Men, making Shakespeare the king's playwright. Until he retired to Stratford (about 1611, apparently), he was with this remarkably stable company. From 1599 the company acted primarily at the Globe theater, in which Shakespeare held a one-tenth interest. Other Elizabethan dramatists are known to have acted, but no other is known also to have been entitled to a share of the profits.

Shakespeare's first eight published plays did not have his name on them, but this is not remarkable; the most popular play of the period, Thomas Kyd's *The Spanish Tragedy*, went through many editions without naming Kyd, and Kyd's authorship is known only because a book on the profession of acting happens to quote (and attribute to Kyd) some lines on the interest of Roman emperors in the drama. What is remarkable is that after 1598 Shakespeare's name commonly appears on printed plays—some of which are not his. Presumably his name was a drawing card, and publishers used it to attract potential buyers. Another indication of his popularity comes from Francis Meres, author of *Palladis Tamia: Wit's Treasury* (1598). In this anthology of snippets accompanied by an essay on literature, many playwrights are mentioned, but Shakespeare's name occurs more often than any other, and Shakespeare is the only playwright whose plays are listed.

From his acting, his playwriting, and his share in a playhouse, Shakespeare seems to have made considerable money. He put it to work, making substantial investments in Stratford real estate. As early as 1597 he bought New Place, the second-largest house in Stratford. His family moved in soon afterward, and the house remained in the family until a granddaughter died in 1670. When Shakespeare made his will in 1616, less than a month before he died, he sought to leave his property intact to his descendants. Of small bequests to relatives and to friends (including three actors, Richard Burbage, John Heminges, and Henry Condell), that to his wife of the second-best bed has provoked the most comment. It has sometimes been taken as a sign of an unhappy marriage (other supposed signs are the apparently hasty marriage, his wife's seniority of eight years, and his residence in London without his family). Perhaps the second-best bed was the bed the couple had slept in, the best bed being reserved for visitors. In any case, had Shakespeare not excepted it, the bed would have gone (with the rest of his household possessions) to his daughter and her husband.

On 25 April 1616 Shakespeare was buried within the chancel of the church at Stratford. An unattractive monument to his memory, placed on a wall near the grave, says that he died on 23 April. Over the grave itself are the lines, perhaps by Shakespeare, that (more than his literary fame) have kept his bones undisturbed in the crowded burial ground where old bones were often dislodged to make way for new:

> Good friend, for Jesus' sake forbear
> To dig the dust enclosed here.
> Blessed be the man that spares these stones
> And cursed be he that moves my bones.

A Note on the Anti-Stratfordians, Especially Baconians and Oxfordians

Not until 1769—more than a hundred and fifty years after Shakespeare's death—is there any record of anyone expressing doubt about Shakespeare's authorship of the plays and poems. In 1769, however, Herbert Lawrence nominated Francis Bacon (1561–1626) in *The Life and Adventures of Common Sense*. Since then, at least two dozen other nominees have been offered, including Christopher Marlowe, Sir Walter Raleigh, Queen Elizabeth I, and Edward de Vere, 17th earl of Oxford. The impulse behind all anti-Stratfordian movements is the scarcely concealed snobbish opinion that "the man from Stratford" simply could not have written the plays because he was a country fellow without a university education and without access to high society. Anyone, the argument goes, who used so many legal terms, medical terms, nautical terms, and so forth, and who showed some familiarity with classical writing, must have attended a university, and anyone who knew so much about courtly elegance and courtly deceit must himself have moved among courtiers. The plays do indeed reveal an author whose interests were exceptionally broad, but specialists in any given field—law, medicine, arms and armor, and so on—soon find that the plays do not reveal deep knowledge in specialized matters; indeed, the playwright often gets technical details wrong.

The claim on behalf of Bacon, forgotten almost as soon as it was put forth in 1769, was independently reasserted by Joseph C. Hart in 1848. In 1856 it was reaffirmed by W. H. Smith in a book, and also by Delia Bacon in an article; in 1857 Delia Bacon published a book, arguing that Francis Bacon had directed a group of intellectuals who wrote the plays.

Francis Bacon's claim has largely faded, perhaps because it was advanced with such evident craziness by Ignatius Donnelly, who in *The Great Cryptogram* (1888) claimed to break a code in the plays that proved Bacon had written not only the plays attributed to Shakespeare but also other Renaissance works, for instance the plays of Christopher Marlowe and the essays of Montaigne.

Consider the last two lines of the Epilogue in *The Tempest*:

As you from crimes would pardoned be,
Let your indulgence set me free.

What was Shakespeare—sorry, Francis Bacon, Baron Verulam—*really* saying in these two lines? According to Baconians, the lines are an anagram reading, "Tempest of Francis Bacon, Lord Verulam; do ye ne'er divulge me, ye words." Ingenious, and it is a pity that in the quotation the letter *a* appears only twice in the cryptogram, whereas in the deciphered message it appears three times. Oh, no problem; just alter "Verulam" to "Verul'm" and it works out very nicely.

Most people understand that with sufficient ingenuity one can torture any text and find in it what one wishes. For instance: Did Shakespeare have a hand in the King James Version of the Bible? It was nearing completion in 1610, when Shakespeare was forty-six years old. If you look at the 46th Psalm and count forward for forty-six words, you will find the word *shake*. Now if you go to the end of the psalm and count backward forty-six words, you will find the word *spear*. Clear evidence, according to some, that Shakespeare slyly left his mark in the book.

Bacon's candidacy has largely been replaced in the twentieth century by the candidacy of Edward de Vere (1550–1604), 17th earl of Oxford. The basic ideas behind the Oxford theory, advanced at greatest length by Dorothy and Charlton Ogburn in *This Star of England* (1952, rev. 1955), a book of 1297 pages, and by Charlton Ogburn in *The Mysterious William Shakespeare* (1984), a book of 892 pages, are these: (1) The man from Stratford could not possibly have had the mental equipment and the experience to have written the plays—only a courtier could have written them; (2) Oxford had the requisite background (social position, education, years at Queen Elizabeth's court); (3) Oxford did not wish his authorship to be known for two basic reasons: writing for the public theater was a vulgar pursuit, and the plays show so much courtly and royal disreputable behavior that they would have compromised Oxford's position at court. Oxfordians offer countless details to support the claim. For example, Hamlet's phrase "that ever I was born to set it right" (1.5.89) barely conceals "E. Ver, I was born to set it right," an unambiguous announcement of de Vere's authorship, according to *This Star of England* (p. 654). A second example: Consider Ben

Jonson's poem entitled "To the Memory of My Beloved Master William Shakespeare," prefixed to the first collected edition of Shakespeare's plays in 1623. According to Oxfordians, when Jonson in this poem speaks of the author of the plays as the "swan of Avon," he is alluding not to William Shakespeare, who was born and died in Stratford-on-Avon and who throughout his adult life owned property there; rather, he is alluding to Oxford, who, the Ogburns say, used "William Shakespeare" as his pen name, and whose manor at Bilton was on the Avon River. Oxfordians do not offer any evidence that Oxford took a pen name, and they do not care that Oxford had sold the manor in 1581, forty-two years before Jonson wrote his poem. Surely a reference to the Shakespeare who was born in Stratford, who had returned to Stratford, and who had died there only seven years before Jonson wrote the poem is more plausible. And exactly why Jonson, who elsewhere also spoke of Shakespeare as a playwright, and why Heminges and Condell, who had acted with Shakespeare for about twenty years, should speak of Shakespeare as the author in their dedication in the 1623 volume of collected plays is never adequately explained by Oxfordians. Either Jonson, Heminges and Condell, and numerous others were in on the conspiracy, or they were all duped—equally unlikely alternatives. Another difficulty in the Oxford theory is that Oxford died in 1604, and some of the plays are clearly indebted to works and events later than 1604. Among the Oxfordian responses are: At his death Oxford left some plays, and in later years these were touched up by hacks, who added the material that points to later dates. *The Tempest*, almost universally regarded as one of Shakespeare's greatest plays and pretty clearly dated to 1611, does indeed date from a period after the death of Oxford, but it is a crude piece of work that should not be included in the canon of works by Oxford.

The anti-Stratfordians, in addition to assuming that the author must have been a man of rank and a university man, usually assume two conspiracies: (1) a conspiracy in Elizabethan and Jacobean times, in which a surprisingly large number of persons connected with the theater knew that the actor Shakespeare did not write the plays attributed to him but for some reason or other pretended that he did; (2) a conspiracy of today's Stratfordians, the professors who teach Shakespeare in the colleges and universities, who are said to have a vested interest in preserving Shakespeare as the author of the plays they teach. In fact, (1) it is inconceivable that the secret of Shakespeare's nonauthorship could have been preserved by all of the people who supposedly were in on the conspiracy, and (2) academic fame awaits any scholar today who can disprove Shakespeare's authorship.

The Stratfordian case is convincing not only because hundreds or even thousands of anti-Stratford arguments—of the sort that say "ever I was born" has the secret double meaning "E. Ver, I was born"—add up to nothing at all but also because irrefutable evidence connects the man from Stratford with the London theater and with the authorship of particular plays. The anti-Stratfordians do not seem to understand that it is not enough to dismiss the Stratford case by saying that a fellow from the provinces simply couldn't have written the plays. Nor do they understand that it is not enough to dismiss all of the evidence connecting Shakespeare with the plays by asserting that it is perjured.

The Shakespeare Canon

We return to William Shakespeare. Thirty-seven plays as well as some nondramatic poems are generally held to constitute the Shakespeare canon, the body of authentic works. The exact dates of composition of most of the works are highly uncertain, but evidence of a starting point and/or of a final limiting point often provides a framework for informed guessing. For example, *Richard II* cannot be earlier than 1595, the publication date of some material to which it is indebted; *The Merchant of Venice* cannot be later than 1598, the year Francis Meres mentioned it. Sometimes arguments for a date hang on an alleged topical allusion, such as the lines about the unseasonable weather in *A Midsummer Night's Dream*, 2.1.81–117, but such an allusion, if indeed it is an allusion to an event in the real world, can be variously interpreted, and in any case there is always the possibility that a topical allusion was inserted years later, to bring the play up to date. (The issue of alterations in a text between the time that Shakespeare drafted it and the time that it was printed—alterations due to censorship or playhouse practice or Shakespeare's own second thoughts—will be discussed in "The Play Text as a Collaboration" later in this overview.) Dates are often attributed on the basis of style, and although conjectures about style usually rest on other conjectures (such as Shakespeare's development as a playwright, or the appropriateness of lines to character), sooner or later one must rely on one's literary sense. There is no documentary proof, for example, that *Othello* is not as early as *Romeo and Juliet*, but one feels that *Othello* is a later, more mature work, and because the first record of its performance is 1604, one is glad enough to set its composition at that date and not push it back into Shakespeare's early years. (*Romeo and Juliet* was first published in 1597, but evidence suggests that it was written a little earlier.) The following chronology, then, is indebted not only to facts but also to informed guesswork and sensitivity. The dates, necessarily imprecise for some works, indicate something like a scholarly consensus concerning the time of original composition. Some plays show evidence of later revision.

Plays. The first collected edition of Shakespeare, published in 1623, included thirty-six plays. These are all accepted as Shakespeare's, though for one of them, *Henry VIII*, he is thought to have had a collaborator. A thirty-seventh play, *Pericles*, published in 1609 and attributed to Shakespeare on the title page, is also widely accepted as being partly by Shakespeare even though it is not included in the 1623 volume. Still another play not in the 1623 volume, *The Two Noble Kinsmen*, was first published in 1634, with a title page attributing it to John Fletcher and Shakespeare. Probably most students of the subject now believe that Shakespeare did indeed have a hand in it. Of the remaining plays attributed at one time or another to Shakespeare, only one, *Edward III*, anonymously published in 1596, is now regarded by some scholars as a serious candidate. The prevailing opinion, however, is that this rather simpleminded play is not Shakespeare's; at most he may have revised some passages, chiefly scenes with the Countess of

Salisbury. We include *The Two Noble Kinsmen* but do not include *Edward III* in the following list.

1588–94	*The Comedy of Errors*
1588–94	*Love's Labor's Lost*
1589–91	*2 Henry VI*
1590–91	*3 Henry VI*
1589–92	*1 Henry VI*
1592–93	*Richard III*
1589–94	*Titus Andronicus*
1593–94	*The Taming of the Shrew*
1592–94	*The Two Gentlemen of Verona*
1594–96	*Romeo and Juliet*
1595	*Richard II*
1595–96	*A Midsummer Night's Dream*
1596–97	*King John*
1594–96	*The Merchant of Venice*
1596–97	*1 Henry IV*
1597	*The Merry Wives of Windsor*
1597–98	*2 Henry IV*
1598–99	*Much Ado About Nothing*
1598–99	*Henry V*
1599	*Julius Caesar*
1599–1600	*As You Like It*
1599–1600	*Twelfth Night*
1600–1601	*Hamlet*
1601–1602	*Troilus and Cressida*
1602–1604	*All's Well That Ends Well*
1603–1604	*Othello*
1604	*Measure for Measure*
1605–1606	*King Lear*
1605–1606	*Macbeth*
1606–1607	*Antony and Cleopatra*
1605–1608	*Timon of Athens*
1607–1608	*Coriolanus*
1607–1608	*Pericles*
1609–10	*Cymbeline*
1610–11	*The Winter's Tale*
1611	*The Tempest*

1612–13	*Henry VIII*
1613	*The Two Noble Kinsmen*

Poems. In 1989 Donald W. Foster published a book in which he argued that "A Funeral Elegy for Master William Peter," published in 1612, ascribed only to the initials W.S., *may* be by Shakespeare. Foster later published an article in a scholarly journal, *PMLA* 111 (1996), in which he asserted the claim more positively. The evidence begins with the initials, and includes the fact that the publisher and the printer of the elegy had published Shakespeare's *Sonnets* in 1609. But such facts add up to rather little, especially because no one has found any connection between Shakespeare and William Peter (an Oxford graduate about whom little is known, who was murdered at the age of twenty-nine). The argument is based chiefly on statistical examinations of word patterns, which are said to correlate with Shakespeare's known work. Despite such correlations, however, many readers feel that the poem does not sound like Shakespeare. True, Shakespeare has a great range of styles, but his work is consistently imaginative and interesting. Many readers find neither of these qualities in "A Funeral Elegy."

1592–93	*Venus and Adonis*
1593–94	*The Rape of Lucrece*
1593–1600	*Sonnets*
1600–1601	*The Phoenix and the Turtle*

Shakespeare's English

1. Spelling and Pronunciation. From the philologist's point of view, Shakespeare's English is modern English. It requires footnotes, but the inexperienced reader can comprehend substantial passages with very little help, whereas for the same reader Chaucer's Middle English is a foreign language. By the beginning of the fifteenth century the chief grammatical changes in English had taken place, and the final unaccented -*e* of Middle English had been lost (though it survives even today in spelling, as in *name*); during the fifteenth century the dialect of London, the commercial and political center, gradually displaced the provincial dialects, at least in writing; by the end of the century, printing had helped to regularize and stabilize the language, especially spelling. Elizabethan spelling may seem erratic to us (there were dozens of spellings of *Shakespeare*, and a simple word like *been* was also spelled *beene* and *bin*), but it had much in common with our spelling. Elizabethan spelling was conservative in that for the most part it reflected an older pronunciation (Middle English) rather than the sound of the language as it was then spoken, just as our spelling continues to reflect medieval pronunciation—most obviously in the now silent but formerly pronounced letters in a word such as *knight*. Elizabethan pronunciation, though not identical with ours, was much closer to ours than to that of the Middle Ages. Incidentally, though no one can be certain about what Elizabethan English sounded like, specialists tend to believe it was rather like the speech of a modern stage Irishman (*time* apparently was pronounced *toime*, *old* pronounced *awld*, *day* pronounced *die*, and *join* pronounced *jine*) and not at all like the Oxford speech that most of us think it was.

An awareness of the difference between our pronunciation and Shakespeare's is crucial in three areas—in accent, or number of syllables (many metrically regular lines may look irregular to us); in rhymes (which may not look like rhymes); and in puns (which may not look like puns). Examples will be useful. Some words that were at least on occasion stressed differently from today are *aspèct*, *còmplete*, *fòrlorn*, *revènue*, and *sepùlcher*. Words that sometimes had an additional syllable are *emp[e]ress*, *Hen[e]ry*, *mon[e]th*, and *villain* (three syllables, *vil-lay-in*). An additional syllable is often found in possessives, like *moon's* (pronounced *moones*), and in words ending in *-tion* or *-sion*. Words that had one less syllable than they now have are *needle* (pronounced *neel*) and *violet* (pronounced *vilet*). Among rhymes now lost are *one* with *loan*, *love* with *prove*, *beast* with *jest*, *eat* with *great*. (In reading, trust your sense of metrics and your ear, more than your eye.) An example of a pun that has become obliterated by a change in pronunciation is Falstaff's reply to Prince Hal's "Come, tell us your reason" in *1 Henry IV*: "Give you a reason on compulsion? If reasons were as plentiful as blackberries, I would give no man a reason upon compulsion, I" (2.4.237–40). The *ea* in *reason* was pronounced rather like a long *a*, like the *ai* in *raisin*, hence the comparison with blackberries.

Puns are not merely attempts to be funny; like metaphors they often involve bringing into a meaningful relationship areas of experience normally seen as remote. In *2 Henry IV*, when Feeble is conscripted, he stoically says, "I care not. A man can die but once. We owe God a death" (3.2.242–43), punning on *debt,* which was the way *death* was pronounced. Here an enormously significant fact of life is put into simple commercial imagery, suggesting its commonplace quality. Shakespeare used the same pun earlier in *1 Henry IV,* when Prince Hal says to Falstaff, "Why, thou owest God a death," and Falstaff replies, " 'Tis not due yet: I would be loath to pay him before his day. What need I be so forward with him that calls not on me?" (5.1.126–29).

Sometimes the puns reveal a delightful playfulness; sometimes they reveal aggressiveness, as when, replying to Claudius's "But now, my cousin Hamlet, and my son," Hamlet says, "A little more than kin, and less than kind!" (1.2.64–65). These are Hamlet's first words in the play, and we already hear him warring verbally against Claudius. Hamlet's "less than kind" probably means (1) Hamlet is not of Claudius's family or nature, *kind* having the sense it still has in our word *mankind*; (2) Hamlet is not kindly (affectionately) disposed toward Claudius; (3) Claudius is not naturally (but rather unnaturally, in a legal sense incestuously) Hamlet's father. The puns evidently were not put in as sops to the groundlings; they are an important way of communicating a complex meaning.

2. Vocabulary. A conspicuous difficulty in reading Shakespeare is rooted in the fact that some of his words are no longer in common use—for example, words concerned with armor, astrology, clothing, coinage, hawking, horsemanship, law, medicine, sailing, and war. Shakespeare had a large vocabulary—something near thirty thousand words—but it was not so much a vocabulary of big words as a vocabulary drawn from a wide range of life, and it is partly his ability to call upon a great body of concrete language that gives his plays the sense of being in close contact with life. When the right word did not already exist, he made it up. Among words thought to be his coinages are *accommodation, all-knowing, amazement, bare-faced, countless, dexterously, dislocate, dwindle, fancy-free, frugal, indistinguishable, lackluster, laughable, overawe, premeditated, sea change, star-crossed*. Among those that have not survived are the verb *convive*, meaning to feast together, and *smilet*, a little smile.

Less overtly troublesome than the technical words but more treacherous are the words that seem readily intelligible to us but whose Elizabethan meanings differ from their modern ones. When Horatio describes the Ghost as an "erring spirit," he is saying not that the ghost has sinned or made an error but that it is wandering. Here is a short list of some of the most common words in Shakespeare's plays that often (but not always) have a meaning other than their most usual modern meaning:

'a	he
abuse	deceive
accident	occurrence
advertise	inform
an, and	if
annoy	harm
appeal	accuse
artificial	skillful
brave	fine, splendid
censure	opinion
cheer	(1) face (2) frame of mind
chorus	a single person who comments on the events
closet	small private room
competitor	partner
conceit	idea, imagination
cousin	kinsman
cunning	skillful
disaster	evil astrological influence
doom	judgment
entertain	receive into service

envy	malice
event	outcome
excrement	outgrowth (of hair)
fact	evil deed
fancy	(1) love (2) imagination
fell	cruel
fellow	(1) companion (2) low person (often an insulting term if addressed to someone of approximately equal rank)
fond	foolish
free	(1) innocent (2) generous
glass	mirror
hap, haply	chance, by chance
head	army
humor	(1) mood (2) bodily fluid thought to control one's psychology
imp	child
intelligence	news
kind	natural, acting according to nature
let	hinder
lewd	base
mere(ly)	utter(ly)
modern	commonplace
natural	a fool, an idiot
naughty	(1) wicked (2) worthless
next	nearest
nice	(1) trivial (2) fussy
noise	music
policy	(1) prudence (2) stratagem
presently	immediately
prevent	anticipate
proper	handsome
prove	test
quick	alive
sad	serious
saw	proverb
secure	without care, incautious
silly	innocent

sensible	capable of being perceived by the senses
shrewd	sharp
so	provided that
starve	die
still	always
success	that which follows
tall	brave
tell	count
tonight	last night
wanton	playful, careless
watch	keep awake
will	lust
wink	close both eyes
wit	mind, intelligence

All glosses, of course, are mere approximations; sometimes one of Shakespeare's words may hover between an older meaning and a modern one, and as we have seen, his words often have multiple meanings.

3. Grammar. A few matters of grammar may be surveyed, though it should be noted at the outset that Shakespeare sometimes made up his own grammar. As E. A. Abbott says in *A Shakespearian Grammar,* "Almost any part of speech can be used as any other part of speech": a noun as a verb ("he childed as I fathered"); a verb as a noun ("She hath made compare"); or an adverb as an adjective ("a seldom pleasure"). There are hundreds, perhaps thousands, of such instances in the plays, many of which at first glance would not seem at all irregular and would trouble only a pedant. Here are a few broad matters.

Nouns: The Elizabethans thought the *-s* genitive ending for nouns (as in *man's*) derived from *his*; thus the line " 'gainst the count his galleys I did some service," for "the count's galleys."

Adjectives: By Shakespeare's time adjectives had lost the endings that once indicated gender, number, and case. About the only difference between Shakespeare's adjectives and ours is the use of the now redundant *more* or *most* with the comparative ("some more fitter place") or superlative

("This was the most unkindest cut of all"). Like double comparatives and double superlatives, double negatives were acceptable; Mercutio "will not budge for no man's pleasure."

Pronouns: The greatest change was in pronouns. In Middle English *thou, thy,* and *thee* were used among familiars and in speaking to children and inferiors; *ye, your,* and *you* were used in speaking to superiors (servants to masters, nobles to the king) or to equals with whom the speaker was not familiar. Increasingly the "polite" forms were used in all direct address, regardless of rank, and the accusative *you* displaced the nominative *ye.* Shakespeare sometimes uses *ye* instead of *you,* but even in Shakespeare's day *ye* was archaic, and it occurs mostly in rhetorical appeals.

Thou, thy, and *thee* were not completely displaced, however, and Shakespeare occasionally makes significant use of them, sometimes to connote familiarity or intimacy and sometimes to connote contempt. In *Twelfth Night* Sir Toby advises Sir Andrew to insult Cesario by addressing him as *thou:* "If thou thou'st him some thrice, it shall not be amiss" (3.2.46–47). In *Othello* when Brabantio is addressing an unidentified voice in the dark he says, "What are you?" (1.1.91), but when the voice identifies itself as the foolish suitor Roderigo, Brabantio uses the contemptuous form, saying, "I have charged thee not to haunt about my doors" (93). He uses this form for a while, but later in the scene, when he comes to regard Roderigo as an ally, he shifts back to the polite *you,* beginning in line 163, "What said she to you?" and on to the end of the scene. For reasons not yet satisfactorily explained, Elizabethans used *thou* in addresses to God—"O God, thy arm was here," the king says in *Henry V* (4.8.108)—and to supernatural characters such as ghosts and witches. A subtle variation occurs in *Hamlet.* When Hamlet first talks with the Ghost in 1.5, he uses *thou,* but when he sees the Ghost in his mother's room, in 3.4, he uses *you,* presumably because he is now convinced that the Ghost is not a counterfeit but is his father.

Perhaps the most unusual use of pronouns, from our point of view, is the neuter singular. In place of our *its, his* was often used, as in "How far that little candle throws *his* beams." But the use of a masculine pronoun for a neuter noun came to seem unnatural, and so *it* was used for the possessive as well as the nominative: "The hedge-sparrow fed the cuckoo so long / That it had it head bit off by it young." In the late sixteenth century the possessive form *its* developed, apparently by analogy with the -*s* ending used to indicate a genitive noun, as in *book*'s, but *its* was not yet common usage in Shakespeare's day. He seems to have used *its* only ten times, mostly in his later plays. Other usages, such as "you have seen Cassio and she together" or the substitution of *who* for *whom,* cause little problem even when noticed.

Verbs, Adverbs, and Prepositions: Verbs cause almost no difficulty: The third person singular present form commonly ends in -*s,* as in modern English (e.g., "He blesses"), but sometimes in -*eth* (Portia explains to Shylock that mercy "blesseth him that gives and him that takes"). Broadly speaking, the -*eth* ending was old-fashioned or dignified or "literary" rather than colloquial, except for the words *doth, hath,* and *saith.* The -*eth* ending (regularly used in the King James Bible, 1611) is very rare in Shakespeare's dramatic prose, though not surprisingly it occurs twice in the rather formal prose summary of the narrative poem *Lucrece.* Sometimes a plural subject, especially if it has collective force, takes a verb ending in -*s,* as in "My old bones aches." Some of our strong or irregular preterites (such as *broke*) have a different form in Shakespeare (*brake*); some verbs that now have a weak or regular preterite (such as *helped*) in Shakespeare have a strong or irregular preterite (*holp*). Some adverbs that today end in -*ly* were not inflected: "grievous sick," "wondrous strange." Finally, prepositions often are not the ones we expect: "We are such stuff as dreams are made on," "I have a king here to my flatterer."

Again, none of the differences (except meanings that have substantially changed or been lost) will cause much difficulty. But it must be confessed that for some elliptical passages there is no widespread agreement on meaning. Wise editors resist saying more than they know, and when they are uncertain they add a question mark to their gloss.

Shakespeare's Theater

In Shakespeare's infancy, Elizabethan actors performed wherever they could—in great halls, at court, in the courtyards of inns. These venues implied not only different audiences but also different playing conditions. The innyards must have made rather unsatisfactory theaters: on some days they were unavailable because carters bringing goods to London used them as depots; when available, they had to be rented from the innkeeper. In 1567, presumably to avoid such difficulties, and also to avoid regulation by the Common Council of London, which was not well disposed toward theatricals, one John Brayne, brother-in-law of the carpenter turned actor James Burbage, built the Red Lion in an eastern suburb of London. We know nothing about its shape or its capacity; we can say only that it may have been the first building in Europe constructed for the purpose of giving plays since the end of antiquity, a thousand years earlier. Even after the building of the Red Lion theatrical activity continued in London in makeshift circumstances, in marketplaces and inns, and always uneasily. In 1574 the Common Council required that plays and playing places in London be licensed because

> sundry great disorders and inconveniences have been found to ensue to this city by the inordinate haunting of great multitudes of people, specially youth, to plays, interludes, and shows, namely occasion of frays and quarrels, evil practices of incontinency in great inns having chambers and secret places adjoining to their open stages and galleries.

The Common Council ordered that innkeepers who wished licenses to hold performance put up a bond and make contributions to the poor.

The requirement that plays and innyard theaters be licensed, along with the other drawbacks of playing at inns and presumably along with the success of the Red Lion, led James Burbage to rent a plot of land northeast of the city walls, on property outside the jurisdiction of the city. Here he built England's second playhouse, called simply the Theatre. About all that is known of its construction is that it was wood. It soon had imitators, the most famous being the Globe (1599), essentially an amphitheater built across the Thames (again outside the city's jurisdiction), constructed with timbers of the Theatre, which had been dismantled when Burbage's lease ran out.

Admission to the theater was one penny, which allowed spectators to stand at the sides and front of the stage that jutted into the yard. An additional penny bought a seat in a covered part of the theater, and a third penny bought a more comfortable seat and a better location. It is notoriously difficult to translate prices into today's money, since some things that are inexpensive today would have been expensive in the past and vice versa—a pipeful of tobacco (imported, of course) cost a lot of money, about three pennies, and an orange (also imported) cost two or three times what a chicken cost—but perhaps we can get some idea of the low cost of the penny admission when we realize that a penny could also buy a pot of ale. An unskilled laborer made about five or sixpence a day, an artisan about twelve pence a day, and the hired actors (as opposed to the sharers in the company, such as Shakespeare) made about ten pence a performance. A printed play cost five or sixpence. Of course a visit to the theater (like a visit to a baseball game today) usually cost more than the admission since the spectator probably would also buy food and drink. Still, the low entrance fee meant that the theater was available to all except the very poorest people, rather as movies and most athletic events are today. Evidence indicates that the audience ranged from apprentices who somehow managed to scrape together the minimum entrance fee and to escape from their masters for a few hours, to prosperous members of the middle class and aristocrats who paid the additional fee for admission to the galleries. The exact proportion of men to women cannot be determined, but women of all classes certainly were present. Theaters were open every afternoon but Sundays for much of the year, except in times of plague, when they were closed because of fear of infection. By the way, no evidence suggests the presence of toilet facilities. Presumably the patrons relieved themselves by making a quick trip to the fields surrounding the playhouses.

There are four important sources of information about the

structure of Elizabethan public playhouses—drawings, a contract, recent excavations, and stage directions in the plays. Of drawings, only the so-called de Witt drawing (c. 1596) of the Swan—really his friend Aernout van Buchell's copy of Johannes de Witt's drawing—is of much significance. The drawing, the only extant representation of the interior of an Elizabethan theater, shows an amphitheater of three tiers, with a stage jutting from a wall into the yard or

Johannes de Witt, a Continental visitor to London, made a drawing of the Swan theater in about the year 1596. The original drawing is lost; this is Aernout van Buchell's copy of it.

center of the building. The tiers are roofed, and part of the stage is covered by a roof that projects from the rear and is supported at its front on two posts, but the groundlings, who paid a penny to stand in front of the stage or at its sides, were exposed to the sky. (Performances in such a playhouse were held only in the daytime; artificial illumination was not used.) At the rear of the stage are two massive doors; above the stage is a gallery.

The second major source of information, the contract for the Fortune (built in 1600), specifies that although the Globe (built in 1599) is to be the model, the Fortune is to be square, eighty feet outside and fifty-five inside. The stage is to be forty-three feet broad, and is to extend into the middle of the yard, i.e., it is twenty-seven and a half feet deep.

The third source of information, the 1989 excavations of the Rose (built in 1587), indicate that the Rose was fourteen-sided, about seventy-two feet in diameter with an inner yard almost fifty feet in diameter. The stage at the Rose was about sixteen feet deep, thirty-seven feet wide at the rear, and twenty-seven feet wide downstage. The relatively small dimensions and the tapering stage, in contrast to the rectangular stage in the Swan drawing, surprised theater historians and have made them more cautious in generalizing about the Elizabethan theater. Excavations at the Globe have not yielded much information, though some historians believe that the fragmentary evidence suggests a larger theater, perhaps one hundred feet in diameter.

From the fourth chief source, stage directions in the plays, one learns that entrance to the stage was by the doors at the rear (*"Enter one citizen at one door, and another at the other"*). A curtain hanging across the doorway—or a curtain hanging between the two doorways—could provide a place where a character could conceal himself, as Polonius does, when he wishes to overhear the conversation between Hamlet and Gertrude. Similarly, withdrawing a curtain from the doorway could "discover" (reveal) a character or two. Such discovery scenes are very rare in Elizabethan drama, but a good example occurs in *The Tempest* (5.1.171), where a stage direction tells us, *"Here Prospero discovers Ferdinand and Miranda playing at chess."* There was also some sort of playing space "aloft" or "above" to represent, for instance, the top of a city's walls or a room above the street. Doubtless each theater had its own peculiarities, but perhaps we can talk about a "typical" Elizabethan theater if we realize that no theater need exactly fit the description, just as no mother is the average mother with 2.7 children.

This hypothetical theater is wooden, round, or polygonal (in *Henry V* Shakespeare calls it a "wooden *O*"), capable of holding some eight hundred spectators who stood in the yard around the projecting elevated stage—these spectators were the "groundlings"—and some fifteen hundred additional spectators who sat in the three roofed galleries. The stage, protected by a "shadow" or "heavens" or roof, is entered from two doors; behind the doors is the "tiring house" (attiring house, i.e., dressing room), and above the stage is some sort of gallery that may sometimes hold spectators but can be used (for example) as the bedroom from which Romeo—according to a stage direction in one text—"goeth down." Some evidence suggests that a throne can be lowered onto the platform stage, perhaps from the "shadow"; certainly characters can descend from the stage through a trap or traps into the cellar or "hell." Sometimes this space beneath the stage accommodates a sound-effects man or musician (in *Antony and Cleopatra* "*music of the hautboys* [oboes] *is under the stage*") or an actor (in *Hamlet* the "*Ghost cries under the stage*"). Most characters simply walk on and off through the doors, but because there is no curtain in front of the platform, corpses will have to be carried off (Hamlet obligingly clears the stage of Polonius's corpse, when he says, "I'll lug the guts into the neighbor room"). Other characters may have fallen at the rear, where a curtain on a doorway could be drawn to conceal them.

Such may have been the "public theater," so called because its inexpensive admission made it available to a wide range of the populace. Another kind of theater has been called the "private theater" because its much greater admission charge (sixpence versus the penny for general admission at the public theater) limited its audience to the wealthy or the prodigal. The private theater was basically a large room, entirely roofed and therefore artificially illuminated, with a stage at one end. The theaters thus were distinct in two ways: One was essentially an amphitheater that catered to the general public; the other was a hall that catered to the wealthy. In 1576 a hall theater was established in Blackfriars, a Dominican priory in London that had been suppressed in 1538 and confiscated by the Crown and thus was not under the city's jurisdiction. All the actors in this Blackfriars theater were boys about eight to thirteen years old (in the public theaters similar boys played female parts; a boy Lady Macbeth played to a man Macbeth). Near the end of this section on Shakespeare's theater we will talk at some length about possible implications in this convention of using boys to play female roles, but for the moment we should say that it doubtless accounts for the relative lack of female roles in Elizabethan drama. Thus, in *A Midsummer Night's Dream*, out of twenty-one named roles, only four are female; in *Hamlet*, out of twenty-four, only two (Gertrude and Ophelia) are female. Many of Shakespeare's characters have fathers but no mothers—for instance, King Lear's daughters. We need not bring in Freud to explain the disparity; a dramatic company had only a few boys in it.

To return to the private theaters, in some of which all of the performers were children—the "eyrie of . . . little eyases" (nest of unfledged hawks—2.2.347–48) which Rosencrantz mentions when he and Guildenstern talk with Hamlet. The theater in Blackfriars had a precarious existence, and ceased operations in 1584. In 1596 James Burbage, who had already made theatrical history by building the Theatre, began to construct a second Blackfriars theater. He died in 1597, and for several years this second Blackfriars theater was used by a troupe of boys, but in 1608 two of Burbage's sons and five other actors (including Shakespeare) became joint operators of the theater, using it in the winter when the open-air Globe was unsuitable. Perhaps such a smaller theater, roofed, artificially illuminated, and with a tradition of a wealthy audience, exerted an influence in Shakespeare's late plays.

Performances in the private theaters may well have had intermissions during which music was played, but in the public theaters the action was probably uninterrupted, flowing from scene to scene almost without a break. Actors would enter, speak, exit, and others would immediately enter and establish (if necessary) the new locale by a few properties and by words and gestures. To indicate that the scene took place at night, a player or two would carry a torch. Here are some samples of Shakespeare establishing the scene:

> This is Illyria, lady.   (*Twelfth Night*, 1.2.2)
>
> Well, this is the Forest of Arden.   (*As You Like It*, 2.4.14)
>
> This castle has a pleasant seat; the air
> Nimbly and sweetly recommends itself
> Unto our gentle senses.   (*Macbeth*, 1.6.1–3)
>
> The west yet glimmers with some streaks of day.
>   (*Macbeth*, 3.3.5)

Sometimes a speech will go far beyond evoking the minimal setting of place and time, and will, so to speak, evoke the social world in which the characters move. For instance, early in the first scene of *The Merchant of Venice* Salerio suggests an explanation for Antonio's melancholy. (In the following passage, *pageants* are decorated wagons, floats, and *cursy* is the verb "to curtsy," or "to bow.")

> Your mind is tossing on the ocean,
> There where your argosies with portly sail—
> Like signiors and rich burghers on the flood,
> Or as it were the pageants of the sea—
> Do overpeer the petty traffickers
> That cursy to them, do them reverence,
> As they fly by them with their woven wings.   (1.1.8–14)

Late in the nineteenth century, when Henry Irving produced the play with elaborate illusionistic sets, the first scene showed a ship moored in the harbor, with fruit vendors and dock laborers, in an effort to evoke the bustling and exotic life of Venice. But Shakespeare's words give us this exotic, rich world of commerce in his highly descriptive language when Salerio speaks of "argosies with portly sail" that fly with "woven wings"; equally important, through Salerio Shakespeare conveys a sense of the orderly, hierarchical society in which the lesser ships, "the petty traffickers," curtsy and thereby "do . . . reverence" to their superiors, the merchant prince's ships, which are "Like signiors and rich burghers."

On the other hand, it is a mistake to think that except for verbal pictures the Elizabethan stage was bare. Although Shakespeare's Chorus in *Henry V* calls the stage an "unworthy scaffold" (Prologue 1.10) and urges the spectators to "eke out our performance with your mind" (Prologue 3.35), there was considerable spectacle. The last act of *Macbeth*, for instance, has five stage directions calling for *"drum and colors,"* and another sort of appeal to the eye is indicated by the stage direction *"Enter Macduff, with Macbeth's head."* Some scenery and properties may have been substantial; doubtless a throne was used, but the pillars supporting the roof would have served for the trees on which Orlando pins his poems in *As You Like It.*

Having talked about the public theater—"this wooden *O*"—at some length, we should mention again that Shakespeare's plays were performed also in other locales. Alvin Kernan, in *Shakespeare, the King's Playwright: Theater in the Stuart Court 1603–1613* (1995), points out that "several of [Shakespeare's] plays contain brief theatrical performances, set always in a court or some noble house. When Shakespeare portrayed a theater, he did not, except for the choruses in *Henry V*, imagine a public theater" (p. 195). (Examples include episodes in *The Taming of the Shrew*, *A Midsummer Night's Dream*, *Hamlet*, and *The Tempest*.)

A Note on the Use of Boy Actors in Female Roles

Until fairly recently, scholars were content to mention that the convention existed; they sometimes also mentioned that it continued the medieval practice of using males in female roles, and that other theaters, notably in ancient Greece and in China and Japan, also used males in female roles. (In classical Noh drama in Japan, males still play the female roles.) Prudery may have been at the root of the academic failure to talk much about the use of boy actors, or maybe there really is not much more to say than that it was a convention of a male-centered culture (Stephen Greenblatt's view, in *Shakespearean Negotiations* [1988]). Further, the very nature of a convention is that it is not thought about: Hamlet is a Dane and Julius Caesar is a Roman, but in Shakespeare's plays they speak English, and we in the audience never give this odd fact a thought. Similarly, a character may speak in the presence of others and we understand, again without thinking about it, that he or she is not heard by the figures on the stage (the aside); a character alone on the stage may speak (the soliloquy), and we do not take the character to be unhinged; in a realistic (box) set, the fourth wall, which allows us to see what is going on, is miraculously missing. The no-nonsense view, then, is that the boy actor was an accepted convention, accepted unthinkingly—just as today we know that Kenneth Branagh is not Hamlet, Al Pacino is not Richard III, and Denzel Washington is not the Prince of Aragon. In this view, the audience takes the performer for the role, and that is that; such is the argument we now make for race-free casting, in which African-Americans and Asians can play roles of persons who lived in medieval Denmark and ancient Rome. But gender perhaps is different, at least today. It is a matter of abundant academic study: The Elizabethan theater is now sometimes called a transvestite theater, and we hear much about cross-dressing.

Shakespeare himself in a very few passages calls attention to the use of boys in female roles. At the end of *As You Like It* the boy who played Rosalind addresses the audience, and says, "O men, . . . if I were a woman, I would kiss as many of you as had beards that pleased me." But this is in the Epilogue; the plot is over, and the actor is stepping out of the play and into the audience's everyday world. A second reference to the practice of boys playing female roles occurs in *Antony and Cleopatra*, when Cleopatra imagines that she and Antony will be the subject of crude plays, her role being performed by a boy:

>   The quick comedians
> Extemporally will stage us, and present
> Our Alexandrian revels: Antony
> Shall be brought drunken forth, and I shall see
> Some squeaking Cleopatra boy my greatness.   (5.2.216–20)

In a few other passages, Shakespeare is more indirect. For instance, in *Twelfth Night* Viola, played of course by a boy, disguises herself as a young man and seeks service in the house of a lord. She enlists the help of a Captain, and (by way of explaining away her voice and her beardlessness) says,

> I'll serve this duke
> Thou shalt present me as an eunuch to him.   (1.2.55–56)

In *Hamlet*, when the players arrive in 2.2, Hamlet jokes with the boy who plays a female role. The boy has grown since Hamlet last saw him: "By'r Lady, your ladyship is nearer to heaven than when I saw you last by the altitude of a chopine" (a lady's thick-soled shoe). He goes on: "Pray God your voice . . . be not cracked" (434–38).

Exactly how sexual, how erotic, this material was and is, is now much disputed. Again, the use of boys may have been unnoticed, or rather not thought about—an unexamined convention—by most or all spectators most of the time, perhaps *all* of the time, except when Shakespeare calls the convention to the attention of the audience, as in the passages just quoted. Still, an occasional bit seems to invite erotic thoughts. The clearest example is the name that Rosalind takes in *As You Like It*, Ganymede—the beautiful youth whom Zeus abducted. Did boys dressed to play female roles carry homoerotic appeal for straight men (Lisa Jardine's view, in *Still Harping on Daughters* [1983]), or for gay men, or for some or all women in the audience? Further, when the boy actor played a woman who (for the purposes of the plot) disguised herself as a male, as Rosalind, Viola, and Portia do—so we get a boy playing a woman playing a man—what sort of appeal was generated, and for what sort of spectator?

Some scholars have argued that the convention empowered women by letting female characters display a freedom unavailable in Renaissance patriarchal society; the convention, it is said, undermined rigid gender distinctions. In this view, the convention (along with plots in which female characters for a while disguised themselves as young men) allowed Shakespeare to say what some modern gender

critics say: Gender is a constructed role rather than a bio-
logical given, something we make, rather than a fixed binary
opposition of male and female (see Juliet Dusinberre, in
Shakespeare and the Nature of Women [1975]). On the other
hand, some scholars have maintained that the male disguise
assumed by some female characters serves only to reaffirm
traditional social distinctions since female characters who
don male garb (notably Portia in *The Merchant of Venice*
and Rosalind in *As You Like It*) return to their female garb
and at least implicitly (these critics say) reaffirm the status
quo. (For this last view, see Clara Claiborne Park, in an
essay in *The Woman's Part*, ed. Carolyn Ruth Swift Lenz et
al. [1980].) Perhaps no one answer is right for all plays; in
As You Like It cross-dressing empowers Rosalind, but in
Twelfth Night cross-dressing comically traps Viola.

Shakespeare's Dramatic Language: Costumes, Gestures and Silences; Prose and Poetry

Because Shakespeare was a dramatist, not merely a poet,
he worked not only with language but also with costume,
sound effects, gestures, and even silences. We have already
discussed some kinds of spectacle in the preceding section,
and now we will begin with other aspects of visual language;
a theater, after all, is literally a "place for seeing." Consider
the opening stage direction in *The Tempest*, the first play in
the first published collection of Shakespeare's plays: *"A
tempestuous noise of thunder and Lightning heard: Enter a
Ship-master, and a Boteswain."*

Costumes: What did that shipmaster and that boatswain
wear? Doubtless they wore something that identified them
as men of the sea. Not much is known about the costumes
that Elizabethan actors wore, but at least three points are
clear: (1) many of the costumes were splendid versions of
contemporary Elizabethan dress; (2) some attempts were
made to approximate the dress of certain occupations and of
antique or exotic characters such as Romans, Turks, and
Jews; (3) some costumes indicated that the wearer was

supernatural. Evidence for elaborate Elizabethan clothing can be found in the plays themselves and in contemporary comments about the "sumptuous" players who wore the discarded clothing of noblemen, as well as in account books that itemize such things as "a scarlet cloak with two broad gold laces, with gold buttons down the sides."

The attempts at approximation of the dress of certain occupations and nationalities also can be documented from the plays themselves, and it derives additional confirmation from a drawing of the first scene of Shakespeare's *Titus Andronicus*—the only extant Elizabethan picture of an identifiable episode in a play. (See pp. xxxviii–xxxix.) The drawing, probably done in 1594 or 1595, shows Queen Tamora pleading for mercy. She wears a somewhat medieval-looking robe and a crown; Titus wears a toga and a wreath, but two soldiers behind him wear costumes fairly close to Elizabethan dress. We do not know, however, if the drawing represents an actual stage production in the public theater, or perhaps a private production, or maybe only a reader's visualization of an episode. Further, there is some conflicting evidence: In *Julius Caesar* a reference is made to Caesar's doublet (a close-fitting jacket), which, if taken literally, suggests that even the protagonist did not wear Roman clothing; and certainly the lesser characters, who are said to wear hats, did not wear Roman garb.

It should be mentioned, too, that even ordinary clothing can be symbolic: Hamlet's "inky cloak," for example, sets him apart from the brightly dressed members of Claudius's court and symbolizes his mourning; the fresh clothes that are put on King Lear partly symbolize his return to sanity. Consider, too, the removal of disguises near the end of some plays. For instance, Rosalind in *As You Like It* and Portia and Nerissa in *The Merchant of Venice* remove their male attire, thus again becoming fully themselves.

Gestures and Silences: Gestures are an important part of a dramatist's language. King Lear kneels before his daughter Cordelia for a benediction (4.7.57–59), an act of humility that contrasts with his earlier speeches banishing her and that contrasts also with a comparable gesture, his ironic

kneeling before Regan (2.4.153–55). Northumberland's
failure to kneel before King Richard II (3.3.71–72) speaks
volumes. As for silences, consider a moment in *Coriolanus*:
Before the protagonist yields to his mother's entreaties
(5.3.182), there is this stage direction: *"Holds her by the
hand, silent."* Another example of "speech in dumbness"
occurs in *Macbeth*, when Macduff learns that his wife and
children have been murdered. He is silent at first, as Malcolm's speech indicates: "What, man! Ne'er pull your hat
upon your brows. Give sorrow words" (4.3.208–9). (For
a discussion of such moments, see Philip C. McGuire's
Speechless Dialect: Shakespeare's Open Silences [1985].)

Of course when we think of Shakespeare's work, we think
primarily of his language, both the poetry and the prose.

Prose: Although two of his plays (*Richard II* and *King John*)
have no prose at all, about half the others have at least one
quarter of the dialogue in prose, and some have notably
more: *1 Henry IV* and *2 Henry IV*, about half; *As You Like It*

and *Twelfth Night*, a little more than half; *Much Ado About Nothing*, more than three quarters; and *The Merry Wives of Windsor*, a little more than five-sixths. We should remember that despite Molière's joke about M. Jourdain, who was amazed to learn that he spoke prose, most of us do not speak prose. Rather, we normally utter repetitive, shapeless, and often ungrammatical torrents; prose is something very different—a sort of literary imitation of speech at its most coherent.

Today we may think of prose as "natural" for drama; or even if we think that poetry is appropriate for high tragedy we may still think that prose is the right medium for comedy. Greek, Roman, and early English comedies, however, were written in verse. In fact, prose was not generally considered a literary medium in England until the late fifteenth century; Chaucer tells even his bawdy stories in verse. By the end of the 1580s, however, prose had established itself on the English comic stage. In tragedy, Marlowe made some use of prose, not simply in the speeches of clownish servants but even in the speech of a tragic hero, Doctor Faustus. Still, before Shakespeare, prose normally was used in the theater only for special circumstances: (1) letters and proclamations, to set them off from the poetic dialogue; (2) mad characters, to indicate that normal thinking has become disordered; and (3) low comedy, or speeches uttered by clowns even when they are not being comic. Shakespeare made use of these conventions, but he also went far beyond them. Sometimes he begins a scene in prose and then shifts into verse as the emotion is heightened; or conversely, he may shift from verse to prose when a speaker is lowering the emotional level, as when Brutus speaks in the Forum.

Shakespeare's prose usually is not prosaic. Hamlet's prose includes not only small talk with Rosencrantz and Guildenstern but also princely reflections on "What a piece of work is a man" (2.2.312). In conversation with Ophelia, he shifts from light talk in verse to a passionate prose denunciation of women (3.1.103), though the shift to prose here is perhaps also intended to suggest the possibility of madness. (Consult Brian Vickers, *The Artistry of Shakespeare's Prose* [1968].)

Poetry: Drama in rhyme in England goes back to the Middle Ages, but by Shakespeare's day rhyme no longer dominated poetic drama; a finer medium, blank verse (strictly speaking, unrhymed lines of ten syllables, with the stress on every second syllable) had been adopted. But before looking at unrhymed poetry, a few things should be said about the chief uses of rhyme in Shakespeare's plays. (1) A couplet (a pair of rhyming lines) is sometimes used to convey emotional heightening at the end of a blank verse speech; (2) characters sometimes speak a couplet as they leave the stage, suggesting closure; (3) except in the latest plays, scenes fairly often conclude with a couplet, and sometimes, as in *Richard II*, 2.1.145–46, the entrance of a new character within a scene is preceded by a couplet, which wraps up the earlier portion of that scene; (4) speeches of two characters occasionally are linked by rhyme, most notably in *Romeo and Juliet*, 1.5.95–108, where the lovers speak a sonnet between them; elsewhere a taunting reply occasionally rhymes with the previous speaker's last line; (5) speeches with sententious or gnomic remarks are sometimes in rhyme, as in the duke's speech in *Othello* (1.3.199–206); (6) speeches of sardonic mockery are sometimes in rhyme—for example, Iago's speech on women in *Othello* (2.1.146–58)—and they sometimes conclude with an emphatic couplet, as in Bolingbroke's speech on comforting words in *Richard II* (1.3.301–2); (7) some characters are associated with rhyme, such as the fairies in *A Midsummer Night's Dream*; (8) in the early plays, especially *The Comedy of Errors* and *The Taming of the Shrew*, comic scenes that in later plays would be in prose are in jingling rhymes; (9) prologues, choruses, plays-within-the-play, inscriptions, vows, epilogues, and so on are often in rhyme, and the songs in the plays are rhymed.

Neither prose nor rhyme immediately comes to mind when we first think of Shakespeare's medium: It is blank verse, unrhymed iambic pentameter. (In a mechanically exact line there are five iambic feet. An iambic foot consists of two syllables, the second accented, as in *away*; five feet make a pentameter line. Thus, a strict line of iambic pentameter contains ten syllables, the even syllables being stressed more heavily than the odd syllables. Fortunately, Shakespeare usually varies the line somewhat.) The first speech in *A Midsummer Night's Dream*, spoken by Duke Theseus to his betrothed, is an example of blank verse:

> Now, fair Hippolyta, our nuptial hour
> Draws on apace. Four happy days bring in
> Another moon; but, O, methinks, how slow
> This old moon wanes! She lingers my desires,
> Like to a stepdame, or a dowager,
> Long withering out a young man's revenue.   (1.1.1–6)

As this passage shows, Shakespeare's blank verse is not mechanically unvarying. Though the predominant foot is the iamb (as in *apace* or *desires*), there are numerous variations. In the first line the stress can be placed on "fair," as the regular metrical pattern suggests, but it is likely that "Now" gets almost as much emphasis; probably in the second line "Draws" is more heavily emphasized than "on," giving us a trochee (a stressed syllable followed by an unstressed one); and in the fourth line each word in the phrase "This old moon wanes" is probably stressed fairly heavily, conveying by two spondees (two feet, each of two stresses) the oppressive tedium that Theseus feels.

In Shakespeare's early plays much of the blank verse is end-stopped (that is, it has a heavy pause at the end of each line), but he later developed the ability to write iambic pentameter verse paragraphs (rather than lines) that give the illusion of speech. His chief techniques are (1) enjambing, i.e., running the thought beyond the single line, as in the first three lines of the speech just quoted; (2) occasionally replacing an iamb with another foot; (3) varying the position of the chief pause (the caesura) within a line; (4) adding an occasional unstressed syllable at the end of a line, traditionally called a feminine ending; and (5) beginning or ending a speech with a half line.

Shakespeare's mature blank verse has much of the rhythmic flexibility of his prose; both the language, though richly figurative and sometimes dense, and the syntax seem natural. It is also often highly appropriate to a particular character. Consider, for instance, this speech from *Hamlet*, in which Claudius, King of Denmark ("the Dane"), speaks to Laertes:

> And now, Laertes, what's the news with you?
> You told us of some suit. What is't, Laertes?
> You cannot speak of reason to the Dane
> And lose your voice. What wouldst thou beg, Laertes,
> That shall not be my offer, not thy asking?   (1.2.42–46)

Notice the short sentences and the repetition of the name "Laertes," to whom the speech is addressed. Notice, too, the shift from the royal "us" in the second line to the more intimate "my" in the last line, and from "you" in the first three lines to the more intimate "thou" and "thy" in the last two lines. Claudius knows how to ingratiate himself with Laertes.

For a second example of the flexibility of Shakespeare's blank verse, consider a passage from *Macbeth*. Distressed by the doctor's inability to cure Lady Macbeth and by the imminent battle, Macbeth addresses some of his remarks to the doctor and others to the servant who is arming him. The entire speech, with its pauses, interruptions, and irresolution (in "Pull't off, I say," Macbeth orders the servant to remove the armor that the servant has been putting on him), catches Macbeth's disintegration. (In the first line, *physic* means "medicine," and in the fourth and fifth lines, *cast the water* means "analyze the urine.")

> Throw physic to the dogs, I'll none of it.
> Come, put mine armor on. Give me my staff.
> Seyton, send out.—Doctor, the thanes fly from me.—
> Come, sir, dispatch. If thou couldst, doctor, cast
> The water of my land, find her disease
> And purge it to a sound and pristine health,
> I would applaud thee to the very echo,
> That should applaud again.—Pull't off, I say.—
> What rhubarb, senna, or what purgative drug,
> Would scour these English hence? Hear'st thou of them?
>
> (5.3.47–56)

Blank verse, then, can be much more than unrhymed iambic pentameter, and even within a single play Shakespeare's blank verse often consists of several styles, depending on the speaker and on the speaker's emotion at the moment.

The Play Text as a Collaboration

Shakespeare's fellow dramatist Ben Jonson reported that the actors said of Shakespeare, "In his writing, whatsoever he penned, he never blotted out line," i.e., never crossed out material and revised his work while composing. None of Shakespeare's plays survives in manuscript (with the possible exception of a scene in *Sir Thomas More*), so we cannot fully evaluate the comment, but in a few instances the published work clearly shows that he revised his manuscript. Consider the following passage (shown here in facsimile) from the best early text of *Romeo and Juliet*, the Second Quarto (1599):

Ro. Would I were sleepe and peace so sweet to rest
The grey eyde morne smiles on the frowning night,
Checkring the Easterne Clouds with streaks of light,
And darknesse fleckted like a drunkard reeles,
From forth daies pathway, made by *Tytans* wheeles.
Hence will I to my ghostly Friers close cell,
His helpe to craue, and my deare hap to tell.

                                  Exit.

     Enter Frier alone with a basket.   (night,
Fri. The grey-eyed morne smiles on the frowning
Checking the Easterne clowdes with streaks of light:
And fleckeld darknesse like a drunkard reeles,
From forth daies path, and *Titans* burning wheeles:
Now ere the sun aduance his burning eie,

Romeo rather elaborately tells us that the sun at dawn is
dispelling the night (morning is smiling, the eastern clouds
are checked with light, and the sun's chariot—Titan's
wheels—advances), and he will seek out his spiritual father,
the Friar. He exits and, oddly, the Friar enters and says pretty
much the same thing about the sun. Both speakers say that
"the gray-eyed morn smiles on the frowning night," but there
are small differences, perhaps having more to do with the
business of printing the book than with the author's
composition: For Romeo's "checkring," "fleckted," and
"pathway," we get the Friar's "checking," "fleckeld," and
"path." (Notice, by the way, the inconsistency in Elizabethan
spelling: Romeo's "clouds" become the Friar's "clowdes.")
    Both versions must have been in the printer's copy, and it
seems safe to assume that both were in Shakespeare's manuscript. He must have written one version—let's say he first
wrote Romeo's closing lines for this scene—and then he
decided, no, it's better to give this lyrical passage to the
Friar, as the opening of a new scene, but he neglected to
delete the first version. Editors must make a choice, and they
may feel that the reasonable thing to do is to print the text as
Shakespeare intended it. But how can we know what he
intended? Almost all modern editors delete the lines from

Romeo's speech, and retain the Friar's lines. They don't do this because they know Shakespeare's intention, however. They give the lines to the Friar because the first published version (1597) of *Romeo and Juliet* gives only the Friar's version, and this text (though in many ways inferior to the 1599 text) is thought to derive from the memory of some actors, that is, it is thought to represent a performance, not just a script. Maybe during the course of rehearsals Shakespeare—an actor as well as an author—unilaterally decided that the Friar should speak the lines; if so (remember that we don't know this to be a fact) his final intention was to give the speech to the Friar. Maybe, however, the actors talked it over and settled on the Friar, with or without Shakespeare's approval. On the other hand, despite the 1597 version, one might argue (if only weakly) on behalf of giving the lines to Romeo rather than to the Friar, thus: (1) Romeo's comment on the coming of the daylight emphasizes his separation from Juliet, and (2) the figurative language seems more appropriate to Romeo than to the Friar. Having said this, in the Signet edition we have decided in this instance to draw on the evidence provided by earlier text and to give the lines to the Friar, on the grounds that since Q1 reflects a production, in the theater (at least on one occasion) the lines were spoken by the Friar.

A playwright sold a script to a theatrical company. The script thus belonged to the company, not the author, and author and company alike must have regarded this script not as a literary work but as the basis for a play that the actors would create on the stage. We speak of Shakespeare as the author of the plays, but readers should bear in mind that the texts they read, even when derived from a single text, such as the First Folio (1623), are inevitably the collaborative work not simply of Shakespeare with his company—doubtless during rehearsals the actors would suggest alterations—but also with other forces of the age. One force was governmental censorship. In 1606 parliament passed "an Act to restrain abuses of players," prohibiting the utterance of oaths and the name of God. So where the earliest text of *Othello* gives us "By heaven" (3.3.106), the first Folio gives "Alas," presumably reflecting the compliance of stage practice with the law. Similarly, the 1623 version of *King Lear* omits the oath "Fut" (probably from "By God's foot") at 1.2.142, again presumably reflecting the line as it was spoken on the stage. Editors who seek to give the reader the play that Shakespeare initially conceived—the "authentic" play conceived by the solitary Shakespeare—probably will restore the missing oaths and references to God. Other editors, who see the play as a collaborative work, a construction made not only by Shakespeare but also by actors and compositors and even government censors, may claim that what counts is the play as it was actually performed. Such editors regard the censored text as legitimate, since it is the play that was (presumably) finally put on. A performed text, they argue, has more historical reality than a text produced by an editor who has sought to get at what Shakespeare initially wrote. In this view, the text of a play is rather like the script of a film; the script is not the film, and the play text is not the performed play. Even if we want to talk about the play that Shakespeare "intended," we will find ourselves talking about a script that he handed over to a company with the intention that it be implemented by actors. The "intended" play is the one that the actors—we might almost say "society"—would help to construct.

Further, it is now widely held that a play is also the work of readers and spectators, who do not simply receive meaning, but who create it when they respond to the play. This idea is fully in accord with contemporary poststructuralist critical thinking, notably Roland Barthes's "The Death of the Author," in *Image-Music-Text* (1977) and Michel Foucault's "What Is an Author?", in *The Foucault Reader* (1984). The gist of the idea is that an author is not an isolated genius; rather, authors are subject to the politics and other social structures of their age. A dramatist especially is a worker in a collaborative project, working most obviously with actors—parts may be written for particular actors—but working also with the audience. Consider the words of Samuel Johnson, written to be spoken by the actor David Garrick at the opening of a theater in 1747:

> The stage but echoes back the public voice;
> The drama's laws, the drama's patrons give,
> For we that live to please, must please to live.

The audience—the public taste as understood by the playwright—helps to determine what the play is. Moreover, even members of the public who are not part of the playwright's immediate audience may exert an influence through censorship. We have already glanced at governmental censorship, but there are also other kinds. Take one of Shakespeare's most beloved characters, Falstaff, who appears in three of Shakespeare's plays, the two parts of *Henry IV* and *The Merry Wives of Windsor*. He appears with this name in the earliest printed version of the first of these plays, *1 Henry IV*, but we know that Shakespeare originally called him (after an historical figure) Sir John Oldcastle. Oldcastle appears in Shakespeare's source (partly reprinted in the Signet edition of *1 Henry IV*), and a trace of the name survives in Shakespeare's play, 1.2.43–44, where Prince Hal punningly addresses Falstaff as "my old lad of the castle." But for some reason—perhaps because the family of the historical Oldcastle complained—Shakespeare had to change the name. In short, the play as we have it was (at least in this detail) subject to some sort of censorship. If we think that a text should present what we take to be the author's intention, we probably will want to replace *Falstaff* with *Oldcastle*. But if we recognize that a play is a collaboration, we may welcome the change, even if it was forced on Shakespeare. Somehow *Falstaff*, with its hint of *false-staff*, i.e., inadequate prop, seems just right for this fat knight who, to our delight, entertains the young prince with untruths. We can go as far as saying that, at least so far as a play is concerned, an insistence on the author's original intention (even if we could know it) can sometimes impoverish the text.

The tiny example of Falstaff's name illustrates the point that the text we read is inevitably only a version—something in effect produced by the collaboration of the playwright with his actors, audiences, compositors, and editors—of a fluid text that Shakespeare once wrote, just as the *Hamlet* that we see on the screen starring Kenneth Branagh is not the *Hamlet* that Shakespeare saw in an open-air playhouse starring Richard Burbage. *Hamlet* itself, as we shall note in a moment, also exists in several versions. It is not surprising that there is now much talk about the *instability* of Shakespeare's texts.

Because he was not only a playwright but was also an actor and a shareholder in a theatrical company, Shakespeare probably was much involved with the translation of the play from a manuscript to a stage production. He may or may not have done some rewriting during rehearsals, and he may or may not have been happy with cuts that were made. Some plays, notably *Hamlet* and *King Lear*, are so long that it is most unlikely that the texts we read were acted in their entirety. Further, for both of these plays we have more than one early text that demands consideration. In *Hamlet*, the Second Quarto (1604) includes some two hundred lines not found in the Folio (1623). Among the passages missing from the Folio are two of Hamlet's reflective speeches, the "dram of evil" speech (1.4.13–38) and "How all occasions do inform against me" (4.4.32–66). Since the Folio has more numerous and often fuller stage directions, it certainly looks as though in the Folio we get a theatrical version of the play, a text whose cuts were probably made—this is only a hunch, of course—not because Shakespeare was changing his conception of Hamlet but because the playhouse demanded a modified play. (The problem is complicated, since the Folio not only cuts some of the Quarto but adds some material. Various explanations have been offered.)

Or take an example from *King Lear*. In the First and Second Quarto (1608, 1619), the final speech of the play is given to Albany, Lear's surviving son-in-law, but in the First Folio version (1623), the speech is given to Edgar. The Quarto version is in accord with tradition—usually the highest-ranking character in a tragedy speaks the final words. Why does the Folio give the speech to Edgar? One possible answer is this: The Folio version omits some of Albany's speeches in earlier scenes, so perhaps it was decided (by Shakespeare? by the players?) not to give the final lines to so pale a character. In fact, the discrepancies are so many between the two texts, that some scholars argue we do not simply have texts showing different theatrical productions. Rather, these scholars say, Shakespeare substantially revised the play, and we really have two versions of *King Lear* (and of *Othello* also, say some)—two different plays—not simply two texts, each of which is in some ways imperfect.

In this view, the 1608 version of *Lear* may derive from Shakespeare's manuscript, and the 1623 version may derive from his later revision. The Quartos have almost three hundred lines not in the Folio, and the Folio has about a hundred lines not in the Quartos. It used to be held that all the texts were imperfect in various ways and from various causes—some passages in the Quartos were thought to have been set from a manuscript that was not entirely legible, other passages were thought to have been set by a compositor who was new to setting plays, and still other passages were thought to have been provided by an actor who misremembered some of the lines. This traditional view held that an editor must draw on the Quartos and the Folio in order to get Shakespeare's "real" play. The new argument holds (although not without considerable strain) that we have two authentic plays, Shakespeare's early version (in the Quarto) and Shakespeare's—or his theatrical company's—revised version (in the Folio). Not only theatrical demands but also Shakespeare's own artistic sense, it is argued, called for extensive revisions. Even the titles vary: Q1 is called *True Chronicle Historie of the life and death of King Lear and his three Daughters*, whereas the Folio text is called *The Tragedie of King Lear*. To combine the two texts in order to produce what the editor thinks is the play that Shakespeare intended to write is, according to this view, to produce a text that is false to the history of the play. If the new view is correct, and we do have texts of two distinct versions of *Lear* rather than two imperfect versions of one play, it supports in a textual way the poststructuralist view that we cannot possibly have an unmediated vision of (in this case) a play by Shakespeare; we can only recognize a plurality of visions.

Editing Texts

Though eighteen of his plays were published during his lifetime, Shakespeare seems never to have supervised their publication. There is nothing unusual here; when a playwright sold a play to a theatrical company he surrendered his ownership to it. Normally a company would not publish the play, because to publish it meant to allow competitors to acquire the piece. Some plays did get published: Apparently hard-up actors sometimes pieced together a play for a publisher; sometimes a company in need of money sold a play; and sometimes a company allowed publication of a play that no longer drew audiences. That Shakespeare did not concern himself with publication is not remarkable; of his contemporaries, only Ben Jonson carefully supervised the publication of his own plays.

In 1623, seven years after Shakespeare's death, John Heminges and Henry Condell (two senior members of Shakespeare's company, who had worked with him for about twenty years) collected his plays—published and unpublished—into a large volume, of a kind called a folio. (A folio is a volume consisting of large sheets that have been folded once, each sheet thus making two leaves, or four pages. The size of the page of course depends on the size of the sheet—a folio can range in height from twelve to sixteen inches, and in width from eight to eleven; the pages in the 1623 edition of Shakespeare, commonly called the First Folio, are approximately thirteen inches tall and eight inches wide.) The eighteen plays published during Shakespeare's lifetime had been issued one play per volume in small formats called quartos. (Each sheet in a quarto has been folded twice, making four leaves, or eight pages, each page being about nine inches tall and seven inches wide, roughly the size of a large paperback.)

Heminges and Condell suggest in an address "To the great variety of readers" that the republished plays are presented in better form than in the quartos:

Before you were abused with diverse stolen and surreptitious copies, maimed and deformed by the frauds and stealths of injurious impostors that exposed them; even those, are now offered to your view cured and perfect of their limbs, and all the rest absolute in their numbers, as he [i.e., Shakespeare] conceived them.

There is a good deal of truth to this statement, but some of the quarto versions are better than others; some are in fact preferable to the Folio text.

Whoever was assigned to prepare the texts for publication in the first Folio seems to have taken the job seriously and yet not to have performed it with uniform care. The sources of the texts seem to have been, in general, good unpublished copies or the best published copies. The first play in the collection, *The Tempest*, is divided into acts and scenes, has unusually full stage directions and descriptions of spectacle, and concludes with a list of the characters, but the editor was not able (or willing) to present all of the succeeding texts so fully dressed. Later texts occasionally show signs of carelessness: in one scene of *Much Ado About Nothing* the names of actors, instead of characters, appear as speech prefixes, as they had in the Quarto, which the Folio reprints; proofreading throughout the Folio is spotty and apparently was done without reference to the printer's copy; the pagination of *Hamlet* jumps from 156 to 257. Further, the proofreading was done while the presses continued to print, so that each play in each volume contains a mix of corrected and uncorrected pages.

Modern editors of Shakespeare must first select their copy; no problem if the play exists only in the Folio, but a considerable problem if the relationship between a Quarto and the Folio—or an early Quarto and a later one—is unclear. In the case of *Romeo and Juliet*, the First Quarto (Q1), published in 1597, is vastly inferior to the Second (Q2), published in 1599. The basis of Q1 apparently is a version put together from memory by some actors. Not surprisingly, it garbles many passages and is much shorter than Q2. On the other hand, occasionally Q1 makes better sense than Q2. For instance, near the end of the play, when the parents have assembled and learned of the deaths of Romeo and Juliet, in Q2 the Prince says (5.3.208–9),

Come, *Montague;* for thou art early vp
To see thy sonne and heire, now earling downe.

The last three words of this speech surely do not make sense, and many editors turn to Q1, which instead of "now earling downe" has "more early downe." Some modern editors take only "early" from Q1, and print "now early down"; others take "more early," and print "more early down." Further, Q1 (though, again, quite clearly a garbled and abbreviated text) includes some stage directions that are not found in Q2, and today many editors who base their text on Q2 are glad to add these stage directions, because the directions help to give us a sense of what the play looked like on Shakespeare's stage. Thus, in 4.3.58, after Juliet drinks the potion, Q1 gives us this stage direction, not in Q2: *"She falls upon her bed within the curtains."*

In short, an editor's decisions do not end with the choice of a single copy text. First of all, editors must reckon with Elizabethan spelling. If they are not producing a facsimile, they probably modernize the spelling, but ought they to preserve the old forms of words that apparently were pronounced quite unlike their modern forms—*lanthorn, alablaster*? If they preserve these forms are they really preserving Shakespeare's forms or perhaps those of a compositor in the printing house? What is one to do when one finds *lanthorn* and *lantern* in adjacent lines? (The editors of this series in general, but not invariably, assume that words should be spelled in their modern form, unless, for instance, a rhyme is involved.) Elizabethan punctuation, too, presents problems. For example, in the First Folio, the only text for the play, Macbeth rejects his wife's idea that he can wash the blood from his hand (2.2.60–62):

> No: this my Hand will rather
> The multitudinous Seas incarnardine,
> Making the Greene one, Red.

Obviously an editor will remove the superfluous capitals, and will probably alter the spelling to "incarnadine," but what about the comma before "Red"? If we retain the comma, Macbeth is calling the sea "the green one." If we drop the comma, Macbeth is saying that his bloody hand will make the sea ("the Green") *uniformly* red.

An editor will sometimes have to change more than spelling and punctuation. Macbeth says to his wife (1.7.46–47):

> I dare do all that may become a man,
> Who dares no more, is none.

For two centuries editors have agreed that the second line is unsatisfactory, and have emended "no" to "do": "Who dares do more is none." But when in the same play (4.2.21–22) Ross says that fearful persons

Floate vpon a wilde and violent Sea
Each way, and moue,

need we emend the passage? On the assumption that the compositor misread the manuscript, some editors emend "each way, and move" to "and move each way"; others emend "move" to "none" (i.e., "Each way and none"). Other editors, however, let the passage stand as in the original. The editors of the Signet Classic Shakespeare have restrained themselves from making abundant emendations. In their minds they hear Samuel Johnson on the dangers of emendation: "I have adopted the Roman sentiment, that it is more honorable to save a citizen than to kill an enemy." Some departures (in addition to spelling, punctuation, and lineation) from the copy text have of course been made, but the original readings are listed in a note following the play, so that readers can evaluate the changes for themselves.

Following tradition, the editors of the Signet Classic Shakespeare have prefaced each play with a list of characters, and throughout the play have regularized the names of the speakers. Thus, in our text of *Romeo and Juliet*, all speeches by Juliet's mother are prefixed "Lady Capulet," although the 1599 Quarto of the play, which provides our copy text, uses at various points seven speech tags for this one character: *Capu. Wi.* (i.e., Capulet's wife), *Ca. Wi.*, *Wi.*, *Wife*, *Old La.* (i.e., Old Lady), *La.*, and *Mo.* (i.e., Mother). Similarly, in *All's Well That Ends Well*, the character whom we regularly call "Countess" is in the Folio (the copy text) variously identified as *Mother, Countess, Old Countess, Lady*, and *Old Lady*. Admittedly there is some loss in regularizing, since the various prefixes may give us a hint of the way Shakespeare (or a scribe who copied Shakespeare's manuscript) was thinking of the character in a particular scene—for instance, as a mother, or as an old lady. But too much can be made of these differing prefixes, since the social relationships implied are *not* always relevant to the given scene.

We have also added line numbers and in many cases act and scene divisions as well as indications of locale at the beginning of scenes. The Folio divided most of the plays into acts and some into scenes. Early eighteenth-century editors increased the divisions. These divisions, which provide a convenient way of referring to passages in the plays, have been retained, but when not in the text chosen as the basis for the Signet Classic text they are enclosed within square brackets, [ ], to indicate that they are editorial additions. Similarly, though no play of Shakespeare's was equipped with indications of the locale at the heads of scene divisions, locales have here been added in square brackets for the convenience of readers, who lack the information that costumes, properties, gestures, and scenery afford to spectators. Spectators can tell at a glance they are in the throne room, but without an editorial indication the reader may be puzzled for a while. It should be mentioned, incidentally, that there are a few authentic stage directions—perhaps Shakespeare's, perhaps a prompter's—that suggest locales, such as *"Enter Brutus in his orchard,"* and *"They go up into the Senate house."* It is hoped that the bracketed additions in the Signet text will provide readers with the sort of help provided by these two authentic directions, but it is equally hoped that the reader will remember that the stage was not loaded with scenery.

Shakespeare on the Stage

Each volume in the Signet Classic Shakespeare includes a brief stage (and sometimes film) history of the play. When we read about earlier productions, we are likely to find them eccentric, obviously wrongheaded—for instance, Nahum Tate's version of *King Lear*, with a happy ending, which held the stage for about a century and a half, from the late seventeenth century until the end of the first quarter of the nineteenth. We see engravings of David Garrick, the greatest actor of the eighteenth century, in eighteenth-century garb as King Lear, and we smile, thinking how absurd the production must have been. If we are more thoughtful, we say, with the English novelist L. P. Hartley, "The past is a foreign country: they do things differently there." But if the eighteenth-century staging is a foreign country, what of the plays of the late sixteenth and seventeenth centuries? A foreign language, a foreign theater, a foreign audience.

Probably all viewers of Shakespeare's plays, beginning with Shakespeare himself, at times have been unhappy with the plays on the stage. Consider three comments about production that we find in the plays themselves, which suggest Shakespeare's concerns. The Chorus in *Henry V* complains that the heroic story cannot possibly be adequately staged:

> But pardon, gentles all,
> The flat unraisèd spirits that hath dared
> On this unworthy scaffold to bring forth
> So great an object. Can this cockpit hold
> The vasty fields of France? Or may we cram
> Within this wooden *O* the very casques
> That did affright the air at Agincourt?
>
> . . . .
>
> Piece out our imperfections with your thoughts.
>
> (Prologue 1.8–14, 23)

Second, here are a few sentences (which may or may not represent Shakespeare's own views) from Hamlet's longish lecture to the players:

> Speak the speech, I pray you, as I pronounced it to you, trippingly on the tongue. But if you mouth it, as many of our players do, I had as lief the town crier spoke my lines. . . . O, it offends me to the soul to hear a robustious periwig-pated fellow tear a passion to tatters, to very rags, to split the ears of the groundlings. . . . And let those that play your clowns speak no more than is set down for them, for there be of them that will themselves laugh, to set on some quantity of barren spectators to laugh too, though in the meantime some necessary question of the play be then to be considered. That's villainous and shows a most pitiful ambition in the fool that uses it. (3.2.1–47)

Finally, we can quote again from the passage cited earlier in this introduction, concerning the boy actors who played the female roles. Cleopatra imagines with horror a theatrical version of her activities with Antony:

> The quick comedians
> Extemporally will stage us, and present
> Our Alexandrian revels: Antony
> Shall be brought drunken forth, and I shall see

Some squeaking Cleopatra boy my greatness
I' th' posture of a whore.   (5.2.216–21)

It is impossible to know how much weight to put on such passages—perhaps Shakespeare was just being modest about his theater's abilities—but it is easy enough to think that he was unhappy with some aspects of Elizabethan production. Probably no production can fully satisfy a playwright, and for that matter, few productions can fully satisfy *us;* we regret this or that cut, this or that way of costuming the play, this or that bit of business.

One's first thought may be this: Why don't they just do "authentic" Shakespeare, "straight" Shakespeare, the play as Shakespeare wrote it? But as we read the plays—words written to be performed—it sometimes becomes clear that we do not know *how* to perform them. For instance, in *Antony and Cleopatra* Antony, the Roman general who has succumbed to Cleopatra and to Egyptian ways, says, "The nobleness of life / Is to do thus" (1.1.36–37). But what is "thus"? Does Antony at this point embrace Cleopatra? Does he embrace and kiss her? (There are, by the way, very few scenes of kissing on Shakespeare's stage, possibly because boys played the female roles.) Or does he make a sweeping gesture, indicating the Egyptian way of life?

This is not an isolated example; the plays are filled with lines that call for gestures, but we are not sure what the gestures should be. *Interpretation* is inevitable. Consider a passage in *Hamlet*. In 3.1, Polonius persuades his daughter, Ophelia, to talk to Hamlet while Polonius and Claudius eavesdrop. The two men conceal themselves, and Hamlet encounters Ophelia. At 3.1.131 Hamlet suddenly says to her, "Where's your father?" Why does Hamlet, apparently out of nowhere—they have not been talking about Polonius—ask this question? Is this an example of the "antic disposition" (fantastic behavior) that Hamlet earlier (1.5.172) had told Horatio and others—including us—he would display? That is, is the question about the whereabouts of her father a seemingly irrational one, like his earlier question (3.1.103) to Ophelia, "Ha, ha! Are you honest?" Or, on the other hand, has Hamlet (as in many productions) suddenly glimpsed Polonius's foot protruding from beneath a drapery at the rear? That is, does Hamlet ask the question because he has suddenly seen something suspicious and now is testing Ophelia? (By the way, in productions that do give Hamlet a physical cue, it is almost always Polonius rather than Claudius who provides the clue. This itself is an act of interpretation on the part of the director.) Or (a third possibility) does Hamlet get a clue from Ophelia, who inadvertently betrays the spies by nervously glancing at their place of hiding? This is the interpretation used in the BBC television version, where Ophelia glances in fear toward the hiding place just after Hamlet says "Why wouldst thou be a breeder of sinners?" (121–22). Hamlet, realizing that he is being observed, glances here and there *before* he asks "Where's your father?" The question thus is a climax to what he has been doing while speaking the preceding lines. Or (a fourth interpretation) does Hamlet suddenly, without the aid of any clue whatsoever, intuitively (insightfully, mysteriously, wonderfully) sense that someone is spying? Directors must decide, of course—and so must readers.

Recall, too, the preceding discussion of the texts of the plays, which argued that the texts—though they seem to be before us in permanent black on white—are unstable. The Signet text of *Hamlet*, which draws on the Second Quarto (1604) and the First Folio (1623) is considerably longer than any version staged in Shakespeare's time. Our version, even if spoken very briskly and played without any intermission, would take close to four hours, far beyond "the two hours' traffic of our stage" mentioned in the Prologue to *Romeo and Juliet*. (There are a few contemporary references to the duration of a play, but none mentions more than three hours.) Of Shakespeare's plays, only *The Comedy of Errors*, *Macbeth*, and *The Tempest* can be done in less than three hours without cutting. And even if we take a play that exists only in a short text, *Macbeth*, we cannot claim that we are experiencing the very play that Shakespeare conceived, partly because some of the Witches' songs almost surely are non-Shakespearean additions, and partly because we are not willing to watch the play performed without an intermission and with boys in the female roles.

Further, as the earlier discussion of costumes mentioned, the plays apparently were given chiefly in contemporary, that is, in Elizabethan dress. If today we give them in the costumes that Shakespeare probably saw, the plays seem not contemporary but curiously dated. Yet if we use our own dress, we find lines of dialogue that are at odds with what we see; we may feel that the language, so clearly not our own, is inappropriate coming out of people in today's dress. A common solution, incidentally, has been to set the plays in the nineteenth century, on the grounds that this attractively distances the plays (gives them a degree of foreignness, allowing for interesting costumes) and yet doesn't put them into a museum world of Elizabethan England.

Inevitably our productions are adaptations, *our* adaptations, and inevitably they will look dated, not in a century but in twenty years, or perhaps even in a decade. Still, we cannot escape from our own conceptions. As the director Peter Brook has said, in *The Empty Space* (1968):

> It is not only the hair-styles, costumes and make-ups that look dated. All the different elements of staging—the shorthands of behavior that stand for emotions; gestures, gesticulations and tones of voice—are all fluctuating on an invisible stock exchange all the time. . . . A living theatre that thinks it can stand aloof from anything as trivial as fashion will wilt. (p. 16)

As Brook indicates, it is through today's hairstyles, costumes, makeup, gestures, gesticulations, tones of voice—this includes our *conception* of earlier hairstyles, costumes, and so forth if we stage the play in a period other than our own—that we inevitably stage the plays.

It is a truism that every age invents its own Shakespeare, just as, for instance, every age has invented its own classical world. Our view of ancient Greece, a slave-holding society in which even free Athenian women were severely circumscribed, does not much resemble the Victorians' view of ancient Greece as a glorious democracy, just as, perhaps, our view of Victorianism itself does not much resemble theirs. We cannot claim that the Shakespeare on our stage is the true Shakespeare, but in our stage productions we find a Shakespeare that speaks to us, a Shakespeare that our ancestors doubtless did not know but one that seems to us to be the true Shakespeare—at least for a while.

Our age is remarkable for the wide variety of kinds of staging that it uses for Shakespeare, but one development deserves special mention. This is the now common practice of race-blind or color-blind or nontraditional casting, which allows persons who are not white to play in Shakespeare. Previously blacks performing in Shakespeare were limited to a mere three roles, Othello, Aaron (in *Titus Andronicus*), and the Prince of Morocco (in *The Merchant of Venice*), and there were no roles at all for Asians. Indeed, African-Americans rarely could play even one of these three roles, since they were not welcome in white companies. Ira Aldridge (c.1806–1867), a black actor of undoubted talent, was forced to make his living by performing Shakespeare in England and in Europe, where he could play not only Othello but also—in whiteface—other tragic roles such as King Lear. Paul Robeson (1898–1976) made theatrical history when he played Othello in London in 1930, and there was some talk about bringing the production to the United States, but there was more talk about whether American audiences would tolerate the sight of a black man—a real black man, not a white man in blackface—kissing and then killing a white woman. The idea was tried out in summer stock in 1942, the reviews were enthusiastic, and in the following year Robeson opened on Broadway in a production that ran an astounding 296 performances. An occasional all-black company sometimes performed Shakespeare's plays, but otherwise blacks (and other minority members) were in effect shut out from performing Shakespeare. Only since about 1970 has it been common for nonwhites to play major roles along with whites. Thus, in a 1996–97 production of *Antony and Cleopatra*, a white Cleopatra, Vanessa Redgrave, played opposite a black Antony, David Harewood. Multiracial casting is now especially common at the New York Shakespeare Festival, founded in 1954 by Joseph Papp, and in England, where even siblings such as Claudio and Isabella in *Measure for Measure* or Lear's three daughters may be of different races. Probably most viewers today soon stop worrying about the lack of realism, and move beyond the color of the performers' skin to the quality of the performance.

Nontraditional casting is not only a matter of color or race; it includes sex. In the past, occasionally a distinguished

woman of the theater has taken on a male role—Sarah Bern-
hardt (1844–1923) as Hamlet is perhaps the most famous
example—but such performances were widely regarded
as eccentric. Although today there have been some performances involving cross-dressing (a drag *As You Like It*
staged by the National Theatre in England in 1966 and in the
United States in 1974 has achieved considerable fame in
the annals of stage history), what is more interesting is the
casting of women in roles that traditionally are male but that
need not be. Thus, a 1993–94 English production of *Henry
V* used a woman—*not* cross-dressed—in the role of the governor of Harfleur. According to Peter Holland, who reviewed
the production in *Shakespeare Survey* 48 (1995), "having a
female Governor of Harfleur feminized the city and provided
a direct response to the horrendous threat of rape and murder
that Henry had offered, his language and her body in direct
connection and opposition" (p. 210). Ten years from now
the device may not play so effectively, but today it speaks to
us. Shakespeare, born in the Elizabethan Age, has been dead
nearly four hundred years, yet he is, as Ben Jonson said, "not
of an age but for all time." We must understand, however,
that he is "for all time" precisely because each age finds in
his abundance something for itself and something of itself.

And here we come back to two issues discussed earlier in
this introduction—the instability of the text and, curiously,
the Bacon/Oxford heresy concerning the authorship of the
plays. *Of course* Shakespeare wrote the plays, and we should
daily fall on our knees to thank him for them—and yet there
is something to the idea that he is not their only author.
Every editor, every director and actor, and every reader to
some degree shapes them, too, for when we edit, direct, act,
or read, we inevitably become Shakespeare's collaborator
and re-create the plays. The plays, one might say, are so cunningly contrived that they guide our responses, tell us how
we ought to feel, and make a mark on us, but (for better or
for worse) we also make a mark on them.

—SYLVAN BARNET
Tufts University

Introduction to *Titus Andronicus*

Titus Andronicus has had few admirers and numerous detractors. T. S. Eliot states the detractors' case as directly as any: *Titus* is "one of the stupidest and most uninspired plays ever written, a play in which it is incredible that Shakespeare had any hand at all, a play in which the best passages would be too highly honored by the signature of Peele." Unlike Eliot's notably original view that *Hamlet* "so far from being Shakespeare's masterpiece . . . is most certainly an artistic failure," his remark on *Titus* is a commonplace: Dr. Johnson, Hazlitt, Coleridge, and the editor of the Yale edition denied Shakespeare's authorship of most of the play; the editor of the New Cambridge edition gives much of it to Peele and saves some of the Shakespearean passages only by the desperate expedient of claiming that they are not really bad but are a clever burlesque of bad writing.

The idea that *Titus* may not be entirely Shakespeare's is at least as old as 1687, when Thomas Ravenscroft, who had recently given the stage his adaptation of the play, recorded that he had been told that Shakespeare "only gave some master-touches to one or two of the principal parts or characters." But the evidence that Shakespeare wrote *Titus* is weighty. In 1598 Francis Meres listed it as one of Shakespeare's plays, and in 1623 Heminges and Condell, who had acted with Shakespeare for some twenty years, included *Titus* in the Folio collection of his plays. However displeased we may be by part or all of *Titus*, there is no utterly convincing evidence that it is not entirely by Shakespeare, though an interesting case has been made that he worked in collaboration with George Peele, whose hand some have detected in certain scenes, notably 1.1, 2.1, and 4.1. The chief arguments have to do with certain verbal constructions

2

Peele favored (e.g., a preposition, possessive pronoun, and monosyllabic noun at the end of a sentence, such as "of my right"), and certain words (e.g., "brethren" rather than "brothers"). The evidence—requiring some understanding of statistics—is lucidly summarized by Brian Vickers in *Shakespeare, Co-Author* (2002), but even Vickers' forceful presentation does not convince all readers that Peele was indeed a coauthor.

There are, of course, some inconsistencies that have been offered as proof that Shakespeare was revising an older play. We are told in 2.3.86 that Tamora's infidelity to the Emperor has "made him noted [i.e., notorious] long," although Tamora and the Emperor have been married only one night. But such an inconsistency proves no more about dual authorship than the similar treatment of time in *Othello*, or the apparently contradictory remarks about Macbeth's children. More serious is the shift of the villain's role from Tamora to Aaron, but again it does not prove that Shakespeare is revising an earlier play; probably he found the Moor Aaron coming to life as he worked on him, and Tamora simply fell into the background until the last act, when her part is stronger.

There is no sense trying to dissociate Shakespeare from *Titus;* all the available evidence insists that it is canonical. But neither is there any sense in emphasizing, as has recently been done, its connection with Shakespeare's early historical plays or with his later Roman tragedies. A good deal has been written about the Elizabethan history play as a dramatized sermon on the wounds of civil war, a sermon of special interest to Englishmen whose monarch was an aging and heirless queen. The later Roman plays, too, are seen to have political subjects. It is true, of course, that *Julius Caesar, Antony and Cleopatra,* and *Coriolanus* are all concerned in part with civil war, but it is hard to believe that while witnessing a performance of, say, *Antony and Cleopatra,* Shakespeare's audience fretted about the possibility that England would find itself the battlefield of triumvirs; rather it must have been watching with interest a story in which political themes are subordinated to the doings of a "lass unparalleled" and a general who becomes "the noble ruin of her magic." *Titus* does indeed concern itself, in part of the first scene, with establishing the succession in Rome; Titus is asked (1.1.186) to "help to set a head on headless Rome." But thereafter the motif fades from view until the fifth act, when Lucius, one of Titus' sons, leads an army against the vicious emperor whom Titus in the first scene helped to establish. In 5.3.73 ff. there is a speech stressing the horror of civil war, but it can scarcely be said to be closely related to what has preceded it, and its ascription to a nameless "Roman Lord" suggests that it may well have been an afterthought. There is, furthermore, a curious bit of evidence that Shakespeare regarded the play as less political than did the earliest recorded interpreter, the printer or editor of the second quarto (1600). The first quarto (1594) concludes—as presumably Shakespeare concluded—with some lines about the deceased wicked queen:

> As for that ravenous tiger, Tamora,
> No funeral rite, nor man in mourning weed,
> No mournful bell shall ring her burial;
> But throw her forth to beasts and birds to prey.
> Her life was beastly and devoid of pity,
> And being dead, let birds on her take pity.

When a second edition was called for, it was apparently set up from a copy that had suffered some damage to the foot of the last leaf of text; the person overseeing the publication seems to have mistakenly thought that some lines had been lost at the foot, though in fact nothing was lost but "Finis the Tragedy of Titus Andronicus." He added four lines:

> See justice done on Aaron, that damned Moor,
> By whom our heavy haps had their beginning;
> Then afterwards to order well the state,
> That like events may ne'er it ruinate.

The last two lines, though bad, are appropriate enough and have their parallels in later plays when rather colorless characters assure their fellows that some sort of order is returning to the state, but certainly neither these lines nor the first scene should turn our minds from characters and passions to politics. Shakespeare himself ended the play by calling attention not to political concerns but to the pitiless queen whose body will be left for scavenging birds.

To say that Shakespeare ended his play with a comment on the Queen and not on the state is not to deny that there are substantial passages devoted to the state. But the final lines emphasize the central concern of the play—the passions and deeds that are the stuff of tragedy. Critics tend to suggest that we go to a tragedy so that we may draw political and ethical conclusions, but the tragic dramatists tend to emphasize deeds of horror and passionate responses to these deeds. Even at the end of a play, the emphasis is not on drawing conclusions, but on experiencing emotions. Nobody who witnesses *Hamlet* can feel that the entrance of Fortinbras shifts attention from tragic experiences to ethics and politics; attention is kept on the catastrophic happenings in Denmark.

Ambassador.   The sight is dismal;
   And our affairs from England come too late.
   The ears are senseless that should give us hearing. . . .

Horatio. But since, so jump upon this bloody question,
   You from the Polack wars, and you from England,
   Are here arrived, give order that these bodies
   High on a stage be placèd to the view,
   And let me speak to th' yet unknowing world
   How these things came about. So shall you hear
   Of carnal, bloody, and unnatural acts,
   Of accidental judgments, casual slaughters,
   Of deaths put on by cunning and forced cause,
   And, in this upshot, purposes mistook
   Fall'n on th' inventors' heads.

                                             (*Hamlet* 5.2.368–86)

The violence of *Titus* has often aroused condemnation, as though tragedy did not customarily dramatize violence. It is true that *Titus* has more than its share, but if, for example, we find especially abhorrent the introduction of the severed heads of two of Titus' sons, it is perhaps because we have forgotten (since directors customarily omit the business) a stage direction in the last act of *Macbeth*, "Enter Macduff, with Macbeth's head." Repulsive happenings are not something Shakespeare dramatized in his youth and then outgrew; *Hamlet* concludes with four corpses (there would be a fifth if Horatio had his way), to say nothing of the earlier deaths or the skulls the gravediggers unearth; *King Lear* calls for Gloucester to be blinded before the audience, and it concludes with the (to modern taste) gratuitous introduction of the corpses of Goneril and Regan, who have had the grace to die offstage. The dozen or so deaths in *Titus* are about double the number in *Lear*, and the rape and cannibalism in Titus are unparalleled elsewhere in Shakespeare, but they are not incompatible with the idea of tragedy. Nor are they mere Elizabethan sensationalism. If we recall Clytemnestra exulting over her slaughtered husband, or the incestuous Oedipus entering on the stage with bloody eyeless sockets, or the lecherous Pentheus, whose mother will in a frenzy exult over his severed head, we remember that none of the world's four great tragic dramatists shrinks from dramatizing the demonic and the horrible. We tend, especially if we are readers rather than spectators, to emphasize the wisdom and patience that are allegedly achieved through heroic suffering, but surely we ought to recall, for example, that Hamlet in the last act forces poison down Claudius' throat. Again, we can talk of purgation and reconciliation in *King Lear*, but we must recall that the cries and horrors do not disappear toward the end of the play; it is only seventy-five lines before the end that Lear enters with the dead Cordelia in his arms ("Howl, howl, howl, howl"), and the play closes with a dead march.

Of Shakespeare's early tragedies—*Richard III*, *Titus*, *Richard II*, and *Romeo and Juliet*—*Titus* is certainly the poorest, but it alone has a protagonist who is both noble and flawed, and thus it looks forward to *Julius Caesar* and to the greater tragedies. *Romeo and Juliet*, perhaps the best of Shakespeare's early tragedies, is an incomparably finer piece of work than *Titus*, but its vision of star-crossed lovers is quite different from the tragic vision of *Hamlet*, *Othello*, *Lear*, *Macbeth*, *Antony and Cleopatra*, and *Coriolanus*, whose protagonists in a significant way resemble Titus. In

Romeo and Juliet the lack of any vigorous presentation of evil (in most of the greater tragedies Shakespeare did not hesitate to draw potent villains), the decisive role played by chance, the youth and innocence of the lovers, and the emphasis on reconciliation at the end, all work together to produce a tragedy that strikes us as substantially different from the later tragedies. Of course one can say that the lovers are in some measure responsible for their fates—if they had not loved they might have outlived their parents—but the overall impression is one of innocence destroyed by destiny and released from this transitory world to a timeless realm. *Titus* is something else; in it, as in the great tragedies, deeds recoil on the head of the doers and even well-intentioned deeds may have their painful consequences. Titus offers up Alarbus as a sacrifice to the souls of the dead, and he thereby incurs the hatred of Tamora. Declining to accept the title of emperor, Titus helps to establish Saturninus, who quickly proves to be his foe. Titus nominates Saturninus apparently because he is the elder son—a reasonable basis—but the first two speeches of the play suggest to the hearer that Bassianus rather than Saturninus is the fitter. What Shakespeare is doing, of course, is dramatizing what seems to be an essential tragic fact—a man doing something according to his best lights and according to an impressive but, as it proves, mistaken code. In his dealings with his sons, as well as with Tamora and Saturninus, Titus prefigures the great tragic heroes: Titus' inflexible conception of honor alienates him even from those he loves. He moves, a Titan, in a world of his own, at times heroically silent when lesser men would weep, at times loudly lamenting to the stones when lesser men would be silent. At the start it is said of him,

> A nobler man, a braver warrior,
> Lives not this day within the city walls.

> (1.1.25–26)

His nobility, his bravery, sets him off from others, even from his own sons, and (like Othello's high vision of Desdemona that leads him to kill her when he thinks her unchaste) Titus' virtues themselves become oppressive. His code of honor sets him apart from other men; he becomes increasingly aware of a painful isolation, and he speaks of it grandly, as a tragic hero should. Juliet comes to realize that her "dismal scene [she] needs must act alone"; Macbeth, plotting Banquo's death, keeps even his wife "innocent of the knowledge"; Hamlet speaks "wild and whirling words" and is markedly detached from Horatio, as well as from Claudius, Gertrude, and Ophelia; Lear will "abjure all roofs"; Coriolanus, told that he is banished from Rome, will reply "I banish you." Titus, the earliest of these protagonists, says of himself:

> For now I stand as one upon a rock,
> Environed with a wilderness of sea,
> Who marks the waxing tide grow wave by wave,
> Expecting ever when some envious surge
> Will in his brinish bowels swallow him.
> This way to death my wretched sons are gone,
> Here stands my other son, a banished man,
> And here my brother weeping at my woes:
> But that which gives my soul the greatest spurn
> Is dear Lavinia, dearer than my soul.

> (3.1.93–102)

Like Shakespeare's other tragic figures, he wears the shirt of Nessus and gives vent to his feelings. The speech is a little too self-conscious, the assonance, alliteration, and other repetitions are a little too insistent (*waxing, wave by wave; expecting, ever, envious; brinish bowels; stands, son; weeping, woes; soul, spurn, dear, dearer, soul*), but one would be hard pressed to point to a better passage in the work of any of Shakespeare's early contemporaries other than Marlowe.

Shakespeare must have felt that his chief problem was one of style, not of plot: What sort of rhetoric could effectively present the bloody and unnatural horrors that were the substance of Elizabethan tragedy and of classical tragedy as he knew it? There was, of course, no question of presenting tragic happenings "realistically"; tragedy was concerned with unusual people in unusual situations; its medium was verse, not prose. *Titus* contains a few brief exchanges in prose, and indeed the Clown's prose is notable ("God forbid, I should be so bold to press to heaven in my young days" [4.3.91–92]), but when he wrote *Titus,* Shakespeare must have been unable to conceive of the significant role that prose might play in his tragedies. Even half a century or so after Shakespeare's great achievements in tragic prose, England's best dramatic critic of the time believed that because tragedy shows us "nature wrought up to a higher pitch" it ought to be in verse. (Dryden advocated heroic couplets, however, not blank verse.) The verse drama of Shakespeare's infancy and much of that of his youth was rhymed, heavily alliterative, and rich in laments built on apostrophes, rhetorical questions, and exclamations. To us it seems stiff and foolish, even in the hands of, say, George Gascoigne, who was educated at Cambridge, and who wrote some lyric and satiric verse of considerable merit. Here is a passage from Gascoigne's tragedy *Jocasta,* produced at Gray's Inn in 1566:

Antigone. O doleful day, wherein my sorry sire
    Was born, and yet O more unhappy hour
    When he was crowned king of stately Thebes.
    The Hymenei, in unhappy bed
    And wicked wedlock, wittingly did join
    The guiltless mother with her guilty son,
    Out of which root we be the branches born
    To bear the scourge of their so foul offense.

If a passage with less narrative content is wanted, the following will do to show the tragic lament full-blown:

Antigone. O weary life, why bid'st thou in my breast
    And I contented be that these mine eyes
    Should see her die that gave to me this life,
    And I not 'venge her death by loss of life?
    Who can me give a fountain made of moan,
    That I may weep as much as is my will,
    To souse this sorrow up in swelling tears?

Finally:

> *Oedipus.* O wife, O mother, O both woeful names,
>   O woeful mother, and O woeful wife,
>   O would to God, alas, O would to God,
>   Thou ne'er had been my mother, nor my wife.

That Gascoigne is translating does not obscure the kind or
the quality of his verse. Shakespeare must have been very
familiar with this sort of writing; in *A Midsummer Night's
Dream* he neatly parodies (through Bottom's speech) the
lament of the previous generation:

>   But stay, O spite!
>   But mark, poor knight,
>   What dreadful dole is here!
>   Eyes, do you see?
>   How can it be?
>   O dainty duck! O dear!
>   Thy mantle good,
>   What, stained with blood!
>   Approach, ye Furies fell!
>   O Fates, come, come,
>   Cut thread and thrum;
>   Quail, crush, conclude, and quell!
>   (5.1.268–79)

More subtle, Hotspur's dying words in *1 Henry IV* have a
touch of the same absurd apostrophe and alliteration that
marked the older drama and that are appropriate to this
anachronistic young knight:

>   O Harry, thou hast robbed me of my youth!
>   I better brook the loss of brittle life
>   Than those proud titles thou hast won of me.
>   They wound my thoughts worse than thy sword my flesh.
>   But thoughts, the slaves of life, and life, Time's fool....
>   (5.4.80–84)

In *Titus* there is a good deal of alliteration, balance, and
parallelism, especially in the first two acts:

> Patient yourself, madam, and pardon me
> (1.1.121)

> Rome's readiest champions, repose you here in rest
> (151)

> Clear up, fair Queen, that cloudy countenance.
> Though chance of war hath wrought this change of cheer
> (263–64)

> And curtained with a counsel-keeping cave
> (2.3.24)

On the whole the impression is not that of naïveté; or if there is a suggestion of naïveté, it is that of a highly talented writer infatuated with his medium and occasionally forgetful of the dramatic ends that every speech ought to serve. Despite the abundant (almost comically frequent) horrors, the atmosphere is more that of the hothouse than the slaughterhouse; the horrors exist in elegant luxuriance, and though the groundlings probably were delighted, the author must have felt he was creating a drama that would appeal also to the cultivated, who knew Seneca and Ovid.

The Latin quotations that dot the play are the most apparent sign of the lamp, but the fifty-odd mythological allusions are scarcely less apparent. Despite the classical setting, Shakespeare did not have to strew his play with references to Pyramus, Vulcan, Cerberus, Prometheus, Hecuba, the Styx, Dido and Aeneas, Priam, Virginius, and a host of others. *Julius Caesar* has only a tenth as many mythological allusions, but when he wrote *Titus*, Shakespeare evidently was aiming at something quite different from the spare style he was to use in *Julius Caesar*. In *Titus* he seeks to capture grandeur by abundance. Here is a sample:

> Now climbeth Tamora Olympus' top,
> Safe out of fortune's shot, and sits aloft,
> Secure of thunder's crack or lightning flash,
> Advanced above pale envy's threat'ning reach.
> As when the golden sun salutes the morn,
> And having gilt the ocean with his beams,

> Gallops the zodiac in his glistering coach,
> And overlooks the highest-peering hills;
> So Tamora:
> Upon her wit doth earthly honor wait,
> And virtue stoops and trembles at her frown.
>
> (2.1.1–11)

The simile beginning in line 5 is markedly introduced by the prominent position that "As" occupies in the line, and it is markedly concluded by the similarly prominent "So" in line 9; the explicit allusion to Olympus and the only barely less explicit allusion to Phoebus suggest that Shakespeare is attempting to climb, in Sidney's phrase, to "the height of Seneca his style." (Before the speech is over there will be a reference to Prometheus, and another to Semiramis.) Sidney was speaking, about 1585, of *Gorboduc* (1562), but his words apply to the infinitely superior *Titus:* "it is full of stately speeches and well-sounding phrases."

  This heightened style, as well as the conception of a tragic hero pushed beyond the limits of endurance, surely owes something to Seneca, but Ovid, too, helped shape *Titus*. The grisly business of cooking Chiron and Demetrius and serving them as a meat pie to a parent is Ovidian as well as Senecan; Seneca's *Thyestes* includes such a feast, but so too does Ovid's tale of Procne in *Metamorphoses*. In a sense, the stories are inseparable; in *Thyestes*, Atreus himself compares the feast to that in the legend of Procne, and the basic idea of a parent dining on the flesh of his offspring (a vestige of rituals in which the father killed his son as his son became a competitor?) exists in various myths. In *Titus*, Shakespeare quotes—rather misquotes—bits of Seneca, but he alludes directly not only to the legend of Procne but to its rendition in the *Metamorphoses*. The strong Ovidian influence on Shakespeare's early writing, especially on the narrative poems, is beyond all doubt; Francis Meres said in 1598 what must have seemed commonplace: "The sweet witty soul of Ovid lives in mellifluous and honey-tongued Shakespeare; witness his *Venus and Adonis,* his *Lucrece,* his sugared sonnets." In *Love's Labor's Lost* a pedant, Holofernes, speaks of Ovid, and though Holofernes can scarcely be regarded as a reliable mouthpiece, here he seems to be voicing Shakespeare's opinion, though perhaps a little bumptiously: "For the elegancy, facility, and golden cadence of poesy, . . . Ovidius Naso was the man" (4.2.127).

Ovid's elegancy, facility, and golden cadence had been famous even in antiquity (Quintilian said Ovid was unable to curb his luxuriance—even as Ben Jonson was later to say that Shakespeare "flowed with that facility that sometime it was necessary he should be stopped"), and to English playwrights in the latter part of the sixteenth century Ovid must have seemed with Seneca to be the man to add dignity to the blatant huffings of earlier English tragedy. The earlier tragedies with their abundant "O's" were notably direct; Ovid is often equally direct, but he is also rich in comparisons. Philomela's severed tongue "writhed convulsively," a recent translation says, "like a snake's tail when it has been newly cut off and, dying, tried to reach its mistress' feet." In Arthur Golding's version of Ovid, which Shakespeare surely knew, the passage runs thus:

> And with a pair of pinsons fast did catch her by the
>   tongue,
> And with his sword did cut it off. The stump whereon it
>   hung
> Did patter still. The tip fell down, and quivering on the
>   ground
> As though that it had murmured it made a certain sound,
> And as an adder's tail cut off doth skip a while, even so
> The tip of Philomela's tongue did wriggle to and fro,
> And nearer to her mistressward in dying still did go.

Here is Ovid's description (in Golding's words) of Pyramus' wound: Pyramus drew

> His sword, the which among his guts he thrust, and by
>   and by
> Did draw it from the bleeding wound beginning for to
>   die,
> And cast himself upon his back. The blood did spin
>   on high

As when a conduit pipe is cracked, the water bursting
    out
Doth shoot itself a great way off and pierce the air about.

Probably Shakespeare felt that his description of the mutilated Lavinia was in the best Ovidian manner:

> Why dost not speak to me?
> Alas, a crimson river of warm blood,
> Like to a bubbling fountain stirred with wind,
> Doth rise and fall between thy rosèd lips,
> Coming and going with thy honey breath.
>
> (2.4.21–25)

In *Lucrece*, probably written in 1593, within three or four
years of *Titus* and possibly within the same year, Shakespeare wrote:

> And from the purple fountain Brutus drew
> The murd'rous knife, and, as it left the place,
> Her blood, in poor revenge, held it in chase.
>
> (1734–36)

To defend *Lucrece* would be even more difficult than to
defend *Titus*, but it ought to be evident that Shakespeare is
attempting to make art out of violence. For naked violence
we must turn, say, to *Lear*, where a woman plucks an old
man's beard, urges her husband to gouge out the old man's
eyes, and stabs a servant in the back. In *Titus* the horror is for
the most part elevated, or at least veiled by ingenuity.

This is not to say that Shakespeare's treatment of horror
in *Titus* is entirely successful for modern audiences, though
a few productions, notably those of Brook and of Warner,
have won wide acclaim. These successes have helped us to
accept the fact that, in its day, and for a couple of decades
after, the play was popular; as late as 1614 Ben Jonson
grumbled that *Titus* still had its admirers. It is a remarkable
achievement, superior in character, in plot, and in language
to *The Spanish Tragedy*, and it rivals Marlowe, whose plays
are the only other major plays of the period. Its exuberance,
though in places distressing, is a sign of imaginative fertility

that was later to be splendidly husbanded. True, in many ways it is a play of its age, and Alan C. Dessen has pointed out (in an essay that we include in this volume) that every successful modern production pays a price of one sort or another. True, in many ways *Titus* is a play of its age, but in our age of horrors we can see that it is also a play for our time.

—SYLVAN BARNET

[*Dramatis Personae*

Saturninus, son to the late Emperor of Rome, afterward
  Emperor
Bassianus, brother to Saturninus
Titus Andronicus, a noble Roman
Marcus Andronicus, Tribune, and brother to Titus
Lucius ⎫
Quintus ⎬ sons to Titus Andronicus
Martius ⎪
Mutius ⎭
Young Lucius, a boy, son to Lucius
Publius, son to Marcus Andronicus
Sempronius ⎫
Caius ⎬ kinsmen to Titus Andronicus
Valentine ⎭
Aemilius, a noble Roman
Alarbus ⎫
Demetrius ⎬ sons to Tamora
Chiron ⎭
Aaron, a Moor, beloved by Tamora
A Captain
A Messenger
A Clown
Tamora, Queen of the Goths
Lavinia, daughter to Titus Andronicus
Nurse, and a blackamoor Infant
Romans, Goths, Senators, Tribunes, Officers, Soldiers,
  and Attendants

Scene: Rome, and the countryside near it]

The Most Lamentable Roman Tragedy
of Titus Andronicus

[ACT 1

Scene 1. *Rome. Before the Capitol.*]

*[Flourish.°¹] Enter the Tribunes and Senators aloft;
and then enter Saturninus and his followers at one
door, and Bassianus and his followers [at the other,]
with drums and trumpets.*

Saturninus. Noble patricians, patrons of my right,
  Defend the justice of my cause with arms;
  And, countrymen, my loving followers,
  Plead my successive title° with your swords.
  I am his first-born son that was the last   *5*
  That ware the imperial diadem of Rome;
  Then let my father's honors live in me,
  Nor wrong mine age° with this indignity.

Bassianus. Romans, friends, followers, favorers of my
      right,
  If ever Bassianus, Caesar's son,   *10*

---

1 The degree sign (°) indicates a footnote, which is keyed to the
text by line number. Text references are printed in **bold** type; the
annotation follows in roman type. 1.1.s.d. **Flourish** trumpet fanfare
4 **successive title** right to the succession 8 **age** i.e., seniority

Were gracious° in the eyes of royal Rome,
Keep° then this passage to the Capitol,
And suffer not dishonor to approach
The imperial seat, to virtue consecrate,
15 To justice, continence,° and nobility;
But let desert in pure election shine,
And, Romans, fight for freedom in your choice.

Marcus. [*With the crown*] Princes, that strive by fac-
    tions and by friends
Ambitiously for rule and empery,°
20 Know that the people of Rome, for whom we stand
A special party, have by common voice,
In election for the Roman empery,
Chosen Andronicus, surnamèd Pius
For many good and great deserts to Rome.
25 A nobler man, a braver warrior,
Lives not this day within the city walls.
He by the senate is accited° home
From weary wars against the barbarous Goths;
That with his sons, a terror to our foes,
30 Hath yoked° a nation strong, trained up in arms.
Ten years are spent since first he undertook
This cause of Rome, and chastisèd with arms
Our enemies' pride: five times he hath returned
Bleeding to Rome, bearing his valiant sons
35 In coffins from the field.°
And now at last, laden with honor's spoils,
Returns the good Andronicus to Rome,
Renownèd Titus, flourishing in arms.
Let us entreat, by honor of his name,
40 Whom worthily you would have now succeed,

---

11 **gracious** acceptable   12 **Keep** guard   15 **continence** restraint
19 **empery** dominion (but in line 22 *empery* = emperor)   27 **accited**
summoned   30 **yoked** subjugated   35 **field** (this word is followed
by: "and at this day/To the monument of that Andronici/Done
sacrifice of expiation,/And slain the noblest prisoner of the Goths."
These lines, omitted from the second and third quartos and from
the Folio, are inconsistent with the ensuing action, in which Alarbus
is sacrificed. Perhaps Shakespeare neglected to cancel them in
the manuscript after deciding to make Alarbus' execution part of the
action)

And in the Capitol and Senate's right,°
Whom you pretend° to honor and adore,
That you withdraw you and abate your strength,
Dismiss your followers, and, as suitors should,
Plead your deserts in peace and humbleness.   45

Saturninus. How fair° the tribune speaks to calm my
     thoughts!

Bassianus. Marcus Andronicus, so I do affy°
In thy uprightness and integrity,
And so I love and honor thee and thine,
Thy noble brother Titus and his sons,   50
And her to whom my thoughts are humbled all,
Gracious Lavinia, Rome's rich ornament,
That I will here dismiss my loving friends;
And to my fortunes and the people's favor
Commit my cause in balance to be weighed.   55
                              Exit [*his*] *soldiers.*

Saturninus. Friends, that have been thus forward in
     my right,
I thank you all, and here dismiss you all,
And to the love and favor of my country
Commit myself, my person, and the cause.°
                         [*Exeunt his followers.*]
Rome, be as just and gracious unto me   60
As I am confident and kind° to thee.
Open the gates and let me in.

Bassianus. Tribunes, and me, a poor competitor.°
     [*Flourish.*] *They go up into the Senate house.*

                    Enter a Captain.

Captain. Romans, make way! The good Andronicus,
Patron° of virtue, Rome's best champion,   65
Successful in the battles that he fights,
With honor and with fortune is returned
From where he circumscribèd with his sword

41 **the Capitol and Senate's right** the right of the Capitol and the
Senate   42 **pretend** claim   46 **fair** courteously   47 **affy** trust   59
cause affair   61 **confident and kind** trusting and natural(ly devoted)
63 **competitor** candidate   65 **Patron** representative

And brought to yoke the enemies of Rome.

*Sound drums and trumpets, and then enter two
of Titus' sons, and then two men bearing a
coffin covered with black, then two other sons,
then Titus Andronicus, and then Tamora, the
Queen of Goths, and her three sons, [Alarbus,]
Chiron, and Demetrius, with Aaron the Moor,
and others as many as can be; then set down the
coffin, and Titus speaks.*

70 *Titus.* Hail, Rome, victorious in thy mourning weeds!°
        Lo, as the bark that hath discharged his fraught°
        Returns with precious lading to the bay
        From whence at first she weighed her anchorage,°
        Cometh Andronicus, bound with laurel boughs,
75   To re-salute his country with his tears,
        Tears of true joy for his return to Rome.
        Thou° great defender of this Capitol,
        Stand gracious to the rites that we intend!
        Romans, of five and twenty valiant sons,
80   Half of the number that King Priam had,
        Behold the poor remains, alive and dead!
        These that survive let Rome reward with love;
        These that I bring unto their latest° home,
        With burial amongst their ancestors.
        Here Goths have given me leave to sheathe my
85   sword.
        Titus, unkind° and careless of thine own,
        Why suffer'st thou thy sons, unburied yet,
        To hover on the dreadful shore of Styx?°
        Make way to lay them by their brethren.°
                                    They open the tomb.
90   There greet in silence, as the dead are wont,
        And sleep in peace, slain in your country's wars!
        O sacred receptacle of my joys,
        Sweet cell of virtue and nobility,

70 **weeds** apparel   71 **his fraught** its freight   73 **anchorage** anchors
77 **Thou** i.e., Jupiter   83 **latest** last   86 **unkind** unnatural   88 **Styx**
river surrounding Hades   89 **brethren** (trisyllabic here and occasionally elsewhere: "breth-e-rin")

How many sons hast thou of mine in store,
That thou wilt never render to me more! 95

Lucius. Give us the proudest prisoner of the Goths,
That we may hew his limbs, and on a pile
Ad manes fratrum° sacrifice his flesh,
Before this earthy prison of their bones,
That so the shadows be not unappeased, 100
Nor we disturbed with prodigies° on earth.

Titus. I give him you, the noblest that survives,
The eldest son of this distressèd queen.

Tamora. Stay, Roman brethren! Gracious conqueror,
Victorious Titus, rue the tears I shed, 105
A mother's tears in passion° for her son:
And if thy sons were ever dear to thee,
O, think my son to be as dear to me!
Sufficeth not that we are brought to Rome,
To beautify thy triumphs° and return, 110
Captive to thee and to thy Roman yoke,
But must my sons be slaughtered in the streets,
For valiant doings in their country's cause?
O, if to fight for king and commonweal
Were piety in thine, it is in these. 115
Andronicus, stain not thy tomb with blood.
Wilt thou draw near the nature of the gods?
Draw near them then in being merciful;
Sweet mercy is nobility's true badge.
Thrice-noble Titus, spare my first-born son. 120

Titus. Patient° yourself, madam, and pardon me.
These are their brethren, whom your Goths beheld
Alive and dead, and for their brethren slain
Religiously they ask a sacrifice.
To this your son is marked, and die he must, 125
T' appease their groaning shadows that are gone.

Lucius. Away with him! And make a fire straight,

---

98 **Ad manes fratrum** to the ghosts of our brothers (Latin)
101 **prodigies** ominous disturbances 106 **passion** violent emotion
110 **triumphs** triumphal processions 121 **Patient** calm

And with our swords, upon a pile of wood,
Let's hew his limbs till they be clean consumed.

                              Exit Titus' sons with Alarbus.

130 *Tamora.* O cruel, irreligious piety!

Chiron. Was never Scythia° half so barbarous.

Demetrius. Oppose° not Scythia to ambitious Rome.
  Alarbus goes to rest, and we survive
  To tremble under Titus' threat'ning look.
135 Then, madam, stand resolved, but hope withal°
  The selfsame gods that armed the Queen of Troy°
  With opportunity of sharp revenge
  Upon the Thracian tyrant in his tent
  May favor Tamora, the Queen of Goths,
140 (When Goths were Goths and Tamora was queen)
  To quit° the bloody wrongs upon her foes.

            Enter the sons of Andronicus again.

Lucius. See, lord and father, how we have performed
  Our Roman rites! Alarbus' limbs are lopped,
  And entrails feed the sacrificing fire,
145 Whose smoke like incense doth perfume the sky.
  Remaineth naught but to inter our brethren,
  And with loud 'larums° welcome them to Rome.

Titus. Let it be so, and let Andronicus
  Make this his latest farewell to their souls.

                        *Sound trumpets, and lay the coffin
                                            in the tomb.*

150 In peace and honor rest you here, my sons,
  Rome's readiest champions, repose you here in rest,
  Secure from worldly chances and mishaps!
  Here lurks no treason, here no envy° swells,
  Here grow no damnèd drugs,° here are no storms,

---

131 **Scythia** a region in southern Russia noted for its savage inhabitants 132 **Oppose** compare 135 **withal** with this 136 **Queen of Troy** Hecuba (who murdered the sons of Polymnestor—*the Thracian tyrant* of line 138—in revenge for his murder of her son) 141 **quit** requite, repay 147 **'larums** alarums, calls to arms 153 **envy** malice 154 **drugs** poisonous plants

No noise, but silence and eternal sleep: 155
In peace and honor rest you here, my sons!

Enter Lavinia.

Lavinia. In peace and honor live Lord Titus long,
My noble lord and father, live in fame!
Lo, at this tomb my tributary° tears
I render for my brethren's obsequies,   160
And at thy feet I kneel, with tears of joy
Shed on this earth for thy return to Rome.
O, bless me here with thy victorious hand,
Whose fortunes Rome's best citizens applaud.

Titus. Kind Rome, that hast thus lovingly reserved   165
The cordial° of mine age to glad my heart!
Lavinia, live, outlive thy father's days
And fame's eternal date,° for virtue's praise!

[*Enter above Marcus Andronicus, Saturninus,
Bassianus, and others.*]

Marcus. Long live Lord Titus, my belovèd brother,
Gracious triumpher in the eyes of Rome!   170

Titus. Thanks, gentle tribune, noble brother Marcus.

Marcus. And welcome, nephews, from successful wars,
You that survive, and you that sleep in fame!
Fair lords, your fortunes are alike in all,
That in your country's service drew your swords,   175
But safer triumph is this funeral pomp,
That hath aspired° to Solon's happiness°
And triumphs over chance in honor's bed.
Titus Andronicus, the people of Rome,
Whose friend in justice thou hast ever been,   180
Send thee by me, their tribune and their trust,
This palliament° of white and spotless hue,
And name thee in election for the empire
With these our late-deceasèd emperor's sons:

159 **tributary** given as tribute 166 **cordial** comfort (literally: stimulant to the heart) 168 **date** duration 177 **aspired** risen 177 **Solon's happiness** (Solon said: "Call no man happy until he is dead") 182 **palliament** robe

185   *Be candidatus°* then, and put it on,
    And help to set a head on headless Rome.

    Titus. A better head her glorious body fits
    Than his that shakes for age and feebleness:
    What° should I don this robe and trouble you?
190   Be chosen with proclamations today,
    Tomorrow yield up rule, resign my life,
    And set abroad new business for you all?
    Rome, I have been thy soldier forty years,
    And led my country's strength successfully,
195   And buried one and twenty valiant sons,
    Knighted in field, slain manfully in arms,
    In right and service of their noble country:
    Give me a staff of honor for mine age,
    But not a scepter to control the world.
200   Upright he held it, lords, that held it last.

    Marcus. Titus, thou shalt obtain and ask° the empery.

    Saturninus. Proud and ambitious tribune, canst thou
      tell?

    Titus. Patience, Prince Saturninus.

    Saturninus.   Romans, do me right.
    Patricians, draw your swords and sheathe them not
205   Till Saturninus be Rome's emperor.
    Andronicus, would thou were shipped to hell
    Rather than rob me of the people's hearts.

    Lucius. Proud Saturnine, interrupter of the good
    That noble-minded Titus means to thee!

210   *Titus*. Content thee, Prince, I will restore to thee
    The people's hearts, and wean them from them-
      selves.

    Bassianus. Andronicus, I do not flatter thee,
    But honor thee, and will do till I die.
    My faction if thou strengthen with thy friends,

---

185 **candidatus** candidate (Latin; literally: clad in white)   189
What why   201 **obtain and ask** i.e., obtain if you ask for

I will most thankful be, and thanks to men   *215*
Of noble minds is honorable meed.°

Titus. People of Rome, and people's tribunes here,
I ask your voices and your suffrages:
Will ye bestow them friendly on Andronicus?

Tribunes. To gratify the good Andronicus,   *220*
And gratulate° his safe return to Rome,
The people will accept whom he admits.°

Titus. Tribunes, I thank you, and this suit I make,
That you create our emperor's eldest son,
Lord Saturnine; whose virtues will, I hope,   *225*
Reflect on Rome as Titan's° rays on earth,
And ripen justice in this commonweal:
Then, if you will elect by my advice,
Crown him and say, "Long live our emperor!"

Marcus. With voices and applause of every sort,   *230*
Patricians and plebeians, we create
Lord Saturninus Rome's great emperor,
And say "Long live our Emperor Saturnine!"
            [*A long flourish till they come down.*]

Saturninus. Titus Andronicus, for thy favors done
To us in our election° this day,   *235*
I give thee thanks in° part of thy deserts,
And will with deeds requite thy gentleness:°
And for an onset,° Titus, to advance
Thy name and honorable family,
Lavinia will I make my empress,°   *240*
Rome's royal mistress, mistress of my heart,
And in the sacred Pantheon° her espouse.
Tell me, Andronicus, doth this motion° please thee?

Titus. It doth, my worthy lord, and in this match

---

216 **meed** reward   221 **gratulate** rejoice at   222 **admits** approves
226 **Titan's** the sun god's   235 **election** (here, as often in Shakespeare, *-ion* is disyllabic)   236 **in** as   237 **gentleness** nobility
238 **onset** beginning   240 **empress** (here, and often elsewhere in
Titus, trisyllabic: "em-per-es")   242 **Pantheon** temple dedicated to
all the gods   243 **motion** proposal

245   I hold me highly honored of your grace,
And here in sight of Rome to Saturnine,
King and commander of our commonweal,
The wide world's emperor, do I consecrate
My sword, my chariot, and my prisoners,
250   Presents well worthy Rome's imperious° lord.
Receive them then, the tribute that I owe,
Mine honor's ensigns° humbled at thy feet.

Saturninus. Thanks, noble Titus, father of my life!
How proud I am of thee and of thy gifts
255   Rome shall record, and when I do forget
The least of these unspeakable deserts,
Romans, forget your fealty° to me.

Titus. [*To Tamora*] Now, madam, are you prisoner to
an emperor,
To him that, for your honor and your state,
260   Will use you nobly and your followers.

Saturninus. [*Aside*] A goodly lady, trust me, of the
hue
That I would choose, were I to choose anew.
[*Aloud*] Clear up, fair Queen, that cloudy coun-
tenance.
Though chance of war hath wrought this change
of cheer,°
265   Thou com'st not to be made a scorn in Rome.
Princely shall be thy usage every way.
Rest on my word, and let not discontent
Daunt all your hopes. Madam, he° comforts you
Can make you greater than the Queen of Goths.
270   Lavinia, you are not displeased with this?

Lavinia. Not I, my lord, sith° true nobility
Warrants° these words in princely courtesy.

Saturninus. Thanks, sweet Lavinia. Romans, let us go.

---

250 **imperious** imperial   252 **ensigns** tokens   257 **fealty** loyalty
264 **cheer** countenance   268 **he** he who   271 **sith** since   272 **War-
rants** justifies

Ransomless here we set our prisoners free.
Proclaim our honors, lords, with trump and drum.   275

Bassianus. Lord Titus, by your leave, this maid is
  mine.

Titus. How, sir! Are you in earnest then, my lord?

Bassianus. Ay, noble Titus, and resolved withal
  To do myself this reason and this right.

Marcus. Suum cuique° is our Roman justice.   280
  This prince in justice seizeth but his own.

Lucius. And that he will, and shall, if Lucius live.

Titus. Traitors, avaunt!° Where is the Emperor's
  guard?
  Treason, my lord! Lavinia is surprised!°

Saturninus. Surprised! By whom?

Bassianus.   By him that justly may   285
  Bear his betrothed from all the world away.
        [*Exeunt Marcus and Bassianus, with Lavinia.*]

Mutius. Brothers, help to convey her hence away,
  And with my sword I'll keep this door° safe.
        [*Exeunt Lucius, Quintus, and Martius.*]

Titus. Follow, my lord, and I'll soon bring her back.
        [*During the fray, exeunt Saturninus, Tamora,
          Demetrius, Chiron, and Aaron.*]

Mutius. My lord, you pass not here.   290

Titus. What, villain boy! Barr'st me my way in Rome?
        [*He stabs Mutius.*]

Mutius. [*Dying*] Help, Lucius, help!

                [*Enter Lucius.*]

Lucius. My lord, you are unjust, and more than so,

---

280 **Suum cuique** to each his own (Latin) 283 **avaunt** be gone
284 **surprised** suddenly taken 288 **door** (disyllabic)

In wrongful quarrel you have slain your son.

295 *Titus*. Nor thou, nor he, are any sons of mine:
 My sons would never so dishonor me.
 Traitor, restore Lavinia to the Emperor.

Lucius. Dead if you will, but not to be his wife
 That is another's lawful promised love.   [*Exit*.]

*Enter aloft the Emperor with Tamora and her
two sons and Aaron the Moor*.

300 *Saturninus*. No, Titus, no; the Emperor needs her not,
 Nor her, nor thee, nor any of thy stock:
 I'll trust by leisure° him that mocks me once;
 Thee never, nor thy traitorous haughty sons,
 Confederates all thus to dishonor me.
305 Was none in Rome to make a stale°
 But Saturnine? Full well, Andronicus,
 Agree these deeds with that proud brag of thine,
 That saidst I begged the empire at thy hands.

Titus. O monstrous! What reproachful words are
 these?

Saturninus. But go thy ways, go, give that changing
310 piece°
 To him that flourished for her with his sword:
 A valiant son-in-law thou shalt enjoy,
 One fit to bandy° with thy lawless sons,
 To ruffle° in the commonwealth of Rome.

315 *Titus*. These words are razors to my wounded heart.

Saturninus. And therefore, lovely Tamora, Queen of
 Goths,
 That like the stately Phoebe° 'mongst her nymphs
 Dost overshine the gallant'st dames of Rome,
 If thou be pleased with this my sudden choice,
320 Behold, I choose thee, Tamora, for my bride,

302 **by leisure** slowly 305 **stale** laughingstock 310 **changing piece**
fickle wench 313 **bandy** contend, bicker 314 **ruffle** brawl 317
Phoebe Diana, goddess of the moon

And will create thee Empress of Rome.
Speak, Queen of Goths, dost thou applaud my
    choice?
And here I swear by all the Roman gods,
Sith priest and holy water are so near,
And tapers burn so bright, and everything   325
In readiness for Hymenaeus° stand,
I will not re-salute the streets of Rome,
Or climb my palace, till from forth this place
I lead espoused my bride along with me.

Tamora. And here in sight of heaven to Rome I
    swear,   330
If Saturnine advance the Queen of Goths,
She will a handmaid be to his desires,
A loving nurse, a mother to his youth.

Saturninus. Ascend, fair Queen, Pantheon. Lords, ac-
    company
Your noble emperor and his lovely bride,   335
Sent by the heavens for Prince Saturnine,
Whose wisdom hath her fortune conquerèd.
There shall we consummate our spousal rites.
                    Exeunt omnes° [*except Titus*].

Titus. I am not bid° to wait upon this bride.
Titus, when wert thou wont to walk alone,   340
Dishonored thus and challengèd° of wrongs?

            Enter Marcus and Titus' sons [*Lucius,
               Quintus, and Martius*].

Marcus. O Titus, see, O, see, what thou hast done!
In a bad quarrel slain a virtuous son.

Titus. No, foolish tribune, no; no son of mine,
Nor thou, nor these, confederates in the deed   345
That hath dishonored all our family,
Unworthy brother, and unworthy sons!

326 **Hymenaeus** god of marriage   338s.d. **omnes** all (Latin)   339
bid asked   341 **challengèd** accused

Lucius. But let us give him burial as becomes;°
　　Give Mutius burial with our brethren.

350 *Titus.* Traitors, away! He rests not in this tomb:
　　This monument five hundred years hath stood,
　　Which I have sumptuously re-edified:°
　　Here none but soldiers and Rome's servitors
　　Repose in fame; none basely slain in brawls.
355 　Bury him where you can, he comes not here.

Marcus. My lord, this is impiety in you.
　　My nephew Mutius' deeds do plead for him;
　　He must be buried with his brethren.

　　　　　Titus' two sons speak:

[*Quintus, Martius.*] And shall, or him we will accompany.

360 *Titus.* And shall? What villain was it spake that word?

　　　　　Titus' son speaks.

[*Quintus.*] He that would vouch it in any place but here.

Titus. What, would you bury him in my despite?°

Marcus. No, noble Titus, but entreat of thee
　　To pardon Mutius and to bury him.

365 *Titus.* Marcus, even thou hast stroke upon my crest,
　　And with these boys mine honor thou hast wounded.
　　My foes I do repute° you every one,
　　So trouble me no more, but get you gone.

Martius. He is not with himself; let us withdraw.

370 *Quintus.* Not I, till Mutius' bones be buried.
　　　　　　　　The brother and the sons kneel.

Marcus. Brother, for in that name doth nature plead—

Quintus. Father, and in that name doth nature speak—

---

348 **becomes** is fitting　352 **re-edified** rebuilt　362 **in my despite** in spite of me　367 **repute** consider

Titus. Speak thou no more, if all the rest will speed.°

Marcus. Renownèd Titus, more than half my soul—

Lucius. Dear father, soul and substance of us all—   375

Marcus. Suffer° thy brother Marcus to inter
His noble nephew here in virtue's nest,
That died in honor and Lavinia's cause.
Thou art a Roman, be not barbarous:
The Greeks upon advice° did bury Ajax°   380
That slew himself; and wise Laertes' son°
Did graciously plead for his funerals:
Let not young Mutius then, that was thy joy,
Be barred his entrance here.

Titus.   Rise, Marcus, rise.
The dismal'st day is this that e'er I saw,   385
To be dishonored by my sons in Rome!
Well, bury him, and bury me the next.

They put him in the tomb.

Lucius. There lie thy bones, sweet Mutius, with thy
friends,
Till we with trophies do adorn thy tomb.
They all kneel and say:

[*All.*] No man shed tears for noble Mutius,   390
He lives in fame that died in virtue's cause.

Marcus. My lord, to step out of these dreary dumps,°
How comes it that the subtle Queen of Goths
Is of a sudden thus advanced in Rome?

Titus. I know not, Marcus, but I know it is;   395
(Whether° by device° or no, the heavens can tell.)
Is she not then beholding° to the man
That brought her for this high good turn so far?
Yes, and will nobly him remunerate.

373 **if all the rest will speed** if the rest is to go well (?) if the rest of
you wish to live (?) 376 **Suffer** allow 380 **advice** deliberation
380 **Ajax** (when Achilles' arms were given to Odysseus, Ajax in a
fury stabbed himself) 381 **Laertes' son** Odysseus 392 **dumps** blues,
melancholy state 396 **Whether** (probably pronounced "where")
396 **device** plot 397 **beholding** beholden, indebted

*Enter the Emperor, Tamora and her two sons, with
the Moor at one door. Enter at the other door
Bassianus and Lavinia, with others.*

400 *Saturninus.* So Bassianus, you have played your prize:°
　　God give you joy, sir, of your gallant bride!

　　Bassianus. And you of yours, my lord! I say no more,
　　Nor wish no less, and so I take my leave.

　　Saturninus. Traitor, if Rome have law, or we have
　　　power,
405 　Thou and thy faction shall repent this rape.

　　Bassianus. Rape, call you it, my lord, to seize my own,
　　My true-betrothèd love, and now my wife?
　　But let the laws of Rome determine all;
　　Meanwhile am I possessed of that is mine.

410 *Saturninus.* 'Tis good, sir; you are very short with us,
　　But if we live we'll be as sharp with you.

　　Bassianus. My lord, what I have done, as best I may
　　Answer I must, and shall do with my life.
　　Only thus much I give your grace to know—
415 　By all the duties that I owe to Rome,
　　This noble gentleman, Lord Titus here,
　　Is in opinion° and in honor wronged,
　　That, in the rescue of Lavinia,
　　With his own hand did slay his youngest son,
420 　In zeal to you, and highly moved to wrath
　　To be controlled° in that he frankly° gave.
　　Receive him then to favor, Saturnine,
　　That hath expressed himself in all his deeds
　　A father and a friend to thee and Rome.

425 *Titus.* Prince Bassianus, leave to plead° my deeds;
　　'Tis thou and those that have dishonored me.
　　Rome and the righteous heavens be my judge,
　　How I have loved and honored Saturnine!

400 **played your prize** won your contest 417 **opinion** reputation
421 **controlled** opposed 421 **frankly** generously 425 **leave to
plead** cease pleading

Tamora. My worthy lord, if ever Tamora
    Were gracious in those princely eyes of thine,   430
    Then hear me speak indifferently° for all;
    And at my suit, sweet, pardon what is past.

Saturninus. What, madam! Be dishonored openly,
    And basely put it up° without revenge?

Tamora. Not so, my lord, the gods of Rome forfend°   435
    I should be author° to dishonor you!
    But on mine honor dare I undertake°
    For good Lord Titus' innocence in all,
    Whose fury not dissembled speaks his griefs:
    Then at my suit look graciously on him;   440
    Lose not so noble a friend on vain suppose,°
    Nor with sour looks afflict his gentle heart.
    [*Aside*] My lord, be ruled by me, be won at last,
    Dissemble all your griefs and discontents—
    You are but newly planted in your throne—   445
    Lest then the people, and patricians too,
    Upon a just survey, take Titus' part,
    And so supplant you for ingratitude,
    Which Rome reputes to be a heinous sin.
    Yield at entreats:° and then let me alone.°   450
    I'll find a day to massacre them all,
    And race° their faction and their family,
    The cruel father and his traitorous sons,
    To whom I suèd for my dear son's life;
    And make them know what 'tis to let a queen   455
    Kneel in the streets and beg for grace in vain.
    [*Aloud*] Come, come, sweet Emperor—come, An-
        dronicus—
    Take up this good old man, and cheer the heart
    That dies in tempest of thy angry frown.

Saturninus. Rise, Titus, rise, my empress hath pre-
        vailed.   460

---

431 **indifferently** impartially   434 **put it up** (the figure is of putting
up, or sheathing, a sword)   435 **forfend** forbid   436 **author** agent
437 **undertake** assert   441 **vain suppose** empty supposition   450 **at
entreats** to entreaties   450 **let me alone** i.e., leave it to me   452 **race**
root out

Titus. I thank your Majesty, and her, my lord.
These words, these looks, infuse new life in me.

Tamora. Titus, I am incorporate in Rome,
A Roman now adopted happily,
465   And must advise the Emperor for his good.
This day all quarrels die, Andronicus.
And let it be mine honor, good my lord,
That I have reconciled your friends and you.
For you, Prince Bassianus, I have passed
470   My word and promise to the Emperor
That you will be more mild and tractable.
And fear not, lords, and you, Lavinia;
By my advice, all humbled on your knees,
You shall ask pardon of his Majesty.

[*Lucius.*] We do, and vow to heaven, and to his high-
475   ness,
That what we did was mildly as we might,°
Tend'ring° our sister's honor and our own.

Marcus. That on mine honor here do I protest.

Saturninus. Away, and talk not, trouble us no more.

Tamora. Nay, nay, sweet Emperor, we must all be
480   friends.
The tribune and his nephews kneel for grace.
I will not be denied. Sweet heart, look back.

Saturninus. Marcus, for thy sake, and thy brother's
here,
And at my lovely Tamora's entreats,
485   I do remit these young men's heinous faults.
Stand up.
Lavinia, though you left me like a churl,
I found a friend, and sure as death I swore
I would not part° a bachelor from the priest.
490   Come, if the Emperor's court can feast two brides,
You are my guest, Lavinia, and your friends.

476 **mildly as we might** as mild as we might do   477 **Tend'ring**
having regard for   489 **part** depart

This day shall be a love-day,° Tamora.

Titus. Tomorrow, and° it please your Majesty
To hunt the panther and the hart with me,
With horn and hound we'll give your Grace bon-
   jour.°　　　　　　　　　　　　　　　　　*495*

Saturninus. Be it so, Titus, and gramercy° too.

                                  Exeunt.

   Sound trumpets. Manet° [*Aaron the*] *Moor*.

---

492 **love-day** day appointed to settle disputes (with a pun on day for love) 493 **and** if 495 **bonjour** good morning (French) 496 **gramercy** thanks 496s.d. **Manet** remains (Latin. Clearly this and the next scene are continuous; the Folio's incorrect division into acts is retained merely to facilitate reference)

[ACT 2

Scene 1. *Rome. Before the palace.*
Aaron alone.]

Aaron. Now climbeth Tamora Olympus'° top,
    Safe out of fortune's shot, and sits aloft,
    Secure of° thunder's crack or lightning flash,
    Advanced above pale envy's° threat'ning reach.
5   As when the golden sun salutes the morn,
    And having gilt the ocean with his beams,
    Gallops° the zodiac in his glistering coach,
    And overlooks° the highest-peering hills;
    So Tamora:
10   Upon her wit doth earthly honor wait,
    And virtue stoops and trembles at her frown.
    Then, Aaron, arm thy heart, and fit thy thoughts
    To mount aloft with thy imperial mistress,
    And mount her pitch,° whom thou in triumph long
15   Hast prisoner held, fettered in amorous chains,
    And faster bound to Aaron's charming° eyes
    Than is Prometheus° tied to Caucasus.
    Away with slavish weeds° and servile thoughts!
    I will be bright and shine in pearl and gold
20   To wait upon this new-made empress.
    To wait, said I? To wanton with this queen,

2.1.1 **Olympus** Mount Olympus (reputed home of the gods) 3 **of** from
4 **envy's** hate's 7 **Gallops** gallops through 8 **overlooks** looks down
upon 14 **mount her pitch** rise to the highest point of her flight (a
term from falconry) 16 **charming** spellbinding 17 **Prometheus**
a Titan fettered to a rock in the Caucasus because he stole fire from
heaven 18 **weeds** apparel

This goddess, this Semiramis,° this nymph,
This siren, that will charm Rome's Saturnine
And see his shipwreck and his commonweal's.
Hollo! What storm is this?　　　　　　　　　　25

Enter Chiron and Demetrius, braving.°

Demetrius. Chiron, thy years wants° wit, thy wits
　　wants edge,
And manners, to intrude where I am graced,°
And may for aught thou knowest affected° be.

Chiron. Demetrius, thou dost overween° in all,
And so in this, to bear me down with braves.°　　30
'Tis not the difference of a year or two
Makes me less gracious,° or thee more fortunate;
I am as able and as fit as thou
To serve, and to deserve my mistress' grace;
And that my sword upon thee shall approve,°　　35
And plead my passions for Lavinia's love.

Aaron. Clubs, clubs!° These lovers will not keep the
　　peace.

Demetrius. Why, boy, although our mother, unad-
　　vised,°
Gave you a dancing-rapier° by your side,
Are you so desperate grown, to threat your friends?　40
Go to; have your lath° glued within your sheath,
Till you know better how to handle it.

Chiron. Meanwhile, sir, with the little skill I have,
Full well shalt thou perceive how much I dare.
　　　　　　　　　　　　　　　　They draw.

Demetrius. Ay, boy, grow ye so brave?

Aaron.　　　　　　　　　　Why, how now, lords!　45

22 **Semiramis** legendary Assyrian queen, noted for her lust and
beauty 25s.d. **braving** challenging 26 **wants** (the ending *-s* is
frequently found with a plural subject) 27 **graced** favored 28
affected loved 29 **overween** arrogantly presume 30 **braves** threats
32 **gracious** acceptable 35 **approve** prove 37 **Clubs, clubs** (the
cry raised to call the watch to separate brawlers in London)
38 **unadvised** unwisely 39 **dancing-rapier** ornamental light sword
41 **lath** wooden (stage) sword

So near the Emperor's palace dare ye draw,
And maintain such a quarrel openly?
Full well I wot° the ground of all this grudge.
I would not for a million of gold
50   The cause were known to them it most concerns,
Nor would your noble mother for much more
Be so dishonored in the court of Rome.
For shame, put up.°

Demetrius.   Not I, till I have sheathed
My rapier in his bosom, and withal
55   Thrust those reproachful speeches down his throat,
That he hath breathed in my dishonor here.

Chiron. For that I am prepared and full resolved,
Foul-spoken coward, that thund'rest with thy tongue
And with thy weapon nothing dar'st perform.

60   *Aaron.* Away, I say!
Now, by the gods that warlike Goths adore,
This petty brabble° will undo us all.
Why, lords, and think you not how dangerous
It is to jet° upon a prince's right?
65   What, is Lavinia then become so loose,
Or Bassianus so degenerate,
That for her love such quarrels may be broached
Without controlment, justice, or revenge?
Young lords, beware! And should the Empress know
70   This discord's ground,° the music would not please.

Chiron. I care not, I, knew she and all the world:
I love Lavinia more than all the world.

Demetrius. Youngling, learn thou to make some meaner° choice.
Lavinia is thine elder brother's hope.

75   *Aaron.* Why, are ye mad? Or know ye not, in Rome
How furious and impatient they be,

48 **wot** know   53 **put up** sheathe your weapons   62 **brabble** brawl
64 **jet** encroach   70 **ground** reason (with a pun on the musical
meaning: bass to a descant)   73 **meaner** lower

And cannot brook competitors in love?
I tell you, lords, you do but plot your deaths
By this device.

Chiron.   Aaron, a thousand deaths
Would I propose° to achieve her whom I love.   80

Aaron. To achieve her how?

Demetrius.   Why makes thou it so strange?°
She is a woman, therefore may be wooed;
She is a woman, therefore may be won;
She is Lavinia, therefore must be loved.
What, man! More water glideth by the mill   85
Than wots the miller of, and easy it is
Of a cut loaf to steal a shive,° we know:
Though Bassianus be the Emperor's brother,
Better than he have worn Vulcan's badge.°

Aaron. [*Aside*] Ay, and as good as Saturninus may.   90

Demetrius. Then why should he despair that knows
     to court it
With words, fair looks, and liberality?
What, hast not thou full often stroke a doe,
And borne her cleanly by the keeper's nose?

Aaron. Why then, it seems, some certain snatch° or so   95
Would serve your turns.

Chiron.   Ay, so the turn were served.

Demetrius. Aaron, thou hast hit it.

Aaron.   Would you had hit it too,
Then should not we be tired with this ado.
Why, hark ye, hark ye! And are you such fools
To square° for this? Would it offend you then   100
That both should speed?°

---

80 **propose** be willing to meet   81 **Why makes thou it so strange**
why do you seem surprised   87 **shive** slice   89 **Vulcan's badge** i.e.,
the horns of cuckoldry (Vulcan's wife, Venus, deceived him with
Mars)   95 **snatch** catch (the likelihood that there is also a sexual
meaning here is increased by *turns* in the next line, a word often
denoting sexual acts)   100 **square** quarrel   101 **speed** prosper

Chiron.   Faith, not me.

Demetrius. Nor me, so I were one.

Aaron. For shame, be friends, and join for that you
          jar.°
          'Tis policy° and stratagem must do

105   That you affect,° and so must you resolve,
      That what you cannot as you would achieve,
      You must perforce° accomplish as you may.
      Take this of me, Lucrece° was not more chaste
      Than this Lavinia, Bassianus' love.

110   A speedier course than ling'ring languishment
      Must we pursue, and I have found the path.
      My lords, a solemn° hunting is in hand.
      There will the lovely Roman ladies troop:
      The forest walks are wide and spacious,

115   And many unfrequented plots° there are
      Fitted by kind° for rape and villainy.
      Single° you thither then this dainty doe,
      And strike her home by force, if not by words:
      This way, or not at all, stand you in hope.

120   Come, come, our empress, with her sacred wit
      To villainy and vengeance consecrate,
      Will we acquaint withal what we intend,
      And she shall file our engines° with advice,
      That will not suffer you to square yourselves,

125   But to your wishes' height advance you both.
      The Emperor's court is like the House of Fame,°
      The palace full of tongues, of eyes, and ears:
      The woods are ruthless,° dreadful, deaf, and dull;
      There speak, and strike, brave boys, and take your
          turns,

130   There serve your lust shadowed from heaven's eye,
      And revel in Lavinia's treasury.

103 **for that you jar** to get what you quarrel over   104 **policy** cunning   105 **affect** desire   107 **perforce** necessarily   108 **Lucrece**
Roman lady noted for her chastity; she killed herself when Sextus
Tarquinius raped her   112 **solemn** ceremonious   115 **unfrequented
plots** unvisited areas   116 **kind** nature   117 **Single** single out (a
hunting term)   123 **file our engines** sharpen our minds   126 **House
of Fame** (Ovid and Chaucer have notable poems on it; Fame =
Rumor, and the House of Fame is full of gossip)   128 **ruthless**
pitiless

Chiron. Thy counsel, lad, smells of no cowardice.

Demetrius. Sit fas aut nefas,° till I find the stream
  To cool this heat, a charm to calm these fits,
  Per Stygia, per manes vehor.°   *Exeunt. 135*

[Scene 2. *A forest near Rome.*]

  *Enter Titus Andronicus and his three sons [and
  Marcus], making a noise with hounds and horns.*

Titus. The hunt is up, the morn is bright and gray,°
  The fields are fragrant, and the woods are green:
  Uncouple° here, and let us make a bay,°
  And wake the Emperor and his lovely bride,
  And rouse the Prince, and ring a hunter's peal,   5
  That all the court may echo with the noise.
  Sons, let it be your charge, as it is ours,
  To attend the Emperor's person carefully:
  I have been troubled in my sleep this night,
  But dawning day new comfort hath inspired.   10

  *Here a cry° of hounds, and wind horns in a peal: then
    enter Saturninus, Tamora, Bassianus, Lavinia,
    Chiron, Demetrius, and their attendants.*

  Many good morrows to your Majesty!
  Madam, to you as many and as good!
  I promisèd your Grace a hunter's peal.

Saturninus. And you have rung it lustily, my lords,
  Somewhat too early for new-married ladies.   15

Bassianus. Lavinia, how say you?

133 **Sit fas aut nefas** be it right or wrong (Latin)   135 **Per Stygia,
per manes vehor** I am carried through Stygian (infernal) regions,
through ghosts (Latin, derived from Seneca's *Hippolytus*, line 1177)
2.2.1 **gray** sky blue (?)   3 **Uncouple** unleash the hounds   3 **make a
bay** keep up the cry of the hounds   10s.d. **cry** deep barking

Lavinia.   I say, no;
  I have been broad awake two hours and more.

Saturninus. Come on then, horse and chariots let us
      have,
  And to our sport. [*To Tamora*] Madam, now shall
      ye see
  Our Roman hunting.

20 *Marcus.*   I have dogs, my lord,
  Will rouse the proudest panther in the chase,
  And climb the highest promontory top.

Titus. And I have horse will follow where the game
  Makes way and runs like swallows o'er the plain.

Demetrius. Chiron, we hunt not, we, with horse nor
25   hound,
  But hope to pluck a dainty doe to ground.   *Exeunt.*

[Scene 3. *The forest.*]

Enter Aaron alone, [*with a bag of gold*].

Aaron. He that had wit would think that I had none,
  To bury so much gold under a tree
  And never after to inherit° it.
  Let him that thinks of me so abjectly°
5   Know that this gold must coin a stratagem,
  Which, cunningly effected, will beget
  A very excellent piece of villainy.
  And so repose, sweet gold, for their unrest,
  That have their alms out of the Empress' chest.
                        [*Hides the gold.*]

Enter Tamora alone to the Moor.

10 *Tamora.* My lovely Aaron, wherefore look'st thou sad

2.3.3 **inherit** possess 4 **abjectly** contemptuously

When every thing doth make a gleeful boast?°
The birds chaunt melody on every bush,
The snakes lies rollèd in the cheerful sun,
The green leaves quiver with the cooling wind,
And make a checkered shadow on the ground: 15
Under their sweet shade, Aaron, let us sit,
And whilst the babbling echo mocks the hounds,
Replying shrilly to the well-tuned horns
As if a double hunt were heard at once,
Let us sit down and mark their yellowing° noise: 20
And after conflict such as was supposed
The wandering prince and Dido° once enjoyed,
When with a happy storm they were surprised
And curtained with a counsel-keeping cave,
We may, each wreathèd in the other's arms,   25
(Our pastimes done) possess a golden slumber,
Whiles hounds and horns and sweet melodious birds
Be unto us as is a nurse's song
Of lullaby to bring her babe asleep.

Aaron. Madam, though Venus govern your desires,   30
Saturn is dominator° over mine:
What signifies my deadly-standing° eye,
My silence and my cloudy melancholy,
My fleece of woolly hair that now uncurls
Even as an adder when she doth unroll   35
To do some fatal execution?
No, madam, these are no venereal° signs:
Vengeance is in my heart, death in my hand,
Blood and revenge are hammering in my head.
Hark, Tamora, the empress of my soul,   40
Which never hopes more heaven than rests in thee,
This is the day of doom for Bassianus:
His Philomel° must lose her tongue today,

11 **boast** display   20 **yellowing** loudly calling   22 **The wandering prince and Dido** Aeneas and the Queen of Carthage (see Virgil's *Aeneid* IV)   31 **Saturn is dominator** the planet Saturn (whose influence allegedly caused sluggishness) dominates   32 **deadly-standing** fixed in a deathlike stare (?)   37 **venereal** erotic   43 **Philomel** (Philomela was ravished by Tereus, who then cut out her tongue; later she communicated her plight by weaving the story into a tapestry. See 2.4.26–27, 38–39; 4.1.47–48; 5.2.195–96)

Thy sons make pillage of her chastity,
45 And wash their hands in Bassianus' blood.
Seest thou this letter? Take it up, I pray thee,
And give the King this fatal-plotted scroll.
Now question me no more; we are espied.
Here comes a parcel of our hopeful booty,°
50 Which dreads not yet their lives' destruction.

Enter Bassianus and Lavinia.

Tamora. Ah, my sweet Moor, sweeter to me than life!

Aaron. No more, great Empress, Bassianus comes.
Be cross with him, and I'll go fetch thy sons
To back thy quarrels whatsoe'er they be.   [*Exit.*]

55 *Bassianus.* Who have we here? Rome's royal Empress,
Unfurnished of° her well-beseeming troop?
Or is it Dian, habited° like her,
Who hath abandonèd her holy groves
To see the general hunting in this forest?

60 *Tamora.* Saucy controller° of my private steps!
Had I the power that some say Dian had,
Thy temples should be planted presently°
With horns, as was Actaeon's,° and the hounds
Should drive upon thy new-transformèd limbs,
65 Unmannerly intruder as thou art!

Lavinia. Under your patience, gentle Empress,
'Tis thought you have a goodly gift in horning,°
And to be doubted° that your Moor and you
Are singled forth to try experiments:
70 Jove shield your husband from his hounds today!
'Tis pity they should take him for a stag.

Bassianus. Believe me, Queen, your swart Cimmerian°

49 **parcel of our hopeful booty** part of the victims we hope for
56 **Unfurnished of** unaccompanied by   57 **habited** dressed   60 **controller** critic   62 **presently** immediately   63 **Actaeon** legendary hunter who spied on Diana bathing; she transformed him into a stag and his own hounds killed him   67 **horning** (an unfaithful wife was said to give her husband horns)   68 **doubted** suspected
72 **Cimmerian** dweller in darkness

Doth make your honor of his body's hue,
Spotted,° detested, and abominable.
Why are you sequest'rèd from all your train,　　　75
Dismounted from your snow-white goodly steed,
And wand'red hither to an obscure plot,
Accompanied but with a barbarous Moor,
If foul desire had not conducted you?

Lavinia. And, being intercepted in your sport,　　　80
Great reason that my noble lord be rated°
For sauciness. I pray you, let us hence,
And let her joy° her raven-colored love;
This valley fits the purpose passing well.

Bassianus. The King my brother shall have notice° of
this.　　　85

Lavinia. Ay, for these slips have made him noted°
long.
Good king, to be so mightily abused!

Tamora. Why, I have patience to endure all this.

　　　　Enter Chiron and Demetrius.

Demetrius. How now, dear sovereign, and our gracious mother,
Why doth your Highness look so pale and wan?　　　90

Tamora. Have I not reason, think you, to look pale?
These two have ticed° me hither to this place,
A barren detested vale, you see it is;
The trees, though summer, yet forlorn and lean,
Overcome with moss and baleful mistletoe:　　　95
Here never shines the sun; here nothing breeds,
Unless the nightly owl or fatal raven:
And when they showed me this abhorrèd pit,
They told me, here, at dead time of the night
A thousand fiends, a thousand hissing snakes,　　　100
Ten thousand swelling toads, as many urchins,°
Would make such fearful and confusèd cries,

74 **Spotted** infected　81 **rated** berated, rebuked　83 **joy** enjoy　85
notice (monosyllabic, pronounced "notes")　86 **noted** notorious
92 **ticed** enticed　101 **urchins** hedgehogs

As any mortal body hearing it
Should straight fall mad, or else die suddenly.
105 No sooner had they told this hellish tale,
But straight they told me they would bind me here
Unto the body of a dismal yew,
And leave me to this miserable death.
And then they called me foul adulteress,
110 Lascivious Goth,° and all the bitterest terms
That ever ear did hear to such effect.
And, had you not by wondrous fortune come,
This vengeance on me had they executed:
Revenge it, as you love your mother's life,
115 Or be ye not henceforth called my children.

Demetrius. This is a witness that I am thy son.
                                   Stab[s] him.

Chiron. And this for me, struck home to show my
    strength.   [*Stabs Bassianus.*]

Lavinia. Ay come, Semiramis, nay, barbarous
    Tamora!
For no name fits thy nature but thy own!

Tamora. Give me the poniard! You shall know, my
120   boys,
Your mother's hand shall right your mother's
    wrong.

Demetrius. Stay, madam; here is more belongs to her.
First thrash the corn, then after burn the straw.
This minion stood upon° her chastity,
125 Upon her nuptial vow, her loyalty,
And with that painted° hope braves your mighti-
    ness:
And shall she carry this unto her grave?

Chiron. And if she do, I would I were an eunuch.
Drag hence her husband to some secret hole,

---

110 **Goth** (possibly a pun on "goat," an animal believed to be lascivious)   124 **minion stood upon** hussy made a fuss about   126 **painted** specious, unreal

And make his dead trunk pillow to our lust.   130

Tamora. But when ye have the honey we desire,
Let not this wasp outlive us both to sting.

Chiron. I warrant you, madam, we will make that
sure.
Come, mistress, now perforce we will enjoy
That nice-preservèd honesty° of yours.   135

Lavinia. O Tamora! Thou bearest a woman's face—

Tamora. I will not hear her speak; away with her.

Lavinia. Sweet lords, entreat her hear me but a word.

Demetrius. Listen, fair madam, let it be your glory
To see her tears, but be your heart to them   140
As unrelenting flint to drops of rain.

Lavinia. When did the tiger's young ones teach the
dam?°
O, do not learn° her wrath; she taught it thee.
The milk thou suck'st from her did turn to marble;
Even at thy teat thou hadst thy tyranny.   145
Yet every mother breeds not sons alike,
[*To Chiron*] Do thou entreat her show a woman's
pity.

Chiron. What! Wouldst thou have me prove myself
a bastard?

Lavinia. 'Tis true; the raven doth not hatch a lark:
Yet have I heard—O could I find it now!—   150
The lion, moved with pity, did endure
To have his princely paws pared all away.
Some say that ravens foster forlorn children,
The whilst their own birds famish in their nests:
O, be to me, though thy hard heart say no,   155
Nothing so kind but something pitiful!°

---

135 **nice-preservèd honesty** fastidiously guarded chastity   142 **dam**
mother   143 **learn** teach   156 **Nothing so kind but something pitiful** i.e., not so kind as the raven, but somewhat pitying

Tamora. I know not what it means; away with her!

Lavinia. O, let me teach thee for my father's sake,
    That gave thee life when well he might have slain
      thee.
160   Be not obdurate, open thy deaf ears.

Tamora. Hadst thou in person ne'er offended me,
    Even for his sake am I pitiless.
    Remember, boys, I poured forth tears in vain
    To save your brother from the sacrifice,
165   But fierce Andronicus would not relent.
    Therefore away with her, and use her as you will;
    The worse to her, the better loved of me.

Lavinia. O Tamora, be called a gentle queen,
    And with thine own hands kill me in this place!
170   For 'tis not life that I have begged so long;
    Poor I was slain when Bassianus died.

Tamora. What begg'st thou then? Fond° woman, let
    me go.

Lavinia. 'Tis present death I beg, and one thing more
    That womanhood denies° my tongue to tell.
175   O, keep me from their worse than killing lust,
    And tumble me into some loathsome pit,
    Where never man's eye may behold my body.
    Do this, and be a charitable murderer.

Tamora. So should I rob my sweet sons of their fee.
180   No, let them satisfice their lust on thee.

Demetrius. Away! For thou hast stayed us here too
    long.

Lavinia. No grace? No womanhood? Ah beastly crea-
    ture!
    The blot and enemy to our general name!°
    Confusion° fall—

Chiron. Nay, then I'll stop your mouth. Bring thou
185   her husband.

172 **Fond** foolish   174 **denies** forbids   183 **our general name** i.e.,
womankind   184 **Confusion** destruction

This is the hole where Aaron bid us hide him.
[*Demetrius throws the corpse into a pit and then covers it with branches. Exeunt Demetrius and Chiron, dragging Lavinia.*]

Tamora. Farewell, my sons, see that you make her
    sure.
Ne'er let my heart know merry cheer indeed
Till all the Andronici be made away.°
Now will I hence to seek my lovely Moor,   190
And let my spleenful° sons this trull° deflower.
                                                    [*Exit.*]

    Enter Aaron with two of Titus' sons [Quintus and Martius].

[*Aaron.*] Come on, my lords, the better foot before!
Straight will I bring you to the loathsome pit
Where I espied the panther fast asleep.

Quintus. My sight is very dull, whate'er it bodes.   195

Martius. And mine, I promise you. Were it not for
    shame,
Well could I leave our sport to sleep awhile.
                                          [*He falls into the pit.*]

Quintus. What, art thou fallen? What subtle hole is
    this,
Whose mouth is covered with rude-growing briers,
Upon whose leaves are drops of new-shed blood   200
As fresh as morning dew distilled on flowers?
A very fatal place it seems to me.
Speak, brother, hast thou hurt thee with the fall?

Martius. O, brother, with the dismal'st object hurt
That ever eye with sight made heart lament.   205

Aaron. [*Aside*] Now will I fetch the King to find them
    here,
That he thereby may have a likely guess
How these were they that made away his brother.
                                                    Exit.

189 **made away** killed   191 **spleenful** lustful   191 **trull** strumpet

Martius. Why dost not comfort me and help me out
210   From this unhallowed and bloodstainèd hole?

Quintus. I am surprisèd° with an uncouth° fear,
        A chilling sweat o'erruns my trembling joints;
        My heart suspects more than mine eye can see.

Martius. To prove thou hast a true-divining heart,
215   Aaron and thou look down into this den
        And see a fearful sight of blood and death.

Quintus. Aaron is gone, and my compassionate heart
        Will not permit mine eyes once to behold
        The thing whereat it trembles by surmise.
220   O, tell me who it is, for ne'er till now
        Was I a child to fear I know not what.

Martius. Lord Bassianus lies berayed° in blood,
        All on a heap, like to a slaughtered lamb,
        In this detested, dark, blood-drinking pit.

225 *Quintus.* If it be dark, how dost thou know 'tis he?

Martius. Upon his bloody finger he doth wear
        A precious ring that lightens all this hole,
        Which, like a taper in some monument,
        Doth shine upon the dead man's earthy cheeks,
230   And shows the ragged entrails° of this pit:
        So pale did shine the moon on Pyramus,
        When he by night lay bathed in maiden blood.
        O brother, help me with thy fainting hand—
        If fear hath made thee faint, as me it hath—
235   Out of this fell° devouring receptacle,
        As hateful as Cocytus'° misty mouth.

Quintus. Reach me thy hand, that I may help thee out;
        Or, wanting° strength to do thee so much good,
        I may be plucked into the swallowing womb
240   Of this deep pit, poor Bassianus' grave.
        I have no strength to pluck thee to the brink.

---

211 **surprisèd** dumfounded   211 **uncouth** strange   222 **berayed** defiled   230 **ragged entrails** rugged interior   235 **fell** savage   236
Cocytus river in Hades   238 **wanting** lacking

Martius. Nor I no strength to climb without thy help.

Quintus. Thy hand once more; I will not loose again
    Till thou art here aloft or I below:
    Thou canst not come to me; I come to thee.   *245*
                                          [*Falls in.*]

        Enter the Emperor and Aaron the Moor.

Saturninus. Along with me! I'll see what hole is here,
    And what he is that now is leaped into it.
    Say, who art thou, that lately didst descend
    Into this gaping hollow of the earth?

Martius. The unhappy sons of old Andronicus,   *250*
    Brought hither in a most unlucky hour,
    To find thy brother Bassianus dead.

Saturninus. My brother dead! I know thou dost but
       jest:
    He and his lady both are at the lodge,
    Upon the north side of this pleasant chase;   *255*
    'Tis not an hour since I left them there.

Martius. We know not where you left them all alive,
    But, out alas! Here have we found him dead.

        Enter Tamora, Andronicus, and Lucius.

Tamora. Where is my lord the King?

Saturninus. Here, Tamora, though grieved with killing
       grief.   *260*

Tamora. Where is thy brother, Bassianus?

Saturninus. Now to the bottom dost thou search° my
       wound;
    Poor Bassianus here lies murderèd.

Tamora. Then all too late I bring this fatal writ,
    The complot° of this timeless° tragedy;   *265*
    And wonder greatly that man's face can fold°

---

262 **search** probe   265 **complot** plot   265 **timeless** untimely   266
fold hide (in the creases of a hypocritical smile)

In pleasing smiles such murderous tyranny.
She giveth Saturnine a letter.

Saturninus. (*Reads the letter.*) "And if° we miss to
    meet him handsomely°—
    Sweet huntsman, Bassianus 'tis we mean—
270 Do thou so much as dig the grave for him.
    Thou know'st our meaning. Look for thy reward
    Among the nettles at the elder tree
    Which overshades the mouth of that same pit
    Where we decreed to bury Bassianus.
275 Do this and purchase us thy lasting friends."
    O, Tamora! Was ever heard the like?
    This is the pit, and this the elder tree.
    Look, sirs, if you can find the huntsman out
    That should° have murdered Bassianus here.

280 *Aaron.* My gracious lord, here is the bag of gold.

Saturninus. [*To Titus*] Two of thy whelps, fell° curs
    of bloody kind,°
    Have here bereft my brother of his life.
    Sirs, drag them from the pit unto the prison,
    There let them bide until we have devised
285 Some never-heard-of torturing pain for them.

Tamora. What, are they in this pit? O wondrous thing!
    How easily murder is discoverèd!

Titus. High Emperor, upon my feeble knee
    I beg this boon, with tears not lightly shed,
290 That this fell fault of my accursèd sons,
    Accursèd, if the faults be proved in them—

Saturninus. If it be proved! You see, it is apparent.°
    Who found this letter? Tamora, was it you?

Tamora. Andronicus himself did take it up.

295 *Titus.* I did, my lord, yet let me be their bail,
    For by my father's reverend tomb I vow
    They shall be ready at your Highness' will

268 **And if** if   268 **handsomely** handily   279 **should** was to   281
fell savage   281 **kind** nature   292 **apparent** obvious

To answer their suspicion° with their lives.

Saturninus. Thou shalt not bail them; see thou follow
me.
Some bring the murdered body, some the murderers. *300*
Let them not speak a word; the guilt is plain,
For by my soul were there worse end than death,
That end upon them should be executed.

Tamora. Andronicus, I will entreat the King.
Fear not° thy sons; they shall do well enough. *305*

Titus. Come, Lucius, come, stay not to talk with them.
[*Exeunt.*]

[Scene 4. *The forest.*]

*Enter the Empress' sons with Lavinia, her hands cut
off, and her tongue cut out, and ravished.*

Demetrius. So, now go tell, and if° thy tongue can
speak,
Who 'twas that cut thy tongue and ravished thee.

Chiron. Write down thy mind, bewray° thy meaning
so,
And if thy stumps will let thee play the scribe.

Demetrius. See how with signs and tokens she can
scrowl.° *5*

Chiron. Go home, call for sweet° water, wash thy
hands.

Demetrius. She hath no tongue to call nor hands to
wash,
And so let's leave her to her silent walks.

298 **their suspicion** i.e., the suspicion they are under   305 **Fear not**
do not fear for   2.4.1 **and if** if (as in line 4)   3 **bewray** reveal   5
scrowl scrawl (with a pun on "scroll"?)   6 **sweet** perfumed

Chiron. And 'twere my cause,° I should go hang
 myself.

Demetrius. If thou hadst hands to help thee knit the
10 cord.   *Exeunt* [*Chiron and Demetrius*].

  Enter Marcus from hunting.

Marcus. Who is this? My niece, that flies away so fast!
 Cousin,° a word, where is your husband?
 If I do dream, would all my wealth would wake me!
 If I do wake, some planet strike me down,
15 That I may slumber an eternal sleep!
 Speak, gentle niece, what stern ungentle hands
 Hath lopped and hewed and made thy body bare
 Of her two branches, those sweet ornaments,
 Whose circling shadows kings have sought to sleep
  in,
20 And might not gain so great a happiness
 As half thy love? Why dost not speak to me?
 Alas, a crimson river of warm blood,
 Like to a bubbling fountain stirred with wind,
 Doth rise and fall between thy rosèd lips,
25 Coming and going with thy honey breath.
 But, sure, some Tereus° hath deflowered thee,
 And, lest thou shouldst detect° him, cut thy tongue.
 Ah, now thou turn'st away thy face for shame!
 And, notwithstanding all this loss of blood,
30 As from a conduit with three issuing spouts,
 Yet do thy cheeks look red as Titan's° face
 Blushing to be encount'red with a cloud.
 Shall I speak for thee? Shall I say 'tis so?
 O, that I knew thy heart, and knew the beast,
35 That I might rail at him to ease my mind!
 Sorrow concealèd, like an oven stopped,
 Doth burn the heart to cinders where it is.
 Fair Philomela, why she but lost her tongue,

---

9 **cause** case 12 **Cousin** (commonly used of any near relative other
than a parent, child, or sibling) 26 **Tereus** ravisher of Philomela
(see note to 2.3.43) 27 **detect** expose 31 **Titan's** the sun god's

And in a tedious sampler° sewed her mind:
But lovely niece, that mean is cut from thee;   40
A craftier Tereus, cousin, hast thou met,
And he hath cut those pretty fingers off,
That could have better sewed than Philomel.
O, had the monster seen those lily hands
Tremble like aspen leaves upon a lute,   45
And make the silken strings delight to kiss them,
He would not then have touched them for his life!
Or, had he heard the heavenly harmony
Which that sweet tongue hath made,
He would have dropped his knife, and fell asleep   50
As Cerberus° at the Thracian poet's feet.
Come, let us go and make thy father blind,
For such a sight will blind a father's eye.
One hour's storm will drown the fragrant meads;
What will whole months of tears thy father's eyes?   55
Do not draw back, for we will mourn with thee:
O, could our mourning ease thy misery!   *Exeunt.*

39 **tedious sampler** laboriously executed tapestry 51 **Cerberus**
three-headed dog who guarded the entrance to Hades; he was lulled
by Orpheus, *the Thracian poet*

[ACT 3

Scene 1. *Rome. A street.*]

Enter the Judges and Senators with Titus' two
sons bound, passing on the stage to the place of
execution, and Titus going before, pleading.

Titus. Hear me, grave fathers! Noble tribunes, stay!
    For pity of mine age, whose youth was spent
    In dangerous wars, whilst you securely slept;
    For all my blood in Rome's great quarrel shed,
5   For all the frosty nights that I have watched,
    And for these bitter tears, which now you see
    Filling the agèd wrinkles in my cheeks,
    Be pitiful to my condemnèd sons,
    Whose souls is not corrupted as 'tis thought.
10   For two and twenty sons I never wept,
    Because they died in honor's lofty bed;

Andronicus lieth down° and the Judges pass by him.

    For these, tribunes, in the dust I write
    My heart's deep languor° and my soul's sad tears:
    Let my tears staunch° the earth's dry appetite;
15   My sons' sweet blood will make it shame and blush.
    O earth, I will befriend thee more with rain,
    That shall distill from these two ancient ruins,
    Than youthful April shall with all his show'rs:
    In summer's drought I'll drop upon thee still,°

3.1.11s.d. **lieth down** i.e., prostrates himself 13 **languor** grief
14 **staunch** satisfy, satiate 19 **still** continuously

56

In winter with warm tears I'll melt the snow,   20
And keep eternal springtime on thy face,
So° thou refuse to drink my dear sons' blood.

Enter Lucius, with his weapon drawn.

O reverend tribunes! O gentle agèd men!
Unbind my sons, reverse the doom° of death,
And let me say, that never wept before,   25
My tears are now prevailing orators.

Lucius. O noble father, you lament in vain,
The tribunes hear you not, no man is by,
And you recount your sorrows to a stone.

Titus. Ah, Lucius, for thy brothers let me plead.   30
Grave tribunes, once more I entreat of you.

Lucius. My gracious lord, no tribune hears you speak.

Titus. Why, 'tis no matter, man, if they did hear
They would not mark me, if they did mark
They would not pity me, yet plead I must,   35
And bootless° unto them.
Therefore I tell my sorrows to the stones,
Who though they cannot answer my distress,
Yet in some sort they are better than the tribunes,
For that they will not intercept° my tale: 40
When I do weep they humbly at my feet
Receive my tears and seem to weep with me;
And were they but attirèd in grave weeds,°
Rome could afford no tribunes like to these.
A stone is soft as wax, tribunes more hard than
   stones: 45
A stone is silent and offendeth not,
And tribunes with their tongues doom men to death.
But wherefore stand'st thou with thy weapon
   drawn?

Lucius. To rescue my two brothers from their death,
For which attempt the judges have pronounced   50

22 **So** provided that   24 **doom** judgment   36 **bootless** in vain   40
intercept interrupt   43 **grave weeds** solemn apparel

My everlasting doom of banishment.

Titus. O happy man! They have befriended thee.
Why, foolish Lucius, dost thou not perceive
That Rome is but a wilderness of tigers?
55   Tigers must prey, and Rome affords no prey
But me and mine. How happy art thou then,
From these devourers to be banishèd!
But who comes with our brother Marcus here?

Enter Marcus with Lavinia.

Marcus. Titus, prepare thy agèd eyes to weep,
60   Or if not so, thy noble heart to break.
I bring consuming sorrow to thine age.

Titus. Will it consume me? Let me see it then.

Marcus. This was thy daughter.

Titus.   Why, Marcus, so she is.

Lucius. Ay me! This object° kills me!

65   *Titus.* Faint-hearted boy, arise, and look upon her.
Speak, Lavinia, what accursèd hand
Hath made thee handless in thy father's sight?
What fool hath added water to the sea,
Or brought a faggot to bright-burning Troy?
70   My grief was at the height before thou cam'st,
And now like Nilus° it disdaineth bounds.
Give me a sword, I'll chop off my hands too,
For they have fought for Rome, and all in vain;
And they have nursed this woe, in feeding life;
75   In bootless prayer have they been held up,
And they have served me to effectless use.
Now all the service I require of them
Is that the one will help to cut the other.
'Tis well, Lavinia, that thou hast no hands,
80   For hands to do Rome service is but vain.

Lucius. Speak, gentle sister, who hath mart'red° thee?

Marcus. O, that delightful engine° of her thoughts,

64 **object** sight 71 **Nilus** the Nile 81 **mart'red** mutilated 82 **engine** instrument

That blabbed° them with such pleasing eloquence,
Is torn from forth that pretty hollow cage,
Where like a sweet melodious bird it sung   85
Sweet varied notes, enchanting every ear!

Lucius. O, say thou for her, who hath done this deed?

Marcus. O, thus I found her, straying in the park,
Seeking to hide herself, as doth the deer
That hath received some unrecuring° wound.   90

Titus. It was my dear, and he that wounded her
Hath hurt me more than had he killed me dead;
For now I stand as one upon a rock,
Environed with a wilderness of sea,
Who marks the waxing tide grow wave by wave,   95
Expecting ever when some envious° surge
Will in his brinish bowels swallow him.
This way to death my wretched sons are gone,
Here stands my other son, a banished man,
And here my brother weeping at my woes: 100
But that which gives my soul the greatest spurn°
Is dear Lavinia, dearer than my soul.
Had I but seen thy picture in this plight,
It would have madded me: what shall I do
Now I behold thy lively° body so?   105
Thou hast no hands to wipe away thy tears,
Nor tongue to tell me who hath mart'red thee.
Thy husband he is dead, and for his death
Thy brothers are condemned, and dead by this.°
Look, Marcus! Ah, son Lucius, look on her!   110
When I did name her brothers, then fresh tears
Stood on her cheeks, as doth the honey-dew
Upon a gath'red lily almost withered.

Marcus. Perchance she weeps because they killed her
        husband,
Perchance because she knows them innocent.   115

83 **blabbed** freely spoke   90 **unrecuring** incurable   96 **envious** malicious   101 **spurn** thrust   105 **lively** living   109 **by this** by this time

Titus. If they did kill thy husband, then be joyful,
    Because the law hath ta'en revenge on them.
    No, no, they would not do so foul a deed;
    Witness the sorrow that their sister makes.
120   Gentle Lavinia, let me kiss thy lips,
    Or make some sign how I may do thee ease.°
    Shall thy good uncle, and thy brother Lucius,
    And thou, and I, sit round about some fountain,
    Looking all downwards, to behold our cheeks
125   How they are stained, like meadows yet not dry
    With miry slime left on them by a flood?
    And in the fountain shall we gaze so long
    Till the fresh taste be taken from that clearness,°
    And made a brine-pit with our bitter tears?
130   Or shall we cut away our hands, like thine?
    Or shall we bite our tongues, and in dumb shows°
    Pass the remainder of our hateful days?
    What shall we do? Let us, that have our tongues,
    Plot some device of further misery,
135   To make us wondered at in time to come.

Lucius. Sweet father, cease your tears, for at your
    grief
    See how my wretched sister sobs and weeps.

Marcus. Patience, dear niece. Good Titus, dry thine
    eyes.

Titus. Ah, Marcus, Marcus! Brother, well I wot
140   Thy napkin° cannot drink a tear of mine,
    For thou, poor man, hast drowned it with thine own.

Lucius. Ah, my Lavinia, I will wipe thy cheeks.

Titus. Mark, Marcus, mark! I understand her signs:
    Had she a tongue to speak, now would she say
145   That to her brother which I said to thee:
    His napkin, with his true tears all bewet,
    Can do no service on her sorrowful cheeks.
    O, what a sympathy° of woe is this!

121 **do thee ease** bring you relief 128 **clearness** i.e., clear pool 131 **dumb shows** silent signs 140 **napkin** handkerchief 148 **sympathy** agreement

As far from help as Limbo is from bliss!

Enter Aaron the Moor alone.

Aaron. Titus Andronicus, my lord the Emperor   150
　Sends thee this word, that, if thou love thy sons,
　Let Marcus, Lucius, or thyself, old Titus,
　Or any one of you, chop off your hand
　And send it to the King: he for the same
　Will send thee hither both thy sons alive,   155
　And that shall be the ransom for their fault.

Titus. O, gracious Emperor! O, gentle Aaron!
　Did ever raven sing so like a lark,
　That gives sweet tidings of the sun's uprise?
　With all my heart, I'll send the Emperor my hand.   160
　Good Aaron, wilt thou help to chop it off?

Lucius. Stay, father! For that noble hand of thine
　That hath thrown down so many enemies
　Shall not be sent; my hand will serve the turn.
　My youth can better spare my blood than you,   165
　And therefore mine shall save my brothers' lives.

Marcus. Which of your hands hath not defended Rome
　And reared aloft the bloody battle-ax,
　Writing destruction on the enemy's castle?
　O, none of both but are of high desert: 170
　My hand hath been but idle; let it serve
　To ransom my two nephews from their death,
　Then have I kept it to a worthy end.

Aaron. Nay, come, agree whose hand shall go along,
　For fear they die before their pardon come.   175

Marcus. My hand shall go.

Lucius.　　　　　　　　By heaven, it shall not go.

Titus. Sirs, strive no more; such with'red herbs as these
　Are meet° for plucking up, and therefore mine.

Lucius. Sweet father, if I shall be thought thy son,
　Let me redeem my brothers both from death.   180

178 **meet** fit

Marcus. And, for our father's sake and mother's care,
Now let me show a brother's love to thee.

Titus. Agree between you; I will spare my hand.

Lucius. Then I'll go fetch an ax.

185 *Marcus.* But I will use the ax.
                    Exeunt [Lucius and Marcus].

Titus. Come hither, Aaron. I'll deceive them both;
Lend me thy hand, and I will give thee mine.

Aaron. [*Aside*] If that be called deceit, I will be honest,
And never whilst I live deceive men so:
190 But I'll deceive you in another sort,
And that you'll say, ere half an hour pass.
                    He cuts off Titus' hand.

Enter Lucius and Marcus again.

Titus. Now stay your strife, what shall be is dis-
     patched.
Good Aaron, give his Majesty my hand;
Tell him it was a hand that warded° him
195 From thousand dangers; bid him bury it;
More hath it merited, that let it have.
As for my sons, say I account of them
As jewels purchased at an easy price,
And yet dear too because I bought mine own.

200 *Aaron.* I go, Andronicus, and for thy hand
Look by and by to have thy sons with thee.
[*Aside*] Their heads, I mean. O, how this villainy
Doth fat° me with the very thoughts of it!
Let fools do good, and fair men call for grace,
205 Aaron will have his soul black like his face.   *Exit.*

Titus. O, here I lift this one hand up to heaven,
And bow this feeble ruin to the earth.
If any power pities wretched tears,
To that I call! [*To Lavinia*] What, wouldst thou
     kneel with me?

194 **warded** guarded   203 **fat** delight (literally: "nourish")

Do then, dear heart, for heaven shall hear our
    prayers,   210
Or with our sighs we'll breathe the welkin dim,°
And stain the sun with fog, as sometime clouds
When they do hug him in their melting bosoms.

Marcus. O brother, speak with possibility,
  And do not break into these deep extremes.   215

Titus. Is not my sorrow deep, having no bottom?
  Then be my passions° bottomless with them.

Marcus. But yet let reason govern thy lament.

Titus. If there were reason for these miseries,
  Then into limits could I bind my woes: 220
  When heaven doth weep, doth not the earth
    o'erflow?
  If the winds rage, doth not the sea wax mad,
  Threat'ning the welkin with his big-swoll'n face?
  And wilt thou have a reason for this coil?°
  I am the sea; hark, how her sighs doth flow!   225
  She is the weeping welkin, I the earth:
  Then must my sea be movèd with her sighs,
  Then must my earth with her continual tears
  Become a deluge, overflowed and drowned,
  For why° my bowels° cannot hide her woes,   230
  But like a drunkard must I vomit them.
  Then give me leave, for losers will have leave
  To ease their stomachs° with their bitter tongues.

    Enter a Messenger, with two heads and a hand.

Messenger. Worthy Andronicus, ill art thou repaid
  For that good hand thou sent'st the Emperor.   235
  Here are the heads of thy two noble sons,
  And here's thy hand in scorn to thee sent back;
  Thy grief their sports, thy resolution mocked:

---

211 **breathe the welkin dim** becloud the heavens with our breath
217 **passions** outbursts   224 **coil** fuss   230 **For why** because   230
bowels (thought to be the seat of compassion; akin to the modern
use of "heart")   233 **stomachs** feeling

That° woe is me to think upon thy woes,
240 More than remembrance of my father's death.

[*Exit.*]

Marcus. Now let hot Etna cool in Sicily,
And be my heart an ever-burning hell!
These miseries are more than may be borne!
To weep with them that weep doth ease some deal,°
245 But sorrow flouted at is double death.

Lucius. Ah, that this sight should make so deep a
wound,
And yet detested life not shrink° thereat!
That ever death should let life bear his name,°
Where life hath no more interest but to breathe!

[*Lavinia kisses Titus.*]

250 *Marcus.* Alas, poor heart, that kiss is comfortless
As frozen water to a starvèd° snake.

Titus. When will this fearful slumber° have an end?

Marcus. Now, farewell, flatt'ry, die Andronicus,
Thou dost not slumber: see thy two sons' heads,
255 Thy warlike hand, thy mangled daughter here,
Thy other banished son with this dear° sight
Struck pale and bloodless, and thy brother, I,
Even like a stony image cold and numb.
Ah! Now no more will I control thy griefs:
260 Rend off thy silver hair, thy other hand
Gnawing with thy teeth, and be this dismal sight
The closing up of our most wretched eyes:
Now is a time to storm; why art thou still?

Titus. Ha, ha, ha!

Marcus. Why dost thou laugh? It fits not with this
265 hour.

Titus. Why, I have not another tear to shed.
Besides, this sorrow is an enemy,

239 **That** so that   244 **some deal** somewhat   247 **shrink** slip away
248 **bear his name** i.e., be called "life"   251 **starvèd** numbed
252 **fearful slumber** i.e., nightmare existence   256 **dear** heartfelt

And would usurp upon my wat'ry eyes
And make them blind with tributary° tears;
Then which way shall I find Revenge's Cave?   270
For these two heads do seem to speak to me,
And threat me I shall never come to bliss
Till all these mischiefs be returned again,
Even in their throats that hath committed them.
Come, let me see what task I have to do.   275
You heavy° people, circle me about,
That I may turn me to each one of you,
And swear unto my soul to right your wrongs.
The vow is made. Come, brother, take a head;
And in this hand the other will I bear.   280
And Lavinia, thou shalt be employed in these arms,
Bear thou my hand, sweet wench, between thy
   teeth:°
As for thee, boy, go, get thee from my sight.
Thou art an exile, and thou must not stay.
Hie to the Goths, and raise an army there,   285
And, if ye love me, as I think you do,
Let's kiss and part, for we have much to do.
                                   Exeunt [all but Lucius].

Lucius. Farewell, Andronicus, my noble father,
   The woefull'st man that ever lived in Rome!
Farewell, proud Rome, till Lucius come again;   290
   He loves his pledges dearer than his life.
Farewell, Lavinia, my noble sister;
   O, would thou wert as thou tofore° hast been!
But now nor Lucius nor° Lavinia lives
   But in oblivion and hateful griefs.   295
If Lucius live, he will requite your wrongs,
   And make proud Saturnine and his empress
Beg at the gates, like Tarquin° and his queen.

269 **tributary** paid as tribute 276 **heavy** sad 282 **teeth** (possibly
Shakespeare intended to delete "teeth" from the manuscript, and
substituted the less grotesque "arms" above it; if so, the compositor
mistakenly took "arms" to be part of the previous line, and to make
sense of it he perhaps altered something like "employed in this" to
"employed in these arms") 293 **tofore** formerly 294 **nor ... nor**
neither ... nor 298 **Tarquin** Roman king whose rule was overthrown when his son (of the same name) raped Lucrece

Now will I to the Goths and raise a pow'r,
300   To be revenged on Rome and Saturnine.

                                        Exit Lucius.

[Scene 2. *Rome. Within Titus' house.*]

A banket.° Enter Andronicus, Marcus, Lavinia,
        and the boy [*Lucius*].

Titus. So, so, now sit, and look you eat no more
      Than will preserve just so much strength in us
      As will revenge these bitter woes of ours.
      Marcus, unknit that sorrow-wreathen knot:°
5   Thy niece and I, poor creatures, want our hands,
      And cannot passionate° our tenfold grief
      With folded arms. This poor right hand of mine
      Is left to tyrannize upon my breast;
      Who, when my heart all mad with misery
10   Beats in this hollow prison of my flesh,
      Then thus I thump it down.
      [*To Lavinia*] Thou map° of woe, that thus dost talk
          in signs,
      When thy poor heart beats with outrageous beating,
      Thou canst not strike it thus to make it still.
15   Wound it with sighing,° girl, kill it with groans;
      Or get some little knife between thy teeth,
      And just against thy heart make thou a hole,
      That all the tears that thy poor eyes let fall
      May run into that sink,° and soaking in
20   Drown the lamenting fool° in sea-salt tears.

Marcus. Fie, brother, fie! Teach her not thus to lay
      Such violent hands upon her tender life.

3.2.s.d. **banket** light meal   4 **knot** i.e., Marcus' folded arms, a sign
of heavy thoughts   6 **passionate** passionately express   12 **map** picture   15 **Wound it with sighing** (sighing was believed to shorten life)
19 **sink** sewer   20 **fool** (here, as often, implying affection and pity)

Titus. How now! Has sorrow made thee dote already?
Why, Marcus, no man should be mad but I.
What violent hands can she lay on her life!   25
Ah, wherefore dost thou urge the name of hands,
To bid Aeneas° tell the tale twice o'er,
How Troy was burnt and he made miserable?
O, handle not the theme, to talk of hands,
Lest we remember still that we have none.   30
Fie, fie, how franticly I square° my talk,
As if we should forget we had no hands,
If Marcus did not name the word of hands!
Come, let's fall to; and, gentle girl, eat this.
Here is no drink? Hark, Marcus, what she says—   35
I can interpret all her martyred signs—
She says she drinks no other drink but tears,
Brewed with her sorrow, meshed° upon her cheeks.
Speechless complainer, I will learn thy thought;
In thy dumb action will I be as perfect°   40
As begging hermits in their holy prayers:
Thou shalt not sigh, nor hold thy stumps to heaven,
Nor wink,° nor nod, nor kneel, nor make a sign,
But I of these will wrest an alphabet,
And by still° practice learn to know thy meaning.   45

Boy. Good grandsire, leave these bitter deep laments.
Make my aunt merry with some pleasing tale.

Marcus. Alas, the tender boy, in passion moved,
Doth weep to see his grandsire's heaviness.

Titus. Peace, tender sapling, thou art made of tears,   50
And tears will quickly melt thy life away.
                    Marcus strikes the dish with a knife.
What dost thou strike at, Marcus, with thy knife?

Marcus. At that that I have killed, my lord—a fly.

Titus. Out on thee, murderer! Thou kill'st my heart;
Mine eyes are cloyed with view of tyranny: 55
A deed of death done on the innocent

27 **Aeneas** (see Virgil's *Aeneid* 2.2) 31 **square** shape 38 **meshed**
mashed, brewed 40 **perfect** fully knowing 43 **wink** shut the eyes
45 **still** constant

    Becomes not Titus' brother. Get thee gone;
    I see thou art not for my company.

Marcus. Alas, my lord, I have but killed a fly.

60 *Titus.* "But!" How, if that fly had a father and mother?
    How would he hang his slender gilded wings,
    And buzz lamenting doings in the air!
    Poor harmless fly,
    That, with his pretty buzzing melody,
    Came here to make us merry! And thou hast killed
65   him.

Marcus. Pardon me, sir; it was a black ill-favored°
    fly,
    Like to the Empress' Moor. Therefore I killed him.

Titus. O, O, O,
    Then pardon me for reprehending thee,
70   For thou hast done a charitable deed.
    Give me thy knife, I will insult on° him,
    Flattering myself, as if it were the Moor,
    Come hither purposely to poison me.
                        [He strikes at it.]
    There's for thyself, and that's for Tamora.
75   Ah, sirrah!°
    Yet I think we are not brought so low
    But that between us we can kill a fly
    That comes in likeness of a coal-black Moor.

Marcus. Alas, poor man! Grief has so wrought on
    him,
80   He takes false shadows for true substances.

Titus. Come, take away.° Lavinia, go with me:
    I'll to thy closet,° and go read with thee
    Sad stories chancèd° in the times of old.
    Come, boy, and go with me; thy sight is young,
85   And thou shalt read when mine begin to dazzle.
                             Exeunt.

66 **ill-favored** ugly 71 **insult on** exult over 75 **sirrah** (common term of address to an inferior) 81 **take away** clear the table 82 **closet** private room 83 **chancèd** that happened

[ACT 4

Scene 1. *Rome. Before Titus' house.*]

Enter Lucius' son and Lavinia running after him;
and the boy flies from her with his books under
his arm. Enter Titus and Marcus.

Boy. Help, grandsire, help! My aunt Lavinia
  Follows me everywhere, I know not why.
  Good uncle Marcus, see how swift she comes.
  Alas, sweet aunt, I know not what you mean.

Marcus. Stand by me, Lucius, do not fear thine aunt.   *5*

Titus. She loves thee, boy, too well to do thee harm.

Boy. Ay, when my father was in Rome she did.

Marcus. What means my niece Lavinia by these signs?

Titus. Fear her not, Lucius. Somewhat doth she mean.
  See, Lucius, see, how much she makes of thee: *10*
  Somewhither would she have thee go with her.
  Ah, boy, Cornelia° never with more care
  Read to her sons than she hath read to thee
  Sweet poetry and Tully's *Orator*.°
  Canst thou not guess wherefore she plies thee thus?   *15*

Boy. My lord, I know not, I, nor can I guess,
  Unless some fit or frenzy do possess her:
  For I have heard my grandsire say full oft,

4.1.12 **Cornelia** mother of the Gracchi, two famous tribunes   14
Tully's Orator Cicero's *De oratore* (or his *Orator ad M. Brutum*)

Extremity of griefs would make men mad;
20   And I have read that Hecuba of Troy
Ran mad for sorrow. That made me to fear,
Although, my lord, I know my noble aunt
Loves me as dear as e'er my mother did,
And would not, but in fury,° fright my youth,
25   Which made me down to throw my books and fly,
Causeless perhaps. But pardon me, sweet aunt:
And, madam, if my uncle Marcus go,
I will most willingly attend° your ladyship.

Marcus. Lucius, I will.

30 *Titus.* How now, Lavinia? Marcus, what means this?
Some book there is that she desires to see.
Which is it, girl, of these? Open them, boy.
But thou art deeper read, and better skilled.
Come, and take choice of all my library,
35   And so beguile thy sorrow, till the heavens
Reveal the damned contriver of this deed.
Why lifts she up her arms in sequence thus?

Marcus. I think she means that there were more than
one
Confederate in the fact.° Ay, more there was,
40   Or else to heaven she heaves them for revenge.

Titus. Lucius, what book is that she tosseth° so?

Boy. Grandsire, 'tis Ovid's *Metamorphosis;°*
My mother gave it me.

Marcus.   For love of her that's gone,
Perhaps she culled it from among the rest.

45 *Titus.* Soft! So busily she turns the leaves!
Help her! What would she find? Lavinia, shall I
read?
This is the tragic tale of Philomel,
And treats of Tereus' treason and his rape;

24 **but in fury** except in madness   28 **attend** wait on   39 **fact** crime
41 **tosseth** turns the pages of   42 **Metamorphosis** (so spelled in the
title of an Elizabethan translation by Golding, with which Shakespeare was familiar; properly *Metamorphoses*)

And rape, I fear, was root of thy annoy.

Marcus. See, brother, see, note how she quotes° the
    leaves.   *50*

Titus. Lavinia, wert thou thus surprised, sweet girl,
    Ravished and wronged, as Philomela was,
    Forced in the ruthless, vast,° and gloomy woods?
    See, see!
    Ay, such a place there is, where we did hunt—   *55*
    O, had we never, never hunted there—
    Patterned by° that the poet here describes,
    By nature made for murders and for rapes.

Marcus. O, why should nature build so foul a den,
    Unless the gods delight in tragedies?   *60*

Titus. Give signs, sweet girl, for here are none but
    friends,
    What Roman lord it was durst do the deed:
    Or slunk not Saturnine, as Tarquin erst,°
    That left the camp to sin in Lucrece' bed?

Marcus. Sit down, sweet niece: brother, sit down by
    me.   *65*
    Apollo, Pallas, Jove, or Mercury,
    Inspire me, that I may this treason find!
    My lord, look here: look here, Lavinia.
                        He writes his name with his staff,
                        and guides it with feet and mouth.
    This sandy plot is plain;° guide if thou canst,
    This after me.° I have writ my name   *70*
    Without the help of any hand at all.
    Cursed be that heart that forced us to this shift!°
    Write thou, good niece, and here display at last
    What God will have discovered° for revenge.
    Heaven guide thy pen to print thy sorrows plain,   *75*
    That we may know the traitors and the truth!
                        She takes the staff in her mouth and guides
                        it with her stumps and writes.

50 **quotes** examines   53 **vast** desolate   57 **Patterned by** after the
pattern   63 **erst** once   69 **plain** flat   70 **after me** as I do   72 **shift**
device   74 **discovered** revealed

O, do ye read, my lord, what she hath writ?

[*Titus*.] "*Stuprum*.° Chiron. Demetrius."

Marcus. What, what! The lustful sons of Tamora
80   Performers of this heinous, bloody deed?

Titus. Magni Dominator poli,
    Tam lentus audis scelera? tam lentus vides?°

Marcus. O, calm thee, gentle lord! Although I know
    There is enough written upon this earth
85   To stir a mutiny in the mildest thoughts,
    And arm the minds of infants to exclaims.°
    My lord, kneel down with me; Lavinia, kneel;
    And kneel, sweet boy, the Roman Hector's° hope;
    And swear with me, as, with the woeful fere°
90   And father of that chaste dishonored dame,
    Lord Junius Brutus° sware for Lucrece' rape,
    That we will prosecute by good advice°
    Mortal revenge upon these traitorous Goths,
    And see their blood, or die with this reproach.

95 *Titus*. 'Tis sure enough, and you knew how,
    But if you hunt these bear-whelps, then beware:
    The dam will wake; and if she wind ye° once,
    She's with the lion deeply still in league,
    And lulls him whilst she playeth on her back,
100   And when he sleeps will she do what she list.°
    You are a young huntsman, Marcus, let alone;
    And, come, I will go get a leaf of brass,
    And with a gad° of steel will write these words,
    And lay it by. The angry northern wind
105   Will blow these sands like Sibyl's leaves° abroad,
    And where's our lesson then? Boy, what say you?

Boy. I say, my lord, that if I were a man,

78 **Stuprum** rape (Latin) 81–82 **Magni Dominator … lentus vides?** ruler of the great heavens, are you so slow to hear and to see crimes? (Latin; derived from Seneca's *Hippolytus*, lines 668–69) 86 **exclaims** exclamations 88 **the Roman Hector's** i.e., Andronicus (Titus is compared to Hector, Troy's champion) 89 **fere** spouse 91 **Junius Brutus** chief of those who drove the Tarquins from Rome 92 **by good advice** after careful deliberation 97 **and if she wind ye** if she get wind of (smell) you 100 **list** please 103 **gad** spike, stylus 105 **Sibyl's leaves** leaves on which the Sibyl wrote prophecies

> Their mother's bedchamber should not be safe
> For these base bondmen to the yoke of Rome.

Marcus. Ay, that's my boy! Thy father hath full oft   *110*
  For his ungrateful country done the like.

Boy. And, uncle, so will I, and if I live.

Titus. Come, go with me into mine armory:
  Lucius, I'll fit thee, and withal my boy
  Shall carry from me to the Empress' sons   *115*
  Presents that I intend to send them both.
  Come, come; thou'lt do my message, wilt thou not?

Boy. Ay, with my dagger in their bosoms, grandsire.

Titus. No, boy, not so; I'll teach thee another course.
  Lavinia, come. Marcus, look to my house.   *120*
  Lucius and I'll go brave it° at the court;
  Ay, marry,° will we, sir; and we'll be waited on.°
                                                    Exeunt.

Marcus. O heavens, can you hear a good man groan,
  And not relent, or not compassion him?
  Marcus, attend him in his ecstasy,°   *125*
  That hath more scars of sorrow in his heart
  Than foemen's marks upon his batt'red shield,
  But yet so just that he will not revenge.
  Revenge the heavens° for old Andronicus!   *Exit.*

---

121 **brave it** behave defiantly   122 **marry** (an interjection, from "By the Virgin Mary")   122 **be waited on** i.e., not be ignored   125 **ecstasy** fit of madness   129 **Revenge the heavens** may the heavens take revenge

[Scene 2. *Rome. Within the palace.*]

Enter Aaron, Chiron, and Demetrius, at one
door, and at the other door young Lucius and
another, with a bundle of weapons and verses
writ upon them.

Chiron. Demetrius, here's the son of Lucius,
He hath some message to deliver us.

Aaron. Ay, some mad message from his mad grandfather.

Boy. My lords, with all the humbleness I may,
5   I greet your honors from Andronicus.
        [*Aside*] And pray the Roman gods confound° you
        both.

Demetrius. Gramercy,° lovely Lucius, what's the news?

Boy. [*Aside*] That you are both deciphered, that's the
        news,
        For villains marked with rape. [*Aloud*] May it
        please you,
10   My grandsire, well-advised,° hath sent by me
        The goodliest weapons of his armory
        To gratify your honorable youth,
        The hope of Rome; for so he bid me say;
        And so I do, and with his gifts present
15   Your lordships; whenever you have need,
        You may be armèd and appointed° well.
        And so I leave you both, [*aside*] like bloody villains.
                                                        Exit.

Demetrius. What's here? A scroll, and written round
        about?

4.2.6 **confound** destroy   7 **Gramercy** thanks   10 **well-advised** in
sound mind   16 **appointed** equipped

Let's see:
>*Integer vitae, scelerisque purus,*　　　　20
>*Non eget Mauri jaculis, nec arcu.°*

Chiron. O, 'tis a verse in Horace; I know it well:
I read it in the grammar long ago.

Aaron. Ay, just; a verse in Horace; right, you have it.
　[*Aside*] Now, what a thing it is to be an ass!　　　　25
Here's no sound jest! The old man hath found their
　guilt,
And sends them weapons wrapped about with lines
That wound, beyond their feeling, to the quick.
But were our witty° empress well afoot,
She would applaud Andronicus' conceit.°　　　　30
But let her rest in her unrest awhile.
　[*Aloud*] And now, young lords, was't not a happy
　star
Led us to Rome, strangers, and more than so,
Captives, to be advancèd to this height?
It did me good, before the palace gate　　　　35
To brave the tribune in his brother's hearing.

Demetrius. But me more good, to see so great a lord
Basely insinuate° and send us gifts.

Aaron. Had he not reason, Lord Demetrius?
Did you not use his daughter very friendly?　　　　40

Demetrius. I would we had a thousand Roman dames
At such a bay,° by turn to serve our lust.

Chiron. A charitable wish and full of love.

Aaron. Here lacks but your mother for to say amen.

Chiron. And that would she for twenty thousand
more.　　　　45

Demetrius. Come, let us go, and pray to all the gods
For our belovèd mother in her pains.

20–21 **Integer vitae ... nec arcu** the man of upright life and free
from crime has no need of a Moor's javelins or bow (Latin; from
Horace, *Odes*, 1.22.1–2) 29 **witty** wise 30 **conceit** idea, design
38 **insinuate** curry favor 42 **At such a bay** thus cornered

Aaron. [*Aside*] Pray to the devils, the gods have given
    us over.

                            Trumpets sound.

Demetrius. Why do the Emperor's trumpets flourish
    thus?

50 *Chiron.* Belike,° for joy the Emperor hath a son.

Demetrius. Soft! Who comes here?

    Enter Nurse with a blackamoor child.

Nurse.   God morrow, lords.
    O, tell me, did you see Aaron the Moor?

Aaron. Well, more or less, or ne'er a whit at all,
    Here Aaron is; and what with Aaron now?

55 *Nurse.* O gentle Aaron, we are all undone!
    Now help, or woe betide thee evermore!

Aaron. Why, what a caterwauling dost thou keep!
    What dost thou wrap and fumble° in thy arms?

Nurse. O, that which I would hide from heaven's eye,
60   Our Empress' shame and stately Rome's disgrace!
    She is delivered, lords, she is delivered.

Aaron. To whom?

Nurse.   I mean, she is brought abed.

Aaron. Well, God give her good rest! What hath he
    sent her?

Nurse. A devil.

Aaron.   Why, then she is the devil's dam;°
65   A joyful issue.

Nurse. A joyless, dismal, black, and sorrowful issue!
    Here is the babe, as loathsome as a toad
    Amongst the fair-faced breeders of our clime.
    The Empress sends it thee, thy stamp, thy seal,

50 **Belike** probably   58 **fumble** clumsily bundle up   64 **dam** mother

And bids thee christen it with thy dagger's point.   70

Aaron. Zounds,° ye whore! Is black so base a hue?
  Sweet blowse,° you are a beauteous blossom, sure.

Demetrius. Villain, what hast thou done?

Aaron. That which thou canst not undo.

Chiron. Thou hast undone our mother.   75

Aaron. Villain, I have done° thy mother.

Demetrius. And therein, hellish dog, thou hast undone
  her.
  Woe to her chance,° and damned her loathèd
  choice!
  Accursed the offspring of so foul a fiend!

Chiron. It shall not live.   80

Aaron. It shall not die.

Nurse. Aaron, it must; the mother wills it so.

Aaron. What, must it, nurse? Then let no man but I
  Do execution on my flesh and blood.

Demetrius. I'll broach° the tadpole on my rapier's
  point.   85
  Nurse, give it me; my sword shall soon dispatch it.

Aaron. Sooner this sword shall plow thy bowels up.
  Stay, murderous villains! Will you kill your brother?
  Now, by the burning tapers of the sky,
  That shone so brightly when this boy was got,°   90
  He dies upon my scimitar's sharp point
  That touches this my first-born son and heir!
  I tell you, younglings, not Enceladus,°
  With all his threat'ning band of Typhon's brood,
  Nor great Alcides,° nor the god of war,   95
  Shall seize this prey out of his father's hands.

71 **Zounds** (an interjection, from "By God's wounds") 72 **blowse**
ruddy wench (here, ironic) 76 **done** had sexual intercourse with
78 **chance** luck 85 **broach** impale 90 **got** begat 93 **Enceladus**
one of the Titans (sons of Typhon) who fought the Olympians 95
Alcides Hercules

What, what, ye sanguine,° shallow-hearted boys!
Ye white-limed walls!° Ye alehouse painted signs!
Coal-black is better than another hue,
100 In that it scorns to bear another hue;
For all the water in the ocean
Can never turn the swan's black legs to white,
Although she lave° them hourly in the flood.
Tell the Empress from me, I am of age
105 To keep mine own, excuse it how she can.

Demetrius. Wilt thou betray thy noble mistress thus?

Aaron. My mistress is my mistress, this my self,
The vigor and the picture of my youth:
This before all the world do I prefer;
110 This mauger° all the world will I keep safe,
Or some of you shall smoke° for it in Rome.

Demetrius. By this our mother is forever shamed.

Chiron. Rome will despise her for this foul escape.°

Nurse. The Emperor in his rage will doom her death.

115 *Chiron.* I blush to think upon this ignomy.°

Aaron. Why, there's the privilege your beauty bears:
Fie, treacherous hue, that will betray with blushing
The close enacts° and counsels of thy heart!
Here's a young lad framed of another leer:°
120 Look, how the black slave smiles upon the father,
As who should say, "Old lad, I am thine own."
He is your brother, lords, sensibly fed
Of that self blood° that first gave life to you,
And from your womb where you imprisoned were
125 He is enfranchisèd and come to light:
Nay, he is your brother by the surer side,°
Although my seal be stampèd in his face.

97 **sanguine** pink-cheeked 98 **white-limed walls** (perhaps a reference to the "whited sepulchers" of Matthew 23:27) 103 **lave** wash
110 **mauger** in spite of 111 **smoke** suffer 113 **escape** escapade
115 **ignomy** ignominy 118 **close enacts** secret resolutions 119
leer complexion 122–23 **sensibly fed/Of that self blood** i.e., his
body draws on the same blood 126 **the surer side** i.e., the mother's
side

Nurse. Aaron, what shall I say unto the Empress?

Demetrius. Advise thee, Aaron, what is to be done,
  And we will all subscribe° to thy advice: *130*
  Save thou the child, so° we may all be safe.

Aaron. Then sit we down and let us all consult.
  My son and I will have the wind of you:°
  Keep there; now talk at pleasure of your safety.

Demetrius. How many women saw this child of his?   *135*

Aaron. Why, so, brave lords! When we join in league,
  I am a lamb: but if you brave the Moor,
  The chafèd° boar, the mountain lioness,
  The ocean swells not so as Aaron storms.
  But say again, how many saw the child?   *140*

Nurse. Cornelia the midwife, and myself,
  And no one else but the delivered Empress.

Aaron. The Empress, the midwife, and yourself:
  Two may keep counsel when the third's away.
  Go to the Empress, tell her this I said.   *145*

                      He kills her.

  Wheak, wheak!
  So cries a pig preparèd to the spit.

Demetrius. What mean'st thou, Aaron? Wherefore
  didst thou this?

Aaron. O, lord, sir, 'tis a deed of policy!°
  Shall she live to betray this guilt of ours?   *150*
  A long-tongued babbling gossip? No, lords, no.
  And now be it known to you my full intent.
  Not far one Muliteus my countryman
  His° wife but yesternight was brought to bed;
  His child is like to her, fair as you are.   *155*
  Go pack° with him, and give the mother gold,
  And tell them both the circumstance of all,°

130 **subscribe** agree 131 **so** provided that 133 **have the wind of
you** i.e., keep you safely in our view (as game is watched, down
wind) 138 **chafèd** enraged 149 **policy** cunning 153–54 **country-
man/His** countryman's 156 **pack** conspire 157 **circumstance of
all** all the details

And how by this their child shall be advanced,
And be receivèd for the Emperor's heir,
160 And substituted in the place of mine,
To calm this tempest whirling in the court;
And let the Emperor dandle him for his own.
Hark ye, lords; you see I have given her physic,°
And you must needs bestow her funeral;
165 The fields are near, and you are gallant grooms.
This done, see that you take no longer days,°
But send the midwife presently to me.
The midwife and the nurse well made away,
Then let the ladies tattle what they please.

170 *Chiron.* Aaron, I see, thou wilt not trust the air
With secrets.

Demetrius.   For this care of Tamora,
Herself and hers are highly bound to thee.   *Exeunt.*

Aaron. Now to the Goths, as swift as swallow flies,
There to dispose this treasure in mine arms,
175 And secretly to greet the Empress' friends.
Come on, you thick-lipped slave, I'll bear you
        hence;
For it is you that puts us to our shifts.°
I'll make you feed on berries and on roots,
And feed on curds and whey, and suck the goat,
180 And cabin° in a cave, and bring you up
To be a warrior and command a camp.   *Exit.*

163 **physic** medicine   166 **days** time   177 **puts us to our shifts**
causes us to use stratagems   180 **cabin** dwell

[Scene 3. *Rome. A street.*]

Enter Titus, old Marcus, [his son Publius,] young
Lucius, and other gentlemen, with bows; and
Titus bears the arrows with letters on the ends
of them.

Titus. Come, Marcus, come; kinsmen, this is the way.
　Sir boy, let me see your archery;
　Look ye draw home° enough, and 'tis there straight.
　Terras Astraea reliquit.°
　Be you remem b'red,° Marcus: she's gone, she's
　　fled.　　　　　　　　　　　　　　　　　　　　　5
　Sirs, take you to your tools. You, cousins, shall
　Go sound the ocean, and cast your nets;
　Happily° you may catch her in the sea;
　Yet there's as little justice as at land:
　No, Publius and Sempronius, you must do it;　　　　10
　'Tis you must dig with mattock and with spade,
　And pierce the inmost center of the earth:
　Then, when you come to Pluto's region,°
　I pray you deliver him this petition:　　　　　　　　15
　Tell him, it is for justice and for aid,
　And that it comes from old Andronicus,
　Shaken with sorrows in ungrateful Rome.
　Ah, Rome! Well, well; I made thee miserable
　What time° I threw the people's suffrages
　On him that thus doth tyrannize o'er me.　　　　　20
　Go, get you gone, and pray be careful all,
　And leave you not a man of war unsearched:
　This wicked Emperor may have shipped her hence,
　And, kinsmen, then we may go pipe for° justice.

Marcus. O, Publius, is not this a heavy case,　　　　25

4.3.3 **home** fully　4 **Terras Astraea reliquit** Astraea (goddess of justice) has left the earth (Latin; from Ovid, *Metamorphoses*, 1.150)
5 **Be you remem b'red** remember　8 **Happily** perhaps　13 **Pluto's
region** Hades　19 **What time** when　24 **pipe for** i.e., whistle vainly
for

To see thy noble uncle thus distract?

Publius. Therefore, my lords, it highly us concerns
    By day and night t' attend him carefully,
    And feed his humor° kindly as we may,
30   Till time beget some careful remedy.

Marcus. Kinsmen, his sorrows are past remedy.
    But° . . .
    Join with the Goths, and with revengeful war
    Take wreak° on Rome for this ingratitude,
35   And vengeance on the traitor Saturnine.

Titus. Publius, how now! How now, my masters!
    What, have you met with her?

Publius. No, my good lord, but Pluto sends you word,
    If you will have revenge from hell, you shall:
40   Marry, for Justice, she is so employed,
    He thinks, with Jove in heaven, or somewhere else,
    So that perforce you must needs stay a time.

Titus. He doth me wrong to feed me with delays.
    I'll dive into the burning lake below,
45   And pull her out of Acheron° by the heels.
    Marcus, we are but shrubs, no cedars we,
    No big-boned men framed of the Cyclops'° size;
    But metal, Marcus, steel to the very back,
    Yet wrung with wrongs more than our backs can
        bear:
50   And sith° there's no justice in earth nor hell,
    We will solicit heaven, and move the gods
    To send down Justice for to wreak° our wrongs.
    Come, to this gear.° You are a good archer, Marcus.
                 He gives them the arrows.
    Ad Jovem, that's for you: here, *Ad Apollinem*:
55   *Ad Martem*,° that's for myself:

29 **humor** mood, caprice 32 **But** (a catchword indicates that the
line begins "But," though the line itself was omitted) 34 **wreak**
vengeance 45 **Acheron** river in Hades 47 **Cyclops** giants (in
Homer's *Odyssey*) 50 **sith** since 52 **wreak** avenge 53 **gear** affair
54–55 **Ad Jovem ... Ad Apollinem:/Ad Martem** to Jove ... to
Apollo; to Mars (Latin)

Here, boy, to Pallas: here, to Mercury:
To Saturn, Caius, not to Saturnine;
You were as good to shoot° against the wind.
To it, boy! Marcus, loose when I bid.
Of my word, I have written to effect;   60
There's not a god left unsolicited.

Marcus. Kinsmen, shoot all your shafts into the court:
   We will afflict the Emperor in his pride.

Titus. Now, masters, draw. O, well said, Lucius!
   Good boy, in Virgo's° lap; give it Pallas.   65

Marcus. My lord, I aim a mile beyond the moon;
   Your letter is with Jupiter by this.

Titus. Ha, ha!
   Publius, Publius, what hast thou done!
   See, see, thou hast shot off one of Taurus' horns.   70

Marcus. This was the sport, my lord: when Publius
      shot,
   The bull being galled, gave Aries such a knock
   That down fell both the Ram's horns in the court,
   And who should find them but the Empress' villain?
   She laughed, and told the Moor he should not
      choose   75
   But give them to his master for a present.

Titus. Why, there it goes! God give his lordship joy!

Enter the Clown,° with a basket and two pigeons in it.

   News, news from heaven! Marcus, the post is come.
   Sirrah, what tidings? Have you any letters?
   Shall I have justice? What says Jupiter?   80

Clown. Ho, the gibbet maker!° He says that he hath

---

58 **You were as good to shoot** you would do as much good by shooting 65 **Virgo's** the Virgin's (sign of the zodiac, as are *Taurus*—the
bull—in line 70, and *Aries*—the ram—in line 72) 77s.d. **Clown**
rustic fellow 81 **gibbet maker** (apparently "Jupiter"—which in the
original text is spelled "Jubiter"—was pronounced rather like "gib-
beter," i.e., gibbet maker)

taken them down again, for the man must not be
hanged till the next week.

Titus. But what says Jupiter, I ask thee?

85 *Clown*. Alas, sir, I know not Jubiter; I never drank
with him in all my life.

Titus. Why, villain, art not thou the carrier?

Clown. Ay, of my pigeons, sir, nothing else.

Titus. Why, didst thou not come from heaven?

90 *Clown*. From heaven? Alas, sir, I never came there!
God forbid, I should be so bold to press to heaven
in my young days. Why, I am going with my
pigeons to the tribunal plebs,° to take up a matter
of brawl betwixt my uncle and one of the Emperal's
95 men.

Marcus. Why, sir, that is as fit as can be to serve for
your oration; and let him deliver the pigeons to the
Emperor from you.

Titus. Tell me, can you deliver an oration to the
100 Emperor with a grace?

Clown. Nay, truly, sir, I could never say grace in all
my life.

Titus. Sirrah, come hither: make no more ado,
But give your pigeons to the Emperor:
105 By me thou shalt have justice at his hands.
Hold, hold, meanwhile, here's money for thy
charges.°
Give me pen and ink. Sirrah, can you with a grace
deliver up a supplication?

Clown. Ay, sir.

110 *Titus*. Then here is a supplication for you. And when
you come to him, at the first approach you must

93 **tribunal plebs** (malaprop for *tribunus plebis,* "Tribune of the
plebs"; *Emperal,* later in the sentence, is another malaprop)   106
charges i.e., pigeons

kneel, then kiss his foot, then deliver up your
pigeons, and then look for your reward. I'll be at
hand, sir! See you do it bravely.°

Clown. I warrant you, sir, let me alone.   *115*

Titus. Sirrah, hast thou a knife? Come, let me see it.
Here, Marcus, fold it in the oration,
For thou hast made it like an humble suppliant.
And when thou hast given it to the Emperor,
Knock at my door, and tell me what he says.   *120*

Clown. God be with you, sir; I will.   *Exit.*

Titus. Come, Marcus, let us go. Publius, follow me.
                                                    Exeunt.

[Scene 4. *Rome. Before the palace.*]

Enter Emperor and Empress and her two sons.
The Emperor brings the arrows in his hand that
Titus shot at him.

Saturninus. Why, lords, what wrongs are these! Was
          ever seen
An emperor in Rome thus overborne,
Troubled, confronted thus, and for the extent°
Of egal° justice used in such contempt?
My lords, you know, as know the mightful gods,   *5*
However these disturbers of our peace
Buzz in the people's ears, there naught hath passed
But even° with law against the willful sons
Of old Andronicus. And what and if
His sorrows have so overwhelmed his wits,   *10*
Shall we be thus afflicted in his wreaks,°
His fits, his frenzy, and his bitterness?

114 **bravely** well 4.4.3 **extent** exercise 4 **egal** equal 8 **even**
agreeing 11 **wreaks** vengeful acts

And now he writes to heaven for his redress!
See, here's to Jove, and this to Mercury,
15   This to Apollo, this to the god of war.
Sweet scrolls to fly about the streets of Rome!
What's this but libeling against the Senate,
And blazoning° our unjustice everywhere?
A goodly humor, is it not, my lords?
20   As who would say, in Rome no justice were.
But if I live, his feignèd ecstasies°
Shall be no shelter to these outrages,
But he and his shall know that justice lives
In Saturninus' health; whom, if he sleep,
25   He'll so awake, as he in fury shall
Cut off the proud'st conspirator that lives.

Tamora. My gracious lord, my lovely Saturnine,
Lord of my life, commander of my thoughts,
Calm thee, and bear the faults of Titus' age,
30   Th' effects of sorrow for his valiant sons,
Whose loss hath pierced him deep and scarred his
    heart,
And rather comfort his distressèd plight
Than prosecute the meanest or the best
For these contempts. [*Aside*] Why, thus it shall
    become
35   High-witted Tamora to gloze° with all.
But, Titus, I have touched thee to the quick,
Thy lifeblood out:° if Aaron now be wise,
Then is all safe, the anchor in the port.

            Enter Clown.

How now, good fellow? Wouldst thou speak with
us?

40 *Clown.* Yea, forsooth, and your mistress-ship be em-
    perial.

Tamora. Empress I am, but yonder sits the Emperor.

Clown. 'Tis he. God and Saint Stephen give you

---

18 **blazoning** proclaiming   21 **ecstasies** fits of madness   35 **gloze** use
specious words   37 **Thy lifeblood out** when your blood is out

godden.° I have brought you a letter and a couple
of pigeons here.   45

>   *He [i.e., Saturninus] reads the letter.*

Saturninus. Go, take him away, and hang him presently.

Clown. How much money must I have?

Tamora. Come, sirrah, you must be hanged.

Clown. Hanged! By lady,° then I have brought up a
neck° to a fair end.   *Exit [with guards].*   50

Saturninus. Despiteful and intolerable wrongs!
Shall I endure this monstrous villainy?
I know from whence this same device proceeds.
May this be borne as if his traitorous sons,
That died by law for murder of our brother,   55
Have by my means been butchered wrongfully.
Go, drag the villain hither by the hair,
Nor age nor honor shall shape privilege:°
For this proud mock I'll be thy slaughter-man—
Sly frantic wretch, that holp'st to make me great,   60
In hope thyself should govern Rome and me.

>   *Enter nuntius,° Aemilius.*

What news with thee, Aemilius?

Aemilius. Arm, my lords. Rome never had more cause.
The Goths have gathered head,° and with a power°
Of high-resolvèd men, bent to the spoil,   65
They hither march amain, under conduct°
Of Lucius, son to old Andronicus;
Who threats, in course of this revenge, to do
As much as ever Coriolanus° did.

---

44 **godden** good evening   49 **By lady** (an interjection, from "By
Our Lady")   50 **neck** (possibly with a pun on "knack," which means
"deceitful trick")   58 **shape privilege** provide immunity   61s.d.
nuntius messenger (Latin)   64 **gathered head** raised an army   64
power army   66 **conduct** leadership   69 **Coriolanus** (this Roman
hero who became Rome's enemy is the protagonist in Shakespeare's
last tragedy)

70 *Saturninus.* Is warlike Lucius general of the Goths?
        These tidings nip me, and I hang the head
        As flowers with frost or grass beat down with
            storms.
        Ay, now begins our sorrows to approach:
        'Tis he the common people love so much;
75   Myself hath often heard them say,
        When I have walkèd like a private man,
        That Lucius' banishment was wrongfully,
        And they have wished that Lucius were their
            emperor.

    Tamora. Why should you fear? Is not your city
        strong?

80 *Saturninus.* Ay, but the citizens favor Lucius,
        And will revolt from me to succor him.

    Tamora. King, be thy thoughts imperious, like thy
        name.
        Is the sun dimmed, that gnats do fly in it?
        The eagle suffers little birds to sing
85   And is not careful° what they mean thereby,
        Knowing that with the shadow of his wings
        He can at pleasure stint° their melody:
        Even so mayst thou the giddy men of Rome.
        Then cheer thy spirit: for know, thou Emperor,
90   I will enchant the old Andronicus
        With words more sweet, and yet more dangerous,
        Than baits to fish, or honey-stalks° to sheep;
        Whenas the one is wounded with the bait,
        The other rotted with delicious feed.

95 *Saturninus.* But he will not entreat his son for us.

    Tamora. If Tamora entreat him, then he will:
        For I can smooth, and fill his agèd ears
        With golden promises, that, were his heart
        Almost impregnable, his old ears deaf,
100 ·   Yet should both ear and heart obey my tongue.

    85 **careful** worried   87 **stint** stop   92 **honey-stalks** clover

[*To Aemilius*] Go thou before to be our ambassa-
   dor:
Say that the Emperor requests a parley
Of warlike Lucius, and appoint the meeting
Even at his father's house, the old Andronicus.

Saturninus. Aemilius, do this message honorably,   *105*
   And if he stand in° hostage for his safety,
   Bid him demand what pledge will please him best.

Aemilius. Your bidding shall I do effectually.   *Exit*.

Tamora. Now will I to that old Andronicus,
   And temper° him with all the art I have,   *110*
   To pluck proud Lucius from the warlike Goths.
   And now, sweet Emperor, be blithe again,
   And bury all thy fear in my devices.

Saturninus. Then go successantly,° and plead to him.

                              Exeunt.

---

106 **stand in** insist upon   110 **temper** work upon   114 **successantly**
one after the other (?)

[ACT 5

Scene 1. *A plain near Rome*.]

*Enter Lucius, with an army of Goths, with drums
and soldiers.*

Lucius. Approvèd° warriors, and my faithful friends,
　I have receivèd letters from great Rome,
　Which signifies what hate they bear their Emperor,
　And how desirous of our sight they are.
5　Therefore, great lords, be, as your titles witness,
　Imperious, and impatient of your wrongs;
　And wherein Rome hath done you any scath,°
　Let him make treble satisfaction.

Goth. Brave slip,° sprung from the great Andronicus,
10　Whose name was once our terror, now our comfort,
　Whose high exploits and honorable deeds
　Ingrateful Rome requites with foul contempt,
　Be bold° in us: we'll follow where thou lead'st,
　Like stinging bees in hottest summer's day,
15　Led by their master to the flow'rèd fields,
　And be advengèd on cursèd Tamora.

[Other Goths.] And as he saith, so say we all with him.

Lucius. I humbly thank him, and I thank you all.
　But who comes here, led by a lusty Goth?

5.1.1 **Approvèd** tested 7 **scath** harm 9 **slip** offshoot 13 **bold** confident

*Enter a Goth, leading of Aaron with his child
in his arms.*

Goth. Renownèd Lucius, from our troops I strayed   20
  To gaze upon a ruinous monastery,
  And, as I earnestly did fix mine eye
  Upon the wasted° building, suddenly
  I heard a child cry underneath a wall.
  I made unto the noise, when soon I heard   25
  The crying babe controlled with this discourse:
  "Peace, tawny° slave, half me and half thy dame.°
  Did not thy hue bewray° whose brat° thou art,
  Had nature lent thee but thy mother's look,
  Villain, thou mightst have been an emperor: 30
  But where the bull and cow are both milk-white,
  They never do beget a coal-black calf.
  Peace, villain, peace!" Even thus he rates° the babe,
  "For I must bear thee to a trusty Goth,
  Who, when he knows thou art the Empress' babe,   35
  Will hold thee dearly for thy mother's sake."
  With this, my weapon drawn, I rushed upon him,
  Surprised him suddenly, and brought him hither,
  To use as you think needful of the man.

Lucius. O worthy Goth, this is the incarnate devil   40
  That robbed Andronicus of his good hand.
  This is the pearl that pleased your Empress' eye,
  And here's the base fruit of her burning lust.
  Say, wall-eyed° slave, whither wouldst thou convey
  This growing image of thy fiendlike face?   45
  Why dost not speak? What, deaf? Not a word?
  A halter, soldiers! Hang him on this tree,
  And by his side his fruit of bastardy.

Aaron. Touch not the boy; he is of royal blood.

Lucius. Too like the sire for ever being good.   50
  First hang the child, that he may see it sprawl—

23 **wasted** ruined 27 **tawny** black 27 **dame** mother 28 **bewray** reveal 28 **brat** young offspring 33 **rates** berates 44 **wall-eyed** glaring (literally: having a whitish iris)

A sight to vex the father's soul withal.

Aaron. Get me a ladder.° Lucius, save the child,
And bear it from me to the Empress.
55 If thou do this, I'll show thee wondrous things
That highly may advantage thee to hear.
If thou wilt not, befall what may befall,
I'll speak no more but "Vengeance rot you all!"

Lucius. Say on, and if it please me which thou
     speak'st,
60 Thy child shall live, and I will see it nourished.

Aaron. And if it please thee! Why, assure thee,
     Lucius,
'Twill vex thy soul to hear what I shall speak;
For I must talk of murders, rapes, and massacres,
Acts of black night, abominable deeds,
65 Complots of mischief, treason, villainies
Ruthful° to hear, yet piteously performed:°
And this shall all be buried in my death,
Unless thou swear to me my child shall live.

Lucius. Tell on thy mind, I say thy child shall live.

70 *Aaron.* Swear that he shall, and then I will begin.

Lucius. Who should I swear by? Thou believest no
     god:
That granted, how canst thou believe an oath?

Aaron. What if I do not? As indeed I do not;
Yet, for I know thou art religious,
75 And hast a thing within thee callèd conscience,
With twenty popish tricks and ceremonies,
Which I have seen thee careful to observe,
Therefore I urge thy oath; for that I know
An idiot holds his bauble° for a god,
80 And keeps the oath which by that god he swears,
To that I'll urge him: therefore thou shalt vow
By that same god, what god soe'er it be,

53 **Get me a ladder** i.e., hang me rather than the child   66 **Ruthful**
pitiful   66 **piteously performed** i.e., performed, which excites pity
79 **bauble** carved head at the end of a court fool's stick

That thou adorest and hast in reverence,
To save my boy, to nourish and bring him up;
Or else I will discover naught to thee.   85

Lucius. Even by my god I swear to thee I will.

Aaron. First know thou, I begot him on the Empress.

Lucius. O most insatiate and luxurious° woman!

Aaron. Tut, Lucius, this was but a deed of charity
To° that which thou shalt hear of me anon.   90
'Twas her two sons that murdered Bassianus;
They cut thy sister's tongue and ravished her,
And cut her hands, and trimmed her as thou sawest.

Lucius. O detestable villain! Call'st thou that trimming?

Aaron. Why, she was washed, and cut, and trimmed, and 'twas   95
Trim sport for them which had the doing of it.

Lucius. O barbarous, beastly villains, like thyself!

Aaron. Indeed, I was their tutor to instruct them.
That codding° spirit had they from their mother,
As sure a card as ever won the set.°   100
That bloody mind, I think, they learned of me,
As true a dog as ever fought at head.°
Well, let my deeds be witness of my worth.
I trained° thy brethren to that guileful hole,
Where the dead corpse of Bassianus lay;   105
I wrote the letter that thy father found,
And hid the gold within that letter mentioned,
Confederate with the Queen and her two sons;
And what not done, that thou hast cause to rue,
Wherein I had no stroke of mischief in it?   110
I played the cheater° for thy father's hand,
And when I had it drew myself apart,

---

88 **luxurious** lustful   90 **To** in comparison with   99 **codding** lustful   100 **set** game   102 **at head** (a courageous bulldog went for the bull's nose)   104 **trained** lured   111 **cheater** officer appointed to look after escheats or property forfeited to the Crown

And almost broke my heart with extreme laughter.
I pried me through the crevice of a wall,
115 When for his hand he had his two sons' heads;
Beheld his tears and laughed so heartily
That both mine eyes were rainy like to his:
And when I told the Empress of this sport,
She sounded° almost at my pleasing tale,
120 And for my tidings gave me twenty kisses.

Goth. What, canst thou say all this and never blush?

Aaron. Ay, like a black dog, as the saying is.

Lucius. Art thou not sorry for these heinous deeds?

Aaron. Ay, that I had not done a thousand more.
125 Even now I curse the day—and yet, I think,
Few come within the compass of my curse—
Wherein I did not some notorious ill:
As kill a man or else devise his death,
Ravish a maid or plot the way to do it,
130 Accuse some innocent and forswear° myself,
Set deadly enmity between two friends,
Make poor men's cattle break their necks,
Set fire on barns and haystalks in the night,
And bid the owners quench them with their tears.
135 Oft have I digged up dead men from their graves
And set them upright at their dear friends' door,
Even when their sorrows almost was forgot,
And on their skins, as on the bark of trees,
Have with my knife carvèd in Roman letters,
140 "Let not your sorrow die, though I am dead."
But, I have done a thousand dreadful things
As willingly as one would kill a fly,
And nothing grieves me heartily indeed,
But that I cannot do ten thousand more.

145 *Lucius.* Bring down the devil, for he must not die
So sweet a death as hanging presently.

Aaron. If there be devils, would I were a devil,
To live and burn in everlasting fire,

119 **sounded** swooned 130 **forswear** perjure

So I might have your company in hell,
But to torment you with my bitter tongue!   150

Lucius. Sirs, stop his mouth, and let him speak no
    more.

Enter Aemilius.

Goth. My lord, there is a messenger from Rome   155
    Desires to be admitted to your presence.

Lucius. Let him come near.
    Welcome, Aemilius, what's the news from Rome?

Aemilius. Lord Lucius, and you princes of the Goths,
    The Roman Emperor greets you all by me;
    And, for he understands you are in arms,
    He craves a parley at your father's house,
    Willing you to demand your hostages,   160
    And they shall be immediately delivered.

Goth. What says our general?

Lucius. Aemilius, let the Emperor give his pledges
    Unto my father and my uncle Marcus,
    And we will come. March away.   [*Exeunt.*]   165

[Scene 2. *Rome. Before Titus' house.*]

Enter Tamora and her two sons, disguised [*as
    Revenge attended by Rape and Murder*].

Tamora. Thus, in this strange and sad habiliment,°
    I will encounter with Andronicus,
    And say I am Revenge, sent from below
    To join with him and right his heinous wrongs.
    Knock at his study, where, they say, he keeps°   5
    To ruminate strange plots of dire revenge;
    Tell him Revenge is come to join with him,
    And work confusion° on his enemies.

5.2.1 **sad habiliment** dismal apparel   5 **keeps** dwells   8 **confusion**
destruction

They knock, and Titus [above] opens his study door.

Titus. Who doth molest my contemplation?
10   Is it your trick to make me ope the door,
        That so my sad decrees may fly away,
        And all my study be to no effect?
        You are deceived: for what I mean to do
        See here in bloody lines I have set down.
15   And what is written shall be executed.

Tamora. Titus, I am come to talk with thee.

Titus. No, not a word. How can I grace my talk,
        Wanting a hand to give that accord?°
        Thou hast the odds of° me, therefore no more.

Tamora. If thou didst know me, thou wouldst talk
20   with me.

Titus. I am not mad, I know thee well enough.
        Witness this wretched stump, witness these crimson
            lines,
        Witness these trenches made by grief and care,
        Witness the tiring day and heavy night,
25   Witness all sorrow, that I know thee well
        For our proud Empress, mighty Tamora:
        Is not thy coming for my other hand?

Tamora. Know thou, sad man, I am not Tamora;
        She is thy enemy, and I thy friend.
30   I am Revenge, sent from th' infernal kingdom
        To ease the gnawing vulture of thy mind,
        By working wreakful° vengeance on thy foes.
        Come down and welcome me to this world's light;
        Confer with me of murder and of death:
35   There's not a hollow cave or lurking place,
        No vast obscurity or misty vale,
        Where bloody murder or detested rape
        Can couch° for fear, but I will find them out,

---

18 **give that accord** i.e., provide appropriate gestures   19 **odds of**
advantage over   32 **wreakful** avenging   38 **couch** lie hidden

And in their ears tell them my dreadful name,
Revenge, which makes the foul offender quake.   40

Titus. Art thou Revenge? And art thou sent to me,
To be a torment to mine enemies?

Tamora. I am, therefore come down and welcome me.

Titus. Do me some service ere I come to thee.
Lo, by thy side where Rape and Murder stands;   45
Now give some surance° that thou art Revenge;
Stab them, or tear them on thy chariot wheels;
And then I'll come and be thy wagoner,
And whirl along with thee about the globes.
Provide thee two proper palfreys,° black as jet,   50
To hale thy vengeful wagon swift away,
And find out murder in their guilty caves:
And when thy car° is loaden with their heads,
I will dismount, and by thy wagon wheel
Trot like a servile footman all day long,   55
Even from Hyperion's° rising in the east,
Until his very downfall in the sea.
And day by day I'll do this heavy task,
So° thou destroy Rapine° and Murder there.

Tamora. These are my ministers and come with me.   60

Titus. Are them thy ministers? What are they called?

Tamora. Rape and Murder; therefore callèd so,
'Cause they take vengeance of such kind of men.

Titus. Good Lord, how like the Empress' sons they are!
And you the Empress! But we worldly° men   65
Have miserable, mad, mistaking eyes.
O sweet Revenge, now do I come to thee:
And, if one arm's embracement will content thee,
I will embrace thee in it by and by.   [*Exit above.*]

Tamora. This closing° with him fits his lunacy.   70

---

46 **surance** assurance   50 **proper palfreys** excellent horses   53 **car**
chariot   56 **Hyperion's** the sun god's   59 **So** provided that   59
Rapine rape   65 **worldly** mortal, of this world   70 **closing** agreement

Whate'er I forge° to feed his brainsick humors,
Do you uphold and maintain in your speeches,
For now he firmly takes me for Revenge,
And, being credulous in this mad thought,
75   I'll make him send for Lucius his son;
And, whilst I at a banket hold him sure,
I'll find some cunning practice° out of hand,°
To scatter and disperse the giddy Goths,
Or at the least make them his enemies.
80   See, here he comes, and I must ply my theme.

[Enter Titus.]

Titus. Long have I been forlorn, and all for thee.
Welcome, dread Fury, to my woeful house:
Rapine and Murder, you are welcome too:
How like the Empress and her sons you are!
85   Well are you fitted, had you but a Moor:
Could not all hell afford you such a devil?
For well I wot the Empress never wags°
But in her company there is a Moor;
And, would you represent our queen aright,
90   It were convenient° you had such a devil:
But welcome, as you are. What shall we do?

Tamora. What wouldst thou have us do, Andronicus?

Demetrius. Show me a murderer, I'll deal with him.

Chiron. Show me a villain that hath done a rape,
95   And I am sent to be revenged on him.

Tamora. Show me a thousand that hath done thee
          wrong,
And I will be revengèd on them all.

Titus. Look round about the wicked streets of Rome,
And when thou find'st a man that's like thyself,
100   Good Murder, stab him; he's a murderer.
Go thou with him, and when it is thy hap°
To find another that is like to thee,

71 **forge** invent   77 **practice** scheme   77 **out of hand** on the spur
of the moment   87 **wags** moves   90 **convenient** fitting   101 **hap**
chance

Good Rapine, stab him; he is a ravisher.
Go thou with them, and in the Emperor's court
There is a queen attended by a Moor;   105
Well shalt thou know her by thine own proportion,
For up and down she doth resemble thee;
I pray thee, do on them some violent death;
They have been violent to me and mine.

Tamora. Well hast thou lessoned us; this shall we do.   110
But would it please thee, good Andronicus,
To send for Lucius, thy thrice valiant son,
Who leads towards Rome a band of warlike Goths,
And bid him come and banquet at thy house:
When he is here, even at thy solemn° feast,   115
I will bring in the Empress and her sons,
The Emperor himself, and all thy foes,
And at thy mercy shall they stoop and kneel,
And on them shalt thou ease thy angry heart.
What says Andronicus to this device?   120

Titus. Marcus, my brother! 'Tis sad Titus calls.

Enter Marcus.

Go, gentle Marcus, to thy nephew Lucius;
Thou shalt inquire him out among the Goths.
Bid him repair° to me and bring with him
Some of the chiefest princes of the Goths: 125
Bid him encamp his soldiers where they are;
Tell him the Emperor and the Empress too
Feast at my house, and he shall feast with them.
This do thou for my love, and so let him,
As he regards his agèd father's life.   130

Marcus. This will I do, and soon return again.   [*Exit.*]

Tamora. Now will I hence about thy business,
And take my ministers along with me.

Titus. Nay, nay, let Rape and Murder stay with me,
Or else I'll call my brother back again,   135
And cleave to no revenge but Lucius.

115 **solemn** ceremonious   124 **repair** come

Tamora. [*Aside to her sons*] What say you, boys? Will
    you abide with him,
    Whiles I go tell my lord the Emperor
    How I have governed our determined jest?°
140   Yield to his humor, smooth and speak him fair,°
    And tarry with him till I turn again.

Titus. [*Aside*] I knew them all, though they supposed
    me mad;
    And will o'erreach them in their own devices,
    A pair of cursèd hellhounds and their dame.

145 *Demetrius.* Madam, depart at pleasure, leave us here.

Tamora. Farewell, Andronicus: Revenge now goes
    To lay a complot° to betray thy foes.

Titus. I know thou dost; and, sweet Revenge, farewell.
                              [*Exit Tamora.*]

Chiron. Tell us, old man, how shall we be employed?

150 *Titus.* Tut, I have work enough for you to do.
    Publius, come hither, Caius, and Valentine!

      [*Enter Publius and others.*]

Publius. What is your will?

Titus. Know you these two?

Publius. The Empress' sons, I take them: Chiron,
155   Demetrius.

Titus. Fie, Publius, fie! Thou art too much deceived;
    The one is Murder, and Rape is the other's name:
    And therefore bind them, gentle Publius:
    Caius and Valentine, lay hands on them:
160   Oft have you heard me wish for such an hour,
    And now I find it: therefore bind them sure;
    And stop their mouths if they begin to cry.   [*Exit.*]

---

139 **governed our determined jest** managed the jest we agreed ("determined") upon 140 **smooth and speak him fair** flatter and speak
courteously to him 147 **complot** plot

Chiron. Villains, forbear! We are the Empress' sons.

Publius. And therefore do we what we are commanded.
   Stop close their mouths, let them not speak a word: *165*
   Is he sure bound? Look that you bind them fast.

  Enter Titus Andronicus with a knife, and Lavinia with
                 a basin.

Titus. Come, come, Lavinia; look, thy foes are bound.
   Sirs, stop their mouths, let them not speak to me,
   But let them hear what fearful words I utter.
   O villains, Chiron and Demetrius!   *170*
   Here stands the spring whom you have stained with
      mud,
   This goodly summer with your winter mixed.
   You killed her husband, and, for that vile fault
   Two of her brothers were condemned to death,
   My hand cut off and made a merry jest: *175*
   Both her sweet hands, her tongue, and that more dear
   Than hands or tongue, her spotless chastity,
   Inhuman traitors, you constrained and forced.
   What would you say if I should let you speak?
   Villains, for shame you could not beg for grace.   *180*
   Hark, wretches, how I mean to martyr you.
   This one hand yet is left to cut your throats,
   Whiles that Lavinia 'tween her stumps doth hold
   The basin that receives your guilty blood.
   You know your mother means to feast with me,   *185*
   And calls herself Revenge, and thinks me mad:
   Hark, villains, I will grind your bones to dust,
   And with your blood and it I'll make a paste,
   And of the paste a coffin° I will rear,
   And make two pasties of your shameful heads,   *190*
   And bid that strumpet, your unhallowed dam,
   Like to the earth, swallow her own increase.°
   This is the feast that I have bid her to,
   And this the banket she shall surfeit on;
   For worse than Philomel you used my daughter,   *195*

189 **coffin** pie crust 192 **increase** offspring

And worse than Progne° I will be revenged.
And now prepare your throats. Lavinia, come,
Receive the blood; and when that they are dead,
Let me go grind their bones to powder small,
200   And with this hateful liquor temper° it,
And in that paste let their vile heads be baked.
Come, come, be every one officious°
To make this banket, which I wish may prove
More stern and bloody than the Centaurs' feast.°
                                        He cuts their throats.
205   So, now bring them in, for I'll play the cook,
And see them ready against° their mother comes.
                                                        Exeunt.

[Scene 3. *Rome. Within Titus' house.*]

*Enter Lucius, Marcus, and the Goths [with Aaron a
prisoner, and an Attendant bearing Aaron's child].*

Lucius. Uncle Marcus, since 'tis my father's mind
    That I repair° to Rome, I am content.

Goth. And ours with thine, befall what fortune will.

Lucius. Good uncle, take you in this barbarous Moor,
5   This ravenous tiger, this accursèd devil;
    Let him receive no sust'nance, fetter him,
    Till he be brought unto the Empress' face
    For testimony of her foul proceedings:
    And see the ambush of our friends be strong;
10   I fear the Emperor means no good to us.

---

196 **Progne** wife of Tereus (Tereus raped and mutilated Progne's
sister, Philomela, and in revenge Progne slaughtered Tereus'—and
her own—son and served him to Tereus) 200 **temper** mix 202
officious busy 204 **Centaurs' feast** (a battle followed the marriage
feast to which the Lapiths invited the Centaurs) 206 **against** in
preparation for the time when   5.3.2 **repair** return

Aaron. Some devil whisper curses in my ear,
   And prompt me, that my tongue may utter forth
   The venomous malice of my swelling heart!

Lucius. Away, inhuman dog! Unhallowed slave!
   Sirs, help our uncle to convey him in.   15
            [*Goths lead Aaron in. Trumpets sound.*]
   The trumpets show the Emperor is at hand.

      Sound trumpets. Enter Emperor and Empress, with
                Tribunes and others.

Saturninus. What, hath the firmament mo° suns than
   one?

Lucius. What boots° it thee to call thyself a sun?

Marcus. Rome's Emperor, and nephew, break the
      parle;°
   These quarrels must be quietly debated.   20
   The feast is ready, which the careful° Titus
   Hath ordained to an honorable end,
   For peace, for love, for league, and good to Rome.
   Please you, therefore, draw nigh, and take your
      places.

Saturninus. Marcus, we will.   25

      Trumpets sounding, enter Titus, like a cook,
      placing the dishes, and Lavinia with a veil over
          her face, [young Lucius, and others].

Titus. Welcome, my lord; welcome, dread Queen;
   Welcome, ye warlike Goths; welcome, Lucius;
   And welcome, all: although the cheer° be poor,
   'Twill fill your stomachs; please you eat of it.

Saturninus. Why art thou thus attired, Andronicus?   30

Titus. Because I would be sure to have all well,
   To entertain your Highness and your Empress.

Tamora. We are beholding to you, good Andronicus.

17 **mo** more   18 **boots** avails   19 **break the parle** interrupt the talk
(i.e., cease quarreling)   21 **careful** full of sorrow   28 **cheer** hospitality

Titus. And if your Highness knew my heart, you were.

35   My lord the Emperor, resolve° me this:
      Was it well done of rash Virginius
      To slay his daughter with his own right hand,
      Because she was enforced,° stained, and deflow'r'd?

Saturninus. It was, Andronicus.

40 *Titus.* Your reason, mighty lord!

Saturninus. Because the girl should not survive her
        shame,
      And by her presence still renew his sorrows.

Titus. A reason mighty, strong, and effectual,
      A pattern, precedent, and lively warrant,
45   For me, most wretched, to perform the like.
      Die, die, Lavinia, and thy shame with thee,
      And with thy shame thy father's sorrow die!
                                  [*He kills her.*]

Saturninus. What hast thou done, unnatural and un-
        kind?°

Titus. Killed her for whom my tears have made me
        blind.
50   I am as woeful as Virginius was,
      And have a thousand times more cause than he
      To do this outrage, and it now is done.

Saturninus. What, was she ravished? Tell who did the
        deed.

Titus. Will't please you eat? Will't please your Highness
        feed?

55 *Tamora.* Why hast thou slain thine only daughter thus?

Titus. Not I; 'twas Chiron and Demetrius:
      They ravished her and cut away her tongue;
      And they, 'twas they, that did her all this wrong.

Saturninus. Go, fetch them hither to us presently.

---

35 **resolve** answer   38 **enforced** forced, raped   48 **unkind** (1) unnatural (2) cruel

Titus. Why, there they are, both bakèd in this pie,　　60
　　Whereof their mother daintily hath fed,
　　Eating the flesh that she herself hath bred.
　　'Tis true, 'tis true; witness my knife's sharp point.
　　　　　　　　　　　　　He stabs the Empress.

Saturninus. Die, frantic wretch, for this accursèd deed.
　　　　　　　　　　　　　[*Kills Titus.*]

Lucius. Can the son's eye behold his father bleed?　　65
　　There's meed for meed,° death for a deadly deed.
　　　　　　　　　　　　　[*Kills Saturninus.*]

Marcus. You sad-faced men, people and sons of Rome,
　　By uproars severed, as a flight of fowl
　　Scattered by winds and high tempestuous gusts,
　　O, let me teach you how to knit again　　70
　　This scattered corn into one mutual sheaf,
　　These broken limbs again into one body.

Roman Lord. Let Rome herself be bane° unto herself,
　　And she whom mighty kingdoms curtsy to,
　　Like a forlorn and desperate castaway,　　75
　　Do shameful execution on herself,
　　But if° my frosty signs and chaps of age,°
　　Grave witnesses of true experience,
　　Cannot induce you to attend my words.
　　[*To Lucius*] Speak, Rome's dear friend, as erst°
　　　　our ancestor,°　　80
　　When with his solemn tongue he did discourse
　　To lovesick Dido's sad attending° ear
　　The story of that baleful° burning night,
　　When subtle Greeks surprised King Priam's Troy;
　　Tell us what Sinon° hath bewitched our ears,　　85
　　Or who hath brought the fatal engine in
　　That gives our Troy, our Rome, the civil wound.
　　My heart is not compact° of flint nor steel;

66 **meed for meed** measure for measure　73 **bane** destruction　77 **But if** unless　77 **frosty signs and chaps of age** i.e., white hair and cracked (wrinkled) skin　80 **erst** formerly　80 **our ancestor** i.e., Aeneas　82 **sad attending** seriously listening　83 **baleful** injurious　85 **Sinon** Greek who persuaded the Trojans to admit the wooden horse　88 **compact** composed

Nor can I utter all our bitter grief,
90   But floods of tears will drown my oratory
And break my utt'rance, even in the time
When it should move ye to attend me most,
And force you to commiseration.
Here's Rome's young captain, let him tell the tale,
95   While I stand by and weep to hear him speak.

Lucius. Then, gracious auditory, be it known to you
That Chiron and the damned Demetrius
Were they that murd'red our Emperor's brother;
And they it were that ravishèd our sister.
100   For their fell° faults our brothers were beheaded,
Our father's tears despised, and basely cozened°
Of that true hand that fought Rome's quarrel out
And sent her enemies unto the grave.
Lastly, myself unkindly banishèd,
105   The gates shut on me, and turned weeping out,
To beg relief among Rome's enemies,
Who drowned their enmity in my true tears
And oped their arms to embrace me as a friend:
I am the turned-forth, be it known to you,
110   That have preserved her welfare in my blood,
And from her bosom took the enemy's point,
Sheathing the steel in my advent'rous body.
Alas, you know I am no vaunter,° I;
My scars can witness, dumb although they are,
115   That my report is just and full of truth.
But, soft!° Methinks, I do digress too much,
Citing my worthless praise. O, pardon me,
For when no friends are by, men praise themselves.

Marcus. Now is my turn to speak. Behold the child:
120   Of this was Tamora deliverèd,
The issue of an irreligious Moor,
Chief architect and plotter of these woes:
The villain is alive in Titus' house,
And as he is to witness, this is true.
125   Now judge what cause had Titus to revenge

100 **fell** savage   101 **cozened** cheated   113 **vaunter** braggart   116 **soft** hold (a common interjection)

These wrongs, unspeakable, past patience,
Or more than any living man could bear.
Now have you heard the truth. What say you,
    Romans?
Have we done aught amiss, show us wherein,
And, from the place where you behold us pleading,   130
The poor remainder of Andronici
Will, hand in hand, all headlong hurl ourselves
And on the ragged° stones beat forth our souls,
And make a mutual closure° of our house.
Speak, Romans, speak, and if you say we shall,   135
Lo, hand in hand, Lucius and I will fall.

Aemilius. Come, come, thou reverend man of Rome,
And bring our Emperor gently in thy hand,
Lucius our Emperor; for well I know
The common voice do cry it shall be so.   140

Marcus. Lucius, all hail, Rome's royal Emperor!
[*To soldiers*] Go, go into old Titus' sorrowful
    house,
And hither hale that misbelieving Moor,
To be adjudged some direful slaught'ring death,
As punishment for his most wicked life.   145
                              [*Exeunt Attendants.*]
Lucius, all hail, Rome's gracious governor!
                              [*Cries of approval.*]

Lucius. Thanks, gentle Romans: may I govern so,
To heal Rome's harms and wipe away her woe!
But, gentle people, give me aim° awhile,
For nature puts me to a heavy task.   150
Stand all aloof; but, uncle, draw you near
To shed obsequious° tears upon this trunk.
O, take this warm kiss on thy pale cold lips,
These sorrowful drops upon thy bloodstained face,
The last true duties of thy noble son!   155

Marcus. Tear for tear and loving kiss for kiss
Thy brother Marcus tenders on thy lips:

133 **ragged** rugged   134 **mutual closure** common end   149 **give me
aim** assist me   152 **obsequious** mourning

O, were the sum of these that I should pay
Countless and infinite, yet would I pay them!

160 *Lucius.* Come hither, boy; come, come, and learn of us
To melt in showers. Thy grandsire loved thee well;
Many a time he danced thee on his knee,
Sung thee asleep, his loving breast thy pillow;
Many a story hath he told to thee,
165 And bid thee bear his pretty tales in mind,
And talk of them when he was dead and gone.

Marcus. How many thousand times hath these poor
lips,
When they were living, warmed themselves on thine!
O, now, sweet boy, give them their latest° kiss.
170 Bid him farewell; commit him to the grave;
Do them° that kindness, and take leave of them.

Boy. O, grandsire, grandsire! Ev'n with all my heart
Would I were dead, so you did live again!
O Lord, I cannot speak to him for weeping;
175 My tears will choke me if I ope my mouth.

[*Enter Attendants with Aaron.*]

Roman. You sad Andronici, have done with woes;
Give sentence on this execrable wretch
That hath been breeder of these dire events.

Lucius. Set him breast-deep in earth and famish him;
180 There let him stand and rave and cry for food:
If anyone relieves or pities him,
For the offense he dies. This is our doom.°
Some stay, to see him fast'ned in the earth.

Aaron. Ah, why should wrath be mute, and fury dumb?
185 I am no baby, I, that with base prayers
I should repent the evils I have done:
Ten thousand worse than ever yet I did
Would I perform, if I might have my will:
If one good deed in all my life I did,

169 **latest** last   171 **them** i.e., "these poor lips" of line 167   182
doom sentence

I do repent it from my very soul.   190

Lucius. Some loving friends convey the Emperor hence,
  And give him burial in his father's grave:
  My father and Lavinia shall forthwith
  Be closèd in our household's monument.
  As for that ravenous tiger, Tamora,   195
  No funeral rite, nor man in mourning weed,
  No mournful bell shall ring her burial;
  But throw her forth to beasts and birds to prey.
  Her life was beastly and devoid of pity,
  And being dead, let birds on her take pity.   *Exeunt.* 200

Textual Note

There is an allusion to a Roman hero named Titus in *A Knack to Know a Knave,* acted in June 1592. Though the allusion may, of course, be to an earlier play on the subject rather than to Shakespeare's play, there is no need to multiply entities; Shakespeare's *Titus Andronicus* may have been on the stage before 1592. The next bit of evidence is a reference of 23 January 1594 in Henslowe's *Diary* to the effect that Sussex's men acted a new piece, "titus & ondronicus." If the allusion in *A Knave* is not to Shakespeare's play, quite possibly *Titus Andronicus* was indeed new in 1594, but it is equally possible that it was "new" only to Sussex's company, or that it had been newly revised. On 6 February 1594 the Stationers' Register entered "a book intituled a Noble Roman Historye of Titus Andronicus." Perhaps this entry alludes to the play, which indeed was published in 1594, though possibly the entry is to some other piece on the same subject. In 1614 Ben Jonson, in the Induction to *Bartholomew Fair,* mentions that Andronicus was seen on the stage as long ago as "fiue and twentie or thirtie yeeres"; strictly, Jonson's reference would date the play 1584–89, though probably he is speaking loosely and his evidence surely does not prohibit a date in the early nineties. The date widely favored is 1592–94, but there is no compelling reason to believe that *Titus* could not have been written in the late eighties.

Only one copy of the first quarto (1594) is known to be extant. Apparently Q1 (i.e., the first quarto) was printed from Shakespeare's manuscript or from a copy of it; a number of stage directions—such as "Enter . . . as many as can be"—suggest an author's hand. In 1600 a second quarto (Q2) was issued. It omits a few lines, adds some, and alters a good deal of punctuation. There is no reason to believe that the alterations represent Shakespeare's revisions; probably all the revisions are a compositor's tamperings. Q3, issued

in 1611, was set up from Q2 and therefore has no authority.
The version in the First Folio (F) is based on Q3 but makes
numerous small alterations (especially in stage directions)
and adds an entire scene (3.2). The new scene is of sufficient
excellence to be Shakespeare's, and though the other
changes in F do not suggest that great effort was made to
give the play in a version much different from that of Q3, the
new scene shows that the editors had access to some unpublished material. The present edition is based on Q1, except for
3.2, which is, of course, based on F. It regularizes speech prefixes (for example, Q1's "Saturnine," "Saturninus," "King,"
"Satur," are all given here as "Saturninus"); it slightly alters
the position of a few stage directions, and it modernizes
spelling and punctuation. The act divisions were first established by F; the scene divisions are the work of later editors
and though of no authenticity they provide a convenient
device for reference. Departures from Q1, other than those
mentioned above and corrections of obvious typographical
errors, are listed below, the adopted reading first, in *italic*
type, followed by the original reading in roman. If the adopted
reading is from Q2, Q3, or F, that fact is indicated in a bracket
following the reading. If there is no such indication, the
adopted reading is an editor's conjecture.

1.1.35 [for the three and a half lines that follow these words in
Q1 see footnote to the line] 69s.d. *her three sons* her two
sonnes 98 *manes* manus 226 *Titan's* [Q2] Tytus 242 *Pantheon*
Pathan 264 *chance* [Q2] change 280 *cuique* cuiqum 317 *Phoebe*
Thebe 358s.d. *speak* speakes 369 *Martius* 3. Sonne 370 *Quin-
tus* 2. Sonne 372 *Quintus* 2. sonne 391 [Q1 follows with s.d.:
"Exit all but Marcus and Titus," and the other early texts also indi-
cate an exit] 399 *Yes . . . remunerate* [F; omitted in the quartos]

2.1.110 *than* this

2.2.1 *morn* [F] Moone

2.3.69 *try* [Q2] trie thy 72 *swart* swartie 160 *ears* [Q3] yeares
210 *unhallowed* [F] vnhollow 222 *berayed* bereaud 231 *Pyramus*
[Q2] Priamus 236 *Cocytus* Ocitus

2.4.27 *him* them 30 *three* their

3.1.146 *his true* her true

3.2 [this scene is found only in F] 39 *complainer* complayne
52 *thy knife* knife 53 *fly* Flys 55 *are cloyed* cloi'd 72 *myself*
my selfes

4.1.50 *quotes* [Q2] coats   88 *hope* [Q2] hop [or "I op"]

4.2.95 *Alcides* [Q2] Alciades

4.3.57 *Saturn* Saturnine   78 *News* [Q2] Clowne. Newes

4.4.5 *know, as know* know   49 *By* be   99 *ears* [F] yeares

5.2.52 *caves* cares   56 *Hyperion's* Epeons   65 *worldly* [Q2] wordlie

5.3.125 *cause*   course   144 *adjudged*   [F]   adiudge   154 *blood-stained* blood slaine   163 *Sung* [Q2] Song

A Possible Source of
Titus Andronicus:
The History of Titus Andronicus

Those Shakespeareans who are embarrassed by *Titus* (but who cannot overlook the strong evidence that he wrote it) sometimes assume that it represents his reworking of an older, and presumably worse, play. No such play has come to light, and though it is possible that Shakespeare's source was a play now extant only in Shakespeare's revision, it seems likely that his source was a prose tale regarded as history. The Folger Shakespeare Library has a unique copy of a mid-eighteenth-century booklet entitled *The History of Titus Andronicus*, which contains a prose narrative (reprinted below) and a ballad. The ballad, of no interest to us, is an abbreviated metrical version of the prose narrative, but this latter seems to be a reprint of a much older piece—quite possibly of a late-sixteenth-century version that may have been Shakespeare's source. Certainly the prose narrative is not indebted to the play: it makes no reference to Shakespeare—as it surely would if it had been written in the eighteenth century—and it includes a good deal of alleged history that Shakespeare does not. Furthermore, some of its characters are unnamed; if the narrative were based on the play, Aaron, for example, would doubtless be mentioned by name, but he is merely called "the wicked Moor."

Put it this way: the extant *History of Titus Andronicus* may well be a reprint of a much older piece, quite possibly a reprint of the tale that Shakespeare dramatized. The *History* is reprinted below, from the only known copy, and for the first time since its publication in the middle of the eighteenth century. Spelling and punctuation have been modernized, and manifest typographical errors have been corrected.

THE

HISTORY

OF

Titus Andronicus,

THE RENOWNED ROMAN GENERAL

who, after he had saved Rome by his valor from being destroyed by the barbarous Goths and lost two and twenty of his valiant sons in ten years' war, was, upon the Emperor's marrying the Queen of the Goths, put to disgrace and banished; but being recalled, the Emperor's son by a first wife was murdered by the Empress' sons and a bloody Moor, and how charging it upon Andronicus' sons, though he cut off his hand to redeem their lives, they were murdered in prison; how his fair daughter Lavinia, being ravished by the Empress' sons, they cut out her tongue, and hands off, etc.; how Andronicus slew them, made pies of their flesh, and presented them to the Emperor and Empress; and then slew them also; with the miserable death he put the wicked Moor to; then at her request slew his daughter and himself to avoid torment.

Reprinted by permission of The Folger Shakespeare Library.

THE

TRAGICAL HISTORY

OF

Titus Andronicus, etc.

Chapter 1

How Rome being besieged by the barbarous Goths and being at the point to yield through famine, it was unexpectedly rescued by Andronicus, with the utter defeat of the enemy, for which he was received in triumph.

When the Roman Empire was grown to its height and the greatest part of the world was subjected to its imperial throne, in the time of Theodosius, a barbarous northern people out of Swedeland, Denmark, and Gothland came into Italy in such numbers, under the leading of Tottilius, their king, that they overrun it with fire and sword, plundering churches, ripping up women with child, and deflowering virgins in so horrid and barbarous a manner that the people fled before them like flocks of sheep.

To oppose this destroying torrent of the Goths, a barbarous people, strangers to Christianity, the Emperor raised a mighty army in Greece, Italy, France, Spain, Germany, and England, and gave battle under the passage of the Alpine mountains, but was overthrown, with the loss of threescore thousand of his men, and flying to Rome, was besieged in it by a numerous host of these barbarians, who pressed so hard to beat down the walls and enter with a miserable slaughter of the citizens that such as could get over the River Tiber fled in a fearful manner to a distant country. The siege lasting ten months, such a famine arose that no unclean thing was left uneaten; dogs, cats, horses, rats and mice were curious dainties; thousands died in the streets of hunger, and most of those that were alive looked more like glass than living creatures; so that being brought to the last extremity, the vulgar sort came about the Emperor's palace and with piteous cries implored him either to find some means to get them food, to stay their fleeting lives, or make the best terms he could and open the gates to the enemy.

This greatly perplexed him; the former he could not do, and the latter he knew would not only uncrown him, if he escaped with his life, but be the ruin of the Roman Empire; yet in the greatest of this extremity he unexpectedly found relief.

Titus Andronicus, a Roman senator and a true lover of his country, hearing in Graecia, where he was governor of the province of Achaia, what straits Rome and his sovereign were brought into by the barbarous nations, got together friends and sold whatever he had of value to hire soldiers; so that with his small army he secretly marched away, and falling upon the mighty army of the enemy (when they were drowned as it were in security, wine, and sleep, resolved to make a general storm the next day, in which they had undoubtedly carried the city), he and his sons, entering their camp, and followed by the rest, made such a slaughter that the cry and confusion were exceeding great; some changed sleep into death, others vomited wine and blood mixed together, through the wounds they received; some lost heads at once, others arms: Tottilius, in this confusion being awakened, had his first care to convey away his queen and two sons, who were newly come to the camp, and then labored to rally his flying men; but being desperately charged by Andronicus, he was thrown from his horse and much wounded, many lives being lost in remounting him; whereupon seeing the slaughter so great by the pale beams of the moon, and not knowing the number of his adversaries, having caused the retreat to be sounded, he fled in great confusion and left the rich spoils of his camp, the wealth of many plundered nations, to Andronicus and his soldiers; who being expert in war, would not meddle with them that night, but stood to their arms till the morning.

Chapter 2

How in ten years' war, with the loss of two and twenty of his valiant sons, he won many famous battles, slew Tottilius, King of the Goths, and did many other brave exploits, etc.

The watch upon the walls of Rome, having heard a confused cry and the clashing of arms, were greatly astonished, but could not think what it should mean; for the camps of the barbarous Goths extended in a large circuit about the famous city; however, the captains of the guards advertised the Emperor of it, who sent out scouts, but they, fearful of approaching too near the enemy in the night, could get certain intelligence only that they heard the groans and cries, as they thought, of dying men. However, the shades of night being dispelled, and the glorious sun raising [?] forth a cheerful light, the porters of the gate espying three men coming towards it, and soon after being come up, knocked with great earnestness, they took the courage to demand what they were and what they required.

"I am," said one of them, "Andronicus, your friend, and desire admittance to speak with the Emperor, since the news I bring will no doubt be pleasing to him."

Upon this, lifting up his helmet, they knew him with joy, knowing him to be a very worthy patriot, thinking he came to do them good, as he had often done in their great distress when the Huns and Vandals invaded the empire some years before and were beaten out by him.

The Emperor no sooner heard he was come, but he ran from his palace to meet him and would not suffer him to kneel, but embraced him tenderly as a brother, saying, "Welcome, Andronicus, in this the time of our greatest misery; it was thy counsel I wanted, to know how to free us from this barbarous enemy, against whose force the city cannot long hold out."

"May it please your Majesty," replied Andronicus, "let those fears be banished, the work is done to you unknown; I and my twenty-five sons, and what friends and soldiers I could get, have this night fallen into their quarters, cut off fifty thousand of them, and their scattered remains with their king are fled."

At this the Emperor was astonished and scarce could believe it, though he very well knew the integrity of Andronicus, till his own captains came and told him the siege was raised with a miserable slaughter, but by whom they knew not, unless the enemy had fallen out among themselves, and the troops they could yet see in view were but inconsiderable. Now these were those that belonged to Andronicus, who as soon as it was day were in pursuit of the enemy under the command of his five-and-twenty sons.

This surprising news was no sooner spread in the city but the joy of the people was exceeding great; and when they knew who was their deliverer, they went in procession and sung his praises. After that he rode in a triumphant chariot through the city, crowned with an oaken garland, the people shouting, trumpets sounding, and all other expressions and demonstrations of joy that a grateful people could afford their deliverer, in which he behaved himself so humble that he gained the love of all.

This was no sooner over, but he desired the Emperor to join what forces he could with those that he had brought and speedily pursue the enemy before he could gather new strength, that he might beat him out of Italy and his other countries where he yet held strong garrisons. This was embraced as good counsel, and the senators, by the Emperor's mandate, assembled with joy, who chose with one consent Andronicus their general. He was not slow in mustering his forces, nor in the speedy pursuit; he found they had passed the Alps and that their army was increased by new supplies, yet he gave them battle, and charging through the thickest of their squadrons hand to hand, slew Tottilius and beat down his standard. Whereupon the Goths fled, and the slaughter continued for many miles, covering all the lanes and roads with the bodies of the dead; and in the pursuit he took the Queen of the Goths captive and brought her to Rome, for which signal victory he had a second triumph and was styled the deliverer of his country. But his joy was a little eclipsed by the loss of five of his sons, who died courageously fighting in battle.

Chapter 3

How the Emperor, weary of so tedious a war, contrary to the mind and persuasions of Andronicus, married the Queen of the Goths and concluded a peace; how she tyrannized and her sons slew the Prince that was betrothed to Andronicus' daughter and hid him in the forest.

The Goths, having found the pleasantness of these fruitful countries, resolved not so to give them over, but, encouraged by Tottilius' two sons, Alaricus and Abonus, sent for fresh forces and made a desolation in the Roman provinces, continuing a ten years' war, wherein the valiant Andronicus, Captain-General of the Empire, gained many victories over them, with great effusion of blood on either side; but those barbarous people still increasing in their numbers, the Emperor, desiring peace, it was agreed to, in consideration he should marry Attava, Queen of the Goths, and in case he should die without issue, her sons might succeed in the Empire. Andronicus opposed this very much, as did many other, knowing, through the Emperor's weakness, that she, being an imperious woman and of a haughty spirit, would govern him as she pleased and enslave the noble Empire to strangers. However, it was carried on with a high hand, and great preparations were made for the royal nuptials, though with very little rejoicing among the people, for what they expected soon followed.

The Queen of the Goths being made Empress, soon began to show her disposition, according to the cruelty of her nation and temper, persuading the easy Emperor to place the Goths in the places of his most trusty friends; and having above all vowed revenge on Andronicus, who most opposed her proceedings, she procured him to be banished; but the people, whose deliverer he had been in their greatest extremity, calling to mind that and his many other good services, rose unanimously in arms and went clamoring to the palace, threatening to fire it and revenge so base an indignity on the Queen, if the decree which had been passed against all reason was not speedily revoked. This put her and the Emperor into such a fears [*sic*] that their request was granted; and now she plotted by more private ways to bring the effects of revenge and implacable hatred about more secretly.

She had a Moor as revengeful as herself, whom she trusted in many great affairs and was usually privy to her secrets, so far that from private dalliances she grew pregnant and brought forth a blackamoor child. This grieved the Emperor extremely, but she allayed his anger by telling him it was conceived by the force of imagination, and brought many suborned women and physicians to testify the like had often happened. This made the Emperor send the Moor into banishment, upon pain of death never to return to Rome. But her lust and the confidence she had put in him as the main engine to bring about her devilish designs made her plot to have that decree revoked; when having got the Emperor into a pleasant humor, she feigned herself sick, telling him withal she had seen a vision which commanded her to call back the innocent Moor from banishment or she should never recover of that sickness. The kind, good-natured Emperor, who could not resist her tears and entreaties, with some difficulty consented to it, provided he should be commanded to keep always out of her sight, lest the like mischance might happen as had been before. This she seemingly consented to, and he was immediately sent for, and the former familiarities continued between them, though more privately.

Andronicus, besides his sons, had a very fair and beautiful daughter, named Lavinia, brought up in all singular virtues, humble, courteous, and modest, insomuch that the Emperor's only son, by a former wife, fell extremely in love with her, seeking her favor by all virtuous and honorable ways, insomuch that after a long courtship, with her father and the Emperor's consent she was betrothed to him.

The Queen of the Goths, hearing this, was much enraged, because from such a marriage might spring princes that might frustrate her ambitious designs, which was to make her sons emperors jointly. Wherefore she labored all she could to frustrate it, by declaring what a disgrace it would be to the Emperor to marry his son to the daughter of a subject, who might have a queen with a kingdom to her dowry. But finding the Prince constant, she resolved to take him out of the way; so it was plotted between her, the Moor, and her two sons that they should invite him to hunt in the great forest on the banks of the River Tiber, and there murder him. This was effected, by shooting him through the back with a poisoned arrow, which came out at his breast, of which wound he fell from his horse and immediately died. Then they digged a very deep pit in a pathway and threw him in, covering it lightly with boughs and sprinkling earth on it; and so returning reported they had lost the Prince in the forest, and though they had sought and called everywhere, they could not find him.

Chapter 4

How the wicked Moor, who had laid with the Empress and got into her favor above all others, betrayed Andronicus' three sons and charged the Prince's murder on them, for which they were cast into a dungeon, and after their father had cut off his hand to save them were beheaded.

The fair Lavinia no sooner heard the Prince was missing but she fell into great sorrow and lamentation, her heart misgiving her of some treachery, and thereupon she entreated her brothers to go in search of him, which they did with all speed. But being dogged by the Moor and the Queen of Goths's two sons, they unluckily coming in the way where the pit was digged, they fell both in upon the dead body and could not by reason of the great depth get out. Their cruel enemies no sooner saw this, but they hasted to the court and sent the guards in search of the murdered Prince, who found Andronicus' two sons with the dead body, which they drew up and carried prisoners to the court, where the Moor and the other two falsely swore against them that they had often heard them threaten revenge on the Prince, because he had put them to the foil, in a tournament at jousting. This, and the circumstances of their being found, with the vehement aggravation, was a sufficient ground to the Emperor to believe, who loved his son entirely and was much grieved for his death, and though they denied it with all the protestations imaginable, and pleaded their innocence, demanded the combat against their accusers, which by the law of arms they ought to have been allowed, they were immediately loaden with irons and cast into a deep dungeon among noisome creatures, as frogs, toads, serpents, and the like, where notwithstanding all the intercessions that were made they continued eating the filth that they found in that place.

At last the Queen, designing to work her revenge on Andronicus, sent the Moor in the Emperor's name, to tell him, if he designed to save his sons from the misery and death that would ensue, he should cut off his right hand and send it to court. This the good-natured father scrupled not to do, no, nor had it been his life to ransom them, he would have freely parted with it; whereupon laying his hand on a block, he gave the wicked Moor his sword, who immediately struck it off and inwardly laughed at the villainy. Then departing with it, he told him his sons should be sent to him in a few hours. But whilst he was rejoicing with the hopes of their delivery, a hearse came to his door with guards, which made his aged heart to tremble. The first thing they presented him was his hand, which they said would not be accepted; and the next was his three sons beheaded. At this woeful sight, overcome with grief, he fainted away on the dead bodies; and when he recovered again, he tore his hoary hair, which age and his lying in winter camps for the defense of his country had made as white as snow, pouring out floods of tears; but found no pity from the hardened villains, who left him with scoffs in the midst of his woeful lamentations with his sorrowful daughter. Yet this was not all, for soon after another to be deplored affliction followed, as shall in the next chapter be shown.

Chapter 5

How the two lustful sons of the Empress, with the assistance of the Moor, in a barbarous manner ravished Lavinia, Andronicus' beautiful daughter, and cut out her tongue and cut off her hands, to prevent discovery; yet she did it by writing in the dust with a wand, etc.

The fair and beautiful Lavinia, for the loss of her lovers [*sic*] and brothers, so basely murdered by treachery, tore her golden hair, shed floods of tears, and with her nails offered violence to that lovely face kings had adored and beheld with admiration. She shunned all company, retiring to woods and groves, to utter her piteous complaints and cries to the senseless trees, when one day, being watched thither by the Moor, he gave notice of it to the Queen's two sons, who, like the wicked Elders and chaste Susanna, had a long time burned in lust yet knew her virtues were proof against all temptations, and therefore it could not be obtained but by violence. So thinking this an opportunity to serve their turns, immediately repaired to the grove and setting the Moor to watch on the outborders, soon found her pensive and sorrowful, yet comely and beautiful in tears, when unawares, before she saw them, like two ravenous tigers, they seized the trembling lady, who struggled all she could and cried out piteously for help; and seeing what their wicked intentions bent at, she offered them her throat, desiring they would bereave her of her life, but not of her honor. However, in a villainous manner, staking her down by the hair of her head and binding her hands behind her, they turned up her nakedness and forced their way into her closet of chastity, taking it by turns, the elder beginning first and the younger seconding him as they had before agreed on; and having tired themselves in satiating their beastly appetites, they began to consider how they should come off when such a villainy was discovered. Whereupon, calling the Moor to them, they asked his advice, who wickedly counseled them to make all sure, seeing they had gone thus far, by cutting out her tongue to hinder her telling tales and her hands off to prevent her writing a discovery. This the cruel wretches did, whilst she in vain entreated them to take away her life, since they had bereaved her of her honor, which was dearer to her. And in this woeful condition they left the lady, who had expired for the loss of blood had not her uncle Marcus happened accidentally, soon after, to come in search of her, who at the woeful sight, overcome with sorrow, could hardly keep life in himself; yet recovering his spirits, he bound up her wounds and conveyed her home.

Poor Andronicus' grief for this sad disaster was so great that no pen can write or words express; much ado they had to restrain him from doing violence upon himself; he cursed the day he was born to see such miseries fall on himself and family, entreating her to tell him, if she could any ways do it by signs, who had so villainously abused her. At last the poor lady, with a flood of tears gushing from her eyes, taking a wand between her stumps, wrote these lines:

> The lustful sons of the proud Empress
> Are doers of this hateful wickedness.

Hereupon he vowed revenge, at the hazard of his own and all their lives, comforting his daughter with this when nothing else would do.

Chapter 6

How Andronicus, feigning himself mad, found means to entrap the Empress' two sons in a forest, where, binding them to a tree, he cut their throats, made pies of their flesh, and served them up to the Emperor and Empress, then slew them, set the Moor quick in the ground, and then killed his daughter and himself.

Andronicus, upon these calamities, feigned himself distracted and went raving about the city, shooting his arrows towards heaven, as in defiance, calling to hell for vengeance, which mainly pleased the Empress and her sons, who thought themselves now secure; and though his friends required justice of the Emperor against the ravishers, yet they could have no redress, he rather threatening them, if they insisted on it; so that finding they were in a bad case and that in all probability their lives would be the next, they conspired together to prevent that mischief and revenge themselves; lying in ambush in the forest when the two sons went a-hunting, they surprised them, and binding them to a tree pitifully crying out for mercy, though they would give none to others, Andronicus cut their throats whilst Lavinia, by his command, held a bowl between her stumps to receive the blood; then conveying the bodies home to his own house privately, he cut the flesh into fit pieces and ground the bones to powder and made of them two mighty pasties, and invited the Emperor and Empress to dinner, who, thinking to make sport with his frantic humor, came; but when they had eat of the pasties, he told them what it was; and thereupon giving the watchword to his friends, they immediately issued out, slew the Emperor's guards, and, lastly, the Emperor and his cruel wife, after they had sufficiently upbraided them with the wicked deeds they had done. Then seizing on the wicked Moor, the fearful villain fell on his knees, promising to discover all. But when he had told how he had killed the Prince, betrayed the three sons of Andronicus by false accusation, and counseled the abuse to the fair Lavinia, they scarce knew what torments sufficient to devise for him; but at last digging a hole, they set him in the ground to the middle alive, smeared him over with honey, and so, between the stinging of bees and wasps and starving, he miserably ended his wretched days. After this, to prevent the torments he expected when these things came to be known, at his daughter's request he killed her; and so, rejoicing he had revenged himself on his enemies to the full, fell on his own sword and died.

times it is Goneril, sometimes it is Edmund, who takes the lead against Lear. In both plays the effect is the same. The forces of evil, no matter who embodies them, work with unabated intensity until the climax is reached.

If then one is looking for parallels, the only parallel to the plot of *Titus* is to be found in the other works of Shakespeare. Greene and Peele are so loose and episodic, so naïve in construction that it is incredible that they should have achieved anything so good as *Titus*. Nor is there any plot of Marlowe's so intricate, so varied, or so well sustained. *Titus* is the expression of a conflict intenser than anything the Elizabethan stage had as yet known. Shakespeare applies in *Titus* those principles of balance and contrast which he had learned from Lyly and had already tested in comedy. He sets up against one another two parties, each led by formidable characters. It is the play of fence between the high incensed points of these mighty opposites that makes the drama. There is nothing like this in Marlowe, whose supermen dominate his plays and dwarf everybody else in them. There is nothing like it in Greene and Peele, who indeed lacked the personality to create a drama of tense conflict.

Titus then resembles Shakespeare's other work, both comedy and tragedy, in that it is built upon the principle of contrast. We have the contrasting pairs or groups: Titus-Aaron, Lavinia-Tamora, Saturninus-Bassianus, the sons of Titus—the sons of Tamora. Not only are members of the opposite party contrasted, there are also contrasts within the same party. Marcus, as we shall see, by his mildness throws into higher relief the sterner traits of Titus. Contrast dominates the play and informs every scene of it. As we have already noted, whatever is fine in the Romans appears finer still in comparison with the vices of their opposites. On the one hand we have courage, stern probity, honor, but also stubbornness, hardness, and stupidity; on the other hand, slipperiness, trickiness, intrigue, the lie, foulness of every sort. None of the dramatists who are supposed to have had a hand in the play could conceive a plan so intricate or adhere to it so closely, once it was conceived. But Shakespeare goes farther. He uses contrast to heighten incident and situation as well as character. Act 2.2 and 3 are admirable examples of Shakespeare's technique. The delightful freshness of dawn and the beauty of the woods are not described for their own sake, still less are they, as some critics assert, a homesick reminiscence of Stratford. They are written in cold blood with the deliberate purpose of accentuating by contrast the horrors that follow. Shakespeare is again borrowing from the technique of Seneca.

There are few things in the play so characteristic of Shakespeare as the function of Marcus. In a world of hard, fierce, revengeful men, he alone is given to gentleness and moderation. Shakespeare often employs this device of a character who embodies a principle standing in stark contrast to the motives that rule the other persons of the play. We have, for instance, Falstaff in *1 Henry IV*. Marcus resembles most closely Henry VI in *2, 3 Henry VI*, the mild, kind king, averse to slaughter and, like Marcus, helpless among so many Kiplingesque heroes. Frequently scholars declare that characters thus marked off are the "mouthpiece" of Shakespeare. However that may be, the technique is just what we should expect to find in a play by Shakespeare. We do not expect to find it in Marlowe, Greene, or Peele.

There is a school of critics who apply the "law of variation" to this technique. They ignore the part that contrast plays in Shakespeare's genuine work and they fasten upon the contrasting elements in *Titus* as evidence of multiple authorship. They usually say that the "poetic" passages, especially the speeches of Marcus, cannot be by the same hand as the rest of the play. Or they declare that the rhetorical speeches of Act 1 are so different from the imaginative verse of Aaron that there must be two poets at work. Anybody who is inclined to follow their lead should study Titania-Bottom, The Nurse–Juliet, Hotspur-Falstaff, Iago-Othello, and then, if he dares, set limits to the unparalleled versatility of Shakespeare.

Act 1 is often condemned as being utterly un-Shakespearean. Anglo-Saxon critics are inclined to apply a verbal yardstick to drama and to ignore construction. The act is not finely enough phrased for such people and so they reject it. Technically it is one of the finest first acts that Shakespeare wrote. It is full of incident and yet it is never confused. It announces the subject boldly and unmistakably, it exploits to the full every device that the staging of those days offered, and it has swiftness, surprise, and a well-sustained interest. It leads up to an effective close. Nothing in the work of Shakespeare's contemporaries can be compared to it for a moment.

The plot is superior to anything that Greene, Peele, Marlowe, or Kyd could achieve, by its quick succession of closely knit incidents, enlivened by many sudden turns and surprises, by its intricacy, in that the fates of so many persons are involved in it and yet the thread is never lost, and by the skill with which all the different threads are bound up into one knot and untied at once in the fifth act. Intricacy with clearness, a firm hand on the story, a swift succession of effective situations logically leading out of what precedes and on to what follows, these are qualities lacking in the dramatists who are supposed to have shared in the composition of *Titus*.

It must be admitted that the plot hinges on several Elizabethan conventions that are now strange to us. For instance the ruse, no matter how transparent, always succeeds, first when Titus is tricked, later when Titus himself takes to deception. Aaron eavesdrops in 2.1—the Elizabethans took in this trick a childish delight which we cannot recapture. Quite suddenly Saturninus falls head over heels in love with Tamora—the Elizabethan believed in these swift and overwhelming effects of passion. Shakespeare is full of them. (See Ruth L. Anderson, *Elizabethan Psychology and Shakespeare's Plays*, Iowa, 1928, p. 120.) Every dramatist must work according to the rules of the game as it is understood in his time. The play is not less likely to be by Shakespeare because it is so full of the conventions of the theater.

We come to an important aspect of the plot which scholars tend to overlook. *Titus* is a political play, and Shakespeare is the most political of all dramatists. His work excited the admiration of statesmen like Gladstone and Bismarck, who both wondered how he managed to penetrate so many secrets of their profession. Shakespeare's political interest shows itself in various ways. He likes to connect his heroes with an action involving the fortunes of the state, he is skillful in tracing the course of political intrigue, and he delights in exposing those kinks of character or intellect which unfit even men of action for public life. The real hero of his political plays is the state. In some plays it is England, in others it is Rome. Now *Titus* centers round an affair of state, and its hero is no particular person but it is Rome herself. All the characters are viewed in their relation to Rome and they are set against Rome as a background. This theme is sustained throughout the play; it dominates the fifth act as the first. No member of that writers' syndicate—large as it is—which the revisionists credit with *Titus* has Shakespeare's deep love of the state or his understanding of the crisscross currents of politics. The intense political interest of *Titus* points to the man who wrote Shakespeare's historical and Roman plays, and it points to no one else.

But even if we grant that *Titus* could not have been written by anybody but Shakespeare, its horrible cruelty still leaves us profoundly dissatisfied. It is not only that Titus is cruel; it is more, he is cruel to the end. He is not a Lear who grows in stature as the play proceeds and whose sufferings purge his character of its baser elements until he emerges a man entirely good. Titus alone of Shakespeare's tragic heroes never arrives at healing self-knowledge. At the beginning of the play we hope that Titus will succeed against his enemies; at the end we wish that he had not. But we must not forget the task that Shakespeare has set himself. He is writing a Senecan play according to the rules, that is to say, a play in which the hero is a man who inexorably pursues revenge and who dies in the act of taking it. Such a plan leaves no room for change of character. Shakespeare, therefore, has been obliged to split what he had to say between Titus and Marcus. Roughly speaking, Lear is a Titus who becomes a Marcus, but a revenge play necessarily precluded this type of development. Shakespeare has not been deluded into thinking revenge is a fine thing. He sets up Marcus to show us the better way. The great fault of the drama from our point of view is that Titus never finds that way. But his stern pursuit of revenge is inherent in the revenge play and Shakespeare could only have got round it by making his hero a kind of Hamlet.

Now if we could absolve Shakespeare of all complicity in the revenge play of *Titus Andronicus,* that might be a good thing. Unfortunately, the evidence makes it quite clear that Shakespeare is at any rate an accessory to the crime, and that he is responsible for the play as it now stands. It is more profitable to consider what probably took place. Everyone knows the cant phrase that Shakespeare "played the sedulous ape" to all and sundry. Even late in life he is asserted to have copied Beaumont and Fletcher. In his apprentice stage he founded himself on Lyly, on Marlowe, and went to Roman comedy, to Plautus. In the same way, in order to learn his craft, he went to Roman tragedy, to Seneca. To understand this, we must remember that the Renaissance entertained an immense admiration for Seneca and that it was the fashion to imitate him. Shakespeare, following the mood of his time, wrote a complete Senecan tragedy, an experiment of unity in harshness and gross cruelty. He makes almost everything harsh, the language, the characters, the incidents. Where he appears to be relenting toward mildness, that is only an artistic device to make the harshness appear all the harsher. It is the very unity of the play that is a criterion of Shakespeare's skill. It is, indeed, this severe unity, which is difficult to achieve, that makes it impossible to entertain the theory that this play was the work of a syndicate of writers or of some young amateur helped out by Shakespeare.

If we turn from the action to the character shown in action, we are just as certainly within the realm of Shakespeare. There is no convincing parallel to the character of Titus outside the works of Shakespeare. He owes, indeed, a few hints to Kyd's *Spanish Tragedy*. Like Kyd's Hieronimo he is an old man angry, seeking revenge for murder, but in the essentials of characterization he is quite different. Titus, like the typical Shakespearean hero, falls by a mixture of good and bad qualities. He is a soldier, and as such, puts loyalty and obedience before everything. In his campaigns he has been accustomed both to judge men swiftly and to act swiftly on his judgment. But he has something of the simplicity of Othello; although he can estimate a man's capacity in the field, he is helpless in the hands of a dishonest schemer at home. Like Lear he is a man grown irascible with age, tolerating no insubordination from his inferiors, from whom he demands that unquestioning obedience which he in turn gives to lawful authority. Shakespeare knew that there is nothing so cruel as the wrath of age. Titus is an old man who retains the strength but has lost the elasticity of youth. His fury, therefore, persists with an obstinacy that it is useless to oppose.

The murders that Titus commits in Act 1 are horrible, just as it is horrible of Lear to banish from his heart Cordelia and Kent, but in neither case is the characterization improbable. Critics are inclined to find both Titus and Lear absurd, but Shakespeare knew more about old age than his critics.

As with many soldiers, the religion of Titus is a firm and somewhat naïve acceptance of the usages consecrated by tradition. He kills Alarbus not so much out of cruelty, but because the traditional rites of religion demand it. He makes Saturninus Emperor for much the same reason. Sacred tradition requires that the eldest son of the Emperor should succeed. He stabs his son Mutius in wrath but also as a soldier exacting that same obedience which is the rule of his own life. Some German scholars doubt whether Shakespeare meant us to approve when Titus kills his son! (Wolfgang Keller in *Shaks. Jbch.*, LXXIV [1938], 146.) Surely in all the blunders of Titus we see the corruption of the best turned to the worst, qualities fine in themselves producing disaster because of Titus' devotion to a false ideal. Further, Titus' habit of loyalty keeps him blind to the dangers that threaten him. His own probity makes it difficult for him to suspect duplicity in others. When the Emperor proves false, his world breaks down and he begins to go mad. The kaleidoscope is shifted to show now one side of his character, and now another. He is not like Marlowe's heroes, the incarnation of a single quality or passion. He is a mixture of virtues and weaknesses, and by a strange irony his virtues are the more devastating. Tamora expresses the fatal defect in his character when she speaks of "cruel irreligious piety." A similar ironic treatment is found in other tragedies of Shakespeare—but nowhere in the work of dramatists who are supposed to have shared in *Titus*. It was indeed far beyond their reach. This irony permeates the play so thoroughly that scholars would find it difficult to prove that any part of *Titus* is not by Shakespeare.

Aaron's character, too, is turned round from side to side so that we can view him from many angles. He is the obvious villain, black like the devil, lustful, cunning, cruel, a consummate dissembler and hypocrite, admiring himself for his superiority in evil and taking a childlike pleasure in contemplating his villainies. Before the days of the dictators, the picture was probably thought to be crude and overdrawn. Shakespeare goes on to mark off Aaron vividly by allowing him an "Oriental" imagination. He is the only man in the play to speak lines afire with romantic poetry (see the opening speech of Act 2), as he is the only character to delight in magnificent dress (2.1.18–20). In this he supplies the strongest possible contrast with the sober Romans, but he is very like the Moorish Prince of Arragon in the *Merchant of Venice*—another parallel that connects Shakespeare with *Titus*. Suddenly at the end of the play another twist is given to Aaron's character. He is a devoted father, through the fact of fatherhood exalted by pride of race and contempt for the white men, ready to go to any lengths to save his offspring. Shakespeare does not make the mistake of softening Aaron to sentimentality by the sight of his child. He remains a killer. Several of these qualities are found in some Moor or other in the Elizabethan drama, but not all together in the same person. It is his many-sidedness that makes Aaron unique. And even when we add up these characteristics we do not obtain the sum of Aaron. There is a fire, a vigor, and a concentration in his personality such as no Elizabethan villain in the early nineties had displayed. The dilemma is not that either Shakespeare or a rival poet created Aaron, it is *aut Shakespeare, aut diabolus*.

Of the minor figures I will only take young Lucius, since he closely resembles Shakespeare's other boys. His character is composed of that mingled web in which Shakespeare delights. He is on the border between child and man. He weeps at the sight of his grandfather's distress. When Lavinia wants one of his books, he runs away from the girl in fear—a touch that while adding horror to horror shows delicate perception of a child's soul. He is full of big words about the great things he is going to do when he grows up. On the other hand he delivers with courage and address the dangerous message entrusted to him, showing an impish humor that we find in other boys of Shakespeare. His speeches are suited to his age by a somewhat simple vocabulary and a certain lilt in their rhythm. This again is characteristic of Shakespeare's presentation of young boys and girls. There is so much delicacy of perception, sympathy,

and humor in the portrait of Lucius that he may take rank
with the best of Shakespeare's boys.

Scholars, of course, might recognize Shakespeare's hand
in particular characters and still assert that he did no more
than just revise the play. But if we look at the characterization broadly, we must say of it what we said of the construction, that it is beyond the reach of anybody but Shakespeare.
It is in the round. On the other hand Marlowe's "figures are
as one dimensional as a line," and the same is true of Greene
and Peele. Besides, the characterization has the peculiar
exuberance, the irrepressible vitality which we find in
Shakespeare's early work and nowhere else. No other playwright of that period could carry such a crowd of persons in
his brain and make them so different from one another and
so alive. More important than this—no other dramatist
writing in 1594 could conceive or depict so intense a conflict
of character. Tamora, Aaron, and Titus are as full of fight as
an egg is of meat. Marlowe may fill one man with consuming passion, Kyd may spin a long intrigue, but only
Shakespeare could combine these things, give intense passions to a crowd of characters, manipulate the action and
reaction of feeling back and forth from one character to
another, and at the same time keep up a long intrigue white
hot with sustained fury. The sheer, unflagging power of
Titus is beyond the reach of anybody but Shakespeare.

Style now remains to be considered as a criterion. There
are two ways of approaching the question—the philological
and the aesthetic. The philologist counts and compares—his
results we have already discussed. It is only necessary to say
here that if parallels prove anything, it is that Shakespeare
wrote *Titus*. Aesthetic consideration is more difficult. You
cannot say of Shakespeare, as you can of Ben Jonson and
Milton, that he had one particular style. He was the dramatist speaking through the minds of his characters, and the
words are those of his characters, not his own. The variations
of Shakespeare's style from play to play or from character to
character within the same play are among the common-
places of criticism.

The question is complicated because Shakespeare was a
slow learner, who made his way by imitating his contemporaries. His early work therefore contains many passages

written in the prevailing fashion which just for that reason offend our taste. Even the great parting scene at dawn in *Romeo and Juliet* is spoiled for us by lines which we find too "conceited" or too fantastic. Indeed, ideas of decorum have changed so much that I doubt if we can read a single play of Shakespeare's without constantly being pulled up by passages that are hard for us to accept.

Let us see what the author of *Titus* was doing. He was writing, as it were, an artificial play, that is one in a particular mode, according to strict, conventional rules. He is writing the rhetorical drama of Seneca. Professor W. F. Schirmer has worked out for us the rhetorical pattern of this play (*Shaks. Jbch.*, LXXI [1935], pp. 11–31). Professor Schirmer shows that Marcus's speech (1.1.18–45) is exactly divided out into three parts. Two of 7 lines each, consisting of a single sentence, frame a middle part of 14 lines. Part 1 reproaches the Romans for their factional spirit and recommends Titus. Part 2 emphasizes his great merits; his noble character, his achievements, the death in battle of his sons. Part 3 seeks to calm down the rivals. Schirmer points out how this exact logical construction corresponds to the best rules of Quintilian or Cicero (p. 19). There is no room here to follow Schirmer further. It is enough to say that he has shown that a large part of the play is severely rhetorical and that in this respect it resembles much of Shakespeare's early work. Indeed, Shakespeare never completely succeeded in freeing himself from the influence of rhetoric. It not only colors his poetry but it also inspires some of his greatest prose speeches. We all recognize that the sheer beauty of Falstaff's style is the result of a training in rhetoric. Intricately designed speech such as we have in *Titus* is common throughout Shakespeare. If we are looking for affinities, I suggest one that is too often neglected—*Titus*, like *Julius Caesar* and *Coriolanus*, is a political play, in which the hero is Rome, and in which a crisis is time and again resolved by rhetoric. The author of all three plays was a fine historian and a fine rhetorician. I submit that it would be difficult to find an affinity more convincing.

But the style, though rhetorical, is not therefore entirely undramatic. The Romans, the Goths, Aaron, all speak a different language. At this period Shakespeare conceived the

Romans as a forthright people, direct in expression, culti-vating simplicity in language as in all things. On great occa-sions their speech can be noble, pity or indignation can move them to poetry, but they are not in the habit of indulging in highfalutin stuff which would lead to a succession of poet-ical speeches. It is true that in trying to be plain Shakespeare is occasionally flat. But on the whole we can say that the lan-guage of the Romans is neat in its plainness and at times it even achieves a kind of monumental dignity. In all his Roman plays Shakespeare aims at some kind of simplicity for his Romans. It is not the same in each play, but then his art ripens.

As we have already noticed, Aaron the Moor speaks with more imagination than anybody else in the play. His ordi-nary language, however, is full of blunt and coarse expres-sions that are never to be found in the Roman speeches. Chiron and Demetrius are even coarser than Aaron. They are marked off by their extensive use of rustic proverbs. The Romans do not use proverbs in this way. Tamora, as Pro-fessor Schirmer has shown, is all deceit and she can sing any tune. She speaks the language of the man she is talking to. Such differentiation is not to be found in Shakespeare's rivals of the nineties. Other playwrights had their own style, which they gave, together with a characteristic rhythm, to all their persons alike. Shakespeare, on the other hand, takes great pains to differentiate, so that when in the 1590's we find characters carefully distinguished by their style, we may with confidence look upon that as a sign of Shake-speare's authorship. This assertion is so painfully obvious that it would not be worth saying if scholars had not applied the law of variation to the style of *Titus* and attempted to make it prove multiple authorship.

RICHARD DAVID

Drams of Eale

Their virtues else—be they as pure as grace,
As infinite as man may undergo—
Shall in the general censure take corruption
From that particular fault: the dram of evil
Doth all the noble substance of a doubt
To his own scandal.

Hamlet's analysis applies to productions of Shakespeare as well as to men. The 1955–56 season promised marvels and in performance displayed an infinity of individual virtues. And yet the total impression was one of disappointment. There was always a dram of evil that finally undermined the most notable production.

Peter Brook's *Titus Andronicus* at Stratford (which came too late for inclusion in my last report) was certainly that. Brook had not only produced the play but had designed scenery, costumes, and musical accompaniment, and he achieved a quite extraordinary unity and concentration of effect. The staging was powerfully simple: three great squared pillars, set angle-on to the audience, fluted, and bronzy-gray in color. The two visible sides could be swung back, revealing inner recesses that might be used as entrances or, in the central pillar, as a two-storied inner stage. This was the tomb of the Andronici, somber and shadowy against the vivid green of the priests' robes and mushroom hats; festooned with lianes it became the murder pit and the forest floor above it; stained a yellowish natural-

From *Shakespeare Survey* 10 (1957), edited by Allardyce Nicoll. Reprinted by permission of Cambridge University Press.

wood color, it provided a background of Roman frugality to
the bereaved and brooding Titus at his family table; blood-
red, it made a macabre eyrie of the upper chamber from
which the Revenger peers out upon his victims, come in fantastic disguise to entrap him. In the court scenes the closed
pillars, supported by heavy side gratings of the same color
and hangings of purple and green, richly suggested the civi-
lized barbarity of late imperial Rome.

Within this frame the whole phantasmagoria unrolled
without hitch or hesitation—from the opening, when the
citizens, in ruffed gowns of shot satin and dark fustian,
broke off their rival acclamations to perform the obsequies
for Titus' sons, marching and countermarching with obsti-
nate purposefulness in a dirgelike quadrille; to the closing
scene, when in the glare of the torches the victims topple forward in succession across the dinner table like a row of
ninepins skittled from behind. It was as if the actors were
engaged in a ritual at once fluent from habitual performance
and yet still practiced with concentrated attention. There
was something puppetlike about them; but puppets manipulated by a master whose genius for improvisation constantly
enlivened his expert routine.

The compulsive and incantatory nature of the production
(which sent some spectators off into faints before ever a
throat was cut) was reinforced by the musical effects, all of a
marvelous directness. The overture was a roll of drum and
cymbal, the dirge for the slain Andronici, so strange and
powerful, no more than the first two bars of "Three Blind
Mice," in the minor and endlessly repeated. A slow seesaw of
two bass notes, a semitone apart, wrought the tension of the
final scene to an unbearable pitch, and ceased abruptly, with
breath-taking effect, as the first morsel of son-pie passed
Tamora's lips. Even more harrowing were the hurrying car-
illon of electronic bells that led up to the abduction of Lavinia
and the slow plucking of harp strings, like drops of blood
falling into a pool, that accompanied her return to the stage.

In speaking of the actors as puppets of the producer's conception, I do not mean to imply that there were not performances of strong individuality but only that, like the dyer's
hand, they were all loyally subdued to what they worked in.
The freest, from the very nature of his part in the play, is

Aaron the Moor, and to him Anthony Quayle brought a rich
gusto, as fetching in the creamy slyness that cheats Titus of
his hand as in the bounce and glory of the defense of his
black baby. But Aaron is a nice fat part for anyone; that Laurence Olivier should succeed in giving equal richness to the
stock Revenger, Titus, was a more unexpected feat. At his
first entry one might almost have accused him of mugging,
so hard did he work with swallowing and pursing, wrinkling
and charming to build up, on the bare bones of the part, a
Great Man, cantankerous, choleric, and at the same time
compelling. Yet by making Titus a "character," in every
sense, he was able not only to gloss over some of the play's
awkwardnesses but to rise (when, all too seldom, the chance
was there) into a freer air than that of Grand Guignol. We
could accept the conqueror's, and patriot's, blazing rage,
that with "Barr'st me my way in Rome?" sweeps his
youngest son out of existence. And the great central scene,
where Titus stands

> as one upon a rock
> Environ'd with a wilderness of sea,
> Who marks the waxing tide grow wave by wave,

so grew and proliferated in the astonishing variety of his
reactions to disaster (the enormous physical agony of the
severed hand was almost unbearable) that with the crowning
frenzy of "I am the sea" Olivier seemed to break through the
illusion and become, not old Hieronimo run mad again, but
madness itself.

As with individual performances, so with individual
scenes. Who could forget the return of the ravishers with
Lavinia? They bring her through the leafy arch that was the
central pillar and leave her standing there, right arm outstretched and head drooping away from it, left arm crooked
with the wrist at her mouth. Her hair falls in disorder over
face and shoulders, and from wrist and wrist-and-mouth trail
scarlet streamers, symbols of her mutilation. The two assas-
sins retreat from her, step by step, looking back at her, on
either side of the stage. Their taunts fall softly, lingeringly,
as if they themselves were in a daze at the horror of their
deed; and the air tingles and reverberates with the slow

plucking of harp strings. Another peak was the scene in which Titus makes his followers shoot arrows into the sky with messages for the gods. Here Brook cheated, bringing on the yokel, who seems to come in answer to the prayers, in a basket from the flies, and writing in a line about "fetching down his pigeons from the walls" to make this plausible. It was certainly in keeping, and added a crowning touch of fantasy to a most fantastical invention.

It was the whole, however, the one extended conjuring trick that held the spectator spellbound—spellbound and yet quite unmoved. What was it that in the last analysis made the evening so unrewarding, the effect so cold beside that of the perhaps more run-of-the-mill *Macbeth*? It was the conviction, unsought but growing irresistibly as the play proceeded, that this piece on which so much labor and ingenuity had been lavished, and to which we had been invited to attend for two and a half hours, was—twaddle. Perhaps this would have been less apparent if producer and company had not worked so hard to persuade us that it was otherwise. The Cambridge Marlowe Society's production in 1954, a shortened version played with frank gusto and dash, had prepared me to find the play itself a straightforward blood-and-thunder entertainment. In striving to make it more than this Brook made it less than nothing. The blood was, we have seen, turned to favors and to prettiness. Severed heads were not allowed to appear unless decently swathed in black velvet and enclosed in ornate funerary caskets. Titus' hand, so swaddled and coffered, was decorously cradled in Lavinia's arms, not carried off between her teeth as the text directs. The pig killing of Chiron and Demetrius occurred offstage and (perhaps to compensate the audience with one maiming in place of another) Titus' final cry of triumph,

Why, there they are both, baked in that pie,

was lopped of its last four words. But no amount of sandpapering and gilding can turn this old shocker into high tragedy à la Racine. Has Shakespeare's *Titus* really any life left in it? The question is not yet answered. Certainly Brook's romantic play of the same name was stillborn.

ALAN C. DESSEN

What Price *Titus*?

To focus upon directors' solutions to the problems posed by the final scene is to call attention to the differing strategies that have been used to deal with (or tame) this troubling, formidable tragedy. In conclusion, let me concentrate again upon those strategies.

One longstanding response to the discomfort caused by this play (as witnessed by the dearth of productions between the age of Shakespeare and 1955) is to ignore it or to pretend that it does not exist. An analogous response to such a "dangerous" script is to joke about it (so that *Titus*, like Falstaff, becomes "the cause that wit is in other men"). To cite but two of the many *Titus* jokes, Kenneth Tynan, "with acknowledgments to Lady Bracknell," quips: "to lose one son may be accounted a misfortune; to lose twenty-four, as Titus does, looks like carelessness." Equally witty is Noel Coward's reported postshow greeting to a Lavinia who had dropped the staff when writing the words in the sand: "Hello, Butterstumps!" On stage such an irreverent approach takes the form of burlesque, as in William Freimuth's 1986–87 Source Theatre Company production in Washington, DC. For example, Freimuth opened his show with a janitor who, carrying a push broom and a blaring radio, placed large rubbish bags and protective bibs over playgoers adjacent to the stage; loud sounds of sawing were then heard at the suggestion that Alarbus's limbs be

From Alan C. Dessen, *Titus Andronicus* (Manchester University Press, 1992), pp. 111–15. Reprinted by permission of Alan C. Dessen.

lopped; the fly scene featured the frustrations of a handless Lavinia trying to join the other Andronici in their meal of chips and dip; and in 5.3 Titus wore an apron with a banner that read: "This is no dress rehearsal. This is it."

Such witty remarks and burlesque choices signal a larger theatrical problem that must be faced by actors and directors. At the Old Vic in 1923 some playgoers laughed at the climactic murders in 5.3, a reaction that apparently had much to do with the absence of *Titus* from the repertoire before 1955. Subsequent directors have therefore gone to considerable lengths to avoid unwanted laughter and, at least in some instances (e.g., Laird Williamson in 1974), have felt frustrated when their audiences tittered at the boys falling into the pit, the fly scene, or the staccato murders. One of the many virtues of the Warner production was Brian Cox's purposeful evocation of such laughter for striking effects. But despite Cox's success and despite the growing recognition of the potential power of this tragedy, many theatrical professionals remain skittish about the risks posed by this play's violent or grotesque moments and worry in particular about evoking a raucous or dismissive laughter that will pull some (or, by a kind of infection, many) spectators out of the show.

As a result, many of the strategies cited throughout this book grow out of attempts to avoid such laughter. Of interest here is a choice made by Mark Rucker in his Santa Cruz production, for if significant laughter followed the four murders in 5.3, his Marcus (Brad Myers) had the option to omit the first three words of his response ("You sad-faced men, people and sons of Rome") so as not to provide a further source of amusement.... To counter or sidestep this problem, some directors (most notably Gerald Freedman) have chosen to stylise some, many, or all scenes and to cut what they perceive to be risky passages or moments. So J. C. Trewin observes that Peter Brook (like Brian Bedford some twenty years later) manipulated his script "so that his actors could let fly without dread of mocking laughter." As Trewin notes, "whenever he spied a possible laugh, he either cut the offending phrase or unmasked his protective atmospherics."

Along with such cuts and adjustments (and the superb acting by Olivier and Quayle), an essential feature of

Brook's success lay in his sense of "ritual." Recognising a "primitive strength" and "a barbaric dignity" in this tragedy, Brook felt that his production "touched audiences directly because we had tapped in it a ritual of bloodshed which was recognized as true." For him, the "completeness" of the play "is linked to a dark flowing current out of which surge the horrors, rhythmically and logically related" so as to produce "a powerful and eventually beautiful barbaric ritual." Freedman also sought to achieve his announced goal (to make his audience "accept the mutilations and decapitations and multiple deaths with belief instead of humour") by means of "masks and music and ritual." The alternative, according to Freedman ("to recreate physical violence on the stage in the manner of the Grand Guignol"), would only "appear ludicrous or stagey" in our age "where violence and destruction are presented to us daily in the newspapers and on television."

Such a "ritual" approach has its advantages, as witnessed by the reception given Brook's landmark production, but, for some playgoers, also has its liabilities. So Rosemary Anne Sisson praises the many achievements of Brook's rendition but then observes that "what he has lost—and it is a dangerous loss—is the physical release of shock upon the audience." According to Sisson, "the symbolic scarlet ribbons of blood grieve us, but calmly," so that "we can neither laugh nor gasp, but only watch and wonder, so that as great demands are made upon the audience as upon the actors." . . . This minority view was also espoused by Evelyn Waugh (who complained of Brook's "squeamishness") and Richard David (who noted that Shakespeare's bloody effects were "turned to favours and to prettiness"). Similar reactions were registered by some reviewers in 1978–80 to Brian Bedford's "restraint" in omitting or playing down the blood and visible horrors and in making substantial cuts from the received script. To some playgoers, especially in the 1970s and 1980s, the choice to stylise or to ritualise this script so as to transform the horrors and avoid unwanted laughter has seemed a poor trade-off, a diminution rather than an enhancement.

To stage those horrors, however, is to take even greater risks. As Douglas Seale notes (in offering a rationale for his

Fascist rendition), the director of *Titus* must decide "whether to play the nightmare for all it is worth, or spare the audience's feelings by avoiding too much realism (or seeming realism)." Seale, Trevor Nunn, Jane Howell, Mark Rucker, and Deborah Warner chose to present that nightmare ("when will this fearful slumber have an end?") without recourse to red ribbons, red China silk, masks, or ritualised action. Thus, Colin Blakely, who had reservations about the "formal, almost ritualized" style and the "symbolic and very cold" violence of the Brook production, argued that in an age "when people can see what violence is really like when they watch the news on television," any on-stage action "would never be as horrible as that picture of the officer pushing a gun into a man's head in Vietnam." One facet of this "realistic" approach to the nightmare element in *Titus* is signalled by the printed sign that greeted playgoers walking into the Pit to see the 1988 remount of the Warner production: "This play contains scenes which some people may find disturbing" (a caveat borne out by the scattering of empty seats after the interval).

The move to "realism," however, has not solved the problems posed by Titus and *Titus*, for, even in a very strong production such as Warner's, some scenes on some evenings prove risible rather than powerful. With such risks and solutions in mind, let me return to the provocative question posed by Freedman (as part of his argument in behalf of the stylised approach). If "the Elizabethans were more receptive to blood and gore as theatre staples" and if "they accepted all the extravagance of emotion and intensity of feeling with a passionate response," how then "does one create a similar response to horror and violence in a modern audience?" Brook and Freedman respond in terms of "ritual"; Seale, Nunn, Howell, Warner, and Rucker opt for various forms of "realism." Clearly, much depends upon the available theatrical personnel, the audience, the theatre, and the mood of the time.

But, as Freedman implies, a significant part of the problem lies in the many (and sometimes subtle) gaps between us and the 1590s, a situation facing interpreters of all of Shakespeare's plays but especially those confronting this early tragedy of blood. The play's literariness (as in its mythological allusions, formal rhetoric, and sometimes leisurely style), its prerealistic approach to psychological and emotional truth, and its distinctive imagery set up a variety of hurdles that must be surmounted by the actor or director who wishes to avoid that damaging laughter so feared by theatrical professionals. Shakespeare, after all, was himself a theatrical professional, but he crafted his playscripts not for us but for actors, playgoers, and theatres that he knew intimately but no longer exist. The problems that arise from such a gap may pertain to all thirty-seven plays but are particularly acute and highly visible in any theatrical interpretation of *Titus*. A scholarly on-the-page demonstration of an imagistic coherence that links the boys at the pit, Titus's hand in Lavinia's mouth, and Marcus's speech after the murders in 5.3 is *not* a solution to the problems facing today's actor and director. Compared to audiences at the Old Vic in 1923 and Stratford in 1955, fewer playgoers today would agree with Ravenscroft that *Titus* "seems rather a heap of Rubbish than a Structure," for a series of successful renditions *have* made a dent in the pejorative view of the script widely held in the theatrical community (as witnessed by the number of productions springing up in widely scattered places in the late 1980s). Such a burgeoning of on-stage renditions cannot help but expand our understanding of the potential in this script. Stanley Wells argues, moreover, that, after the example set by Deborah Warner, "subsequent directors will have far less excuse than before for evading its problems by textual adaptation or by evasive theatricalism." Progress has been and is being made.

Nonetheless, the long tradition of *Titus* bashing has left its mark. The jokes and burlesques continue. Few theatrical professionals are willing to emulate Warner and her cast so as to "trust" the script and their audiences. The gaps between the 1590s and today, moreover, will not go away. No amount of "historical" argument or directorial ingenuity will fully resolve "the *Titus* problem" for today's actor or playgoer.

In response to Brook's 1955 production, Richard David posed the telling question: "Has Shakespeare's *Titus* really any life left in it?" The answer provided by more than thirty years of theatrical experimentation is clearly yes. Those for-

SYLVAN BARNET

Titus Andronicus on Stage and Screen

Ever since the late 1980s reviewers every couple of years find to their surprise that a new production of *Titus Andronicus* is interesting, engaging, and indeed deeply moving. Older theatergoers, however, will remember that Peter Brook's production at Stratford in 1955 also was hailed for showing that *Titus* had been unjustly neglected.

There is no question that *Titus* has undergone long periods of neglect, but it has also had its periods of popularity—and the second half of the twentieth century may be one of them. What is especially interesting, however, is that we cannot claim to have rescued from obscurity a neglected play; *Titus* was popular in its own day. The first record of a specific performance is on January 23, 1594, but the title page of the first edition, published sometime in 1594, says that the play has been acted by three theatrical companies, which suggests that *Titus* had already been on the stage for at least a couple of years. In addition to a few other references to specific public performances in London early in 1594, there is a record of a private performance at Christmas festivities given in Rutland in 1596, in the country house of Sir John Harington of Exton. Nor was this early popularity simply a matter of the appeal that any new play might make. *Titus* was reprinted in 1600 and in 1611—a sign that there must have been a market for it—each time with the assertion that it had been acted by prominent theatrical companies. Moreover, four years after the third printing of *Titus*, in the Induction to *Bartholomew Fair* Ben Jonson cites *Titus* as an enduring favorite of a public with low tastes.

We can't say exactly how *Titus Andronicus* was performed on the Elizabethan stage, but clues in the text indicate that it took advantage of all three performing levels: the platform stage, an upper acting area, and (in 2.3) a trap. The first stage direction in the earliest printed text runs thus:

> Enter the Tribunes and Senators aloft; and then enter Saturninus and his followers at one door, and Bassianus and his followers with drums and trumpets.

Pretty clearly if Saturninus enters "at one door," Bassianus enters at another, since they represent opposed forces. (The De Witt drawing of the Swan [discussed on pages xxviii–xxix] shows two doors at the rear of the thrust stage, with an overhanging gallery.) Possibly one of the stage doors—perhaps equipped with black drapery or with a cloth painted to represent an architectural facade—served also as the tomb, though conceivably the tomb was represented by some sort of structure erected at the rear of the platform. The upper stage was not used only for the initial entrance, "aloft," of the tribunes and senators; at line 63 Bassianus and Saturninus *"go up into the Senate house."* An upper playing area is also used in 5.2; although no stage directions in this scene specify that the action is "aloft," it is clear that when Tamora addresses Titus in his "study," Titus is above, since she asks him to "come down." And in 5.3.130–33, Marcus's words ("headlong hurl ourself/And on the ragged stones beat forth our souls") suggest that he and Lucius are on an upper level. Also worth mentioning is the emphasis on spectacle, implicit in the reference to "drums and trumpets" in the first stage direction. One sometimes reads that the Elizabethan stage was bare, but in fact a good deal of attention was paid to highly visual effects; here the "drums and trumpets" imply at least some dressing up of the stage with supernumeraries, and one may assume that such characters were attractively dressed.

We also get some sense of Elizabethan stage spectacle from a late sixteenth-century illustration of *Titus Andronicus,* the only contemporary drawing illustrating a play by Shakespeare [see pp. xxviii–xxxix]. This pen drawing, in the papers of the Marquis of Bath at Longleat, shows Tamora in the center, crowned and robed, kneeling before Titus, to the left, who wears what passes for a Roman costume. Behind Tamora, at the right, kneel two of her sons, their hands tied, and still further to the right stands a coal-black Aaron brandishing a sword. At the extreme left, behind Titus, stand two attendant soldiers in Elizabethan garb. The drawing is important evidence that for plays set in classical times the Elizabethans used both classical and contemporary clothing, classical clothing for the chief characters, and Elizabethan clothing for the lesser ones. Although the drawing is accompanied by some forty lines of text from several parts of the play, in fact it does not precisely illustrate any scene in the play. Obviously it evokes the first part of the play, when Tamora pleads for her son Alarbus—but why is Aaron (a captive) armed, and why are there not three sons (as the text specifies) rather than two? And why are not Titus's sons shown, since in the play they are present when Tamora pleads for Alarbus? Even if a viewer interprets the picture as showing a slightly later episode, after Alarbus has been sent off to his death, the problem of an armed Aaron remains. In all probability the drawing is based on a somewhat faulty memory of a performance of the play; but it probably does give us a good idea of Elizabethan costuming and of the Elizabethan presentation of the Moor.

From 1642 until 1660, that is, during the Civil War and the reign of Cromwell, until the restoration of King Charles II in 1660, the theaters in England were closed, but they reopened in 1660 and *Titus* may have been performed occasionally during the 1660s; in any case it was mentioned, and it appears in a list of plays assigned to one of the theaters. In 1678 Edward Ravenscroft adapted the play, calling his work *Titus Andronicus or the Rape of Lavinia*. The adaptation, probably performed in 1678, was not published until 1687, when it included an address "To the Reader" in which Ravenscroft claims that he has extensively revised "a heap of rubbish":

> However as if some great Building had been design'd, in the removal we found many Large and Square Stones both usefull and Ornamental to the Fabrick, as now Modell'd: Compare the Old Play with this, you'l finde that none in all that Authors

Works ever receiv'd greater Alterations or Additions, the Language not only refin'd but many scenes entirely New; Besides
most of the Principal Characters heighten'd, and the Plot much
encreas'd.

This version was revived in the mid 1680s, and continued
on the stage until 1724. Curiously, despite Ravenscroft's
claim, his revisions are relatively slight, at least when compared to other revisions of the period, such as John Dryden's
version of *Troilus and Cressida* and Nahum Tate's revision
of *King Lear*. He modernizes some of the language, reas-
signs or moves some speeches (he heightens Aaron's part in
1.1 by giving him lines that Shakespeare gave to Tamora and
Demetrius), invents some new speeches, and sends Titus
offstage to chop off his hand, but Ravenscroft pretty much
follows the original, except that he ends with Aaron, tied to
the rack, being set afire.

To this point the stage history of the play, though not
exceptional, was respectable. But after the 1724 production
of Ravenscroft's version, with the eminent James Quin as
Aaron, *Titus Andronicus*—in the original form and in
Ravenscroft's adaptation—seems to have vanished from the
stage until 1839, when it was given in Philadelphia in an
adaptation by the American actor Nathaniel Harrington
Bannister. No text of Bannister's adaptation survives, but a
commentator wrote that Bannister "excluded the horrors
with infinite skill." As we will see, excluding the horrors, or
at least modifying them, continues to be a preoccupation of
most directors of the play.

In England (and in Scotland and Ireland) Ira Aldridge, a
black American who went to England because he could not
find work with white companies in the United States, played
the role of Aaron between 1849 and 1860. Aldridge did not
confine himself to black roles, but earlier he had been especially successful as Othello, and so it seems natural for him
to have added Aaron to his repertoire. His version of the play
does not survive, but fairly full references to it make it clear
that it was heavily adapted. Not surprisingly, the part of
Aaron—already in many ways highly attractive—was made
more attractive, and, equally unsurprisingly, the violence

was muted. But the changes in Tamora and her children come as a surprise. A reviewer of a production in Hoxton, in 1857, wrote:

> The deflowerment of Lavinia, cutting out her tongue, chopping off her hands, and the numerous decapitations and gross language which occur in the original are totally omitted and a play not only presentable but actually attractive is the result. Aaron is elevated into a noble and lofty character. Tamora, the Queen of Scythia, is a chaste though decidedly strong-minded female, and her connection with the Moor appears to be of a legitimate description; her sons Chiron and Demetrius are dutiful children, obeying the behests of their mother. . . . Thus altered, Mr. Aldridge's conception of the part of Aaron is excellent—gentle and impassioned by turns; now burning with jealousy as he doubts the honor of the Queen; anon, fierce with rage as he reflects upon the wrongs which have been done him—the murder of Alarbus and the abduction of his son; and then all tenderness and emotion in the gentle passages with his infant.

After Aldridge's final production of the play in 1860, *Titus* (even in adapted forms) disappeared from the stage until 1923, when the Old Vic put it on, thereby completing its production of the entire canon. The director, Robert Atkins, sought to do the play in a more or less Elizabethan manner, with few properties and with an emphasis on pageantry. The reviews on the whole were favorable, although the rapid sequence of deaths in the last scene (Titus kills Lavinia and then kills Tamora; Saturninus kills Titus, and Lucius kills Saturninus, all within twenty lines) evoked some laughter. Putting aside productions chiefly of local interest (e.g. a version done at Yale University in 1924), *Titus* next appeared in 1951, in a thirty-minute version by Kenneth Tynan and Peter Myers, staged in London as one of six pieces in an evening of Grand Guignol. (Later, in a review of Peter Brook's production of *Titus* in 1955, Tynan said that he "always had a soft spot for *Titus Andronicus*," a play that is "tragedy naked, godless, and unredeemed, a carnival of carnage in which pity is the first man down. We have since learned how to sweeten tragedy, to make it ennobling, but we would do well to remember that *Titus* is the raw material, 'the thing itself,' the piling of agony on to a human head until it splits.") Curiously, Aaron was omitted. In 1953 the play was performed by the Marlowe Society at Cambridge, and (as part of a cycle of Shakespeare's classical plays) by the Antioch Shakespeare Festival at Yellow Springs, Ohio, but the great production of the 1950s was Peter Brook's, at Stratford-upon-Avon in 1955, with Laurence Olivier as Titus, Vivien Leigh as Lavinia, Maxine Audley as Tamora, and Anthony Quayle as Aaron. Richard David's somewhat cool report of the production is reprinted in this edition, but a few details may be added here. Brook cut about 650 lines, dropping a hundred and fifty from the first scene. Moreover, he occasionally rearranged speeches. For instance, in 1.1 he put Lavinia's rejection of Saturninus before Saturninus's expression of interest in Lavinia, thus making Lavinia's rejection contribute to Saturninus's interest in Tamora. As Richard David points out, Brook muted or stylized much of the violence, for instance by not displaying Titus's severed hand, and by using scarlet ribbons to represent Lavinia's bloody stumps. He also used such visual devices to replace some of the ornate poetry, in this case Marcus's speech (2.4.11–57) describing the maimed Lavinia as a "conduit with three issuing spouts." Still, it should be pointed out that although Brook relegated the deaths of Chiron and Demetrius to offstage, he did keep the other seven onstage murders of the play. In short, although he did not attempt a faithful, museum-piece production, he did demonstrate that Shakespeare's play (with some touching up) could powerfully move an audience. In 1957 he took the production on a tour of six continental capitals, and then brought it to London for thirty-six performances; these, with the 1955 performances, gave the play a total of ninety performances, probably the longest run the play has had.

Other productions in the 1950s included two performances at the Oregon Shakespeare Festival in Ashland in 1956, done without an intermission (i.e. Elizabethan style) on a stage that approximated an Elizabethan stage (a neutral platform with a permanent architectural background), fifteen performances at Joseph Papp's New York Shakespeare

Festival in 1956, and a highly cut version done in 1957 by the Old Vic, on a double bill with an abridged *Comedy of Errors*. The Old Vic production was set in an inn courtyard; Elizabethan strolling players entered, and then, wearing a combination of Elizabethan and classical costume, gave a version of *Titus* that ran about an hour and a half.

In 1963 the Birmingham Repertory performed the play, and in 1967 a Baltimore company staged it in a modern setting: Saturninus, with a retinue of Blackshirts, resembled Mussolini, Titus was dressed like a Prussian officer, and the Goths—envisioned as a liberating army—wore costumes reminiscent of the clothing of American forces in World War II. Also in 1967 Joseph Papp in New York returned to the play, offering a version directed by Gerald Freedman and starring Moses Gunn as Aaron. Freedman's production was somewhat like Peter Brook's in that it ritualized the play, though Freedman went further, using masks, a chorus, and silver and black costumes of no particular period or culture. Freedman explained that he turned to such devices because he had found the 1967 Baltimore modern version unsuccessful; its realism, in his view, called attention to the unreality of the play. *Titus Andronicus*, Freedman said, needs to be stylized if it is to be "meaningful and emotional to a contemporary audience," and if the multiple deaths are to be acceptable rather than ridiculous. (Brook had already said he presented the play in an "unrealistic" manner in order to make the violence of the play "totally real.") Mildred Kuner, in a brief review in *Shakespeare Quarterly* (Autumn 1967) gives a sample of the staging:

> At the end, when the principals meet their death in the banquet scene, the chorus, from the shadows, wove about the victims a red cloth which turned into a black shroud: the dead, in turn, did not collapse but remained upright, as though transformed into stone. Symbolism rather than gory realism was what made this production so stunning.

One other detail of Freedman's production may be cited: when the emperor sends Titus the severed heads of two of his sons, the heads were simply the masks on a platter. It is reported that the audience gasped at the sight of the empty masks.

The 1970s saw several productions of *Titus*, including one by the Royal Shakespeare Theatre in 1972, directed by Trevor Nunn, where, with *Coriolanus*, *Julius Caesar*, and *Antony and Cleopatra*, it was done as part of a series of Roman plays. Nunn said that Shakespeare used Roman settings in order to examine "political motives and social organization," and that the Roman plays "are speaking directly to us now." What did he think *Titus* was saying? In the program, Nunn wrote that "Shakespeare's Elizabethan nightmare has become ours," and that we may already be experiencing a "convulsion which heralds a fall greater than Rome's." The governing idea was that Titus's Rome has become decadent (Saturninus was an effete weakling) and is about to fall. Despite this unpromising reading of the play, there were some successes, notably Colin Blakely's grand, battered Titus, which received considerable praise.

The play has fared better in the 1980s, though not in John Barton's production of 1981, done in a "presentational" rather than a "representational" manner (e.g. actors when not performing sat in the shadows onstage). In practice, Barton's production seemed to mock the play, giving us a fatuous Titus and a Tamora who spoke with a ludicrous accent. A production at Brown University, however, directed by David Burr in 1984, was extremely effective, using a black-and-silver-metal set and presenting Titus and the old guard in leather, against a new world of upstart punks. Unfortunately this production attracted little attention outside of the university. An earlier punk production in New York in a lounge in the East Village in 1983, directed by Kestutis Nakas, was far less successful. Nakas chose to present the play in as ridiculous a fashion as possible: effeminate soldiers equipped with plastic weapons and shields made grand gestures, and meat snacks were served to the audience. The director justified the production by claiming, "If the humor is openly recognized, it'll be gruesome, black humor adding to the tragedy rather than destroying it—which is what happens when you play it straight." The experiment was, as one might have easily predicted, a failure.

The most important production of the late twentieth century was given in the Swan at Stratford-upon-Avon in 1987, directed by Deborah Warner and starring Brian Cox as Titus and Estelle Kohler as Tamora. The stage was relatively bare except for a large aluminum ladder, to which Tamora's defeated sons were tied when they enter Rome, and which was used again when Aaron is hanged. Ritual was *not* used to distance the horrors; although blood was kept to a minimum, the mutilations were realistic. Perhaps more than any other production of the play in the twentieth century, this production showed that a relatively straight version can be deeply moving.

The BBC did a television version in 1985, directed by Jane Howell. It is straightforward for the most part, though masks are used for the followers of Saturninus and Bassianus in 1.1 and for courtiers in 4.4. Howell explained that the Rome of *Titus* "seemed like a society where everyone was faceless except for those in power." She also said she hoped the masks would have "a strange, dislocating effect." A few other special effects were used—for instance, the opening image shows a skull that fades and is replaced by an image of the dead emperor—but on the whole this version is realistic, not stylized and not highly cinematic. That is, Howell did not do much in the way of converting a play into a film. She did, however, occasionally evoke aspects of contemporary society. The costumes of the Goths were inspired by the rock music group Kiss in keeping with her belief that television essentially shows us today's society.

Julie Taymor, best known for directing *The Lion King* on Broadway, has directed a film version of *Titus Andronicus* (1999). She drew on her New York stage production of the play (1994) but in the film she took full advantage of the camera, opening up the play with numerous shots impossible in a stage production. The film begins, however, as her stage production did, with a twentieth-century boy violently playing with toy soldiers in a kitchen, and then being transported to ancient Rome, where he becomes Young Lucius. In the film, a bomb is thrown into the kitchen, and when the smoke clears a Roman soldier invades the home and whisks the boy into an ancient coliseum. In short, our childish fantasies of violence become adult realities. In an interview

Taymor said of the Andronici, who slaughtered a Goth as a sacrifice, "These boys have been given license to kill. I think violence is such an integral part of the human psyche and physicality. . . . Boxing and football and all of these sports are sublimated violent urges. They're codified. I mean, why do we play football in a coliseum?" Taymor emphasized the contemporary relevance of the play by combining images of modern life with images of the past: Chiron and Demetrius are dressed as rock performers, chariots mix with motorcycles, crossbows are used but so are rifles and tanks, togas are worn but so are frock coats, and microphones and bottled beer are in evidence; Titus's severed hand is deposited in a Ziplock bag. In short, Taymor sees *Titus* as relevant to all times, and in interviews she has spoken of contemporary killings in schools, of Bosnia, of mutilations in Rwanda, and of the sort of thing we see daily on television: "I think it is exactly right for our times" (*New York Times,* December 20, 1998), and she has suggested that *Titus* is less violent than such films as *Braveheart* and *Saving Private Ryan*. The end of Taymor's film offers a departure from Shakespeare's play that, given Taymor's comments about violence, is surprising: The Young Lucius takes Aaron's baby out of a cage and, carrying the baby, leaves the coliseum, with the implication that there is some hope for a new life, a hope that the cycle of violence may end.

Bibliographic Note: Many of the titles cited below in the Suggested References, Section 4 (Shakespeare on Stage and Screen) include brief discussions of productions, and the editions of *Titus Andronicus* cited at the beginning of Section 11 include surveys of the stage history of the play. Alan C. Dessen's *Titus Andronicus: Shakespeare in Performance* (1989) offers excellent discussions of many twentieth-century productions, but pays detailed attention especially to those of Peter Brook (1955), Gerald Freedman (1967), Trevor Nunn (1972), Laird Williamson (1974), Jane Howell (BBC TV, 1985), Pat Patton (1986), and Deborah Warner (1987). Martin White, in *Renaissance Drama in Action* (1998), pp. 188–96, discusses ways of staging Act 2, Scene 4.

For a collection of some two dozen reviews of twentieth-century productions, see Philip C. Kolin, *Titus Andronicus: Critical Essays* (1995). *Shakespeare Quarterly* is a good source for reviews of productions—not only in the English-speaking world but also elsewhere—since the middle of the twentieth century. *Shakespeare Survey*, an annual, includes reviews of British productions of the same period. *Shakespeare Bulletin,* though less readily available in libraries, is also an excellent source.

On Julie Taymor's film (1999), for the text, pictures, and director's notes, see her Titus: *The Illustrated Screenplay, Adapted from the Play by William Shakespeare* (2000). David McCandless compares Taymor's stage production (1994) with her screen version, in "A Tale of Two *Tituses:* Julie Taymor's Visions on Stage and Screen," *Shakespeare Quarterly* 53 (2002): 487–511. *Shakespearean Criticism* 73 reprints an important long interview with Taymor from *Cineaste,* as well as some reviews.

The Life of
Timon of Athens

Introduction to *Timon of Athens*

There is general agreement that *Timon of Athens* is an unfinished play. In an influential article in the *Review of English Studies* (1942), Una Ellis-Fermor described *Timon* as "a play such as a great artist might leave behind him, roughed out, worked over in part and then abandoned; full of inconsistencies in form and presentation, with fragments (some of them considerable) bearing the unmistakable stamp of his workmanship scattered throughout." The roughnesses of the play are obvious to any conscientious reader of Shakespeare. The blank verse is often extremely irregular, with many lines that do not fit into the iambic pentameter pattern. There are strange eruptions of prose in verse passages, and there are many inept repetitions of words and phrases from one line to the next. Characters appear, such as the Fool and Page (2.2), who are not properly integrated into the action; there are two conflicting epitaphs for Timon in Act 5; and the Poet and Painter announced at 4.3.355 do not arrive until almost two hundred lines later. The subplot of Alcibiades and his revenge on Athens is so loosely related to the main action which it is intended to parallel that some have suspected a lost scene. We know that the murderer for whom Alcibiades is pleading in Act 3, Scene 5, cannot be Timon, but he is not anyone else in the play, and it is more than an idle curiosity which seeks to know his name.

One detail in the play is the subject of a fascinating study. In "Shakespeare Learns the Value of Money," Terence Spencer discusses the inconsistency in the references to talents. A talent was an ancient coin frequently mentioned in Plutarch and the Bible, and generally taken to be worth half a hundredweight of silver, or well over $1000 in its modern equivalent. The sum of 1000 talents that Timon seeks from the Senators (2.2) is an absurdly large one (more than $1,000,000), and it is possible that Shakespeare really did not know how much a talent was worth. At some point he learned its true value and corrected the references at the beginning of the play, but left others uncorrected. The request for "fifty five hundred talents" in Act 3, Scene 2, seems to mean either fifty or five hundred, depending on how much a talent is worth, and the references to "so many talents" in the same scene should be replaced by actual sums.

This example of the talents is a very neat one for demonstrating that many details in *Timon* need to be revised and corrected and that the play lacks the sort of polishing and tidying up that one would expect from a final draft. The circumstances surrounding the printing of *Timon* (discussed in the Textual Note) lend further support to this idea. There can be no doubt that the play as it appears in Shakespeare's First Folio of 1623 is unfinished. Recently, there has been renewed interest in *Timon* as a collaboration between Shakespeare and Thomas Middleton, first suggested by William Wells in 1920 and Dugdale Sykes in 1924. In the Oxford Shakespeare, edited by Stanley Wells and Gary Taylor, *Timon* appears as a collaborated play.

Miss Ellis-Fermor's thesis has done great harm to the appreciation of *Timon* because it suggests that the play is not only unfinished (in the sense of its lacking any final revision), but that it is a mere collection of jottings and rough sketches without any integral coherence. I would strongly disagree with this point of view. It seems to me that *Timon* is completely finished in conception: its structure makes good sense as a whole, its characters are well adapted to the overall plan, and its style, tone, imagery, and dramatic handling all contribute to a unified imaginative vision.

Because *Timon* is an unusual play, it would be more profitable to try to understand its uniqueness than to compare it unfavorably with the great tragedies that preceded it. The structure of the play is that of a dramatic fable, divided into two sharply contrasted parts. By dramatic fable I mean what other critics have called a morality play or an allegory—that is, a structure that does not proceed rationally and causatively from point to point, but rather one that progresses by a series of unmotivated leaps from one imaginative state to another.

We are not meant to examine the credibility of Timon's financial extravagance, or his total unawareness of his bankruptcy, or his sudden discovery of an inexhaustible supply of gold. We accept these improbabilities as part of our willing suspension of disbelief. The testing of the three false friends in Act 3 moves as in a folktale to its inevitable conclusion, and the faithful servant who remains true while all others are false is a familiar fairy-tale figure. The exact cause of Timon's death is left poetically obscure, and no attempt at all is made to give his sudden change from philanthropy to misanthropy a psychological basis. The structure of the play is schematic, and the dramatic action separates itself into a series of well-defined episodes related to each other analogically rather than causally. One scene is not the source or cause or motive for another, but is, rather, a parallel to it and serves as a comment on it. I should like to look more closely at the structure of *Timon* in order to show that the play is complete and fully imagined within the meaning of a dramatic fable. For this purpose, I will survey the action scene by scene and offer an account of "what happens in *Timon*."

The first sequence of ninety-four lines before Timon appears is of crucial importance for establishing the tone and mood of the play as well as announcing its major themes. We have a Poet and Painter, a Jeweler and Merchant, who have come to peddle their wares to Timon, as patron of the arts and general connoisseur. None of these characters is named, and they represent, as in an allegory, the type functions of their names. Behind the elaborate compliment and self-deprecation of this scene lies a blatant hucksterism that well expresses the rottenness of Athens. The meretriciousness of the Poet and Painter is particularly disturbing, since we expect them to aim higher than merely "to propagate their states." Shakespeare seems nowhere else to have put artists in such an unfavorable light.

The controlling element in the scene is the Poet's allegory of Fortune, which serves as a central fable for the play. The goddess Fortune and her capricious ways much occupied the mind of men in the Middle Ages and Renaissance, and great efforts were made to reconcile the Roman myth with Christian morality. Wealth and all material benefits are the fortuitous and insubstantial gifts of Fortune, the blindfolded goddess who is forever turning the wheel on which her worshipers are placed (the wheel in a gambling casino derives from this one). Timon's alliance with Fortune early in the play clearly foreshadows his ruin, "When Fortune in her shift and change of mood/ Spurns down her late beloved" (1.1.84–85).

Thus, when Timon enters at line 94 with great ceremony, *"addressing himself courteously to every suitor,"* we are already prepared not to accept his munificence at its face value. The pack of suppliants is itself so mixed in degrees of worth that we cannot help agreeing with Dr. Johnson, who said that the play is a "warning against that ostentatious liberality which scatters bounty but confers no benefits, and buys flattery but no friendship." Timon is at his height in this scene, reveling in his philanthropic role. There is, of course, something dreamlike about this early scene, with its mixture of charity, prodigality, and enormous public display. The entrance of Apemantus at line 175 restores some measure of reality, since he at least speaks the truth, however churlish and snarling he may be in his personal manner. He warns Timon of his waste and extravagance, but Apemantus is so unsympathetic in his role of satiric, malcontent railer that he is almost never believed; this is another disturbing element in the play. The young military hero, Alcibiades, also appears in Act 1, Scene 1, but aside from his elaborate military costume, he is a colorless figure and, with the single exception of Act 3, Scene 5, remains so throughout.

In Act 1, Scene 2, Timon is still high and godlike as he presides over an elaborate banquet for his friends. There is a strong visual emphasis on the fact that Timon's bounty shows itself in hedonism and high living more than in old-fashioned benevolence. His ideal of friendship is inseparable from the clubby atmosphere of good food and drink and the Gemütlichkeit of mutual compliment. As Apemantus had said earlier, "He that loves to be flattered is worthy o' th' flatterer" (1.1.229–30). The Masque of Amazons in this scene is an element of spectacle common in Shakespeare's later plays and not very closely related to the action. Incidentally, the only women in the play are these Amazons and the prostitutes, Phrynia and Timandra; the world of Athens is distinctly a man's world.

It is in Act 1, Scene 2, that Flavius, the always loyal steward of Timon, tells us that his master is bankrupt, everything is mortgaged, and utter ruin is imminent. Flavius resembles Apemantus in speaking the truth, but he has a fund of compassion for Timon—"I bleed inwardly for my lord" (210)—while Apemantus cynically delights in misfortune.

The first scene of Act 2 takes us back to the opening of the play, and once again we are plunged into the icy reality of Athens, in which all values are on a strictly cash basis. A Senator who is not named is counting up Timon's debts and is impatiently dispatching his servant to dun him for the money. He loves and honors Timon, of course, "But must not break my back to heal his finger" (2.1.24). The most shocking aspect of this scene is the contempt in which the Senator holds Timon for his generosity:

> If I want gold, steal but a beggar's dog
> And give it Timon—why the dog coins gold.
>
> (5–6)

The Senator is only elaborating on Timon's own formula: "there's none/ Can truly say he gives, if he receives" (1.2.10–11). But Timon's rejection of reciprocity in giving leaves him terribly vulnerable.

The next scene (2.2) marks a new stage in the action, for Timon is now finally aware of his bankruptcy. In an effort to avoid the overwhelming truth, Timon will test his friends by seeking to borrow money from them. This process is accomplished in three satiric scenes in Act 3, written in vivid colloquial style. They are all brief vignettes, very different from each other, and designed to show the varieties of evasive ingenuity. The scene with Lucullus (3.1) is so masterfully done that we are almost convinced that "this is no time to lend money, especially upon bare friendship without security" (44–45). In the next scene (3.2), three Strangers are introduced to serve as choral commentators on what is happening and to arouse our sympathies for Timon. These Strangers are merely non-Athenians without any further specification (although one of them is called Hostilius); they are in no way connected with the plot and appear only to vindicate Timon.

In Act 3, Scene 4, the creditors' servants are again assembled at the house of Timon as they were in Act 2, Scene 2. When Timon enters *"in a rage,"* we have a new development in the action, since Timon now has been stripped of his illusions. His misanthropy proper begins at this point, and he speaks in the highly emotional, freely associative style reserved for those distracted. Timon seems to be on the road to that bitter self-knowledge demanded by tragic recognition, yet he never progresses any further, and the tragedy, at least from the point of view of Aristotle's *Poetics,* remains truncated and fragmentary. In his hysterical, martyrlike sufferings, Timon does not turn inward as do so many of Shakespeare's tragic protagonists; instead, he begins to gloat over the possibility of being brilliantly and histrionically revenged in a mock-banquet.

Act 3, Scene 5, is the first and only full scene of the subplot. It is well written and fully written, with a carefully developed oration by Alcibiades for a friend and fellow soldier who has killed a man to defend his honor. This speech is, by the way, in the direct tradition of the "mercy" speeches of Portia in *The Merchant of Venice* and Isabella in *Measure for Measure.* Although the scene has no plot links with what precedes, it does have a strong thematic connection with it. The Athenian senators show the same ingratitude to a benefactor of their state as they did to Timon. This scene plays an important part in developing the tone and mood of Athens, so that when Timon's mock-banquet and revenge follow in the next scene, we are glad to see the tables turned on the greedy, usurious senators. Alcibiades' banishment in this scene foreshadows the self-exile of Timon at the end of the next scene.

The final scene of Act 3 is carefully written up to provide an effective climax for the first part of the play: "Uncover, dogs, and lap" (86). This is a memorable line, and the dramatic skill with which the discovery and reversal are managed shows Shakespeare at his best. It is a great moment for Timon, who has once again recovered his former stature. One interesting structural element is that Timon in this scene is beginning to take over the role of Apemantus: his grace echoes Apemantus' bitter benediction in Act 1, Scene 2, and in Acts 4 and 5 the verbal echoes become more marked. Another striking feature is the reaction of the guests to Timon's revenge. Here we have an excellent example of the use of sharp contrast to establish an effect. The friends are as untouched by Timon's towering pronouncements as the dunning servants were in Act 3, Scene 4. After having their souls seared by Timon's revelations of their inner corruption, they respond with utter banality: "Push, did you see my cap?", "I have lost my gown," "He gave me a jewel th' other day, and now he has beat it out of my hat. Did you see my jewel?" (110, 111, 113–15) This anticlimax of high comedy concludes when the lost items have been recovered.

Timon's soliloquy outside the walls of Athens in the next scene (4.1) has none of the meditative, soul-searching qualities of the soliloquies in *Hamlet* or *Macbeth;* it is purely an oration by one with no onstage audience. Timon's vision of chaos in this scene is so radical that it fails to be convincing. It is perhaps not more extreme than Lear's speeches on the heath, but it has no psychological terror and passion to support the violent rhetoric, and the intensity of the language seems to be separated from any occasion which might have caused it. This leads to some odd side effects, even to an irreverent feeling of sick humor in some of the most hysterical imprecations:

> Son of sixteen,
> Pluck the lined crutch from thy old limping sire,
> With it beat out his brains.   (13–15)

One of the drawbacks in the writing of a dramatic fable is that one deliberately rejects the kind of psychological thickness that is needed to support statements like the above. The fourth and fifth acts of *Timon* are unsuccessful partly because the impassioned rhetoric cannot sustain itself without an impassioned action.

The brief second scene of Act 4 shows us Timon's servants, "All broken implements of a ruined house" (16), still faithful to him in adversity. They are the counterparts of the false friends, and they modify our possible contempt for Timon. Along with the three Strangers of Act 3, Scene 2, they prevent the play from becoming out-and-out satire.

Act 4, Scene 3, a long and miscellaneous scene, consists chiefly of a series of encounters with Timon. It is worth noting that Timon's cave in the woods seems to be as easily accessible as a good midtown office. These encounters all meet with predictable failure, as we might expect in a dramatic fable, so that their main function seems to be to exhibit

Timon's misanthropy in a number of different guises. One new movement, however, is the sense of world-weariness that comes over Timon, accompanied by a desire to die. It begins at line 380 and culminates in the moving speech:

> My long sickness
> Of health and living now begins to mend,
> And nothing brings me all things.   (5.1.187–89)

At the beginning of Act 4, Scene 3, Timon's parable of the "Twinned brothers of one womb" (3) shows us that he now believes in the Poet's vision of Fortune in the first scene of the play. "All's obliquy" (18), everything is crooked and perverse, and the law of nature no longer rules man. Timon's hate would not be so disturbing if it did not include a petulant self-hate by which he forfeits all neutral ground. He is not the one just man bearing witness against corruption, but as worthless and corrupt as the rest. His primitivism, then, is a mere sham, and there is ironic justification for his finding gold rather than roots. He will use it to fulfill his evil vision and make "Destruction fang mankind" (23).

The appearance of Alcibiades with a brace of whores undercuts his heroic pretensions, and the slangy directness of the whores makes them more interesting than their noble captain. Like other realists in the play, Phrynia and Timandra humor Timon in the hope of gain: "More counsel with more money, bounteous Timon" (168). In their plainspeaking refusal to flatter, they make explicit a theme from the earlier part of the play: "Believe't that we'll do anything for gold" (151).

The word-slinging wit-combat with Apemantus has some of the best and some of the worst speeches in the play. The absolute low point, it seems to me, is the series of insults they hurl at each other. There is not enough inventiveness in either calumniator to go beyond Timon's "Would thou wert clean enough to spit upon" (363)—my entry for the worst line in the play, which gains an added point from Timon's insufferable snobbishness. But the mutual judgments that Timon and Apemantus make of each other are excellently done, and they show an old-fashioned character analysis rare in this play. Apemantus' case against Timon is made so explicitly that we cannot possibly mistake Timon for Shakespeare's mouthpiece. Timon is a naturally disdainful man, who feigns misanthropy out of pique with Fortune; he is an absolutist who cannot make any compromises with the human condition. As Apemantus says, "The middle of humanity thou never knewest, but the extremity of both ends" (301–02). This hits home, but Timon's account of Apemantus' meanness and envy and essentially servile nature also strikes its mark and draws blood.

The meeting with the anonymous Banditti is full of improbability, and their sententiousness and lack of ferocity are disappointing. The encounter with Flavius that closes the scene shows Timon again at his worst, since he is grudgingly forced to admit that there is one honest man. Shadwell got around this difficulty in his version of the play (1678) by introducing an honest woman, Evandra, who is able to regenerate Timon. At this point in the structure of Shakespeare's play, it is clear that Timon must soon die, if only to satisfy the exacerbation of the audience. He has reached such an extreme position that he can go no further in negation. Being a static and flat character, he has already involved himself in tedious repetition.

Act 5, Scene 1, continues the previous scene, with the Poet and Painter forming another exhibit of why Timon took to the woods; we are pleased to see them laboring so hard for rewards they will not receive. The mission from Athens at the end of the scene suggests that some changes have occurred in the city since Timon's departure, although the elaborate, unnecessarily complicated rhetoric of the Senators hints that these changes could not have been very profound. The "heaps and sums" and "figures of their love" inevitably imply that the Senators are ready to offer Timon a handsome bribe. After the announcement of Timon's death and the discovery of his epitaph, the play ends conventionally with a sense of the purgation of evil and the possibility of a new and better life in the once corrupted city.

At the risk of reviewing the plot, I have gone into some detail about the structure of *Timon* in order to show that it is a coherent whole with carefully developed analogies between its parts, and not a mere hodgepodge of first thoughts, jottings, roughings-out, or fragments. Although it has many flaws, it does seem to me a completed play, and one that can satisfactorily be acted in its present form (as it has been in recent years by the Old Vic—twice, the Stratford Festival Company of Canada, and many others). There is no doubt that *Timon* could be improved, but it does make good sense dramatically as it now stands. I would not try to push the argument further than that. A dramatic fable by its very nature has many weaknesses in psychological characterization and tragic development, but it can produce some striking effects of simplicity, symmetry, and dramatic intensity. These excellences of *Timon* have perhaps been best appreciated by William Hazlitt, who in *The Characters of Shakespear's Plays* said that the play

> always appeared to us to be written with as intense a feeling of his subject as any one play of Shakespear. It is one of the few in which he seems to be in earnest throughout, never to trifle nor go out of his way. He does not relax in his efforts, nor lose sight of the unity of his design.

The imagery of *Timon* has an inner consistency that reflects the completeness of the play as a work of the imagination. Images of disease, especially venereal disease, pervade the action, evoking the sort of disgust one finds in *Hamlet* and *Troilus and Cressida*. Man's nature is infected and the soul of the world is sick. Timon's misanthropy itself rages as virulently as any disease. Animal imagery and predatory images of food and eating combine with those of disease to strengthen its negative aspect. In Timon's tirades, especially, all mankind is reduced to Hobbes's fearful state of nature, where the law of the jungle once more prevails. There is much elaborate play on the dog image, since Apemantus was himself a Cynic philosopher, a school derived from the Greek word for dog and thought to have currish properties. William Empson has discussed some of the overtones of this image in the play, and Caroline Spurgeon has pointed to the typical fawning image-cluster of dogs licking candy. The imagery of gold is too obvious to dwell on, but one should remember its double sense of evil and blessing. There are also traditional themes of winter and summer, cold and hot, constriction and flow, which follow the movement of the dramatic action.

Shakespeare seems to be completely in control of the style of *Timon*, which, if it has rough places that need to be revised, has also some extraordinary felicities. The play is not lyric in intent, so that some of the most vivid lyric effects are used negatively to support Timon's cruel imagination. The best passage of this sort is Timon's advice to Alcibiades to wage total war and spare none, for all are hypocritical dissemblers:

> Let not the virgin's cheek
> Make soft thy trenchant sword: for those milk paps,
> That through the window-bars bore at men's eyes,
> Are not within the leaf of pity writ,
> But set them down horrible traitors. (4.3.115–19)

"Window-bars" has sometimes been interpreted to mean the open-work squares on the bodice of a woman's frock, but its literal reference to the bars outside a window seems more natural. We have the image of a young virgin mewed up in her chamber, whose disturbing sexuality as she stands at her window transfixes men and pierces them through. One must struggle against one's natural instincts to overcome these charms, and the lyric expression is used for derogatory purposes. Another more shocking example of twisted lyricism is Timon's advice to Flavius:

> Hate all, curse all, show charity to none,
> But let the famished flesh slide from the bone
> Ere thou relieve the beggar. (536–38)

The physical force of the image is not buried in faded metaphor. Its cruelty is stark and unadorned.

One other stylistic excellence in *Timon* is its epigrammatic conciseness, the ability to pack a complex meaning into a brief phrase. There are many examples of this, some of them, as "feast-won, fast-lost" (2.2.181), founded on proverbs. Flavius' defense of Timon also suggests a proverb, although it is not a recorded one: "Never mind/ Was to be so unwise to be so kind" (5–6). The effect of compression probably depends upon the multiple connotations of "kind" and "unwise"; a paraphrase would demand a good deal of amplification. The most numerous examples of this kind of writing are, I think, in Act 3, Scene 5. Here the conciseness is part of the dramatic plan, and the Senators' brusque questions are ominous in their brevity: "Now, captain?", "What's that?", "How?", "What?", and then the explicit: "Do you dare our anger?" (6, 63, 90, 91, 95) which precedes Alcibiades' banishment. In the carefully articulated rhetoric of Alcibiades' oration, there are many of these pregnant phrases. When the First Senator states as his guiding principle, "He forfeits his own blood that spills another" (88), Alcibiades simply cannot believe what he has heard: "Must it be so? It must not be" (89). The repetition gives special point to the line, as it also does in Alcibiades' final soliloquy:

> I'm worse than mad. I have kept back their foes,
> While they have told their money, and let out
> Their coin upon large interest, I myself
> Rich only in large hurts. All those, for this?
>
> (105–08)

The ironic echoing of "large" prepares us for the antithesis of the final question. The deliberate ambiguity of "this" suggests a wide range of meanings: this banishment, this debasement, this travesty of justice, this perversion of honor and merit—in sum, this evil, corrupt, tyrannical city governed by cynically usurious Senators.

Timon has many of the qualities of satire and high comedy. In the attempt to depict the sophisticated, morally corrupt, and completely money-oriented life of Athens, Shakespeare uses a sharp realism of style expressed in easy colloquial speech. The scenes with the false friends in Act 3 (1, 2, 3) are the best sustained examples of this style. Lucullus' reply to Flaminius' request for money shows an unabashed ironic scorn: "La, la, la, la! 'Nothing doubting,' says he? Alas, good lord, a noble gentleman 'tis, if he would not keep so good a house" (3.1.23–25). Lucullus is completely at his ease, and his use of contracted speech forms throughout this scene indicates an assumed and contemptuous familiarity. Another example of Shakespeare's mastery of the colloquial style is Flavius' report of how the Senators reacted to his request for a loan:

They answer in a joint and corporate voice,
That now they are at fall, want treasure, cannot
Do what they would, are sorry; you are honorable,
But yet they could have wished—they know not;
Something hath been amiss—a noble nature
May catch a wrench—would all were well—'tis pity—
And so, intending other serious matters,
After distasteful looks, and these hard fractions,
With certain half-caps and cold-moving nods,
They froze me into silence.   (2.2.214–23)

"These hard fractions" show Shakespeare's skill at imitating, by syntax and phrase, the halting dishonesty of the Senators. The fragments are those of actual speech, and their disconnectedness is intended to soften the blow on Timon. Even such a glorious spender as Timon "May catch a wrench" and go broke, and, as Lucullus says, "this is no time to lend money, especially upon bare friendship without security" (3.1.44–45).

Another approach to the integrity of *Timon* is to consider the play in the context of Shakespeare's other works. *Timon* has most often been compared with *King Lear*. Coleridge called it an "after vibration" of *Lear*, and A. C. Bradley compared the two plays extensively in his study of Shakespearean tragedy. Both deal with the theme of ingratitude and its overpowering effects on Lear and Timon, who both react with a fierce indictment of man and society. But in *Lear* this indictment touches the protagonist, too, and leads him to a bitter self-awareness which is not present in *Timon*. There is no inward-turning in the latter play, no soul-searching of any sort, which gives it the effect of satire rather than tragedy. Both Lear and Timon are first shown in an atmosphere of false flattery and public adoration. They are soon reduced to primitive nature, but in Lear's case this stripping-down has a necessity lacking in Timon's, who chooses self-exile in the woods and perversely persists in it even after he has found gold. One may also compare Kent and Flavius, the unshakably loyal servants who minister to their masters in adversity, but Kent is individualized as a character by a keen, blunt-speaking wit, whereas Flavius only fulfills a type function. In both plays, the frequent contrast of "nothing" and "all" identifies the extreme nature of the tragic action, which eschews any happy mean between prosperity and adversity.

Timon is especially close to those dark, satirical plays that put a strong emphasis on sexual corruption: *Measure for Measure, Hamlet,* and *Troilus and Cressida.* While *Timon* conveys the strongest sense of sexual disease, it shares a disillusioned view of human nature and an overpowering sense of deceit and hypocrisy with these other plays. It has been suggested that all of these plays (except *Hamlet)* were written for the more fastidious audiences of the Inns of Court or the private theaters. That would help to explain the difficult, closely reasoned, and abstract character of many of their speeches.

There is a specific connection between *Timon* and *Troilus and Cressida* in the characters of Apemantus and Thersites. Both are scurrilous, churlish, and thoroughly unattractive truth-speakers, who, like professional fools, prick the illusions in their plays. Their own reality is never intended to be any alternative to the pretensions they attack, since they are both base and mean-spirited. Perhaps Apemantus, by his profession of Cynic philosophy, is a somewhat more attractive figure than the completely servile Thersites.

The relation of *Timon* to *Coriolanus* is so close that it deserves particular attention. Both plays are based on North's Plutarch for their essential details, and the exile of Alcibiades with his return to conquer his native city is very like the career of Coriolanus. The two are, in fact, parallel lives in Plutarch. The banishment of Alcibiades and Coriolanus is manipulated by a politically and morally corrupt group, whose mediocrity is disturbed by the presence of military heroes. The subsequent plea of the Senators to spare their city is also similar in the two plays. In structure both plays are divided into two distinct parts, one showing the wrong or evil, the other the revenge for it. The opening fable of Fortune's hill in *Timon* parallels the fable of the belly and the members in *Coriolanus;* both provide a convenient set of ideas by which to interpret the action, and both foreshadow what will eventually occur.

One could enumerate many similarities in detail between the two plays, but the larger similarities in conception are more important. *Timon* and *Coriolanus* are both tragedies that cannot be judged by the standards of Aristotle's *Poetics*: in neither play does the tragic protagonist have much awareness of what is happening to him, and there is no tragic recognition at all. Neither Timon nor Coriolanus has any sense of the middle state of man, the mean, the human condition. They are both absolutists, extremists, harsh individualists who wish to be either god or beast, but nothing in between. They are equally insensitive to human failings and weaknesses—even Timon's philanthropy is always public, never personal. Both plays put strong emphasis on public display and have many large scenes of crowded activity. There are very few personal or domestic scenes, and almost no attention at all is devoted to romantic heroines. The soliloquies in both plays are never used for purposes of self-analysis or self-exploration. Stylistically, both plays seem very objective and impersonal, and there are excellent examples in both of a condensed and telegraphic dramatic speech without lyric amplification. Both plays also have a good deal of satire, which draws on an extensive imagery of disease, animals, and food.

In the absence of any external evidence, I agree with E. K. Chambers in placing *Timon* after *Coriolanus* as the last of Shakespeare's tragedies, written sometime around 1608. However, Chambers' dating of *Timon* (in *William Shakespeare*, Vol. 1) is based on assumptions about Shakespeare's psychological and physical condition at the time of composition that are difficult to accept:

> Both *King Lear* and *Timon of Athens* seem to show symptoms of mental disturbance. But mental disturbance may come in waves. It may very likely only be a whimsy of my own that during the attempt at *Timon of Athens* a wave broke, then an illness followed, and that when it passed, the breach between the tragic and the romantic period was complete.

Timon has always been a favorite candidate for the "mythical sorrows of Shakespeare," and Chambers only echoes more than a century of romantic speculation on the dark corners of Shakespeare's soul. Georg Brandes in his *William*

Shakespeare said much the same thing in a more rapturous and unrestrained form:

> all that, in these years, Shakespeare has endured and experienced, thought and suffered, is concentrated into the one great despairing figure of Timon of Athens, "misanthropos," whose savage rhetoric is like a dark secretion of clotted blood and gall, drawn off to assuage pain.

Recently, a number of medical critics have stated that Timon is suffering from the classic symptoms of syphilis, which reach the stage of paresis by Act 4. Perhaps we must then postulate that Shakespeare himself was suffering from the French malady in order to be able to write about it. This is the same order of fallacy as attributing Shakespeare's bird-lore and flowerlore to his close observation of the Warwickshire countryside, despite the fact that they have figured in literary traditions at least as old as the ancient Greeks.

Shakespeare surely tried to protect himself from being taken for a Timonist by making Timon so unattractive and unsympathetic. "[Y]ond despised and ruinous man" (4.3.467) is a lost soul, self-exiled and self-damned by his own evil vision of reality. We cannot have become so uncritically enamored of the power of blackness not to see the truth of Apemantus' judgment:

> Thou hast cast away thyself, being like thyself:
> A madman so long, now a fool. (221–22)

We would not want to accept this, however, as a final appraisal of Timon, whose fierce energy and passion redeem him from the pettiness and rancor of his accusers. "Friendship's full of dregs," but to escape the humdrum complications of the common fate by trying to be either god or beast can be a more agonizing experience. Both Shakespeare's and Molière's misanthropes fascinate us and repel us because their attempt is so heroic, so uncompromising, and so inhuman.

—MAURICE CHARNEY

Dramatis Personae

Timon of Athens
Lucius, and } two flattering lords
Lucullus
Sempronius, another flattering lord
Ventidius, one of Timon's false friends
Apemantus, a churlish philosopher
Alcibiades, an Athenian captain
Poet
Painter
Jeweler
Merchant
[Flavius, steward to Timon]
Flaminius, one of Timon's servants
Servilius, another
[Lucilius, another]
Caphis
Philotus
Titus
Hortensius } several servants to usurers
[Servant to] Varro
[Servant to] Lucius
[Servant to Isidore]
[An Old Athenian]
[Three Strangers]
[A Page]
[A Fool]
[Phrynia } mistresses to Alcibiades
[Timandra
Certain Maskers [as] Cupid [and Amazons]
Certain Senators, certain Thieves, with divers other Servants and Attendants, [Lords, Officers, Soldiers]

[*Scene:* Athens and the neighboring woods]

The Life of Timon of Athens

ACT 1

Scene 1. [*Athens. Timon's house.*]

Enter Poet, Painter, Jeweler, Merchant
at several°1 doors.

Poet. Good day, sir.

Painter.   I am glad y'are well.

Poet. I have not seen you long; how goes the world?

Painter. It wears,° sir, as it grows.

Poet.   Ay that's well known.
  But what particular rarity? What strange,
  Which manifold record° not matches? See,   5
  Magic of bounty,° all these spirits thy power
  Hath conjured to attend. I know the merchant.

Painter. I know them both; th' other's a jeweler.

---

1 The degree sign (°) indicates a footnote, which is keyed to the text by line number. Text references are printed in **bold** type; the annotation follows in roman type.
1.1.s.d. **several** separate (the Poet and Painter enter at one door, the Jeweler and Merchant at another) 3 **wears** wears out 5 **manifold record** many and varied records, history ("record" accented on second syllable) 6 **bounty** generosity

Merchant. O 'tis a worthy lord.

Jeweler.   Nay that's most fixed.°

Merchant. A most incomparable man, breathed,° as it
10   were,
To an untirable and continuate° goodness.
He passes.°

Jeweler.   I have a jewel here—

Merchant. O pray let's see't. For the Lord Timon, sir?

Jeweler. If he will touch the estimate.° But for that—

Poet. [*Aside to Painter*] When we for recompense
15   have praised the vild,°
It stains the glory in that happy° verse
Which aptly sings the good.

Merchant. [*Looking at the jewel*] 'Tis a good form.

Jeweler. And rich. Here is a water,° look ye.

Painter. You are rapt, sir, in some work, some dedication
To the great lord.

20   *Poet.*   A thing slipped idly from me.
Our poesy is as a gum, which oozes
From whence 'tis nourished. The fire i' th' flint
Shows not till it be struck; our gentle flame
Provokes itself,° and like the current flies
25   Each bound it chases.° What have you there?

Painter. A picture, sir. When comes your book forth?

Poet. Upon the heels of my presentment,° sir.
Let's see your piece.

9 **fixed** certain 10 **breathed** exercised, trained 11 **continuate** uninterrupted 12 **passes** surpasses 14 **touch the estimate** offer the
expected price 15 **vild** vile 16 **happy** fortunate 18 **water** luster
(of a jewel) 23–24 **our gentle flame/Provokes itself** i.e., the inspiration of poets is spontaneous, not externally provoked like the "fire
i' th' flint" 25 **Each bound it chases** i.e., the stream flows towards
the shore but rebounds upon contact 27 **presentment** presentation
(to Timon)

Painter.   'Tis a good piece.

Poet. So 'tis; this comes off well and excellent.

Painter. Indifferent.°

Poet.   Admirable. How this grace   30
Speaks his own standing!° What a mental power
This eye shoots forth! How big° imagination
Moves in this lip! To th' dumbness° of the
   gesture
One might interpret.°

Painter. It is a pretty mocking° of the life.   35
Here is a touch—is't good?

Poet.   I will say of it,
It tutors nature; artificial strife°
Lives in these touches, livelier than life.

> *Enter certain Senators, [who pass over the*
>   *stage and exeunt].*

Painter. How this lord is followed!

Poet. The senators of Athens, happy men!   40

Painter. Look, moe!°

Poet. You see this confluence, this great flood of visi-
   tors:
I have in this rough work shaped out a man
Whom this beneath world° doth embrace and hug
With amplest entertainment. My free drift   45
Halts not particularly,° but moves itself
In a wide sea of wax;° no leveled° malice

---

30 **Indifferent** neither good nor bad 31 **standing** dignity, social
status 32 **big** (adverb) 33 **dumbness** silence (as in a dumb show)
34 **interpret** supply words 35 **mocking** imitation 37 **artificial strife**
the striving of art to outdo nature 41 **moe** more 44 **beneath
world** sublunary world (Timon as the moon) 46 **particularly** at
individuals 47 **sea of wax** (either a sea of inspiration as easily
molded as wax—not limited to a mere writing tablet of wax—or
perhaps a waxing sea swelling with inspiration) 47 **leveled** aimed
(at one person)

Infects one comma in the course I hold,
But flies an eagle flight, bold and forth on,
50   Leaving no tract° behind.

Painter. How shall I understand you?

Poet.   I will unbolt to you.
You see how all conditions,° how all minds,
As well of glib and slipp'ry creatures as
Of grave and austere quality, tender down°
55   Their services to Lord Timon. His large fortune,
Upon his good and gracious nature hanging,
Subdues and properties° to his love and tendance°
All sorts of hearts; yea, from the glass-faced°
            flatterer
To Apemantus, that few things loves better
60   Than to abhor himself—even he drops down
The knee before him, and returns in peace
Most rich in Timon's nod.

Painter.   I saw them speak together.

Poet. Sir, I have upon a high and pleasant hill
Feigned° Fortune to be throned. The base o' th'
            mount
65   Is ranked with all deserts,° all kind of natures
That labor on the bosom of this sphere
To propagate their states.° Amongst them all,
Whose eyes are on this sovereign lady fixed,
One do I personate of Lord Timon's frame,°
70   Whom Fortune with her ivory hand° wafts to her,

---

50 **tract** (either "trace" or "track")   52 **conditions** (1) social classes
(2) temperaments   54 **tender down** offer (as one offers money)
57 **properties** appropriates   57 **tendance** attendance   58 **glass-faced**
mirror-faced   64 **Feigned** imagined   65 **deserts** degrees of worth
67 **propagate their states** increase their possessions   69 **frame** (1)
disposition (2) physical stature   70 **ivory hand** hand white and
smooth as ivory (this is the right hand of Fortune, with which she
distributes her favors; with the left or dark hand she takes them
away)

Whose present° grace° to present slaves and ser-
        vants
Translates° his rivals.

Painter.   'Tis conceived to scope.°
    This throne, this Fortune, and this hill, methinks,
    With one man beckoned from the rest below,
    Bowing his head against the steepy mount   75
    To climb his happiness, would be well expressed
    In our condition.

Poet.   Nay, sir, but hear me on.
    All those which were his fellows but of late,
    Some better than his value, on the moment
    Follow his strides, his lobbies fill with tendance, 80
    Rain sacrificial whisperings° in his ear,
    Make sacred even his stirrup, and through him
    Drink° the free air.

Painter.   Ay marry,° what of these?

Poet. When Fortune in her shift and change of mood
    Spurns down her late beloved, all his dependants 85
    Which labored after him to the mountain's top,
    Even on their knees and hands, let him slip down,
    Not one accompanying his declining foot.

Painter. 'Tis common.
    A thousand moral paintings° I can show   90
    That shall demonstrate° these quick° blows of
        Fortune's
    More pregnantly than words. Yet you do well
    To show Lord Timon that mean° eyes have seen
    The foot above the head.°

---

71 **present** (1) existing now (2) immediate   71 **grace** graciousness,
generosity   72 **Translates** transforms   72 **to scope** to the purpose,
just right   81 **sacrificial whisperings** (lines 81–83 suggest the hieratic
atmosphere surrounding Timon, now high in Fortune's favor)   83
Drink breathe   83 **marry** indeed (originally "By Mary")   90 **moral
paintings** allegorical pictures (especially wall hangings)   91 **demonstrate** (accented on second syllable)   91 **quick** (1) swift (2) full
of life   93 **mean** lowly   94 **The foot above the head** i.e., in the
quick changes that Fortune brings, the foot of the lowliest may
suddenly appear above the head of the highest

Trumpets sound. Enter Lord Timon, addressing him-
self courteously to every suitor; [a Messenger from
Ventidius talking with him; Lucilius and other servants
following].

Timon.   Imprisoned is he, say you?

95 *Messenger.* Ay, my good lord; five talents° is his debt,
His means most short, his creditors most strait.°
Your honorable letter he desires
To those have shut him up, which failing,
Periods° his comfort.

Timon.   Noble Ventidius—well.
100 I am not of that feather° to shake off
My friend when he must need me. I do know him
A gentleman that well deserves a help,
Which he shall have. I'll pay the debt and free him.

Messenger. Your lordship ever binds° him.

105 *Timon.* Commend me to him; I will send his ransom,
And being enfranchised bid him come to me.
'Tis not enough to help the feeble up,
But to support him after. Fare you well.

Messenger. All happiness to your honor.   *Exit.*

Enter an Old Athenian.

Old Athenian. Lord Timon, hear me speak.

110 *Timon.*   Freely, good father.

Old Athenian. Thou hast a servant named Lucilius.

Timon. I have so. What of him?

Old Athenian. Most noble Timon, call the man before
thee.

Timon. Attends he here or no? Lucilius!

115 *Lucilius.* Here at your lordship's service.

95 **five talents** (see Introduction, pp.162–63)   96 **strait** strict   99 **Periods**
puts an end to   100 **feather** character   104 **binds** attaches by ties of
gratitude (with play on "free" in line 103)

Old Athenian. This fellow° here, Lord Timon, this thy
　　creature,°
By night frequents my house. I am a man
That from my first have been inclined to thrift,
And my estate deserves an heir more raised
Than one which holds a trencher.°

Timon.　　　　　　　　　　　　Well; what further? 120

Old Athenian. One only daughter have I, no kin else,
On whom I may confer what I have got.
The maid is fair, a° th' youngest for a bride,
And I have bred her at my dearest cost
In qualities of the best. This man of thine　　　　　　125
Attempts her love. I prithee, noble lord,
Join with me to forbid him her resort;°
Myself have spoke in vain.

Timon.　　　　　　　　The man is honest.

Old Athenian. Therefore he will be,° Timon.
His honesty rewards him in itself;　　　　　　　　　130
It must not bear° my daughter.

Timon.　　　　　　　　Does she love him?

Old Athenian. She is young and apt.
Our own precedent° passions do instruct us
What levity's in youth.

Timon.　　　　　　　Love you the maid?

Lucilius. Ay, my good lord, and she accepts of it.　　135

Old Athenian. If in her marriage my consent be miss-
　　ing,
I call the gods to witness, I will choose

---

116 **fellow, creature** (terms of contempt)　120 **trencher** wooden
plate or shallow dish on which meat is served (a servant who waits on
tables would hold a trencher)　123 **a** (a worn down form for "of")
127 **her resort** resort or access to her　129 **Therefore he will be** i.e.,
since Lucilius *is* honest (or honorable), he will therefore show his
honesty by not pursuing the Old Athenian's daughter　131 **bear**
carry away　133 **precedent** former (accented on second syllable)

Mine heir from forth the beggars of the world,
And dispossess her all.°

Timon.   How shall she be endowed,
140   If she be mated with an equal° husband?

Old Athenian. Three talents on the present;° in future,
   all.

Timon. This gentleman of mine hath served me long.
   To build his fortune I will strain a little,
   For 'tis a bond° in men. Give him thy daughter;
145   What you bestow, in him I'll counterpoise,°
   And make him weigh with her.

Old Athenian.   Most noble lord,
   Pawn me to this your honor, she is his.

Timon. My hand to thee, mine honor on my promise.

Lucilius. Humbly I thank your lordship; never may
150   That state or fortune fall into my keeping,
   Which is not owed° to you.
                          Exit [*Lucilius, with Old Athenian*].

Poet. Vouchsafe° my labor, and long live your lordship.

Timon. I thank you; you shall hear from me anon.
   Go not away. What have you there, my friend?

155 *Painter.* A piece of painting, which I do beseech
   Your lordship to accept.

Timon.   Painting is welcome.
   The painting is almost the natural man;
   For since dishonor traffics° with man's nature,
   He is but outside.° These penciled° figures are

---

139 **all** completely   140 **equal** (either socially or financially)   141 **on
the present** at once   144 **bond** obligation   145 **counterpoise** coun-
terbalance   151 **owed** (1) acknowledged to you as the cause of it (2)
due to you as a debt   152 **Vouchsafe** deign to accept   158 **traffics**
deals (pejorative sense)   159 **but outside** merely external, a false
semblance   159 **penciled** painted

Even such as they give out.° I like your work, 160
And you shall find I like it. Wait attendance
Till you hear further from me.

Painter.　　　　　　　　The gods preserve ye.

Timon. Well fare you, gentleman. Give me your hand;
We must needs dine together. Sir, your jewel
Hath suffered under praise.°

Jeweler.　　　　　　What, my lord, dispraise? 165

Timon. A mere° satiety of commendations.
If I should pay you for't as 'tis extolled,
It would unclew° me quite.

Jeweler.　　　　　　My lord, 'tis rated
As those which sell would give.° But you well
　　know,
Things of like value, differing in the owners, 170
Are prizèd by their masters.° Believe't, dear lord,
You mend° the jewel by the wearing it.

Timon. Well mocked.°

Merchant. No, my good lord; he speaks the common
　　tongue°
Which all men speak with him. 175

　　　　　　　Enter Apemantus.

Timon. Look who comes here; will you be chid?

Jeweler. We'll bear with your lordship.

Merchant.　　　　　　He'll spare none.

---

160 **Even such as they give out** i.e., painting, in contrast with human nature, is honest; it makes no pretense to be something other than what it appears to be 165 **under praise** in being praised, since the jewel is beyond praise (but the Jeweler takes it in the sense of "dispraise") 166 **mere** absolute 168 **unclew** undo 169 **As those which sell would give** i.e., at the wholesale price 171 **Are prizèd by their masters** are valued according to the social status of their owners 172 **mend** improve 173 **mocked** simulated (i.e., I know your flattery is only part of your sales talk) 174 **speaks the common tongue** says what everyone is saying

Timon. Good morrow to thee, gentle° Apemantus.

Apemantus. Till I be gentle, stay thou for thy good
     morrow—
180   When thou art Timon's dog, and these knaves
        honest.

Timon. Why dost thou call them knaves, thou know'st
        them not?

Apemantus. Are they not Athenians?

Timon. Yes.

Apemantus. Then I repent not.

185 *Jeweler.* You know me, Apemantus?

Apemantus. Thou know'st I do, I called thee by thy
        name.

Timon. Thou art proud, Apemantus.

Apemantus. Of nothing so much as that I am not like
190   Timon.

Timon. Whither art going?

Apemantus. To knock out an honest Athenian's
        brains.

Timon. That's a deed thou't die for.

195 *Apemantus.* Right, if doing nothing be death by th'
        law.

Timon. How lik'st thou this picture, Apemantus?

Apemantus. The best, for the innocence.°

Timon. Wrought he not well that painted it?

200 *Apemantus.* He wrought better that made the painter,
        and yet he's but a filthy° piece of work.

178 **gentle** (1) well-born (a conventional complimentary epithet) (2)
mild   198 **innocence** (1) harmlessness (2) foolishness   201 **filthy**
contemptible

Painter. Y'are a dog.°

Apemantus. Thy mother's of my generation.° What's she, if I be a dog?

Timon. Wilt dine with me, Apemantus?   205

Apemantus. No. I eat not lords.

Timon. And° thou shouldst, thou'dst anger ladies.

Apemantus. O they eat lords; so they come by great bellies.°

Timon. That's a lascivious apprehension.   210

Apemantus. So, thou apprehend'st it, take it for thy labor.

Timon. How dost thou like this jewel, Apemantus?

Apemantus. Not so well as plain-dealing, which will not cost a man a doit.°   215

Timon. What dost thou think 'tis worth?

Apemantus. Not worth my thinking. How now, poet?

Poet. How now, philosopher?

Apemantus. Thou liest.

Poet. Art not one?   220

Apemantus. Yes.

Poet. Then I lie not.

Apemantus. Art not a poet?

Poet. Yes.

---

202 **dog** (Apemantus is a Cynic philosopher; "cynic" is derived from the Greek word for dog)   203 **generation** (1) breed (2) persons born at about the same time   207 **And** if   208–09 **come by great bellies** become pregnant   215 **doit** a small Dutch coin worth less than a farthing (used as a type expression for any very small sum)

225 *Apemantus*. Then thou liest.° Look in thy last work,
      where thou hast feigned him° a worthy fellow.

Poet. That's not feigned, he is so.

Apemantus. Yes, he is worthy of thee, and to pay thee
      for thy labor. He that loves to be flattered is worthy
230   o' th' flatterer. Heavens, that I were a lord!

Timon. What wouldst do then, Apemantus?

Apemantus. E'en as Apemantus does now: hate a lord
      with my heart.

Timon. What, thyself?

235 *Apemantus*. Ay.

Timon. Wherefore?

Apemantus. That I had no angry wit to be a lord.°
      Art not thou a merchant?

Merchant. Ay, Apemantus.

240 *Apemantus*. Traffic° confound thee, if the gods will
      not.

Merchant. If traffic do it, the gods do it.

Apemantus. Traffic's thy god, and thy god confound
      thee.

        Trumpet sounds. Enter a Messenger.

245 *Timon*. What trumpet's that?

Messenger. 'Tis Alcibiades and some twenty horse,°
      All of companionship.°

Timon. Pray entertain them, give them guide to us.
                                      [*Exeunt some Attendants*.]
      You must needs dine with me. Go not you hence

---

225 **liest** (a play on the old idea that poetry is a *mimesis*, imitation,
mocking, or feigning of reality and therefore a lie) 226 **him** i.e.,
Timon 237 **no angry wit to be a lord** no more wit in my anger than
to wish to be a lord (?) 240 **Traffic** trade, business 246 **horse**
horsemen 247 **All of companionship** all of the same party

Till I have thanked you. When dinner's done   250
Show me this piece. I am joyful of your sights.°

Enter Alcibiades with the rest.

Most welcome, sir.

Apemantus.   So, so.
Their° aches° contract and starve° your supple
    joints!
That there should be small love amongst these
    sweet knaves,
And all this courtesy! The strain of man's bred out   255
Into baboon and monkey.

Alcibiades. Sir, you have saved° my longing, and I
    feed
Most hungerly on your sight.

Timon.   Right welcome, sir.
Ere we depart, we'll share a bounteous time
In different pleasures. Pray you let us in.   260
                    Exeunt [all but Apemantus].

Enter two Lords.

First Lord. What time a day is't, Apemantus?

Apemantus. Time to be honest.

First Lord. That time serves still.°

Apemantus. The most accursèd thou that still omit'st°
    it.   265

Second Lord. Thou art going to Lord Timon's feast?

Apemantus. Ay, to see meat fill knaves and wine heat
    fools.

Second Lord. Fare thee well, fare thee well.

251 **of your sights** at the sight of you   253 **Their** i.e., of Alcibiades
and his soldiers   253 **aches** (the reference is probably to venereal
disease—"aches" is disyllabic, pronounced "aitches")   253 **starve**
destroy   257 **saved** anticipated and so prevented   263 **still** always
264 **omit'st** neglects

270 *Apemantus.* Thou art a fool to bid me farewell twice.

Second Lord. Why, Apemantus?

Apemantus. Shouldst have kept one to thyself, for I
    mean to give thee none.

First Lord. Hang thyself!

275 *Apemantus.* No, I will do nothing at thy bidding.
    Make thy requests to thy friend.

Second Lord. Away, unpeaceable° dog, or I'll spurn
    thee hence.

Apemantus. I will fly like a dog the heels a th' ass.
                                                    [*Exit.*]

First Lord. He's opposite to° humanity. Come, shall
280   we in
    And taste Lord Timon's bounty? He outgoes
    The very heart of kindness.

Second Lord. He pours it out. Plutus, the god of gold,
    Is but his steward; no meed° but he repays
285 Sevenfold above itself. No gift to him
    But breeds the giver a return exceeding
    All use of quittance.°

First Lord.   The noblest mind he carries°
    That ever governed man.

Second Lord.   Long may he live
    In fortunes. Shall we in?

First Lord.   I'll keep you company.   *Exeunt.*

---

277 **unpeaceable** quarrelsome   280 **opposite to** (1) hostile to (2) the
reverse of   284 **meed** (1) merit, desert (2) gift (?)   287 **All use of
quittance** all the customary returns made in repayment of debts (one
meaning of "use" is "interest")   287 **carries** bears

[Scene 2. *Timon's house*.]

Hautboys° playing loud music. A great banquet served in; and then enter Lord Timon, the States,° the Athenian Lords, Ventidius (which Timon redeemed from prison), [and Alcibiades. Steward and others attending.] Then comes dropping after all, Apemantus, discontentedly, like himself.

Ventidius. Most honored Timon,
  It hath pleased the gods to remember my father's
     age,
  And call him to long peace.
  He is gone happy, and has left me rich.
  Then, as in grateful virtue I am bound   5
  To your free° heart, I do return those talents
  Doubled with thanks and service, from whose help
  I derived liberty.

Timon.   O by no means,
  Honest Ventidius. You mistake my love;
  I gave it freely ever, and there's none   10
  Can truly say he gives, if he receives.
  If our betters° play at that game, we must not dare
  To imitate them; faults that are rich are fair.°

Ventidius. A noble spirit.

Timon. Nay, my lords, ceremony° was but devised at
     first   15
  To set a gloss on faint deeds, hollow welcomes,
  Recanting goodness, sorry ere 'tis shown.

1.2.s.d. **Hautboys** oboes s.d. **the States** persons of state, the Senators 6 **free** generous 12 **our betters** those of higher rank 13 **faults that are rich are fair** i.e., the faults of rich persons are made to seem attractive because of their wealth 15 **ceremony** ceremonious attitudes

But where there is true friendship, there needs none.
Pray sit; more welcome are ye to my fortunes
20   Than my fortunes to me.

First Lord. My lord, we always have confessed it.

Apemantus. Ho, ho, confessed it? Hanged it,° have
    you not?

Timon. O Apemantus, you are welcome.

Apemantus. No, you shall not make me welcome.
25   I come to have thee thrust me out of doors.

Timon. Fie, th'art a churl, y'have got a humor° there
    Does not become a man; 'tis much to blame.
    They say, my lords, *Ira furor brevis est,°* but yond
    man is ever angry. Go, let him have a table by
30   himself, for he does neither affect° company, nor is
    he fit for't indeed.

Apemantus. Let me stay at thine apperil,° Timon.
    I come to observe, I give thee warning on't.

Timon. I take no heed of thee. Th'art an Athenian,
35   therefore welcome. I myself would have no power;°
    prithee let my meat make thee silent.

Apemantus. I scorn thy meat; 'twould choke me, for I
    should ne'er flatter thee.° O you gods! What a num-
    ber of men eats Timon, and he sees 'em not! It grieves
40   me to see so many dip their meat in one man's
    blood, and all the madness is, he cheers them up
    too.
    I wonder men dare trust themselves with men.
    Methinks they should invite them without knives:°
45   Good for their meat, and safer for their lives.

---

22 **confessed it? Hanged it** (an allusion to the proverb "Confess and
be hanged") 26 **humor** temperamental quirk (in the old physio-
logical sense of the four humors) 28 **Ira furor brevis est** anger is
a brief fury or madness (Horace, *Epistles,* 1.2.62) 30 **affect** (1) like
(2) seek out 32 **apperil** peril 35 **no power** i.e., to force you to be
silent 37–38 **'twould ... thee** i.e., Apemantus would prefer to choke
on Timon's meat than to flatter him 44 **knives** (dinner guests normally brought their own knives)

There's much example for't; the fellow that sits
next him, now parts bread with him, pledges the
breath of him in a divided draught,° is the readiest
man to kill him. 'T'as been proved. If I were a
huge° man, I should fear to drink at meals,   50
Lest they should spy my windpipe's dangerous
    notes;°
Great men should drink with harness° on their
    throats.

Timon. My lord, in heart;° and let the health go round.

Second Lord. Let it flow this way, my good lord.

Apemantus. Flow this way? A brave° fellow. He keeps   55
his tides° well. Those healths will make thee and
thy state° look ill, Timon.
Here's that which is too weak to be a sinner,
Honest water, which ne'er left man i' th' mire.
This and my food are equals, there's no odds;   60
Feasts° are too proud to give thanks to the gods.

Apemantus' Grace.

Immortal gods, I crave no pelf;°
I pray for no man but myself.
Grant I may never prove so fond°
To trust man on his oath or bond,   65
Or a harlot for her weeping,
Or a dog that seems a-sleeping,
Or a keeper° with my freedom,
Or my friends if I should need 'em.
Amen. So fall to't: 70

---

48 **a divided draught** a drink from a cup that is passed around the
table 50 **huge** important 51 **Lest ... notes** i.e., lest men should
cut my throat when my head is tilted backward (with additional
allusion to the windpipe as a musical instrument, like a bagpipe)
52 **harness** armor 53 **My lord, in heart** (a toast) 55 **brave** excellent
56 **tides** times (with play on the usual sense, linked to "flow")
57 **state** estate, fortune 61 **Feasts** i.e., those who give feasts 62 **pelf**
possessions 64 **fond** foolish 68 **keeper** jailer

Rich men sin, and I eat root.   [*Eats and drinks.*]
Much good dich° thy good heart, Apemantus.

Timon. Captain Alcibiades, your heart's in the field
now.

75 *Alcibiades*. My heart is ever at your service, my lord.

Timon. You had rather be at a breakfast of° enemies
than a dinner of friends.

Alcibiades. So° they were bleeding new, my lord,
there's no meat like 'em; I could wish my best
80   friend at such a feast.

Apemantus. Would all those flatterers were thine enemies then, that then thou mightst kill 'em—and
bid° me to 'em.

First Lord. Might we but have that happiness, my
85   lord, that you would once use our hearts,° whereby
we might express some part of our zeals, we should
think ourselves for ever perfect.°

Timon. O no doubt, my good friends, but the gods
themselves have provided that I shall have much
90   help from you: how had you been my friends else?
Why have you that charitable° title from° thousands, did not you chiefly belong to my heart? I
have told more of you to myself than you can
with modesty speak in your own behalf; and thus
95   far I confirm° you. O you gods, think I, what
need we have any friends, if we should ne'er have
need of 'em? They were the most needless creatures
living should we ne'er have use for 'em, and
would most resemble sweet instruments hung up
100   in cases, that keeps their sounds to themselves.
Why I have often wished myself poorer that I

72 **dich** may it do (?)   76 **of** consisting of (but later in the sentence
it means "with")   78 **So** provided that   83 **bid** invite   85 **use our
hearts** i.e., make trial of the feelings in our hearts   87 **perfect** i.e., in
our happiness in demonstrating our love for Timon   91 **charitable**
loving, kindly   91 **from** from among   95 **confirm** sanction, cor-
roborate (your claims as friends)

might come nearer° to you. We are born to do
benefits; and what better or properer can we call
our own than the riches of our friends? O what a
precious comfort 'tis to have so many like brothers   105
commanding one another's fortunes. O joy's e'en
made away ere't can be born.° Mine eyes cannot
hold out water,° methinks. To forget their faults,°
I drink to you.

Apemantus. Thou weep'st to make them drink,°
Timon.   110

Second Lord. Joy had the like conception° in our eyes,
And at that instant like a babe sprung up.°

Apemantus. Ho, ho! I laugh to think that babe a bastard.

Third Lord. I promise you, my lord, you moved me
much.

Apemantus. Much.   *Sound tucket.°*   115

Timon. What means that trump?

Enter Servant.

How now?

Servant. Please you, my lord, there are certain ladies
most desirous of admittance.

Timon. Ladies? What are their wills?

Servant. There comes with them a forerunner, my   120
lord, which bears that office to signify their pleasures.°

---

102 **nearer** (1) closer to your hearts (2) closer to your financial status
106–07 **e'en ... born** i.e., our weeping for joy seems to destroy joy
before it properly exists   108 **hold out water** keep out tears   108
faults defects   110 **to make them drink** (1) to provide drink for
them (they drink up your tears, and you and your estate, too) (2) to
furnish a pretext for their carousing   111 **the like conception** a similar birth (i.e., accompanied with tears)   112 **like a babe sprung up**
i.e., the sight of Timon's joy immediately caused the birth of a like
joy in the eyes of his friends   115s.d. **tucket** a flourish on a trumpet
121–22 **pleasures** wishes

Timon. I pray let them be admitted.

[*Enter Cupid.*]

Cupid. Hail to thee, worthy Timon, and to all
125   That of his bounties taste. The five best senses
Acknowledge thee their patron, and come freely
To gratulate° thy plenteous bosom. Th' ear,
Taste, touch, all, pleased from thy table rise;
They only now come but to feast thine eyes.°

Timon. They're welcome all; let 'em have kind admit-
130   tance.
Music° make their welcome.   [*Exit Cupid.*]

First Lord. You see, my lord, how ample y'are beloved.

[*Music.*] *Enter Cupid with the Masque*° *of Ladies* [*as*]
Amazons,° *with lutes in their hands, dancing and
playing.*

Apemantus. Hoy-day!°
What a sweep° of vanity comes this way.
135   They dance? They are madwomen.
Like° madness is the glory° of this life,
As this pomp shows to° a little oil and root.
We make ourselves fools to disport° ourselves,
And spend our flatteries to drink° those men
140   Upon whose age we void° it up again
With poisonous spite and envy.°
Who lives that's not depravèd or depraves?°
Who dies that bears not one spurn° to their graves

---

127 **gratulate** (1) greet (2) gratify, please   129 **but to feast thine eyes**
i.e., only to appeal to the sense of sight, whereas at Timon's banquet
all the senses were gratified   131 **Music** i.e., let music   132s.d.
Masque an elaborate allegorical show or entertainment with emphasis on spectacle, music, and dance   132s.d. **Amazons** legendary
female warriors   133 **Hoy-day** (exclamation of surprise)   134 **sweep**
(in reference to the sweeping motion of the dancers)   136 **Like** similar   136 **glory** vainglory   137 **to** compared to   138 **disport** amuse
139 **drink** drink the health of   140 **void** vomit   141 **envy** malice
142 **depravèd or depraves** slandered or a slanderer   143 **spurn** insult

Of their friends' gift?°
I should fear those that dance before me now   145
Would one day stamp upon me. 'T'as been done.
Men shut their doors against a setting sun.

> *The Lords rise from table, with much
> adoring of° Timon, and to show their
> loves, each single out an Amazon, and
> all dance, men with women, a lofty
> strain or two to the hautboys, and cease.*

Timon. You have done our pleasures much grace, fair
  ladies,
Set a fair fashion on° our entertainment,
Which was not half so beautiful and kind.°   150
You have added worth unto't and luster,
And entertained me with mine own device.°
I am to thank you for't.

First Lady. My lord, you take us even at the best.°

Apemantus. Faith, for the worst is filthy, and would   155
  not hold taking,° I doubt me.°

Timon. Ladies, there is an idle banquet° attends you,
  Please you to dispose yourselves.°

All Ladies. Most thankfully, my lord.
                    Exeunt [Cupid and Ladies].

Timon. Flavius.   160

Flavius. My lord.

Timon.   The little casket bring me hither.

Flavius. Yes, my lord. *[Aside]* More jewels yet?

---

144 **gift** giving   147s.d. **adoring of** paying homage to   149 **Set a
fair fashion on** given a pleasant semblance to   150 **kind** gracious
152 **mine own device** (suggests that Timon designed the masque or at
least had the idea for it)   154 **take us even at the best** judge us in the
most favorable and complimentary way   155–56 **would not hold
taking** i.e., sexual "taking" is not possible because of rottenness
caused by venereal disease   156 **doubt me** fear, suspect (reflexive)
157 **idle banquet** trifling dessert or light collation   158 **Please you to
dispose yourselves** if you please to take your places

There is no crossing him in's humor,°
Else I should tell him well, i' faith I should,
When all's spent, he'd be crossed° then, and° he
165   could.
'Tis pity bounty had not eyes behind,
That man might ne'er be wretched for his mind.°

                                        Exit.

First Lord. Where be our men?

Servant. Here, my lord, in readiness.

170 *Second Lord.* Our horses.

               Enter Flavius [with the casket].

Timon. O my friends,
    I have one word to say to you. Look you, my good
      lord,
    I must entreat you honor me so much
    As to advance° this jewel; accept it and wear it,
175 Kind my lord.

First Lord. I am so far already in your gifts—

All. So are we all.

                  Enter a Servant.

Servant. My lord, there are certain nobles of the
      senate newly alighted, and come to visit you.

180 *Timon.* They are fairly° welcome.

Flavius. I beseech your honor, vouchsafe me a word;
      it does concern you near.

Timon. Near? Why then another time I'll hear thee. I
      prithee let's be provided to show them entertain-
185   ment.

Flavius. [*Aside*] I scarce know how.

163 **no crossing him in's humor** no thwarting him in his capricious
disposition   165 **crossed** (1) thwarted (2) have his debts canceled
("crossed" off a list) (3) be given money (have his palm "crossed")
165 **and** if   167 **for his mind** for his generous inclinations   174 **ad-**
vance enhance in value (by your wearing it)   180 **fairly** courteously

Enter another Servant.

Second Servant. May it please your honor, Lord
  Lucius,
Out of his free love, hath presented to you
Four milk-white horses, trapped in silver.°

Timon. I shall accept them fairly. Let the presents   190
  Be worthily entertained.°

         Enter a third Servant.
            How now? What news?

Third Servant. Please you, my lord, that honorable
  gentleman Lord Lucullus entreats your company
  tomorrow to hunt with him, and has sent your
  honor two brace° of greyhounds.   195

Timon. I'll hunt with him, and let them be received
  Not without fair reward.

Flavius. [*Aside*]   What will this come to?
  He commands us to provide, and give great gifts,
  And all out of an empty coffer;
  Nor will he know his purse, or yield° me this,   200
  To show him what a beggar his heart is,
  Being of no power to make his wishes good.
  His promises fly so beyond his state°
  That what he speaks is all in debt; he owes for
    ev'ry word.
  He is so kind that he now pays interest for't;   205
  His land's put to their books.° Well, would I were
  Gently put out of office before I were forced out.
  Happier is he that has no friend to feed
  Than such that do e'en enemies exceed.°
  I bleed inwardly for my lord.   *Exit.* 210

---

189 **trapped in silver** with harness coverings adorned in silver
191 **worthily entertained** appropriately received 195 **two brace** two
pairs 200 **yield** grant 203 **state** estate, possessions 206 **put to
their books** mortgaged (entered on creditors' account books)
209 **Than such that do e'en enemies exceed** (1) than such a number
that surpasses the number of one's enemies (2) than such sort of
friends whose demands go beyond those of one's enemies

Timon. You do yourselves much wrong,
   You bate° too much of your own merits.
   Here, my lord, a trifle of our love.

Second Lord. With more than common thanks I will
   receive it.

215 *Third Lord.* O he's the very soul of bounty.

Timon. And now I remember, my lord, you gave good
   words the other day of a bay courser° I rode on.
   'Tis yours because you liked it.

First Lord. O I beseech you pardon me, my lord, in
220   that.°

Timon. You may take my word, my lord, I know no
   man can justly praise but what he does affect.° I
   weigh° my friend's affection with° mine own. I'll
   tell you true, I'll call to you.°

225 *All Lords.* O none so welcome.

Timon. I take all and your several° visitations
   So kind to heart, 'tis not enough to give.°
   Methinks I could deal° kingdoms to my friends,
   And ne'er be weary. Alcibiades,
230   Thou art a soldier, therefore seldom rich;
   It° comes in charity to thee, for all thy living°
   Is 'mongst the dead, and all the lands thou hast
   Lie in a pitched field. °

Alcibiades. Ay, defiled land,° my lord.

235 *First Lord.* We are so virtuously bound—

Timon. And so am I to you.

212 **bate** abate, undervalue 217 **bay courser** reddish-brown stallion
219–20 **in that** in accepting your gift (because I seemed to solicit it)
222 **affect** like, desire to possess 223 **weigh** consider 223 **with**
equal with 223–24 **I'll tell you true, I'll call to you** I assure you I
will call on you 226 **all and your several** the sum total (an inten-
sive form) 227 **'tis not enough to give** i.e., mere gifts, no matter
how great, cannot truly express the feeling in my heart 228 **deal**
distribute 231 **It** what you receive, a gift 231 **living** (1) existence
(2) property (3) livelihood 233 **pitched field** field prepared for a
battle 234 **defiled land** (a quibble on the proverb, "He that toucheth
pitch shall be defiled," *Ecclesiasticus* 13:1)

Second Lord. So infinitely endeared°—

Timon. All to you.° Lights, more lights!

First Lord. The best of happiness, honor, and fortunes
Keep with you, Lord Timon.   240

Timon. Ready for his friends.   *Exeunt Lords.*

Apemantus.   What a coil's° here,
Serving of becks° and jutting out of bums!°
I doubt whether their legs° be worth the sums
That are given for 'em. Friendship's full of dregs;
Methinks false hearts should never have sound
legs.°   245
Thus honest fools lay out their wealth on curtsies.°

Timon. Now Apemantus, if thou wert not sullen,
I would be good to thee.

Apemantus. No, I'll nothing; for if I should be bribed
too, there would be none left to rail upon° thee,   250
and then thou wouldst sin the faster. Thou giv'st so
long, Timon, I fear me thou wilt give away thyself in paper° shortly. What needs these feasts,
pomps, and vainglories?

Timon. Nay, and you begin to rail on society once, I   255
am sworn not to give regard to you. Farewell, and
come with better music.   *Exit.*

Apemantus. So. Thou wilt not hear me now, thou
shalt not then.°
I'll lock thy heaven° from thee.
O that men's ears should be   260
To counsel deaf, but not to flattery.   *Exit.*

237 **endeared** indebted 238 **All to you** i.e., I am all of these things
to you rather than vice versa 241 **coil** fuss, bustle, confusion
242 **Serving of becks** offering of nods or curtsies 242 **bums** posteri-
ors 243 **legs** (1) bows (cf. "to make a leg") (2) the limbs themselves
245 **sound legs** i.e., legs healthy enough to make obeisances 246
curtsies (1) bows (2) courtesies (a different spelling of the same word)
250 **rail upon** revile 253 **in paper** i.e., in promissory notes and other
paper records of debts 258 **thou shalt not then** you will not be able
to listen to me later, when you are bankrupt 259 **thy heaven** i.e.,
the advice by which I might have saved you from ruin

[ACT 2

Scene 1. *A Senator's house.*]

Enter a Senator.

Senator. And late° five thousand. To Varro and to
　　Isidore
He owes nine thousand, besides my former sum,
Which makes it five and twenty. Still° in motion
Of raging waste? It cannot hold,° it will not.
5　　If I want gold, steal but a beggar's dog
And give it Timon—why the dog coins gold.
If I would sell my horse and buy twenty moe
Better than he—why give my horse to Timon;
Ask nothing, give it him, it foals me straight,°
10　　And able horses. No porter° at his gate,
But rather one that smiles, and still invites
All that pass by. It cannot hold; no reason
Can sound his state in safety.° Caphis, ho!
Caphis, I say!

2.1.1 **late** lately　3 **Still** always　4 **hold** last　9 **straight** immediately
10 **No porter** (because a porter's function is to keep out undesirable
persons)　12–13 **no reason/Can sound his state in safety** i.e., because
Timon is insolvent, no reasonable person can safely fathom or test
his estate ("sound" in its nautical sense)

Enter Caphis.

Caphis.   Here, sir, what is your pleasure?

Senator. Get on your cloak, and haste you to Lord
    Timon;   15
    Importune him for my moneys; be not ceased
    With slight denial; nor then silenced when
    "Commend me to your master" and the cap
    Plays in the right hand, thus°—but tell him,
    My uses° cry to me; I must serve my turn   20
    Out of mine own;° his days and times° are past,
    And my reliances on his fracted° dates
    Have smit my credit. I love and honor him,
    But must not break my back to heal his finger.
    Immediate are my needs, and my relief   25
    Must not be tossed and turned to me in words,
    But find supply immediate. Get you gone;
    Put on a most importunate aspect,°
    A visage of demand; for I do fear,
    When every feather sticks in his own wing,°   30
    Lord Timon will be left a naked gull,°
    Which flashes now a phoenix.° Get you gone.

Caphis. I go, sir.

Senator. Ay, go sir! Take the bonds along with you,
    And have the dates in.° Come!

Caphis.   I will, sir.

Senator.   Go!   35

                             Exeunt.

18–19 **"Commend me ..."** ... **thus** (examples of anticipated ceremonious delays by Timon) 20 **uses** financial needs 21 **mine own**
i.e., my own money 21 **days and times** due dates of his debts
22 **fracted** broken 28 **aspect** (accented on second syllable) 30
sticks in his own wing is returned to the bird to which it belongs
(i.e., when Timon's debts, and the security he has given for them, are
settled) 31 **gull** (1) unfledged bird (2) credulous dupe 32 **phoenix**
a rare legendary bird which immolated itself and was reborn from
its own ashes; a unique or matchless person 35 **have the dates in**
put in the exact dates when the bonds fall due

[Scene 2. *Timon's house*.]

*Enter [Flavius, the] Steward, with many bills in
his hand.*

Flavius. No care, no stop, so senseless of expense
　　That he will neither know how to maintain it,
　　Nor cease his flow of riot.° Takes no accompt
　　How things go from him, nor resumes no care°
5　　Of what is to continue. Never mind
　　Was to be so unwise to be so kind.°
　　What shall be done he will not hear, till feel.
　　I must be round° with him, now he comes from
　　　　hunting.
　　Fie, fie, fie, fie!

*Enter Caphis, [with the Servants of] Isidore
and Varro.*

Caphis. Good even, Varro. What, you come for
10　　money?

Varro's Servant. Is't not your business too?

Caphis. It is; and yours too, Isidore?

Isidore's Servant. It is so.

Caphis. Would we were all discharged.°

15　*Varro's Servant.* I fear it.°

Caphis. Here comes the lord.

Enter Timon and his Train, [and Alcibiades].

Timon. So soon as dinner's done, we'll forth again,

2.2.3 **riot** extravagance, irresponsible reveling 4 **resumes no care**
has no concern 6 **to be so kind** (1) as to be so generous (2) in order
to be so generous 8 **round** blunt 14 **discharged** paid (of a debt)
15 **I fear it** I doubt it

My Alcibiades. [*To Caphis*] With me, what is your
   will?

Caphis. My lord, here is a note of certain dues.

Timon. Dues? Whence are you?

Caphis.   Of Athens here, my lord.   20

Timon. Go to my steward.

Caphis. Please it your lordship, he hath put me off
   To the succession of new days° this month.
   My master is awaked by great occasion
   To call upon his own, and humbly prays you   25
   That with your other noble parts you'll suit°
   In giving him his right.

Timon.   Mine honest friend,
   I prithee but repair° to me next morning.

Caphis. Nay, good my lord—

Timon.   Contain thyself, good friend.

Varro's Servant. One Varro's servant, my good lord—   30

Isidore's Servant. From Isidore; he humbly prays
   your speedy payment.

Caphis. If you did know, my lord, my master's
   wants—

Varro's Servant. 'Twas due on° forfeiture, my lord, six   35
   weeks and past.

Isidore's Servant. Your steward puts me off, my lord,
   and I am sent expressly to your lordship.

Timon. Give me breath.
   I do beseech you, good my lords, keep on;°   40
   I'll wait upon you instantly.
                    [*Exeunt Alcibiades and Lords.*]

23 **To the succession of new days** from one day to the next   26 **That . . .
suit** i.e., that you will act in accordance with your other noble
qualities   28 **repair** return   35 **on** on penalty of   40 **keep on** go
ahead

[*To Flavius*] Come hither. Pray you,
How goes the world,° that I am thus encount'red
With clamorous demands of broken bonds,
And the detention° of long since due debts
Against my honor?

45 *Flavius.*   Please you, gentlemen,
The time is unagreeable to this business.
Your importunacy° cease till after dinner,
That I may make his lordship understand
Wherefore you are not paid.

50 *Timon.* Do so, my friends. See them well entertained.
                                        Exit.

Flavius. Pray draw near.   [*Exit.*]

          Enter Apemantus and Fool.

Caphis. Stay, stay, here comes the fool with Ape-
     mantus.
     Let's ha' some sport with 'em.

Varro's Servant. Hang him, he'll abuse us.

55 *Isidore's Servant.* A plague upon him, dog!

Varro's Servant. How dost, fool?

Apemantus. Dost dialogue with thy shadow?

Varro's Servant. I speak not to thee.

Apemantus. No, 'tis to thyself. [*To the Fool*] Come
60   away.

Isidore's Servant. [*To Varro's Servant*] There's the
     fool hangs on your back already.

Apemantus. No, thou stand'st single,° th'art not on
     him yet.

65 *Caphis.* Where's the fool now?

Apemantus. He last asked the question. Poor rogues
     and usurers' men, bawds between gold and want.

42 **How goes the world** what is going on   44 **detention** withholding
payment   47 **importunacy** urgent solicitation   63 **single** alone

All Servants. What are we, Apemantus?

Apemantus. Asses.

All Servants. Why?   70

Apemantus. That you ask me what you are, and do not know yourselves. Speak to 'em, fool.

Fool. How do you, gentlemen?

All Servants. Gramercies,° good fool. How does your mistress?   75

Fool. She's e'en setting on water to scald° such chickens as you are. Would we could see you at Corinth.°

Apemantus. Good, gramercy.

Enter Page.

Fool. Look you, here comes my mistress' page.   80

Page. [*To the Fool*] Why, how now, captain? What do you in this wise company? How dost thou, Apemantus?

Apemantus. Would I had a rod° in my mouth, that I might answer thee profitably.°   85

Page. Prithee, Apemantus, read me the superscription° of these letters. I know not which is which.

Apemantus. Canst not read?

Page. No.

Apemantus. There will little learning die then that   90
day thou art hanged. This is to Lord Timon, this to Alcibiades. Go, thou wast born a bastard, and thou'lt die a bawd.

74 **Gramercies** thanks   76 **scald** a method of removing feathers from chickens (with suggestions of loss of hair in venereal disease, and of sweating in a heated tub, which was one of the treatments of venereal disease)   78 **Corinth** ancient city noted for licentiousness (hence a cant term for brothel or red-light district)   84 **rod** stick to beat you 85 **profitably** for your profit or improvement   86–87 **superscription** address

Page. Thou wast whelped a dog, and thou shalt fam-
95 ish a dog's death.° Answer not, I am gone.   *Exit*.

Apemantus. E'en so thou outrun'st grace.° Fool, I
will go with you to Lord Timon's.

Fool. Will you leave me there?

Apemantus. If Timon stay at home. You three serve
100 three usurers?

All Servants. Ay; would they served us.

Apemantus. So would I—as good a trick as ever
hangman served thief.

Fool. Are you three usurers' men?

105 *All Servants*. Ay, fool.

Fool. I think no usurer but has a fool to his servant.
My mistress is one, and I am her fool. When men
come to borrow of your masters, they approach
sadly,° and go away merry; but they enter my
110 mistress' house merrily, and go away sadly. The
reason of this?

Varro's Servant. I could render one.

Apemantus. Do it then, that we may account thee a
whoremaster and a knave, which notwithstanding,
115 thou shalt be no less esteemed.

Varro's Servant. What is a whoremaster, fool?

Fool. A fool in good clothes, and something like thee.
'Tis a spirit; sometime't appears like a lord, sometime like a lawyer, sometime like a philosopher,
120 with two stones° moe than's artificial one.° He is
very often like a knight; and generally, in all shapes

94–95 **famish a dog's death** die by famishing, a mean death appropriate for a dog 96 **E'en so thou outrun'st grace** i.e., by leaving
now and not listening to my profitable answer, you will never receive
grace 109 **sadly** gravely 120 **stones** testicles 120 **artificial one**
philosopher's stone (a highly refined substance which could turn
base metals into gold)

that man goes up and down in, from fourscore to
thirteen, this spirit walks in.

Varro's Servant. Thou are not altogether a fool.

Fool. Nor thou altogether a wise man. As much fool-   125
ery as I have, so much wit thou lack'st.

Apemantus. That answer might have become Apemantus.

    Enter Timon and [Flavius, the] Steward.

All Servants. Aside, aside, here comes Lord Timon.

Apemantus. Come with me, fool, come.   130

Fool. I do not always follow lover, elder brother, and
woman;° sometime the philosopher.

Flavius. Pray you, walk near: I'll speak with you
anon.°   *Exeunt [Apemantus, Fool, and Servants].*

Timon. You make me marvel wherefore ere this time
Had you not fully laid my state° before me,   135
That I might so have rated° my expense
As I had leave of means.°

Flavius.   You would not hear me.
At many leisures° I proposed—

Timon.   Go to.°
Perchance some single vantages° you took
When my indisposition° put you back,   140
And that unaptness° made your minister°
Thus to excuse yourself.

Flavius.   O my good lord,
At many times I brought in my accompts,

131–32 **lover, elder brother, and woman** (persons who might be expected to be generous)   133 **anon** soon   135 **state** financial situation
136 **rated** regulated   137 **As I had leave of means** as my means
would allow   138 **At many leisures** i.e., when you were at leisure
138 **Go to** nonsense (an exclamation of impatience)   139 **vantages**
opportunities   140 **indisposition** disinclination   141 **unaptness** un-
readiness to listen   141 **minister** ministration, prompting

Laid them before you; you would throw them off,
145 And say you found them in mine honesty.
When for some trifling present you have bid me
Return so much, I have shook my head and wept;
Yea 'gainst th' authority of manners,° prayed you
To hold your hand more close. I did endure
150 Not seldom, nor no slight checks,° when I have
Prompted° you in the ebb of your estate
And your great flow of debts. My loved lord,
Though you hear now, too late, yet now's a time:
The greatest of your having° lacks a half
To pay your present debts.

155 *Timon.*   Let all my land be sold.

Flavius. 'Tis all engaged,° some forfeited and gone,
And what remains will hardly stop the mouth
Of present dues. The future comes apace.°
What shall defend the interim? And at length
160 How goes our reck'ning?

Timon. To Lacedaemon did my land extend.

Flavius. O my good lord, the world is but a word;
Were it all yours to give it in a breath,
How quickly were it gone!

Timon.   You tell me true.

165 *Flavius.* If you suspect my husbandry or falsehood,°
Call me before th' exactess auditors,
And set me on° the proof. So the gods bless me,
When all our offices° have been oppressed°
With riotous feeders,° when our vaults° have wept
170 With drunken spilth° of wine, when every room
Hath blazed with lights and brayed with minstrelsy,

---

148 **th' authority of manners** the dictates of good manners   150
checks rebukes   151 **Prompted** (in its theatrical sense)   154 **The
greatest of your having** your worth estimated at the highest possible
figure   156 **engaged** mortgaged   158 **apace** swiftly   165 **suspect
my husbandry or falsehood** suspect me of false husbandry or dishonest management   167 **on** to   168 **offices** service rooms of a
household   168 **oppressed** crowded   169 **feeders** servants   169
vaults wine cellars   170 **spilth** spilling

I have retired me to a wasteful cock,°
And set mine eyes at flow.°

Timon.   Prithee no more.

Flavius. Heavens, have I said, the bounty of this lord!
How many prodigal bits° have slaves and peasants   175
This night englutted!° Who is not Timon's?
What heart, head, sword, force, means, but is
    Lord Timon's?
Great Timon, noble, worthy, royal Timon!
Ah, when the means are gone that buy this praise,
The breath is gone whereof this praise is made.   180
Feast-won, fast-lost;° one cloud of winter show'rs,
These flies are couched.°

Timon.   Come, sermon me no further.
No villainous bounty° yet hath passed my heart;
Unwisely, not ignobly, have I given.
Why dost thou weep? Canst thou the conscience°
    lack   185
To think I shall lack friends? Secure° thy heart.
If I would broach the vessels° of my love,
And try the argument° of hearts by borrowing,
Men and men's fortunes could I frankly° use
As I can bid thee speak.

Flavius.   Assurance° bless your thoughts.   190

Timon. And in some sort these wants of mine are
    crowned,°
That I account them blessings; for by these

---

172 **wasteful cock** spigot (of a wine cask) that has not been shut off
173 **And set mine eyes at flow** i.e., following the example of the
"wasteful cock," I have added my tears to the general riot and
superfluity 175 **prodigal bits** wasteful morsels 176 **englutted**
gulped down 181 **Feast-won, fast-lost** the friendship that is won by
giving feasts is quickly lost (with pun on "fast" as noun and adverb)
182 **couched** lying hidden 183 **villainous bounty** generosity for evil
purposes 185 **conscience** reasonableness 186 **Secure** make free
from care or apprehension 187 **broach the vessels** tap the casks
188 **try the argument** test the theme or contents 189 **frankly** freely
190 **Assurance** i.e., may assurance 191 **crowned** given a royal dignity

Shall I try friends. You shall perceive how you
Mistake my fortunes; I am wealthy in my friends.
195   Within there! Flaminius! Servilius!

Enter [Flaminius, Servilius, and Third Servant].

Servants. My lord, my lord.

Timon. I will dispatch you severally.° [*To Servilius*]
You to Lord Lucius, [*to Flaminius*] to Lord Lucullus you; I hunted with his honor today. [*To Third
200   Servant*] You to Sempronius. Commend me to their
loves; and I am proud, say, that my occasions°
have found time to use 'em toward a supply of
money. Let the request be fifty talents.

Flaminius. As you have said, my lord.
[*Exeunt Servants.*]

205 *Flavius.* [*Aside*] Lord Lucius and Lucullus? Humh!

Timon. Go you, sir, to the senators,
Of whom, even to the state's best health,° I have
Deserved this hearing. Bid 'em send o' th' instant
A thousand talents to me.

Flavius.   I have been bold,
210   For that I knew it the most general° way,
To them to use your signet° and your name;
But they do shake their heads, and I am here
No richer in return.

Timon.   Is't true? Can't be?

Flavius. They answer in a joint and corporate voice,
215   That now they are at fall,° want treasure, cannot
Do what they would, are sorry; you are honorable,
But yet they could have wished—they know not;
Something hath been amiss—a noble nature

---

197 **severally** separately   201 **occasions** needs   207 **even to the
state's best health** i.e., Timon, because of his own generosity to the
state in the past, now deserves a loan from them to the very outer-
most limit they can pay (?)   210 **general** usual   211 **signet** signet
ring (as sign of authority to act)   215 **at fall** at ebb tide

May catch a wrench°—would all were well—'tis
   pity—
And so, intending° other serious matters,   220
After distasteful looks, and these hard fractions,°
With certain half-caps° and cold-moving° nods,
They froze me into silence.

Timon.   You gods reward them!
Prithee man look cheerly. These old fellows
Have their ingratitude in them hereditary.   225
Their blood is caked, 'tis cold, it seldom flows;
'Tis lack of kindly° warmth they are not kind;
And nature, as it grows again toward earth,°
Is fashioned for the journey, dull and heavy.
Go to Ventidius. Prithee be not sad;   230
Thou art true and honest; ingeniously° I speak,
No blame belongs to thee. Ventidius lately
Buried his father, by whose death he's stepped
Into a great estate. When he was poor,
Imprisoned, and in scarcity of friends,   235
I cleared him with five talents. Greet him from me,
Bid him suppose some good necessity°
Touches his friend, which craves to be rememb'red
With those five talents. That had, give't these
   fellows
To whom 'tis instant° due. Nev'r speak or think   240
That Timon's fortunes 'mong° his friends can sink.

Flavius. I would I could not think it; that thought is
   bounty's foe.
Being free° itself, it thinks all others so.   *Exeunt.*

---

219 **catch a wrench** accidentally be twisted from its natural bent
220 **intending** pretending 221 **hard fractions** harsh fragments of
speech (conveyed in the broken syntax) 222 **half-caps** half-courteous
salutations 222 **cold-moving** producing cold, frigid 227 **kindly**
(1) natural (2) generous 228 **grows again toward earth** approaches
death and the grave 231 **ingeniously** ingenuously, candidly 237 **good
necessity** valid need 240 **instant** instantly, immediately 241 **'mong**
in the midst of 243 **free** bounteous

[ACT 3

Scene 1. *Lucullus' house*.]

*Flaminius waiting to speak with Lord [Lucullus]
from his Master, enters a Servant to him.*

Servant. I have told my lord of you; he is coming
down to you.

Flaminius. I thank you, sir.

Enter Lucullus.

Servant. Here's my lord.

5   *Lucullus*. [*Aside*] One of Lord Timon's men? A gift
I warrant. Why this hits right; I dreamt of a silver
basin and ewer tonight.°—Flaminius, honest Flaminius, you are very respectively° welcome, sir.
Fill me some wine. [*Exit Servant*.] And how does
10   that honorable, complete,° free-hearted gentleman
of Athens, thy very bountiful good lord and master?

Flaminius. His health is well, sir.

3.1.7 **tonight** last night   8 **respectively** respectfully   10 **complete**
fully equipped or endowed, perfect

Lucullus. I am right glad that his health is well, sir.
And what hast thou there under thy cloak, pretty° 15
Flaminius?

Flaminius. Faith, nothing but an empty box, sir,
which in my lord's behalf I come to entreat your
honor to supply;° who, having great and instant
occasion to use fifty talents, hath sent to your lord- 20
ship to furnish him, nothing doubting your present°
assistance therein.

Lucullus. La, la, la, la! "Nothing doubting," says he?
Alas, good lord, a noble gentleman 'tis, if he would
not keep so good a house.° Many a time and often 25
I ha' dined with him, and told him on't, and come
again to supper to him of purpose to have him
spend less, and yet he would embrace no counsel,
take no warning by my coming. Every man has
his fault, and honesty° is his. I ha' told him on't, 30
but I could ne'er get him from't.

Enter Servant, with wine.

Servant. Please your lordship, here is the wine.

Lucullus. Flaminius, I have noted thee always wise.
Here's to thee.

Flaminius. Your lordship speaks your pleasure.° 35

Lucullus. I have observed thee always for a towardly
prompt spirit,° give thee thy due, and one that
knows what belongs to reason; and canst use the
time well, if the time use thee well.° Good parts°
in thee. [*To Servant*] Get you gone, sirrah. [*Exit* 40
Servant.] Draw nearer, honest Flaminius. Thy
lord's a bountiful gentleman, but thou art wise,
and thou know'st well enough, although thou

---

15 **pretty** (vague epithet of praise) 19 **supply** fill 21 **present** immediate 25 **so good a house** such lavish hospitality 30 **honesty**
generosity 35 **speaks your pleasure** is pleased to say so 36–37 **towardly prompt spirit** well-disposed and well-inclined person 39 **if
the time use thee well** if you strike good fortune 39 **parts** qualities

45 com'st to me, that this is no time to lend money,
especially upon bare friendship without security.
Here's three solidares° for thee. Good boy, wink°
at me, and say thou saw'st me not. Fare thee well.

Flaminius. Is't possible the world should so much
differ,°
And we alive that lived?° Fly, damnèd baseness,
50 To him that worships thee.
                                        [*Throws back the money.*]

Lucullus. Ha? Now I see thou art a fool, and fit for
thy master.   *Exit.*

Flaminius. May these° add to the number that may
scald° thee.
Let molten coin be thy damnation,°
55 Thou disease of a friend, and not himself.
Has friendship such a faint and milky heart
It turns° in less than two nights? O you gods!
I feel my master's passion.° This slave
Unto his honor° has my lord's meat° in him;
60 Why should it thrive and turn to nutriment
When he is turned to poison?
O may diseases only work upon't,
And when he's sick to death, let not that part of
nature°
Which my lord paid for be of any power
65 To expel sickness, but prolong his hour.°   *Exit.*

---

46 **solidares** (perhaps Shakespeare was referring to the Roman "sol-
idus," which was used in England for a shilling) 46 **wink** shut your
eyes 48 **differ** change 49 **And we alive that lived** i.e., the world
changes so swiftly, it is hard to believe that the same people are still
alive 53 **these** (the rejected coins) 53 **scald** i.e., in hell 54 **thy
damnation** the torment you will suffer in hell (perhaps a reference to
the pouring of molten gold down the throat of Marcus Crassus by
the Parthians, thought of as a punishment in hell for avarice)
57 **turns** curdles 58 **passion** anger, suffering (trisyllabic) 58–59
slave/Unto his honor (ironical: "this man who claims to be so devoted to honor") 59 **meat** food (in general, in contradistinction to
"drink") 63 **that part of nature** i.e., that part of his body nourished
by Timon's food 65 **but prolong his hour** i.e., may he have a lin-
gering death

[Scene 2. *A public place.*]

Enter Lucius, with three Strangers.°

Lucius. Who, the Lord Timon? He is my very good
friend and an honorable gentleman.

First Stranger. We know him for no less, though we
are but strangers to him. But I can tell you one
thing, my lord, and which I hear from common   5
rumors: now Lord Timon's happy hours are done
and past, and his estate shrinks from him.

Lucius. Fie, no, do not believe it; he cannot want for
money.

Second Stranger. But believe you this, my lord, that   10
not long ago, one of his men was with the Lord
Lucullus to borrow so many talents,° nay urged
extremely for't, and showed what necessity belonged to't, and yet was denied.

Lucius. How?   15

Second Stranger. I tell you, denied, my lord.

Lucius. What a strange case was that! Now before
the gods I am ashamed on't. Denied that honorable
man? There was very little honor showed in't. For
my own part, I must needs confess, I have received   20
some small kindnesses from him, as money, plate,°
jewels, and suchlike trifles, nothing comparing to
his;° yet had he mistook him° and sent to me, I
should ne'er have denied his occasion° so many
talents.   25

3.2.s.d. **Strangers** foreigners, non-Athenians **12 so many talents**
(an indefinite number probably intended to be replaced, in revision,
by a definite number) **21 plate** utensils for domestic use, especially
of gold or silver **23 his** i.e., Lucullus' **23 mistook him** made a
mistake **24 occasion** need

Enter Servilius.

Servilius. See, by good hap, yonder's my lord; I have sweat to see his honor. My honored lord.

Lucius. Servilius? You are kindly met, sir. Fare thee well; commend me to thy honorable virtuous lord, my very exquisite friend.

30

Servilius. May it please your honor, my lord hath sent—

Lucius. Ha? What has he sent? I am so much endeared° to that lord; he's ever sending. How shall I thank him, think'st thou? And what has he sent now?

35

Servilius. Has only sent his present occasion now, my lord, requesting your lordship to supply his instant use with so many talents.

Lucius. I know his lordship is but merry with me,
He cannot want° fifty five hundred talents.°

40

Servilius. But in the meantime he wants less, my lord.
If his occasion were not virtuous,
I should not urge it half so faithfully.

Lucius. Dost thou speak seriously, Servilius?

45

Servilius. Upon my soul 'tis true, sir.

Lucius. What a wicked beast was I to disfurnish myself against° such a good time, when I might ha' shown myself honorable! How unluckily it happ'ned that I should purchase the day before for a little part,° and undo a great deal of honor!° Servilius, now before the gods I am not able to do—the more beast, I say! I was sending to use

50

33–34 **endeared** indebted   41 **want** (1) be without, lack (2) need, desire   41 **fifty five hundred talents** a huge sum (see Introduction, p. 163)   47–48 **disfurnish myself against** to allow myself to be unprovided for   50–51 **for a little part** for a little business transaction (deliberately vague)   51 **undo a great deal of honor** i.e., lose the anticipated honor of lending to Timon

Lord Timon myself, these gentlemen can witness;
but I would not for the wealth of Athens I had 55
done't now. Commend me bountifully to his good
lordship, and I hope his honor will conceive the
fairest° of me, because I have no power to be kind.
And tell him this from me, I count it one of my
greatest afflictions, say, that I cannot pleasure such 60
an honorable gentleman. Good Servilius, will you
befriend me so far as to use mine own words to
him?

Servilius. Yes, sir, I shall.

Lucius. I'll look you out a good turn, Servilius. 65
                                          Exit Servilius.
True, as you said, Timon is shrunk indeed,
And he that's once denied will hardly speed.°   *Exit.*

First Stranger. Do you observe this, Hostilius?

Second Stranger.   Ay, too well.

First Stranger. Why this is the world's soul, and just
    of the same piece°
Is every flatterer's sport.° Who can call him his
    friend 70
That dips in the same dish? For in my knowing
Timon has been this lord's father,
And kept his° credit with his° purse;
Supported his estate; nay, Timon's money
Has paid his men their wages. He ne'er drinks 75
But Timon's silver treads° upon his lip,
And yet—O see the monstrousness of man
When he looks out in an ungrateful shape°—
He does deny him, in respect of his,°
What charitable men afford to beggars. 80

Third Stranger. Religion groans at it.

57–58 **conceive the fairest** think the best 67 **speed** be successful,
prosper 69 **piece** sort, kind 70 **sport** mockery, diversion (as Lucius
has just made sport of Timon) 73 **kept his** sustained Lucius'
73 **his** i.e., Timon's 76 **treads** presses 78 **shape** form 79 **in respect of his** in relation to what Lucius is worth

First Stranger.   For mine own part,
    I never tasted° Timon in my life,
    Nor came any of his bounties over me
    To mark me for his friend. Yet I protest,
85 For his right° noble mind, illustrious virtue,
    And honorable carriage,°
    Had his necessity made use of me,
    I would have put my wealth into donation,°
    And the best half should have returned° to him,
90 So much I love his heart. But I perceive
    Men must learn now with pity to dispense,
    For policy° sits above conscience.   *Exeunt.*

[Scene 3. *Sempronius' house.*]

*Enter a Third Servant [of Timon] with
Sempronius, another of Timon's friends.*

Sempronius. Must he needs trouble me in't—humh!—
        'bove all others?
    He might have tried Lord Lucius or Lucullus,
    And now Ventidius is wealthy too,
    Whom he redeemed from prison. All these
    Owes their estates unto him.

5 *Third Servant.*   My lord,
    They have all been touched° and found base metal,
    For they have all denied him.

    Sempronius.   How? Have they denied him?
    Has Ventidius and Lucullus denied him,
    And does he send to me? Three? Humh!
10 It shows but little love or judgment in him.

82 **tasted** experienced the qualities of   85 **right** very   86 **carriage**
moral conduct   88 **put my wealth into donation** i.e., treated
my fortune as a gift from Timon   89 **returned** been given back
92 **policy** cunning   3.3.6 **touched** tested (by being rubbed on a touchstone; unlike base metals, gold and silver produced the proper
colored streak)

Must I be his last refuge? His friends, like physi-
    cians,
Thrive, give him over.° Must I take th' cure upon
    me?
Has much disgraced me in't; I'm angry at him
That might have known my place.° I see no sense
    for't,
But his occasions° might have wooed me first;   15
For, in my conscience, I was the first man
That e'er received gift from him.
And does he think so backwardly° of me now
That I'll requite it last? No.
So it may prove an argument° of laughter   20
To th' rest, and I 'mongst lords be thought a fool.
I'd rather than the worth of thrice the sum,
Had° sent to me first, but for my mind's sake;°
I'd such a courage° to do him good. But now re-
    turn,
And with their faint reply this answer join: 25
Who bates° mine honor shall not know my coin.
                                                    Exit.

Third Servant. Excellent. Your lordship's a goodly
    villain. The devil knew not what he did when he
    made man politic;° he crossed himself by't:° and
    I cannot think but in the end the villainies of   30
    man will set him clear.° How fairly° this lord
    strives to appear foul!° Takes virtuous copies to be
    wicked.° Like those° that under hot ardent zeal

---

12 **Thrive, give him over** i.e., prosper on his money while they are
giving him up for dead (?) 14 **my place** i.e., before Lucullus, Lucius,
and Ventidius 15 **occasions** needs 18 **backwardly** (1) poorly (2)
near the end, late 20 **argument** occasion, subject 23 **Had** i.e., he
had (perhaps "H'ad"?) 23 **but for my mind's sake** if only to express
my good will towards him 24 **courage** desire 26 **bates** abates,
undervalues 29 **politic** cunning 29 **he crossed himself by't** i.e.,
the devil thwarted his own purposes by making man his rival in
shrewdness and guile 31 **will set him clear** will make the devil appear innocent (when compared with the "villainies of man") 31
How fairly with what a beautiful appearance 32 **foul** ugly 32–33
Takes virtuous copies to be wicked i.e., models himself on exemplars
of virtue to serve as disguise for his wickedness 33 **those** i.e., religious fanatics (perhaps "zeal" suggests an allusion to Puritans)

would set whole realms on fire, of such a nature is
35   his politic love.
This was my lord's best hope; now all are fled
Save only the gods. Now his friends are dead,
Doors that were ne'er acquainted with their wards°
Many a bounteous year, must be employed
40   Now to guard sure° their master.
And this is all a liberal° course allows;
Who cannot keep his wealth must keep his house.°
                                                        Exit.

[Scene 4. *Timon's house.*]

*Enter Varro's [two Servants], meeting others. All
[the Servants of] Timon's creditors to wait for
his coming out. Then enter [the Servant of]
Lucius; [then Titus] and Hortensius.*

Varro's First Servant. Well met; good morrow, Titus
and Hortensius.

Titus. The like to you, kind Varro.

Hortensius.   Lucius!
What, do we meet together?

Lucius' Servant.   Ay, and I think
One business does command us all;
For mine is money.

5   *Titus.*   So is theirs and ours.

                    Enter Philotus.

Lucius' Servant. And, sir, Philotus' too!

Philotus.   Good day at once.°

38 **wards** locks   40 **sure** securely   41 **liberal** generous   42 **keep his
house** remain at home (for fear of being arrested for debt) 3.4.6
at once to you all

Lucius' Servant. Welcome, good brother. What do
   you think the hour?

Philotus. Laboring for nine.

Lucius' Servant. So much?

Philotus.   Is not my lord seen yet?

Lucius' Servant.   Not yet.

Philotus. I wonder on't; he was wont to shine at seven.   *10*

Lucius' Servant. Ay, but the days are waxed° shorter
   with him.
   You must consider that a prodigal course
   Is like the sun's,
   But not like his recoverable,° I fear.
   'Tis deepest winter in Lord Timon's purse;   *15*
   That is, one may reach deep enough and yet
   Find little.

Philotus.   I am of your fear for that.

Titus. I'll show you how t' observe° a strange event.
   Your lord sends now for money?

Hortensius.   Most true, he does.

Titus. And he wears jewels now of Timon's gift,   *20*
   For which I wait for money.

Hortensius. It is against my heart.°

Lucius' Servant.   Mark how strange it shows,
   Timon in this should pay more than he owes;°
   And e'en as if your lord should wear rich jewels
   And send for money for 'em.   *25*

Hortensius. I'm weary of this charge,° the gods can
   witness.

---

11 **waxed** grown 12–14 **prodigal course ... recoverable** i.e., the
prodigal, like the sun, declines, but cannot renew himself every
day 18 **observe** observe and interpret 22 **against my heart** contrary to my natural feeling 23 **should pay more than he owes** i.e.,
he has given the gifts, and now he is also asked for the money for
them 26 **charge** task

I know my lord hath spent of Timon's wealth,
And now ingratitude makes it worse than stealth.°

Varro's First Servant. Yes, mine's three thousand
crowns. What's yours?

30 *Lucius' Servant.* Five thousand mine.

Varro's First Servant. 'Tis much deep, and it should
seem by th' sum
Your master's confidence° was above mine,°
Else surely his had equaled.

Enter Flaminius.

Titus. One of Lord Timon's men.

35 *Lucius' Servant.* Flaminius? Sir, a word. Pray is my
lord ready to come forth?

Flaminius. No, indeed he is not.

Titus. We attend his lordship; pray signify so much.

Flaminius. I need not tell him that; he knows you are
40 too diligent.   [*Exit.*]

*Enter [Flavius, the] Steward, in a cloak,
muffled.°*

Lucius' Servant. Ha! Is not that his steward muffled
so?
He goes away in a cloud.° Call him, call him.

Titus. Do you hear, sir?

Varro's Second Servant. By your leave, sir.

45 *Flavius.* What do ye ask of me, my friend?

Titus. We wait for certain money here, sir.

Flavius.   Ay,
If money were as certain as your waiting,

28 **stealth** stealing 32 **confidence** trust 32 **mine** i.e., my master's
40s.d. **muffled** wrapped up, especially about the face 42 **in a cloud**
(1) in a state of gloominess and concern (2) covered with a cloud
because he is muffled

'Twere sure enough.
Why then preferred° you not your sums and bills
When your false masters ate of my lord's meat?   50
Then they could smile, and fawn upon° his debts,
And take down th' int'rest° into their glutt'nous
    maws.
You do yourselves but wrong to stir me up;
Let me pass quietly.
Believe't, my lord and I have made an end;   55
I have no more to reckon,° he to spend.

Lucius' Servant. Ay, but this answer will not serve.

Flavius. If 'twill not serve, 'tis not so base as you,
For you serve knaves.   [*Exit.*]

Varro's First Servant. How? What does his cashiered°
    worship mutter?   60

Varro's Second Servant. No matter what; he's poor,
    and that's revenge enough. Who can speak
    broader° than he that has no house to put his head
    in? Such may rail against great buildings.

Enter Servilius.

Titus. O here's Servilius. Now we shall know some   65
    answer.

Servilius. If I might beseech you, gentlemen, to re-
    pair° some other hour, I should derive much
    from't. For take't of my soul,° my lord leans won-
    drously to discontent. His comfortable° temper has   70
    forsook him, he's much out of health, and keeps
    his chamber.

Lucius' Servant. Many do keep their chambers are
    not sick;

49 **preferred** proffered, presented 51 **fawn upon** seek favor by
servility (used especially of dogs) 52 **th' int'rest** i.e., what they
ate was equivalent to the interest due on the money owed them
by Timon 56 **reckon** keep account of 60 **cashiered** dismissed
from employment 63 **broader** more critically 67–68 **repair** come
69 **take't of my soul** take it from my heart (i.e., sincerely) 70 **comfortable** cheerful

And if it be so far beyond his health,
75   Methinks he should the sooner pay his debts,
And make a clear° way to the gods.

Servilius.   Good gods!

Titus. We cannot take this for answer, sir.

Flaminius. (*Within*) Servilius, help! My lord, my lord!

          Enter Timon in a rage.

Timon. What, are my doors opposed against my
          passage?
80   Have I been ever free,° and must my house
Be my retentive° enemy? My jail?
The place which I have feasted,° does it now,
Like all mankind, show me an iron heart?

Lucius' Servant. Put in° now, Titus.

85   *Titus.* My lord, here is my bill.

Lucius' Servant. Here's mine.

Hortensius. And mine, my lord.

Both Varro's Servants. And ours, my lord.

Philotus. All our bills.

Timon. Knock me down with 'em, cleave me to the
90   girdle.°

Lucius' Servant. Alas, my lord—

Timon. Cut my heart in sums.°

Titus. Mine, fifty talents.

76 **clear** (1) free from debt (2) innocent, unstained (because he has
paid his debts) (3) untrammeled, without the obstacle of debts 80
free (1) generous (2) unrestrained 81 **retentive** confining 82 **The
place which I have feasted** i.e., the house itself in which I have given
feasts 84 **Put in** i.e., put in your claim for money 90 **Knock ...
girdle** (Timon chooses to understand "bills" not as "accounts of
money due," but as "weapons"—a bill had a long wooden handle
with a blade or ax-shaped head at one end, and it was capable of
cutting a man through to the belt) 92 **in sums** into sums of money

Timon. Tell out° my blood.

Lucius' Servant. Five thousand crowns, my lord. 95

Timon. Five thousand drops pays that. What yours?
 And yours?

Varro's First Servant. My lord—

Varro's Second Servant. My lord—

Timon. Tear me, take me, and the gods fall upon you.
 Exit Timon.

Hortensius. Faith, I perceive our masters may throw 100
 their caps at their money;° these debts may well be
 called desperate° ones, for a madman owes 'em.
 Exeunt.

Enter Timon [and Flavius].

Timon. They have e'en put my breath from me,° the
 slaves.
 Creditors? Devils!

Flavius. My dear lord— 105

Timon. What if it should be so?

Flavius. My lord—

Timon. I'll have it so. My steward!

Flavius. Here, my lord.

Timon. So fitly?° Go, bid° all my friends again, 110
 Lucius, Lucullus, and Sempronius—all.
 I'll once more feast the rascals.

Flavius.   O my lord,
 You only speak from your distracted soul;
 There's not so much left to furnish out
 A moderate table.

94 **Tell out** count out   100–01 **may throw ... money** may give up
their money for lost   102 **desperate** beyond hope of recovery (cf.
"sperate," recoverable)   103 **put my breath from me** put me out of
breath   110 **fitly** conveniently   110 **bid** invite

115 *Timon.*   Be it not in thy care.°
            Go, I charge thee, invite them all, let in the tide
            Of knaves once more; my cook and I'll provide.

                                                          Exeunt.

                    [Scene 5. *The Senate House*]

        *Enter three Senators at one door, Alcibiades meeting
                    them with Attendants.*

        First Senator. My lord, you have my voice° to't. The
                fault's
            Bloody; 'tis necessary he should die.
            Nothing emboldens sin so much as mercy.

        Second Senator. Most true; the law shall bruise 'em.°

        Alcibiades. Honor, health, and compassion to the
    5   senate.

        First Senator. Now, captain?

        Alcibiades. I am an humble suitor to your virtues;
            For pity is the virtue° of the law,
            And none but tyrants use it cruelly.
    10   It pleases time and fortune to lie heavy
            Upon a friend of mine, who in hot blood
            Hath stepped into the law,° which is past depth°
            To those that, without heed, do plunge into't.
            He is a man, setting his fate° aside,
    15   Of comely virtues;
            Nor did he soil the fact° with cowardice
            (An honor in him which buys out° his fault),

            115 **Be it not in thy care** i.e., let the feast be my concern   3.5.1
            voice vote   4 **bruise 'em** crush them (possibly sinners or wrongdoers
            in general?)   8 **virtue** characteristic excellence   12 **stepped into the
            law** done something to bring him within the jurisdiction of the law
            12 **past depth** beyond any measurable depth   14 **his fate** i.e., this one
            fateful action of his   16 **soil the fact** sully the deed   17 **buys out**
            redeems

But with a noble fury and fair° spirit,
Seeing his reputation touched to death,
He did oppose his foe;   20
And with such sober and unnoted° passion
He did behove° his anger, ere 'twas spent,
As if he had but proved an argument.°

First Senator. You undergo too strict a paradox,°
Striving to make an ugly deed look fair.   25
Your words have took such pains as if they labored
To bring manslaughter into form,° and set
Quarreling upon the head of valor, which indeed
Is valor misbegot, and came into the world
When sects and factions° were newly born.   30
He's truly valiant that can wisely suffer
The worst that man can breathe,°
And make his wrongs his outsides,°
To wear them like his raiment, carelessly,
And ne'er prefer° his injuries to his heart,   35
To bring it into danger.
If wrongs be evils and enforce us kill,
What folly 'tis to hazard life for ill.

Alcibiades. My lord—

First Senator. You cannot make gross sins look clear.°
To revenge is no valor, but to bear.°   40

Alcibiades. My lords, then, under favor,° pardon me,
If I speak like a captain.
Why do fond° men expose themselves to battle,
And not endure all threats? Sleep upon't,

---

18 **fair** excellent 21 **unnoted** not notable, i.e., calm 22 **behove** control 23 **argument** i.e., a *point d'honneur* rather than a personal passion 24 **undergo too strict a paradox** i.e., attempt to argue a position that is excessively paradoxical 27 **form** i.e., a legal and acceptable form 30 **factions** (trisyllabic) 32 **breathe** utter 33 **outsides** mere externals 35 **prefer** present 39 **clear** innocent 40 **bear** tolerate (our wrongs) 41 **under favor** by your leave (a formula of politeness) 43 **fond** foolish

45   And let the foes quietly cut their throats
        Without repugnancy?° If there be
        Such valor in the bearing, what make we
        Abroad?° Why then, women are more valiant
        That stay at home, if bearing° carry it,°
50   And the ass more captain than the lion, the fellow
        Loaden with irons wiser than the judge,
        If wisdom be in suffering. O my lords,
        As you are great, be pitifully good.°
        Who cannot condemn rashness in cold blood?
55   To kill, I grant, is sin's extremest gust,°
        But in defense, by mercy,° 'tis most just.
        To be in anger is impiety;
        But who is man that is not angry?
        Weigh but the crime with this.

Second Senator. You breathe in vain.

60 _Alcibiades._   In vain? His service done
        At Lacedaemon and Byzantium
        Were a sufficient briber for his life.

First Senator. What's that?

Alcibiades.   Why say,° my lords, h'as
        done fair service,
        And slain in fight many of your enemies.
65   How full of valor did he bear himself
        In the last conflict, and made plenteous wounds!

Second Senator. He has made too much plenty with
        'em.
        He's a sworn rioter;° he has a sin° that often
        Drowns him and takes his valor prisoner.
70   If there were no foes, that were enough
        To overcome him. In that beastly fury
        He has been known to commit outrages,

46 **repugnancy** resistance, fighting back   48 **Abroad** i.e., away from home, at battle   49 **bearing** (1) enduring of wrongs (2) childbearing (3) bearing of men in sexual intercourse   49 **carry it** win the day   53 **be pitifully good** i.e., be good in showing pity   55 **gust** (1) taste, relish (2) strong wind or storm   56 **by mercy** in a merciful interpretation   63 **say** let us say, let us admit   68 **rioter** debauchee   68 **sin** i.e., drunkenness

And cherish factions.° 'Tis inferred° to us
His days are foul and his drink dangerous.

First Senator. He dies.

Alcibiades.　　　　　Hard fate. He might have died
　　in war.　　　　　　　　　　　　　　　　　　　　75
My lords, if not for any parts° in him—
Though his right arm might purchase his own time,°
And be in debt to none—yet, more to move you,
Take my deserts to his, and join 'em both.
And for I know your reverend ages love　　　　80
Security,° I'll pawn my victories, all
My honor to you, upon his good returns.°
If by this crime he owes the law his life,
Why, let the war receive 't in valiant gore,
For law is strict, and war is nothing more.　　85

First Senator. We are for law. He dies. Urge it no
　　more,
On height of our displeasure. Friend or brother,
He forfeits his own blood that spills another.

Alcibiades. Must it be so? It must not be.
My lords, I do beseech you know me.

Second Senator.　　　　　　　How?　　90

Alcibiades. Call me to your remembrances.

Third Senator.　　　　　　What?

Alcibiades. I cannot think but your age° has forgot
　　me;
It could not else be I should prove so base
To sue° and be denied such common grace.
My wounds ache at you.

First Senator.　　　　　Do you dare our anger?　　95
'Tis in few words, but spacious in effect:
We banish thee for ever.

73 **cherish factions** foster dissension 73 **inferred** reported 76
parts good qualities 77 **his own time** i.e., his proper time to
die 81 **Security** (1) safety, freedom from care or apprehension
(2) collateral for a debt 82 **good returns** profit on an invest-
ment 92 **your age** i.e., you, because of your age 94 **To sue**
to beg

Alcibiades.   Banish me?
   Banish your dotage, banish usury,
   That makes the senate ugly.

First Senator. If after two days' shine Athens contain
100   thee,
   Attend our weightier judgment.° And, not to swell
      our spirit,°
   He shall be executed presently.°
                              Exeunt [*Senators*].

Alcibiades. Now the gods keep you old enough, that
      you may live
   Only in bone,° that none may look on you.
105   I'm worse than mad. I have kept back their foes,
   While they have told° their money, and let out
   Their coin upon large interest, I myself
   Rich only in large hurts. All those, for this?
   Is this the balsam° that the usuring Senate
110   Pours into captains' wounds? Banishment!
   It comes not ill. I hate not to be banished;
   It is a cause worthy my spleen° and fury,
   That I may strike at Athens. I'll cheer up
   My discontented troops and lay for hearts.°
115   'Tis honor with most lands to be at odds;
   Soldiers should brook° as little wrongs as gods.
                                          Exit.

101 **Attend our weightier judgment** expect a more severe sentence
from us   101 **not to swell our spirit** not to allow our anger any further scope   102 **presently** at once   104 **Only in bone** i.e., be mere
hideous skeletons   106 **told** counted   109 **balsam** balm   112 **spleen**
malice, passionate hatred   114 **lay for hearts** i.e., try to win their
hearts to my cause (or, possibly, try to win the hearts of new followers)   116 **brook** endure

[Scene 6. *A banqueting hall in Timon's house.*]

[*Music. Tables set out, Servants attending.*] Enter
   divers Friends [*of Timon*] *at several doors.*

First Lord. The good time of day to you, sir.

Second Lord. I also wish it to you. I think this honorable lord did but try us this other day.

First Lord. Upon that were my thoughts tiring° when
   we encount'red. I hope it is not so low with him as   5
   he made it seem in the trial of his several friends.

Second Lord. It should not be, by the persuasion of°
   his new feasting.

First Lord. I should think so. He hath sent me an
   earnest inviting, which many my near occasions°   10
   did urge me to put off; but he hath conjured me
   beyond them, and I must needs appear.

Second Lord. In like manner was I in debt to my im-
   portunate business, but he would not hear my
   excuse. I am sorry, when he sent to borrow of me,   15
   that my provision° was out.

First Lord. I am sick of that grief too, as I understand how all things go.°

Second Lord. Every man here's so. What would he
   have borrowed of you?   20

3.6.4 **tiring** feeding (especially, to tear flesh in feeding as does a
bird of prey)   7 **by the persuasion of** on the evidence of   10 **many
my near occasions** my many pressing social obligations   16 **provi-
sion** supply (of money)   17–18 **as I ... go** i.e., on the evidence of his
"new feasting," things seem to be picking up again with Timon

First Lord. A thousand pieces.°

Second Lord. A thousand pieces?

First Lord. What of you?

Second Lord. He sent to me, sir—

   Enter Timon and Attendants.

         Here he comes.

25 *Timon.* With all my heart, gentlemen both; and how
  fare you?

First Lord. Ever at the best, hearing well of your lordship.

Second Lord. The swallow° follows not summer more
30 willing than we your lordship.

Timon. [*Aside*] Nor more willingly leaves winter, such
  summer birds are men.— Gentlemen, our dinner
  will not recompense this long stay. Feast your ears
  with the music awhile, if they will fare so harshly°
35 o' th' trumpet's sound; we shall to't presently.°

First Lord. I hope it remains not unkindly with your
  lordship that I returned you an empty messenger.

Timon. O sir, let it not trouble you.

Second Lord. My noble lord—

40 *Timon.* Ah my good friend, what cheer?

Second Lord. My most honorable lord, I am e'en sick
  of shame that when your lordship this other day
  sent to me, I was so unfortunate a beggar.

Timon. Think not on't, sir.

45 *Second Lord.* If you had sent but two hours before—

21 **pieces** gold coins worth about a pound (but probably used vaguely)
29 **swallow** (cf. the proverb: "Swallows, like false friends, fly away
upon the approach of winter") 34 **fare so harshly** feed on such
rough food 35 **we shall to't presently** we shall sit down to eat immediately

Timon. Let it not cumber your better remembrance.°
                    The banquet brought in.
  Come, bring in all together.

Second Lord. All covered dishes.°

First Lord. Royal cheer,° I warrant you.

Third Lord. Doubt not that, if money and the season   50
  can yield it.

First Lord. How do you? What's the news?

Third Lord. Alcibiades is banished. Hear you of it?

First and Second Lords. Alcibiades banished?

Third Lord. 'Tis so, be sure of it.   55

First Lord. How? How?

Second Lord. I pray you upon what?°

Timon. My worthy friends, will you draw near?

Third Lord. I'll tell you more anon.° Here's a noble
  feast toward.°   60

Second Lord. This is the old man still.°

Third Lord. Will't hold?° Will't hold?

Second Lord. It does; but time will°—and so—

Third Lord. I do conceive.°

Timon. Each man to his stool, with that spur° as he   65
  would to the lip of his mistress. Your diet° shall be
  in all places alike.° Make not a city feast° of it, to

_____

46 **cumber your better remembrance** burden your good memory
48 **covered dishes** (signifies food of high quality) 49 **Royal cheer**
i.e., food fit for a king 57 **upon what** for what cause 59 **anon**
soon 60 **toward** forthcoming 61 **still** ever, without change 62
Will't hold will it last 63 **time will** (presumably a platitude such
as "time will alter all things") 64 **conceive** understand 65 **spur**
spurring, speed 66 **diet** food 67 **in all places alike** the same at all
places of the table (i.e., no need for seating according to rank) 67
city feast a formal London banquet (London is the "City")

let the meat cool ere we can agree upon the first
place. Sit, sit. The gods require our thanks.

70   You great benefactors, sprinkle our society with
thankfulness. For your own gifts, make yourselves
praised. But reserve° still to give, lest your deities
be despised. Lend to each man enough that one
need not lend to another; for were your godheads to
75   borrow of men, men would forsake the gods. Make
the meat be beloved more than the man that gives
it. Let no assembly of twenty be without a score of
villains. If there sit twelve women at the table, let
a dozen of them be as they are. The rest of your
80   fees,° O gods—the senators of Athens, together
with the common leg° of people—what is amiss in
them, you gods, make suitable for destruction. For
these my present friends, as they are to me nothing,
so in nothing bless them, and to nothing are they
85   welcome.
Uncover, dogs, and lap.
                    [*The dishes are uncovered and
                     seen to be full of water.*]

Some speak. What does his lordship mean?

Some other. I know not.

Timon. May you a better feast never behold,
    You knot of mouth-friends.° Smoke° and lukewarm
90   water
    Is your perfection.° This is Timon's last,
    Who, stuck and spangled° with your flatteries,
    Washes it off and sprinkles in your faces
    Your reeking° villainy.   [*Throws the water
                             in their faces.*]
                    Live loathed and long,

---

72 **reserve** i.e., keep something in reserve   80 **fees** property, possessions   81 **leg** limb (as a literal part of the body politic)   90 **knot of
mouth-friends** pack of (1) friends merely in speech (2) friends won
through feeding, "trencher-friends"   90 **Smoke** (1) insubstantiality
(2) mere talk   91 **perfection** highest excellence (?) perfect likeness of
you (?)   92 **stuck and spangled** bespattered and tricked out (as if
with spangles)   94 **reeking** giving off smoke or fumes, stinking

Most smiling, smooth,° detested parasites, 95
Courteous destroyers, affable wolves, meek bears,
You fools of fortune, trencher-friends, time's flies,
Cap-and-knee slaves, vapors, and minute-jacks.°
Of man and beast the infinite° malady
Crust you quite o'er. What, dost thou go? 100
Soft, take thy physic° first; thou too, and thou.
Stay, I will lend thee money, borrow° none.

                         [*Drives them out.*]

What? All in motion? Henceforth be no feast,
Whereat a villain's not a welcome guest.
Burn house, sink Athens, henceforth hated be 105
Of° Timon man and all humanity.   *Exit.*

     Enter the Senators, with other Lords.

First Lord. How now, my lords?

Second Lord. Know you the quality of Lord Timon's
    fury?

Third Lord. Push,° did you see my cap? 110

Fourth Lord. I have lost my gown.

First Lord. He's but a mad lord, and naught but
    humors° sways him. He gave me a jewel th' other
    day, and now he has beat it out of my hat. Did
    you see my jewel? 115

Third Lord. Did you see my cap?

Second Lord. Here 'tis.

Fourth Lord. Here lies my gown.

First Lord. Let's make no stay.

---

95 **smooth** flattering 97–98 **You fools ... minute-jacks** you dupes
of fortune, friends won by feeding, insects that appear only in fair
weather, servile slaves always kneeling or removing caps in deference,
insubstantial creatures, and figures who strike the bell of a clock
(i.e., opportunistic persons) 99 **infinite** unlimited 101 **physic** medicine 102 **borrow** i.e., borrow none from others (?) I will borrow
none (?) 106 **Of** by 110 **Push** (an effeminate expression of
impatience) 113 **humors** whims, caprices

Second Lord. Lord Timon's mad.

120 *Third Lord.*   I feel't upon my bones.

Fourth Lord. One day he gives us diamonds, next day
   stones.

                    Exeunt the Senators [and others].

[ACT 4

Scene 1. *Outside the walls of Athens.*]

Enter Timon.

Timon. Let me look back upon thee. O thou wall
  That girdles in those wolves, dive in the earth,
  And fence not Athens. Matrons, turn incontinent;
  Obedience fail in children. Slaves and fools,
  Pluck the grave wrinkled senate from the bench,   5
  And minister° in their steads. To general filths°
  Convert o' th' instant green° virginity;
  Do't in your parents' eyes. Bankrupts, hold fast
  Rather than render back;° out with your knives,
  And cut your trusters' throats. Bound° servants,
      steal;   10
  Large-handed° robbers your grave masters are,
  And pill° by law. Maid, to thy master's bed,
  Thy mistress is o' th' brothel. Son of sixteen,
  Pluck the lined° crutch from thy old limping sire,
  With it beat out his brains. Piety, and fear,   15

4.1.6 **minister** govern 6 **filths** harlots (or, more generally, immoral acts or corruption) 7 **green** young, inexperienced 9 **render back** repay debts 10 **Bound** under obligation to serve for a stated period 11 **Large-handed** rapacious (usually means "generous") 12 **pill** steal 14 **lined** padded

  Religion to° the gods, peace, justice, truth,
  Domestic awe,° night-rest, and neighborhood,°
  Instruction, manners, mysteries,° and trades,
  Degrees,° observances, customs, and laws,
20 Decline to your confounding contraries,°
  And let confusion° live. Plagues incident to° men,
  Your potent and infectious fevers heap
  On Athens ripe for stroke. Thou cold sciatica,
  Cripple our senators, that their limbs may halt°
25 As lamely as their manners. Lust and liberty°
  Creep in the minds and marrows of our youth,
  That 'gainst the stream of virtue they may strive,
  And drown themselves in riot. Itches, blains,°
  Sow all th' Athenian bosoms, and their crop
30 Be general leprosy. Breath infect breath,
  That their society, as their friendship, may
  Be merely° poison. Nothing I'll bear from thee
  But nakedness, thou detestable° town;
  Take thou that too, with multiplying bans.°
35 Timon will to the woods, where he shall find
  Th' unkindest beast more kinder° than mankind.
  The gods confound—hear me, you good gods all—
  Th' Athenians both within and out that wall.
  And grant, as Timon grows, his hate may grow
40 To the whole race of mankind, high and low.
  Amen.   *Exit.*

16 **Religion to** religious concern for 17 **Domestic awe** the respect appropriate to domestic relations (to parents, home, etc.) 17 **neighborhood** neighborliness 18 **mysteries** crafts, callings 19 **Degrees** social classes 20 **confounding contraries** opposites which destroy each other and so bring on general chaos 21 **confusion** ruin 21 **incident to** natural to 24 **halt** limp 25 **liberty** licentiousness 28 **blains** blisters 32 **merely** utterly 33 **detestable** (primary accent on first syllable) 34 **multiplying bans** ever-increasing curses (?) multiple curses (?) 36 **more kinder** (1) more generous, gracious (2) more natural, closer to the moral law of nature

[Scene 2. *Athens. Timon's house.*]

Enter [Flavius, the] Steward, with two or three Servants.

First Servant. Hear you, master steward, where's our master?
Are we undone, cast off, nothing remaining?

Flavius. Alack, my fellows, what should I say to you?
Let me be recorded° by the righteous gods,
I am as poor as you.

First Servant.   Such a house broke?   5
So noble a master fall'n, all gone, and not
One friend to take his fortune° by the arm,
And go along with him?

Second Servant.   As we do turn our backs
From our companion thrown into his grave,
So his familiars to his buried fortunes°   10
Slink all away, leave their false vows with him,
Like empty purses picked; and his poor self,
A dedicated beggar to the air,°
With his disease of all-shunned poverty,
Walks like contempt alone.

Enter other Servants.

                    More of our fellows.   15

Flavius. All broken implements of a ruined house.

Third Servant. Yet do our hearts wear Timon's livery,

4.2.4 **Let me be recorded** let it be recorded of me   7 **his fortune**
i.e., Timon in his ill fortune   10 **his familiars to his buried fortunes**
those who were the familiar friends of his now buried fortunes (also
suggests "familiar spirit," a personal servant from the spirit world)
13 **A dedicated beggar to the air** a beggar vowed or doomed to wander about in the open air

That see I by our faces; we are fellows° still,
Serving alike in sorrow. Leaked is our bark,
20 And we poor mates stand on the dying deck,
Hearing the surges threat. We must all part
Into this sea of air.°

Flavius.   Good fellows all,
The latest° of my wealth I'll share amongst you.
Wherever we shall meet, for Timon's sake,
25 Let's yet be fellows. Let's shake our heads and say,
As 'twere a knell unto our master's fortunes,
"We have seen better days." Let each take some.

              [*Gives money.*]

Nay, put out all your hands. Not one word more;
Thus part we rich in sorrow, parting poor.

              Embrace, and part several ways.

30 O the fierce wretchedness that glory brings us!
Who would not wish to be from wealth exempt,
Since riches point to° misery and contempt?
Who would be so mocked with glory, or to live°
But in a dream of friendship,
35 To have his pomp and all what state compounds°
But only painted,° like his varnished° friends?
Poor honest lord, brought low by his own heart,
Undone by goodness. Strange, unusual blood,°
When man's worst sin is, he does too much good.
40 Who then dares to be half so kind° again?
For bounty, that makes gods, do still mar men.
My dearest lord, blessed to be° most accursed,
Rich only to be wretched, thy great fortunes
Are made thy chief afflictions. Alas, kind lord,
45 He's flung in rage from this ingrateful seat°
Of monstrous friends;

18 **fellows** fellow servants   22 **this sea of air** i.e., the open air, which
is as comfortless to us as is the sea to sailors on a sinking ship   23
latest last   32 **point to** lead to   33 **to live** i.e., who would wish to
live   35 **all what state compounds** all that worldly splendor is composed of   36 **painted** illusory   36 **varnished** fair-seeming   38
blood disposition   40 **half so kind** i.e., as Timon was, who came to
grief because of it   42 **blessed to be** i.e., blessed with wealth only to
be   45 **seat** residence

Nor has he with him to supply his life,°
Or that° which can command it.
I'll follow and inquire him out.
I'll ever serve his mind with my best will;   50
Whilst I have gold, I'll be his steward still.   *Exit.*

[Scene 3. *Before Timon's cave.*]

Enter Timon in the woods.

Timon. O blessèd breeding sun, draw from the earth
    Rotten humidity;° below thy sister's orb°
    Infect the air. Twinned brothers of one womb,
    Whose procreation, residence, and birth,
    Scarce is dividant°—touch° them with several°
        fortunes,   5
    The greater scorns the lesser. Not nature,
    To whom all sores lay siege, can bear great fortune
    But by contempt of nature.°
    Raise me this beggar, and deny't° that lord,
    The senators shall bear contempt hereditary,°   10
    The beggar native° honor.
    It is the pasture lards the brother's sides,
    The want that makes him lean.° Who dares? Who
        dares

47 **to supply his life** i.e., he has no food and drink   48 **that** i.e.,
money   4.3.2 **Rotten humidity** humidity that causes things to rot
2 **below thy sister's orb** beneath the moon (i.e., in the middle air
between earth and moon)   5 **dividant** divisible, separable   5 **touch**
test   5 **several** different   6–8 **Not nature … nature** i.e., human
nature, which is subjected to all sorts of miseries, when it encounters
good fortune rejects its own natural affection and despises mankind
9 **deny't** i.e., deny to raise   10 **hereditary** i.e., as if they were born
that way and not simply victims of fortune's caprices   11 **native** i.e.,
as if he were born with it   12–13 **It is … lean** i.e., the "twinned
brothers" (line 3) are distinguished by their gifts of fortune; the
rich pasture, and not any intrinsic worth, makes one brother fat and
the other lean

In purity of manhood stand upright
15 And say, this man's a flatterer? If one be,
So are they all, for every grise° of fortune
Is smoothed° by that below. The learned pate°
Ducks to the golden fool.° All's obliquy;°
There's nothing level in our cursèd natures
20 But direct villainy. Therefore be abhorred
All feasts, societies, and throngs of men.
His semblable,° yea himself, Timon disdains;
Destruction fang° mankind. Earth, yield me roots.
                                          [Digs.]

Who seeks for better of thee, sauce° his palate
25 With thy most operant° poison. What is here?
Gold? Yellow, glittering, precious gold?
No, gods, I am no idle votarist.°
Roots, you clear° heavens! Thus much of this will
    make
Black, white; foul, fair; wrong, right;
30 Base, noble; old, young; coward, valiant.
Ha, you gods! Why this? What this, you gods?
    Why this
Will lug your priests and servants from your sides;
Pluck stout men's pillows from below their heads.°
This yellow slave
35 Will knit and break religions, bless th' accursed,
Make the hoar° leprosy adored, place° thieves,
And give them title, knee, and approbation
With senators on the bench. This is it
That makes the wappened° widow wed again;
40 She, whom the spital-house° and ulcerous sores°

---

16 **grise** step   17 **smoothed** flattered, facilitated by flattery   17 **pate** head   18 **Ducks to the golden fool** inclines in deference to the rich fool   18 **obliquy** obliquity, moral crookedness   22 **semblable** anything like himself   23 **fang** (1) seize, as with fangs (2) provide with fangs   24 **sauce** season   25 **operant** potent   27 **no idle votarist** i.e., I have not sworn my vow in an idle or trifling way   28 **clear** pure   33 **Pluck ... heads** i.e., kill even strong men by sudden suffocation   36 **hoar** white   36 **place** elevate to a place or office of dignity   39 **wappened** sexually exhausted   40 **spital-house** hospital (especially for the lower classes and sufferers from loathsome diseases)   40 **ulcerous sores** i.e., those afflicted with ulcerous sores

Would cast the gorge° at, this embalms and spices
To th' April day° again. Come, damned earth,
Thou common whore of mankind, that puts odds
Among the rout of nations,° I will make thee
Do thy right nature.°

                                        March afar off.
            Ha? A drum? Th'art quick,°   45
But yet I'll bury thee. Thou't go,° strong thief,
When gouty keepers of thee cannot stand.
Nay, stay thou out for earnest.°   [*Keeps some gold.*]

        *Enter Alcibiades, with drum and fife, in war-
        like manner; and Phrynia and Timandra.*

Alcibiades. What art thou there? Speak.

Timon. A beast as thou art. The canker° gnaw thy
    heart   50
    For showing me again the eyes of man.

Alcibiades. What is thy name? Is man so hateful to
    thee
    That art thyself a man?

Timon. I am Misanthropos° and hate mankind.
    For thy part, I do wish thou wert a dog,   55
    That I might love thee something.°

Alcibiades.   I know thee well,
    But in thy fortunes am unlearned and strange.°

Timon. I know thee too, and more than that I know
    thee
    I not desire to know. Follow thy drum,
    With man's blood paint the ground gules,° gules.   60

---

41 **cast the gorge** vomit   41–42 **embalms and spices/To th' April
day** i.e., preserves, perfumes, and generally revivifies to a springlike
and youthful amorousness   43–44 **puts odds/Among the rout of nations** sets the disorderly mob of nations at strife with each other
45 **Do thy right nature** i.e., cause strife and dissension   45 **quick** (1)
alive (2) speedily had and lost   46 **go** walk, move   48 **for earnest**
as an installment   50 **canker** (1) ulcerous sore (2) canker-worm
54 **Misanthropos** the man-hater   56 **something** somewhat   57
strange ignorant   60 **gules** red (the heraldic term)

Religious canons, civil laws are cruel;
Then what should war be? This fell° whore of thine
Hath in her more destruction than thy sword,
For all her cherubin look.

Phrynia.   Thy lips rot off.

65 *Timon.* I will not kiss thee; then the rot returns°
To thine own lips again.

Alcibiades. How came the noble Timon to this
change?

Timon. As the moon does, by wanting° light to give.
But then renew° I could not like the moon;
70   There were no suns to borrow of.

Alcibiades. Noble Timon, what friendship may I do
thee?

Timon. None, but to maintain my opinion.°

Alcibiades. What is it, Timon?

Timon. Promise me friendship, but perform none.
75   If thou wilt not promise, the gods plague thee,
For thou art a man. If thou dost perform,
Confound thee, for thou art a man.

Alcibiades. I have heard in some sort of thy miseries.

Timon. Thou saw'st them when I had prosperity.

80 *Alcibiades.* I see them now; then was a blessed time.

Timon. As thine is now, held with a brace° of harlots.

Timandra. Is this th' Athenian minion,° whom the
world
Voiced so regardfully?°

---

62 **fell** destructive 65 **the rot returns** (based on a prevalent belief
that by transmitting a venereal infection to another, one loses it
himself) 68 **wanting** lacking 69 **renew** (1) to become new (2) to
extend a loan (as in the next line) 72 **maintain my opinion** i.e.,
be a misanthropist, too 81 **brace** (usually used for a pair of dogs on
a leash) 82 **minion** favorite, darling 83 **Voiced so regardfully**
spoke of with so much regard

Timon.   Art thou Timandra?

Timandra.   Yes.

Timon. Be a whore still; they love thee not that use
   thee.
   Give them diseases, leaving° with thee their lust.   85
   Make use of thy salt° hours. Season° the slaves
   For tubs and baths;° bring down rose-cheeked
      youth
   To the tub-fast and the diet.°

Timandra.   Hang thee, monster!

Alcibiades. Pardon him, sweet Timandra, for his wits
   Are drowned and lost in his calamities.   90
   I have but little gold of late, brave° Timon,
   The want whereof doth daily make revolt
   In my penurious° band. I have heard, and grieved,
   How cursèd Athens, mindless of thy worth,
   Forgetting thy great deeds, when neighbor states,   95
   But for thy sword and fortune, trod° upon them—

Timon. I prithee beat thy drum° and get thee gone.

Alcibiades. I am thy friend and pity thee, dear Timon.

Timon. How dost thou pity him whom thou dost
   trouble?
   I had rather be alone.

Alcibiades.   Why fare thee well.   100
   Here is some gold for thee.

Timon.   Keep it, I cannot eat it.

Alcibiades. When I have laid proud Athens on a
   heap—

---

85 **leaving** i.e., while they leave   86 **salt** lustful, salacious   86 **Season**
spice   87 **tubs and baths** sweating-tubs and hot baths (used to treat
venereal disease)   88 **tub-fast and the diet** (fasting and special diet
were treatments for venereal disease)   91 **brave** excellent   93 **penuri-
ous** needy   96 **trod** i.e., would have trodden   97 **beat thy drum** i.e.,
let thy drummer give the signal for departure

Timon. War'st thou 'gainst Athens?

Alcibiades.   Ay, Timon, and have cause.

Timon. The gods confound them all in thy conquest,°
105   And thee after when thou hast conquerèd.

Alcibiades. Why me, Timon?

Timon.   That by killing of villains
      Thou wast born to conquer my country.
      Put up° thy gold. Go on, here's gold, go on.
      Be as a planetary plague,° when Jove
110   Will o'er some high-viced city hang his poison
      In the sick air. Let not thy sword skip one.
      Pity not honored age for his white beard:
      He is an usurer. Strike me the counterfeit matron:
      It is her habit° only that is honest,°
115   Herself's a bawd. Let not the virgin's cheek
      Make soft thy trenchant° sword: for those milk
          paps,
      That through the window-bars° bore at men's eyes,
      Are not within the leaf of pity writ,°
      But set them down horrible traitors. Spare not the
          babe
      Whose dimpled smiles from fools exhaust° their
120   mercy:
      Think it a bastard, whom the oracle
      Hath doubtfully° pronounced thy throat shall cut,
      And mince it sans remorse.° Swear against objects.°
      Put armor on thine ears and on thine eyes,
      Whose proof° nor yells of mothers, maids, nor
125   babes,

104 **in thy conquest** i.e., in your victory over them   108 **Put up** put
away   109 **planetary plague** plague caused by the planets   114 **habit**
dress   114 **honest** chaste   116 **trenchant** cutting   117 **window-bars**
lattice work of a window (?) open-work squares of the bodice of a
woman's frock (?)   118 **within the leaf of pity writ** i.e., written down
on the page with the names of those who are to be pitied and spared
120 **exhaust** draw out, elicit   122 **doubtfully** ambiguously   123
mince it sans remorse cut it up without pity   123 **objects** objections,
accusations of cruelty   125 **proof** high quality (of armor), impene-
trability

Nor sight of priests in holy vestments bleeding,
Shall pierce a jot. There's gold to pay thy soldiers.
Make large confusion;° and, thy fury spent,
Confounded be thyself. Speak not, begone.

Alcibiades. Hast° thou gold yet, I'll take the gold thou
 givest me,   130
Not all thy counsel.

Timon. Dost thou or dost thou not, heaven's curse
 upon thee.

Phrynia and Timandra. Give us some gold, good
 Timon; hast thou more?

Timon. Enough to make a whore forswear her trade,
And to make whores, a bawd.° Hold up, you sluts, 135
Your aprons mountant.° You are not oathable,°
Although I know you'll swear, terribly swear
Into strong shudders and to heavenly agues
Th' immortal gods that hear you. Spare your oaths;
I'll trust to your conditions.° Be whores still,° 140
And he whose pious breath seeks to convert you,
Be strong in whore, allure him, burn him up;
Let your close fire predominate his smoke,°
And be no turncoats. Yet may your pains six months
Be quite contrary.° And thatch   145
Your poor thin roofs with burdens of the dead—°
Some that were hanged, no matter.
Wear them, betray with them; whore still;

---

128 **confusion** destruction 130 **Hast** i.e., if you have 135 **And to make whores, a bawd** i.e., and enough to make a bawd give up her trade of making whores (or, perhaps, enough to make a whore set herself up as a bawd, making whores instead of being one) 136 **aprons mountant** rising aprons (a mock heraldic phrase with sexual overtones) 136 **oathable** capable of being placed under oath 140 **conditions** dispositions 140 **still** always 143 **Let ... smoke** i.e., let the hidden fire of your sexuality or disease dominate over the smoke of idle words of he who "seeks to convert you" 144–45 **Yet ... contrary** i.e., may you spend six months of the year in being whores and the other six in repairing the physical damage occasioned by your debaucheries (?) 145–46 **And thatch ... dead** i.e., wear wigs (or possibly false pubes) made from loads of hair taken from the dead (venereal disease was thought to cause loss of hair)

Paint till a horse may mire° upon your face.
A pox of wrinkles!°

150 *Phrynia and Timandra.* Well, more gold. What then?
Believe't that we'll do anything for gold.

Timon. Consumptions° sow
In hollow° bones of man; strike their sharp° shins,
And mar men's spurring. Crack the lawyer's voice,
155 That he may never more false title plead,
Nor sound his quillets° shrilly. Hoar the flamen,°
That scolds against the quality of flesh°
And not believes himself. Down with the nose,°
Down with it flat, take the bridge quite away
160 Of him, that his particular to foresee,
Smells from the general weal.° Make curled-pate
ruffians bald,
And let the unscarred braggarts of the war
Derive some pain from you. Plague all,
That your activity may defeat and quell
165 The source of all erection.° There's more gold.
Do you damn others, and let this damn you,
And ditches grave° you all.

Phrynia and Timandra. More counsel with more
money, bounteous Timon.

Timon. More whore, more mischief first; I have given
you earnest.°

---

148 **mire** sink into the mire or mud (because of the thickness of
cosmetics)   149 **A pox of wrinkles** i.e., a pox on wrinkles, away with
wrinkles (since they can be covered with cosmetics)   152 **Consump-
tions** wasting diseases (here venereal disease)   153 **hollow … sharp**
i.e., the disease will make the bones hollow and the shins painful   156
quillets subtle verbal distinctions   156 **Hoar the flamen** whiten the
priest with disease, or cause his hair to turn white (possible pun on
"whore")   157 **quality of flesh** the nature of the flesh, sexual pleasure   158 **Down with the nose** (an effect of syphilis)   160–61 **his
particular … weal** i.e., to provide for his private advantage or profit,
he abandons the proper scent that contributes to the public good or
welfare   165 **The source of all erection** i.e., sexuality itself   167
grave be a grave for, bury   169 **earnest** a part payment to seal a
bargain

Alcibiades. Strike up the drum towards Athens. Farewell, Timon.   170
  If I thrive well, I'll visit thee again.

Timon. If I hope well,° I'll never see thee more.

Alcibiades. I never did thee harm.

Timon. Yes, thou spok'st well of me.

Alcibiades.   Call'st thou that harm?

Timon. Men daily find it. Get thee away, and take   175
  Thy beagles with thee.

Alcibiades.   We but offend him. Strike!
[*Drum beats.*]   *Exeunt* [*Alcibiades, Phrynia, and
                              Timandra*].

Timon. That nature, being sick of° man's unkindness,
  Should yet be hungry! Common mother, thou,
                             [*Digging*]
  Whose womb unmeasurable and infinite breast
  Teems° and feeds all; whose selfsame mettle,°   180
  Whereof thy proud child, arrogant man, is puffed,°
  Engenders the black toad and adder blue,
  The gilded newt and eyeless venomed worm,
  With all th' abhorrèd births below crisp° heaven
  Whereon Hyperion's quick'ning fire° doth shine;   185
  Yield him, who all the human sons do hate,
  From forth thy plenteous bosom, one poor root.
  Ensear° thy fertile and conceptious° womb;
  Let it no more bring out ingrateful man.
  Go great° with tigers, dragons, wolves, and bears,   190
  Teem with new monsters, whom thy upward face
  Hath to the marbled mansion all above°

---

172 **If I hope well** if my hopes are realized   177 **of** as a result of
180 **Teems** brings forth   180 **mettle** (1) substance (2) vigorous spirit
181 **puffed** puffed up with pride   184 **crisp** with curled clouds (?)
shining, clear (?)   185 **Hyperion's quick'ning fire** (the sun was
thought to have the power of generating some of the lower forms of
insect life)   188 **Ensear** dry up   188 **conceptious** conceiving, pro-
lific   190 **great** pregnant   192 **above** in heaven

Never presented. O, a root, dear thanks!
Dry up thy marrows,° vines and plough-torn leas,
195   Whereof ingrateful man, with liquorish draughts
And morsels unctious,° greases his pure mind,
That from it all consideration° slips—

Enter Apemantus.

More man? Plague, plague!

Apemantus. I was directed hither. Men report
200   Thou dost affect° my manners, and dost use them.

Timon. 'Tis then because thou dost not keep a dog
Whom I would imitate. Consumption° catch thee.

Apemantus. This is in thee a nature but infected,°
A poor unmanly melancholy sprung
From change of future.° Why this spade? This
205   place?
This slave-like habit° and these looks of care?
Thy flatterers yet wear silk, drink wine, lie soft,
Hug their diseased perfumes,° and have forgot
That ever Timon was. Shame not these woods
210   By putting on the cunning of a carper.°
Be thou a flatterer now, and seek to thrive
By that which has undone thee. Hinge thy knee,
And let his very breath whom thou'lt observe
Blow off thy cap;° praise his most vicious strain°
215   And call it excellent. Thou wast told thus.°

194 **marrows** (the type of a rich food, not a necessity of life, produced by the "vines" and "leas")   196 **unctious** (an obsolete variant
form of "unctuous")   197 **consideration** ability to consider   200
affect imitate   202 **Consumption** any wasting disease   203 **infected**
(1) affected, factitious (2) caught like an infection from your changed
circumstances   205 **change of future** i.e., change in your material
prospects   206 **habit** dress, garb   208 **diseased perfumes** diseased
and perfumed mistresses   210 **By ... carper** i.e., by pretending to
the profession of a cynic or railer (which any fool can do)   213–14
let his ... cap kneel so obsequiously close to the person you are paying court to that his breath may blow off your cap   214 **strain** quality
215 **Thou wast told thus** i.e., in your prosperity others spoke to you
in this manner

Thou gav'st thine ears, like tapsters° that bade
    welcome,
To knaves and all approachers. 'Tis most just
That thou turn rascal; hadst thou wealth again,
Rascals should have't. Do not assume my likeness.

Timon. Were I like thee, I'd throw away myself.   220

Apemantus. Thou hast cast away thyself, being like
    thyself:
A madman so long, now a fool. What, think'st
That the bleak air, thy boisterous chamberlain,°
Will put thy shirt on warm? Will these moist° trees,
That have outlived the eagle, page thy heels   225
And skip when thou point'st out?° Will the cold
    brook,
Candied° with ice, caudle° thy morning taste
To cure thy o'er-night's surfeit?° Call the creatures
Whose naked natures live in all the spite
Of wreakful° heaven, whose bare unhoused trunks,   230
To the conflicting elements exposed,
Answer mere nature.° Bid them flatter thee.
O thou shalt find—

Timon.   A fool of thee. Depart.

Apemantus. I love thee better now than e'er I did.

Timon. I hate thee worse.

Apemantus.   Why?

Timon.   Thou flatter'st misery.   235

Apemantus. I flatter not, but say thou art a caitiff.°

---

216 **tapsters** (tavern-keepers or bartenders are proverbial for their indiscriminate hospitality) 223 **chamberlain** one who waits on a king or lord in his bedchamber 224 **moist** damp 226 **point'st out** indicate your desires 227 **Candied** congealed, encrusted 227 **caudle** offer a caudle (a warm, spiced, mildly alcoholic drink given to the sick) 228 **o'er-night's surfeit** previous night's indulgence in drink 230 **wreakful** vengeful 232 **Answer mere nature** correspond to or reflect nature in its barest and most rigorous form 236 **caitiff** wretch

Timon. Why dost thou seek me out?

Apemantus.   To vex thee.

Timon. Always a villain's office° or a fool's.
Dost please thyself in't?

Apemantus.   Ay.

Timon.   What, a knave too?

240 *Apemantus.* If thou didst put this sour cold habit° on
To castigate thy pride, 'twere well; but thou
Dost it enforcedly.° Thou'dst courtier be again
Wert thou not beggar. Willing misery°
Outlives incertain pomp, is crowned before.°
245 The one is filling still,° never complete;
The other, at high wish.° Best state, contentless,
Hath a distracted and most wretched being,
Worse than the worst, content.°
Thou shouldst desire to die, being miserable.

250 *Timon.* Not by his breath° that is more miserable.
Thou art a slave, whom Fortune's tender arm
With favor never clasped, but bred a dog.
Hadst thou, like us, from our first swath° proceeded
The sweet degrees° that this brief world affords
255 To such as may the passive drudges° of it
Freely command, thou wouldst have plunged thyself
In general riot,° melted down thy youth
In different beds of lust, and never learned

---

238 **office** duty   240 **habit** (1) garment (2) outward manner, bearing
242 **enforcedly** i.e., as if you were being forced to do it   243 **Willing
misery** voluntary poverty   244 **is crowned before** comes earlier to
the fulfillment of its desires and wishes   245 **The one is filling still**
i.e., pomp, like a leaky vessel, can never be filled (or fulfilled)   246
The other, at high wish i.e., "willing misery," because it wishes little,
can easily arrive at the height of its wishes   246–48 **Best state ...
content** i.e., a man in even the best material condition, if he is without content or happiness, is confused and wretched, worse than a
man in the poorest condition who is contented   250 **breath** voice
253 **swath** swaddling clothes   253–54 **proceeded/The sweet degrees**
advanced from one stage to the next above it (in sense of academic
"degrees")   255 **passive drudges** submissive menial servants   257
riot debauchery

The icy precepts of respect,° but followed
The sug'red game° before thee. But myself—   260
Who had the world as my confectionary,°
The mouths, the tongues, the eyes, and hearts of
     men
At duty, more than I could frame employment;°
That numberless upon me stuck, as leaves
Do on the oak, have with one winter's brush°   265
Fell° from their boughs, and left me open, bare
For every storm that blows—I to bear this,
That never knew but better, is some burden.
Thy nature did commence in sufferance,° time
Hath made thee hard in't. Why shouldst thou hate
     men?   270
They never flattered thee. What hast thou given?
If thou wilt curse, thy father, that poor rogue,
Must be thy subject; who in spite put stuff
To° some she-beggar and compounded thee
Poor rogue hereditary. Hence, begone.   275
If thou hadst not been born the worst° of men,
Thou hadst been a knave and flatterer.

Apemantus.   Art thou proud yet?

Timon. Ay, that I am not thee.

Apemantus.   I, that I was
     No prodigal.

Timon.   I, that I am one now.
Were all the wealth I have shut up in thee,   280
I'd give thee leave to hang it. Get thee gone.
That° the whole life of Athens were in this!
Thus would I eat it.   [*Eats a root.*]

---

259 **icy precepts of respect** i.e., the chilling rules of reason which
constitute proper social conduct   260 **sug'red game** outwardly sweet
quarry (probably whores)   261 **confectionary** a place where sweet-
meats or candy are made   263 **frame employment** invent work for
265 **winter's brush** i.e., brush of a wintry wind   266 **Fell** fallen   269
sufferance suffering   273–74 **put stuff/To** i.e., made pregnant (contemptuous)   276 **worst** i.e., in social and financial position   282
That i.e., would that

Apemantus.　　　　　　　　　Here, I will mend° thy feast.
　　　　　　　　　　　　　　　　[*Offers him food.*]

Timon. First mend my company, take away thyself.

Apemantus. So I shall mend mine own, by th' lack of
285　　thine.

Timon. 'Tis not well mended so, it is but botched;°
　　If not, I would it were.

Apemantus. What wouldst thou have to° Athens?

Timon. Thee thither in a whirlwind. If thou wilt,
290　　Tell them there I have gold; look, so I have.

Apemantus. Here is no use for gold.

Timon.　　　　　　　　　　　　The best and truest;
　　For here it sleeps and does no hirèd harm.

Apemantus. Where liest a nights, Timon?

Timon.　　　　　　　　　　　Under that's above me.°
　　Where feed'st thou a days, Apemantus?

295　*Apemantus.* Where my stomach finds meat, or rather
　　where I eat it.

Timon. Would poison were obedient and knew my
　　mind!

Apemantus. Where wouldst thou send it?

300　*Timon.* To sauce thy dishes.

Apemantus. The middle of humanity thou never
　　knewest, but the extremity of both ends. When thou
　　wast in thy gilt and thy perfume, they mocked thee
　　for too much curiosity;° in thy rags thou know'st
305　　none, but art despised for the contrary. There's a
　　medlar° for thee; eat it.

---

283 **mend** improve　286 **botched** clumsily repaired (because Apemantus is still present—with himself)　288 **to** in　293 **that's above
me** i.e., that which is above me, the sky　304 **curiosity** carefulness,
fastidiousness　306 **medlar** a fruit like a small brown-skinned apple,
not ready to be eaten until in the early stages of decay

Timon. On what I hate I feed not.

Apemantus. Dost hate° a medlar?

Timon. Ay, though it look like thee.

Apemantus. And° th'hadst hated meddlers° sooner, *310*
thou shouldst have loved thyself better now. What
man didst thou ever know unthrift° that was beloved after° his means?

Timon. Who, without those means thou talk'st of,
didst thou ever know beloved? *315*

Apemantus. Myself.

Timon. I understand thee; thou hadst some means to
keep a dog.°

Apemantus. What things in the world canst thou nearest compare to thy flatterers? *320*

Timon. Women nearest, but men—men are the
things themselves. What wouldst thou do with the
world, Apemantus, if it lay in thy power?

Apemantus. Give it the beasts, to be rid of the men.

Timon. Wouldst thou have thyself fall in the confu- *325*
sion of men,° and remain a beast with the beasts?

Apemantus. Ay, Timon.

Timon. A beastly ambition, which the gods grant
thee t' attain to. If thou wert the lion, the fox
would beguile° thee. If thou wert the lamb, the *330*
fox would eat thee. If thou wert the fox, the lion
would suspect thee, when peradventure° thou wert
accused by the ass. If thou wert the ass, thy dull-

---

308 **hate** ("eat" and "hate" were pronounced alike in Elizabethan
English) 310 **And** if 310 **meddlers** (1) the fruit (2) busybodies,
intriguers (3) those who overindulge in sexual intercourse 312 **unthrift** prodigal, spendthrift 313 **after** in accordance with (i.e., the
true love for an "unthrift" is not in proportion with his bounty) 318
a dog i.e., you had just enough to keep a dog so that something might
love you 325–26 **the confusion of men** i.e., the original Fall in the
Garden of Eden 330 **beguile** trick 332 **peradventure** perchance

ness would torment thee, and still thou liv'dst but
335 as a breakfast to the wolf. If thou wert the wolf,
thy greediness would afflict thee, and oft thou
shouldst hazard thy life for thy dinner. Wert thou
the unicorn,° pride and wrath would confound°
thee, and make thine own self the conquest of thy
340 fury. Wert thou a bear, thou wouldst be killed by
the horse. Wert thou a horse, thou wouldst be
seized by the leopard. Wert thou a leopard, thou
wert german° to the lion, and the spots° of thy
kindred were jurors° on thy life. All thy safety
345 were remotion,° and thy defense absence. What
beast couldst thou be that were not subject to a
beast? And what a beast art thou already, that seest
not thy loss in transformation!°

Apemantus. If thou couldst please me with speaking
350 to me, thou mightst have hit upon it here. The
commonwealth of Athens is become a forest of
beasts.

Timon. How has the ass broke the wall, that thou art
out of the city?

355 *Apemantus.* Yonder comes a poet and a painter.°
The plague of company light upon thee! I will fear
to catch it, and give way.° When I know not what
else to do, I'll see thee again.

Timon. When there is nothing living but thee, thou
360 shalt be welcome. I had rather be a beggar's dog
than Apemantus.

Apemantus. Thou art the cap° of all the fools alive.

---

338 **unicorn** (an untamable beast, who, in his fury to attack the treed
lion, runs his horn into the tree and puts himself at the mercy of the
lion) 338 **confound** destroy 343 **german** akin 343 **spots** (1)
markings (2) moral stains, vices 344 **jurors** witnesses (especially
false ones) 345 **remotion** removal of yourself (to a distance), re-
moteness 348 **in transformation** i.e., in seeking to be transformed
into a beast 355 **a poet and a painter** (they do not actually enter
until the beginning of Act 5) 357 **give way** retire 362 **cap** chief,
summit

Timon. Would thou wert clean enough to spit upon.

Apemantus. A plague on thee, thou art too bad to
    curse.

Timon. All villains that do stand by thee° are pure. 365

Apemantus. There is no leprosy but what thou
    speak'st.

Timon. If I name thee.
  I'll beat thee, but I should infect my hands.

Apemantus. I would my tongue could rot them off.

Timon. Away, thou issue of a mangy dog. 370
  Choler° does kill me that thou art alive;
  I swound° to see thee.

Apemantus. Would thou wouldst burst.

Timon. Away, thou tedious rogue, I am sorry I shall
  lose a stone by thee.   [*Throws a stone at him.*] 375

Apemantus. Beast!

Timon. Slave!

Apemantus. Toad!

Timon. Rogue, rogue, rogue!
  I am sick of this false world, and will love naught 380
  But even the mere necessities upon't.°
  Then, Timon, presently° prepare thy grave.
  Lie where the light foam of the sea may beat
  Thy gravestone daily. Make thine epitaph,
  That death in me° at others' lives may laugh. 385
  [*To the gold*] O thou sweet king-killer, and dear
    divorce
  'Twixt natural° son and sire, thou bright defiler
  Of Hymen's° purest bed, thou valiant Mars,

---

365 **that do stand by thee** compared to you   371 **Choler** anger   372
swound swoon   381 **But even … upon't** i.e., except the bare necessities of life   382 **presently** immediately   385 **in me** by my example
387 **natural** son by birth (does not mean "illegitimate")   388 **Hymen**
Greek god of marriage

Thou ever young, fresh, loved, and delicate wooer,
390 Whose blush° doth thaw the consecrated snow
That lies on Dian's° lap. Thou visible god,
That sold'rest close impossibilities°
And mak'st them kiss; that speak'st with every
    tongue
To every purpose. O thou touch° of hearts,
395 Think thy slave man rebels, and by thy virtue
Set them into confounding odds,° that beasts
May have the world in empire.

Apemantus.   Would 'twere so,
But not till I am dead. I'll say th'hast gold.
Thou wilt be thronged to shortly.

Timon.   Thronged to?

Apemantus.   Ay.

Timon. Thy back, I prithee.

400 *Apemantus*.   Live, and love thy misery.

Timon. Long live so, and so die. I am quit.°

Enter the Banditti.

Apemantus. Moe things like men! Eat, Timon, and
abhor them.   *Exit Apemantus.*

First Bandit. Where should he have this gold? It is
some poor fragment, some slender ort° of his
405 remainder. The mere° want of gold, and the falling-
from° of his friends, drove him into this melancholy.

Second Bandit. It is noised° he hath a mass of treasure.

410 *Third Bandit*. Let us make the assay° upon him. If

---

390 **blush** glow 391 **Dian** Diana, the virgin huntress, Greek goddess
of chastity 392 **sold'rest close impossibilities** joins closely together
things thought to be irreconcilable 394 **touch** touchstone 396 **into
confounding odds** at ruinous strife 401 **quit** rid (of Apemantus)
404 **ort** leftover bit 405 **mere** sheer 405–06 **falling-from** falling-off
408 **noised** rumored 410 **make the assay** put it to the test

he care not for't, he will supply us easily; if he
covetously reserve it, how shall's get it?

Second Bandit. True, for he bears it not about him;
'tis hid.

First Bandit. Is not this he?   *415*

All. Where?

Second Bandit. 'Tis his description.

Third Bandit. He? I know him.

All. Save thee,° Timon.

Timon. Now, thieves?   *420*

All. Soldiers, not thieves.

Timon.   Both too, and women's sons.

All. We are not thieves, but men that much do want.°

Timon. Your greatest want is, you want much of
     meat.°
  Why should you want? Behold, the earth hath
     roots;
  Within this mile break forth a hundred springs;   *425*
  The oaks bear mast,° the briers scarlet hips;°
  The bounteous huswife° nature on each bush
  Lays her full mess° before you. Want? Why want?

First Bandit. We cannot live on grass, on berries,
     water,
  As beasts and birds and fishes.   *430*

Timon. Nor on the beasts themselves, the birds and
     fishes;
  You must eat men. Yet thanks I must you con°
  That you are thieves professed, that you work not
  In holier shapes; for there is boundless theft

---

419 **Save thee** God save thee (a conventional salutation) 422 **want**
need, lack 423 **you want much of meat** you desire (or lack) a good
deal of food (i.e., if you didn't eat so much your wants would be
smaller) 426 **mast** acorns (generally fed to swine) 426 **hips** fruit
of the rose 427 **huswife** housewife 428 **mess** meal 432 **con** offer

435 In limited° professions. Rascal thieves,
     Here's gold. Go, suck the subtle° blood o' th' grape,
     Till the high fever° seethe your blood to froth,
     And so 'scape hanging. Trust not the physician;
     His antidotes are poison, and he slays
440 Moe° than you rob. Take wealth and lives together,
     Do, villain, do, since you protest° to do't.
     Like workmen, I'll example you with thievery:°
     The sun's a thief, and with his great attraction°
     Robs the vast sea. The moon's an arrant thief,
445 And her pale fire she snatches from the sun.
     The sea's a thief, whose liquid surge resolves
     The moon into salt tears.° The earth's a thief,
     That feeds and breeds by a composture° stol'n
     From gen'ral excrement. Each thing's a thief.
450 The laws, your curb and whip, in their rough power
     Has unchecked theft. Love not yourselves; away,
     Rob one another. There's more gold; cut throats,
     All that you meet are thieves. To Athens go,
     Break open shops; nothing can you steal
455 But thieves do lose it. Steal less for this I give you,°
     And gold confound you howsoe'er.° Amen.

     Third Bandit. Has almost charmed me from my profession by persuading me to it.

     First Bandit. 'Tis in the malice of mankind° that he
460 thus advises us, not to have us thrive in our
     mystery.°

---

435 **limited** limited in numbers, restricted (as a guild) 436 **subtle** treacherous 437 **high fever** i.e., of drunkenness 440 **Moe** more 441 **protest** profess 442 **Like . . . thievery** i.e., as one instructs workmen by practical example, so I will give you some precedents for your line of work, thievery 443 **attraction** drawing power 446–47 **whose . . . tears** (the idea is that the sea's tides are stolen from the moon's precipitation) 448 **composture** compost, manure 455 **Steal less for this I give you** i.e., even if you steal less because of the gold I am giving you 456 **howsoe'er** nevertheless 459 **in the malice of mankind** i.e., because of the malice Timon bears to all mankind 461 **mystery** trade, profession

Second Bandit. I'll believe him as an enemy,° and
  give over° my trade.

First Bandit. Let us first see peace in Athens; there
  is no time so miserable but a man may be true.°   465
                                 Exit Thieves.

      Enter [Flavius,] the Steward to Timon.

Flavius. O you gods!
  Is yond despised and ruinous° man my lord?
  Full of decay and failing? O monument
  And wonder° of good deeds evilly bestowed!
  What an alteration of honor° has desp'rate want
    made!   470
  What vilder° thing upon the earth than friends,
  Who can bring noblest minds to basest ends!
  How rarely does it meet with this time's guise,°
  When man was wished° to love his enemies!
  Grant I may ever love, and rather woo   475
  Those that would mischief me than those that do.°
  Has caught me in his eye; I will present
  My honest grief unto him, and as my lord
  Still serve him with my life. My dearest master.

Timon. Away! What art thou?

Flavius.   Have you forgot me, sir?   480

Timon. Why dost ask that? I have forgot all men.
  Then, if thou grunt'st° th'art a man,
  I have forgot thee.

---

462 **I'll believe him as an enemy** i.e., since he is an enemy, I'll do the
opposite of what he advises   463 **give over** give up   464–65 **there
is ... true** i.e., you can become an honest man any time you choose
(therefore, why do it now?)   467 **ruinous** ruined   468–69 **monu-
ment/And wonder** i.e., wonderful monument (memorial or tombstone)   470 **alteration of honor** change (for the worse) in honor
471 **vilder** viler   473 **How ... guise** i.e., how excellently does
Timon's example fit in with the moral tone of these times (spoken
ironically)   474 **wished** desired (by God)   476 **Those ... do** i.e.,
I will love those enemies who are direct and open in their desire to
harm me better than those who harm me under the guise of friendship   482 **grunt'st** i.e., even your claim to be a man is delivered in
an animal grunt (since all men are bestial)

Flavius. An honest poor servant of yours.

485 *Timon.* Then I know thee not.
　　　I never had honest man about me, I; all
　　　I kept were knaves,° to serve in meat to villains.

Flavius. The gods are witness,
　　　Nev'r did poor steward wear a truer grief
490　For his undone lord than mine eyes for you.

Timon. What, dost thou weep? Come nearer. Then
　　　　I love thee
　　　Because thou art a woman, and disclaim'st
　　　Flinty° mankind, whose eyes do never give°
　　　But thorough° lust and laughter. Pity's sleeping.
　　　Strange times, that weep with laughing, not with
495　　　weeping!

Flavius. I beg of you to know me, good my lord,
　　　T' accept my grief, and whilst this poor wealth lasts,
　　　To entertain° me as your steward still.

Timon. Had I a steward
500　So true, so just, and now so comfortable?°
　　　It almost turns my dangerous nature mild.
　　　Let me behold thy face. Surely, this man
　　　Was born of woman.
　　　Forgive my general and exceptless° rashness,
505　You perpetual-sober gods. I do proclaim
　　　One honest man. Mistake me not, but one.
　　　No more I pray—and he's a steward.
　　　How fain would I have hated all mankind,
　　　And thou redeem'st thyself. But all save thee
510　I fell° with curses.
　　　Methinks thou art more honest now than wise;
　　　For, by oppressing° and betraying me,

487 **knaves** (1) servants (2) villains   493 **Flinty** hardhearted   493
give weep   494 **But thorough** except through   498 **entertain** receive into service   500 **comfortable** comforting   504 **exceptless**
making no exceptions   510 **fell** cause to fall, strike down   512 **op-
pressing** distressing

Thou might'st have sooner got another service.°
For many so arrive at second masters
Upon their first lord's neck.° But tell me true—   *515*
For I must ever doubt,° though ne'er so sure—
Is not thy kindness subtle, covetous,
A usuring kindness, as rich men deal° gifts,
Expecting in return twenty for one?

Flavius. No, my most worthy master, in whose breast   *520*
  Doubt and suspect,° alas, are placed too late.
  You should have feared false times when you did
    feast.
  Suspect still° comes where an estate is least.
  That which I show, heaven knows, is merely° love,
  Duty and zeal to your unmatchèd mind,   *525*
  Care of your food and living; and believe it,
  My most honored lord,
  For any benefit that points° to me,
  Either in hope or present, I'd exchange
  For this one wish, that you had power and wealth   *530*
  To requite me by making rich yourself.

Timon. Look thee, 'tis so. Thou singly° honest man,
  Here, take. The gods out of my misery
  Has sent thee treasure. Go, live rich and happy,
  But thus conditioned:° thou shalt build from° men;   *535*
  Hate all, curse all, show charity to none,
  But let the famished flesh slide from the bone
  Ere thou relieve the beggar. Give to dogs
  What thou deniest to men. Let prisons swallow 'em,
  Debts wither 'em to nothing; be men like blasted°
    woods,   *540*
  And may diseases lick up their false bloods.
  And so farewell, and thrive.

---

513 **service** position as a servant   515 **Upon their first lord's neck**
i.e., by treading down their first master and mounting on his neck
(or shoulders)   516 **doubt** suspect, fear   518 **deal** distribute   521
suspect suspicion   523 **still** always   524 **merely** entirely   528 **points**
might accrue   532 **singly** (1) uniquely (2) truly   535 **But thus conditioned** with this condition   535 **from** away from   540 **blasted**
blighted

Flavius. O let me stay and comfort you, my master.

Timon. If thou hat'st curses
545   Stay not; fly, whilst thou art blessed and free.
      Ne'er see thou man, and let me ne'er see thee.
                    Exit [Flavius; and exit Timon into his cave].

[ACT 5

Scene 1. *Before Timon's cave.*]

Enter Poet and Painter; [Timon listens from his cave, unseen].

Painter. As I took note of the place, it cannot be far where he abides.

Poet. What's to be thought of him? Does the rumor hold for true that he's so full of gold?

Painter. Certain. Alcibiades reports it. Phrynia and   5
Timandra had gold of him. He likewise enriched poor straggling soldiers° with great quantity. 'Tis said he gave unto his steward a mighty sum.

Poet. Then this breaking° of his has been but a try° for his friends?   10

Painter. Nothing else. You shall see him a palm° in Athens again, and flourish with the highest. Therefore 'tis not amiss we tender° our loves to him in this supposed distress of his. It will show honestly° in us, and is very likely to load our purposes with   15
what they travail° for, if it be a just and true report that goes of his having.°

5.1.7 **soldiers** i.e., the banditti, who claimed to be soldiers 9 **breaking** going bankrupt 9 **try** test 11 **palm** (cf. Psalm 92:11 "The righteous shall flourish like the palm-tree") 13 **tender** offer 14 **honestly** honorably 16 **travail** (1) labor (2) travel 17 **having** wealth

271

Poet. What have you now to present unto him?

Painter. Nothing at this time but my visitation; only
20   I will promise him an excellent piece.

Poet. I must serve him so too, tell him of an intent
  that's coming toward him.

Painter. Good as the best. Promising is the very air
  o' th' time; it opens the eyes of expectation. Per-
25   formance is ever the duller for his act,° and but
  in the plainer and simpler kind of people, the deed
  of saying° is quite out of use. To promise is most
  courtly and fashionable; performance is a kind of
  will or testament, which argues a great sickness in
30   his judgment that makes it.

        Enter Timon from his cave.

Timon. [*Aside*] Excellent workman, thou canst not
  paint a man so bad as is thyself.

Poet. I am thinking what I shall say I have provided
  for him. It must be a personating of himself;° a
35   satire against the softness° of prosperity, with a
  discovery° of the infinite flatteries that follow youth
  and opulency.

Timon. [*Aside*] Must thou needs stand for° a villain
  in thine own work? Wilt thou whip thine own faults
40   in other men? Do so, I have gold for thee.

Poet. Nay, let's seek him.
  Then do we sin against our own estate,°
  When we may profit meet, and come too late.

Painter. True.
45   When the day serves, before black-cornered night,°

25 **his act** its act, its having been put into action   26–27 **the deed of
saying** i.e., the doing of what a person says he will do   34 **personating of himself** representation of Timon and his situation   35 **soft-
ness** weakness, flabbiness   36 **discovery** revelation (a theatrical term)
38 **stand for** serve as a model for   42 **estate** fortune, material possessions   45 **black-cornered night** i.e., night which creates dark corners
and is obscure like them

Find what thou want'st by free and offered light.
Come.

Timon. [*Aside*] I'll meet you at the turn.°
    What a god's gold, that he is worshiped
    In a baser temple° than where swine feed!   50
    'Tis thou that rig'st the bark and plough'st the
        foam,
    Settlest admirèd reverence° in a slave.
    To thee be worshiped and thy saints for aye;°
    Be° crowned with plagues that thee alone obey.
    Fit I meet them.   [*Comes forward.*]   55

Poet. Hail, worthy Timon.

Painter.   Our late noble master.

Timon. Have I once° lived to see two honest men?

Poet. Sir,
    Having often of your open bounty tasted,
    Hearing you were retired,° your friends fall'n off,   60
    Whose thankless natures, O abhorrèd spirits,
    Not all the whips of heaven are large enough—
    What, to you,
    Whose starlike nobleness gave life and influence°
    To their whole being! I am rapt,° and cannot cover   65
    The monstrous bulk of this ingratitude
    With any size° of words.

Timon.   Let it go;
    Naked, men may see't the better.
    You that are honest, by being what you are,
    Make them° best seen and known.

Painter.   He and myself   70

---

48 **I'll meet you at the turn** i.e., I will match your tricks with better
ones of my own   50 **baser temple** i.e., the human body   52 **Settlest
admirèd reverence** establishes a wondering awe (of his master)
53 **for aye** forever   54 **Be** i.e., may they be   57 **once** indeed (an in-
tensive)   60 **retired** withdrawn   64 **influence** i.e., astrological influence   65 **rapt** carried away with emotion   67 **size** (1) magnitude
(2) starchlike glue used on cloth, especially before painting on it
70 **them** i.e., the thankless natures of his fair-weather friends

Have traveled in the great show'r of your gifts,
And sweetly felt it.

Timon.   Ay, you are honest men.

Painter. We are hither come to offer you our service.

Timon. Most honest men. Why, how shall I requite
you?
75   Can you eat roots and drink cold water? No?

Both. What we can do, we'll do to do you service.

Timon. Y'are honest men. Y'have heard that I have
gold,
I am sure you have. Speak truth, y'are honest men.

Painter. So it is said, my noble lord, but therefore
80   Came not my friend nor I.

Timon. Good honest men. Thou draw'st a counterfeit°
Best in all Athens. Th'art indeed the best;
Thou counterfeit'st most lively.°

Painter.   So-so, my lord.

Timon. E'en so, sir, as I say. And for thy fiction,°
85   Why thy verse swells with stuff so fine and smooth°
That thou art even natural in thine art.°
But for all this, my honest-natured friends,
I must needs say you have little fault;
Marry,° 'tis not monstrous in you, neither wish I
You take much pains to mend.

90   *Both.*   Beseech your honor
To make it known to us.

Timon.   You'll take it ill.

Both. Most thankfully, my lord.

---

81 **counterfeit** (1) representation, picture (2) false representation
83 **most lively** in a most lifelike manner 84 **fiction** imaginative
feigning 85 **smooth** polished (with implication of flattery) 86 **thou ...
art** (1) your writings represent a triumph of nature over art; your art
conceals itself (2) you show your evil natural self in your art-
ful dissimulation 89 **Marry** indeed

Timon. Will you indeed?

Both. Doubt it not, worthy lord.

Timon. There's never a one of you but trusts a knave
 That mightily deceives you.

Both. Do we, my lord? 95

Timon. Ay, and you hear him cog,° see him dis-
 semble,
 Know his gross patchery,° love him, feed him,
 Keep° in your bosom, yet remain assured
 That he's a made-up° villain.

Painter. I know none such, my lord.

Poet. Nor I. 100

Timon. Look you, I love you well; I'll give you gold:
 Rid me these villains from your companies.
 Hang them, or stab them, drown them in a
 draught,°
 Confound° them by some course, and come to me,
 I'll give you gold enough. 105

Both. Name them, my lord, let's know them.

Timon. You that way, and you this; but two in com-
 pany.°
 Each man apart, all single and alone,
 Yet an arch-villain keeps him company.
 [*To one*] If where thou art, two villains shall not be, 110
 Come not near him. [*To the other*] If thou wouldst
 not reside
 But° where one villain is, then him abandon.
 Hence, pack,° there's gold; you came for gold, ye
 slaves.
 [*To one*] You have work for me, there's payment.
 Hence!

96 **cog** cheat 97 **patchery** roguery 98 **Keep** i.e., let him dwell
99 **made-up** complete 103 **draught** privy, sink 104 **Confound** destroy 107 **but two in company** i.e., wherever either of them is, there
is both a poet (or painter) and a villain 112 **But** except 113 **pack**
be off

[*To the other*] You are an alchemist, make gold
115   of that.
       Out, rascal dogs!
                    [*Beats them out, then retires into his cave.*]

       Enter [Flavius, the] Steward, and two Senators.

Flavius. It is vain that you would speak with Timon,
       For he is set so only to himself°
       That nothing but himself, which looks like man,
       Is friendly with him.

120 *First Senator.*   Bring us to his cave.
       It is our part and promise° to th' Athenians
       To speak with Timon.

Second Senator.   At all times alike
       Men are not still the same; 'twas time and griefs
       That framed him thus. Time with his fairer hand
125   Offering the fortunes of his former days,
       The former man may make him. Bring us to him,
       And chance it° as it may.

Flavius.   Here is his cave.
       Peace and content be here. Lord Timon! Timon!
       Look out, and speak to friends. Th' Athenians
130   By two of their most reverend senate greet thee.
       Speak to them, noble Timon.

              Enter Timon out of his cave.

Timon. Thou sun that comforts, burn! Speak and be
       hanged.
       For each true word a blister,° and each false
       Be as a cauterizing to the root o' th' tongue,
       Consuming it with speaking.

135 *First Senator.*   Worthy Timon—

Timon. Of none but such as you, and you of Timon.

---

118 **is set so only to himself** is so completely preoccupied with himself   121 **our part and promise** the role we promised to play
127 **chance it** may it turn out   133 **For each true word a blister** (an
ironic reversal of the proverbial belief that a lie causes a blister on
the tongue)

First Senator. The senators of Athens greet thee,
    Timon.

Timon. I thank them, and would send them back the
    plague,
    Could I but catch it for them.

First Senator.   O forget
    What we are sorry for ourselves in thee.°   140
    The senators, with one consent of love,°
    Entreat thee back to Athens, who have thought
    On special dignities, which vacant lie
    For thy best use and wearing.°

Second Senator.   They confess
    Toward thee forgetfulness too general° gross;   145
    Which now the public body,° which doth seldom
    Play the recanter, feeling in itself
    A lack of Timon's aid, hath sense withal°
    Of it own fall,° restraining° aid to Timon;
    And send forth us to make their sorrowed render,°   150
    Together with a recompense more fruitful°
    Than their offense can weigh down by the dram°—
    Ay, even such heaps and sums of love and wealth
    As shall to thee blot out what wrongs were theirs,
    And write in thee the figures° of their love,   155
    Ever to read them° thine.

Timon.   You witch° me in it;
    Surprise me to the very brink of tears.

---

140 **in thee** i.e., in the wrongs we have caused you   141 **consent of love** harmonious voice of affection   144 **For thy best use and wearing** i.e., only you are suited to fill these dignities with the proper distinction   145 **general** universally   146 **the public body** the senate as representative of the body politic   148 **withal** at the same time   149 **it own fall** its own fall from grace   149 **restraining** keeping back   150 **sorrowed render** sorrowful rendering of an account   151 **fruitful** abundant   152 **weigh down by the dram** i.e., balance in weight even if measured to the last tiny unit   155 **figures** (1) written characters (2) numerals (as in counting money) (3) images, representations   156 **them** i.e., the Athenians as represented in the "figures of their love"   156 **witch** bewitch

Lend me a fool's heart and a woman's eyes,
And I'll beweep these comforts,° worthy senators.

First Senator. Therefore so please thee to return with
160   us,
And of our Athens, thine and ours, to take
The captainship, thou shalt be met with thanks,
Allowed° with absolute power, and thy good name
Live with authority. So soon we shall drive back
165   Of Alcibiades th' approaches wild,
Who like a boar too savage doth root up
His country's peace.

Second Senator.   And shakes his threat'ning sword
Against the walls of Athens.

First Senator.   Therefore, Timon—

Timon. Well, sir, I will; therefore I will, sir, thus:
170   If Alcibiades kill my countrymen,
Let Alcibiades know this of Timon,
That Timon cares not. But if he sack fair Athens,
And take our goodly agèd men by th' beards,
Giving our holy virgins to the stain
175   Of contumelious,° beastly, mad-brained war,
Then let him know, and tell him Timon speaks it,
In pity of our agèd and our youth,
I cannot choose but tell him that I care not,
And let him take't at worst.° For their knives care
    not
180   While you have throats to answer.° For myself,
There's not a whittle° in th' unruly camp°
But I do prize it at my love° before
The reverend'st throat in Athens. So I leave you

---

159 **comforts** pleasures   163 **Allowed** endowed   175 **contumelious**
insolent   179 **take't at worst** put the worst interpretation he wishes
on it   180 **throats to answer** i.e., throats to be cut by the knives of
Alcibiades' soldiers (and voices to protest for yourselves)   181 **whit-
tle** small knife   181 **th' unruly camp** (1) the party of those revolting
against Athens (2) the disorderly, turbulent army (of Alcibiades)
182 **prize it at my love** value it in my esteem

To the protection of the prosperous° gods,
As thieves to keepers.°

Flavius.   Stay not, all's in vain.   185

Timon. Why I was writing of my epitaph;
    It will be seen tomorrow. My long sickness
    Of health and living now begins to mend,
    And nothing° brings me all things. Go, live still;
    Be Alcibiades your plague, you his,   190
    And last° so long enough.

First Senator.   We speak in vain.

Timon. But yet I love my country, and am not
    One that rejoices in the common wrack,°
    As common bruit° doth put it.

First Senator.   That's well spoke.

Timon. Commend me to my loving countrymen.   195

First Senator. These words become° your lips as they
    pass through them.

Second Senator. And enter in our ears like great tri-
    umphers°
    In their applauding gates.°

Timon.   Commend me to them,
    And tell them that to ease them of their griefs,
    Their fears of hostile strokes, their aches,° losses,   200
    Their pangs of love, with other incident throes°
    That nature's fragile vessel doth sustain
    In life's uncertain voyage, I will some kindness do
    them;
    I'll teach them to prevent° wild Alcibiades' wrath.

184 **prosperous** propitious   185 **As thieves to keepers** i.e., as I would
leave thieves to the protection of their jailers   189 **nothing** nothing-
ness, oblivion   191 **last** endure   193 **wrack** destruction   194 **bruit**
rumor   196 **become** befit   197 **triumphers** triumphant marchers
198 **applauding gates** i.e., city gates thronged with those applauding
the   triumph   200 **aches** (two syllables, pronounced "aitches")
201 **incident throes** agonies likely to occur   204 **prevent** anticipate
(but First Senator interprets "to keep from occurring")

205 *First Senator.* I like this well; he will return again.

　　Timon. I have a tree which grows here in my close,°
　　　　That mine own use invites me to cut down,
　　　　And shortly must I fell it. Tell my friends,
　　　　Tell Athens, in the sequence of degree,°
210　　From high to low throughout, that whoso please
　　　　To stop affliction, let him take his haste;
　　　　Come hither ere my tree hath felt the ax,
　　　　And hang himself. I pray you do my greeting.

　　Flavius. Trouble him no further; thus you still° shall
　　　　find him.

215 *Timon.* Come not to me again, but say to Athens,
　　　　Timon hath made his everlasting mansion
　　　　Upon the beachèd verge of the salt flood,°
　　　　Who° once a day with his embossèd° froth
　　　　The turbulent surge shall cover. Thither come,
220　　And let my gravestone be your oracle.°
　　　　Lips, let four words go by and language end.°
　　　　What is amiss, plague and infection mend.
　　　　Graves only be men's works and death their gain.
　　　　Sun, hide thy beams; Timon hath done his reign.
　　　　　　　　　　　　　　　　　　　Exit Timon.

225 *First Senator.* His discontents are unremovably
　　　　Coupled to nature.°

　　Second Senator. Our hope in him is dead. Let us
　　　　return,

---

206 **close** enclosure　209 **sequence of degree** proper order of the
social hierarchy　214 **still** always　217 **beachèd verge of the salt
flood** edge of the sea that forms a beach　218 **Who** i.e., "the beachèd
verge"　218 **embossèd** covered with foam (usually from the mouth
of a hunted animal)　220 **be your oracle** i.e., be consulted by you as
if it were an oracle (a place where divine pronouncements are made,
or the god making such pronouncements)　221 **let four words go
by and language end** i.e., speak only a few more words ("four" is
used indefinitely) and then not speak any further　226 **Coupled to
nature** a part of his nature

And strain° what other means is left unto us
In our dear° peril.

First Senator.   It requires swift foot.   *Exeunt.*

[Scene 2. *Before the walls of Athens.*]

Enter two other Senators with a Messenger.

Third Senator. Thou hast painfully discovered.° Are
        his files°
    As full as thy report?

Messenger.   I have spoke the least.°
    Besides, his expedition° promises
    Present° approach.

Fourth Senator. We stand much hazard if they bring
        not Timon.   5

Messenger. I met a courier, one mine ancient° friend,
    Whom though in general part° we were opposed,
    Yet our old love made a particular° force,
    And made us speak like friends. This man was
        riding
    From Alcibiades to Timon's cave   10
    With letters of entreaty, which imported°
    His fellowship i' th' cause against your city,
    In part for his sake moved.°

228 **strain** exert to the utmost   229 **dear** grievous, dire   5.2.1 **Thou
hast painfully discovered** (1) your revelation was painful to us (2) you
have made your revelation in painstaking detail   1 **files** ranks
2 **spoke the least** reported the minimum   3 **expedition** speed
4 **Present** immediate   6 **ancient** former   7 **in general part** i.e., in
matters of general or public interest   8 **particular** personal   11 **imported** bore as their message (with additional suggestion of "im-
portuned" or urged)   13 **moved** instigated

Enter the other Senators [from Timon].

Third Senator.   Here come our brothers.

First Senator. No talk° of Timon, nothing of him
    expect.
15 The enemy's drum is heard, and fearful scouring°
    Doth choke the air with dust. In, and prepare.
    Ours is the fall, I fear, our foes the snare.°   *Exeunt.*

[Scene 3. *Before Timon's cave.*]

Enter a Soldier in the woods, seeking Timon.

Soldier. By all description this should be the place.
    Who's here? Speak, ho! No answer? What is this?°
    "Timon is dead, who hath outstretched his span.°
    Some beast read this; there does not live a man."°
5   Dead, sure, and this his grave. What's on this tomb
    I cannot read. The character I'll take with wax;°
    Our captain hath in every figure° skill,
    An aged° interpreter, though young in days.
    Before proud Athens he's set down° by this,
10 Whose fall the mark° of his ambition is.   *Exit.*

14 **No talk** i.e., let us not talk   15 **scouring** scurrying about (in preparation for battle)   17 **our foes the snare** i.e., our foes are the snare or trap which will cause the downfall of Athens   5.3.2 **What is this** (presumably the Soldier finds an inscription or trial epitaph composed by Timon in English, which the Soldier can read, whereas the epitaph on Timon's tomb is in Latin, which the Soldier cannot read)   3 **outstretched his span** lived beyond his allotted or desired life span   4 **there does not live a man** i.e., all men left alive are merely beasts   6 **The character I'll take with wax** I will take a wax impression of the letters   7 **figure** written character   8 **aged** experienced   9 **set down** i.e., in a siege   10 **mark** goal

[Scene 4. *Before the walls of Athens*.]

Trumpets sound. Enter Alcibiades with his
powers before Athens.

Alcibiades. Sound to this coward and lascivious town
   Our terrible° approach.   *Sounds a parley.°*

   The Senators appear upon the walls.°

Till now you have gone on, and filled the time
With all licentious measure,° making your wills
The scope° of justice. Till now, myself and such   5
As slept° within the shadow of your power,
Have wandered with our traversed° arms and
   breathed
Our sufferance vainly.° Now the time is flush,°
When crouching marrow in the bearer strong°
Cries, of itself, "No more." Now breathless wrong°   10
Shall sit and pant in your great chairs of ease,°
And pursy° insolence shall break his wind
With fear and horrid° flight.

First Senator.   Noble and young,
   When thy first griefs° were but a mere conceit,°

5.4.2 **terrible** terrifying   2s.d. **Sounds a parley** i.e., by a special
signal on drum or trumpet, Alcibiades calls for a conference with
the enemy to try to make peace   2s.d. **upon the walls** i.e., upon the
upper stage   4 **With all licentious measure** with all kinds of unbridled conduct   5 **scope** extent   6 **slept** (1) were asleep, inactive
(2) lived   7 **traversed** folded across (in resignation)   7–8 **breathed/**
Our sufferance vainly spoke in vain about our sufferings   8 **flush**
ripe   9 **When ... strong** i.e., when the resolute man's courage is
aroused   10 **breathless wrong** wrongdoers breathless through fear
11 **great chairs of ease** comfortably upholstered chairs of state
12 **pursy** short-winded   13 **horrid** horrible   14 **griefs** grievances
14 **conceit** idea

15 Ere thou hadst power or we had cause of fear,
    We sent to thee to give thy rages balm,
    To wipe out our ingratitude with loves
    Above their° quantity.

Second Senator.   So did we woo
20 Transformèd Timon to our city's love
    By humble message and by promisèd means.°
    We were not all unkind, nor all deserve
    The common stroke of war.

First Senator.   These walls of ours
    Were not erected by their hands from whom
    You have received your grief; nor are they such
    That these great tow'rs, trophies, and schools°
25   should fall
    For private faults in them.

Second Senator.   Nor are they living
    Who were the motives that you first went out;°
    Shame that they wanted, cunning in excess
    Hath broke their hearts.° March, noble lord,
30 Into our city with thy banners spread.
    By decimation and a tithèd death,°
    If thy revenges hunger for that food
    Which nature loathes, take thou the destined tenth,
    And by the hazard of the spotted die,°
    Let die the spotted.°

35 *First Senator.*   All have not offended.
    For those that were, it is not square° to take

18 **their** (the antecedent is either "griefs" or "rages" or both)
20 **means** conditions of peace (or possibly "riches") 25 **trophies, and schools** monuments, and public buildings 27 **motives that you first went out** instigators or movers of your
original banishment 28–29 **Shame . . . hearts** i.e., their hearts
were broken with remorse for two common moral failings: lack
of a sense of disgrace for their wrongdoing and excess of crafty
deceit 31 **decimation and a tithèd death** the killing of one
person in ten 34 **by the hazard of the spotted die** by chance,
as in dice ("die" is the singular of "dice") 35 **spotted** (1) guilty
(2) those selected by the "spots" on the dice 36 **square** honest

On those that are, revenge. Crimes, like lands,
Are not inherited. Then, dear countryman,
Bring in thy ranks, but leave without° thy rage.
Spare thy Athenian cradle and those kin   40
Which in the bluster° of thy wrath must fall
With those that have offended. Like a shepherd,
Approach the fold° and cull th' infected forth,
But kill not all together.

Second Senator.   What thou wilt,
Thou rather shalt enforce it with thy smile   45
Than hew to't° with thy sword.

First Senator.   Set but thy foot
Against our rampired° gates, and they shall ope,
So° thou wilt send thy gentle heart before
To say thou't enter friendly.

Second Senator.   Throw thy glove,
Or any token of thine honor else,   50
That thou wilt use the wars as thy redress
And not as our confusion.° All thy powers°
Shall make their harbor° in our town till we
Have sealed° thy full desire.

Alcibiades.   Then there's my glove.
Descend and open your unchargèd ports.°   55
Those enemies of Timon's and mine own
Whom you yourselves shall set out for reproof,°
Fall, and no more. And to atone° your fears
With my more noble meaning,° not a man
Shall pass his quarter,° or offend the stream   60
Of regular justice in your city's bounds,

---

39 **without** outside   41 **bluster** tempest   43 **fold** enclosure for sheep
or the flock itself   46 **hew to't** cut thy way to it   47 **rampired** forti-
fied   48 **So** provided that   52 **confusion** destruction   52 **powers**
armed forces   53 **make their harbor** be billeted   54 **sealed** solemnly
ratified (by fulfilling)   55 **unchargèd ports** unassailed gates   57 **reproof** shame   58 **atone** appease   59 **meaning** intention   60 **quarter**
billet (?) area of duty (?)

But shall be remedied° to your public laws
At heaviest answer.°

Both Senators.   'Tis most nobly spoken.

Alcibiades. Descend, and keep your words.
         [*The Senators descend, and open the gates.*]

                Enter a Soldier.

65 *Soldier.* My noble general, Timon is dead,
      Entombed upon the very hem° o' th' sea,
      And on his gravestone this insculpture° which
      With wax I brought away, whose soft impression
      Interprets° for my poor ignorance.

              Alcibiades reads the epitaph.°

    Alcibiades. "Here lies a wretched corse,° of wretched
70   soul bereft.
      Seek not my name. A plague consume you, wicked
        caitiffs° left.
      Here lie I, Timon, who alive all living men did
        hate.
      Pass by and curse thy fill, but pass, and stay not
        here thy gait."
      These well express in thee thy latter° spirits.
75   Though thou abhorr'dst in us our human griefs,
      Scorn'dst our brains' flow,° and those our droplets
        which
      From niggard° nature fall; yet rich conceit°
      Taught thee to make vast Neptune weep for aye°
      On thy low grave, on faults forgiven. Dead
80   Is noble Timon, of whose memory
      Hereafter more. Bring me into your city,

___

62 **remedied** turned over for remedy   63 **At heaviest answer** for the maximum punishment   66 **hem** edge (the "beachèd verge" of 5.1.217)   67 **insculpture** inscription   69 **Interprets** acts as an interpreter   69s.d. **epitaph** (there are two epitaphs here, both from North's *Plutarch*, and it seems very likely that one of them—probably the first—was intended to be omitted)   70 **corse** corpse   71 **caitiffs** wretches   74 **latter** later, more recent   76 **brains' flow** tears   77 **niggard** stingy   77 **rich conceit** fanciful imagination   78 **for aye** forever

And I will use the olive with my sword,°
Make war breed peace, make peace stint° war,
    make each
Prescribe to other, as each other's leech.°
Let our drums strike.   *Exeunt.*   85

---

82 **use the olive with my sword** i.e., combine the olive branch of peace with the sword of war, show mercy even though I enter your city as a conqueror   83 **stint** cause to stop   84 **leech** physician

Textual Note

Our sole authority for the text of *Timon of Athens* is the First Folio of Shakespeare, published in 1623. It may only be the result of a lucky accident that the play was printed at all, since *Troilus and Cressida* was intended to follow *Romeo and Juliet* in the section of Tragedies, and three pages of *Troilus* were actually set up and printed. But difficulties over the copyright of *Troilus* probably forced Jaggard to stop work on it. He allowed a sufficient number of blank pages for it, and then went on to set up and print *Julius Caesar*. Contrary to Jaggard's expectations, the difficulties with *Troilus* were not quickly resolved. Something had to fill the space left for *Troilus*, and *Timon* was decided on. It is a relatively short play, so that it only partially fills the allotted pages. Signature ii is omitted and there is an awkward gap between pages 98 and 109 (beginning of *Julius Caesar*), despite the blown-up and elaborately decorated list of actors' names that has a page to itself at the end of *Timon*.

Whether *Timon* would have been printed at all if the difficulties with *Troilus* had not occurred is a teasing question, but the condition of its text strongly confirms its role as an afterthought or stopgap. *Timon* is full of the kind of inconsistencies and roughnesses that suggest a play that has not received any final revision (see Introduction). There is no record of a performance of the play during Shakespeare's lifetime, and the possibility seems unlikely. It is obviously not the sort of play that a business-minded publisher would be eager to include in an expensive and speculative venture like the Shakespeare Folio. The text of *Timon* was set up either directly from Shakespeare's "foul papers" (rough draft), or from a transcript of them made by a scribe.

The state of the text has an important bearing on the editing of the play. If *Timon* is indeed a play that has not received that final revision and polishing necessary to put it into actable (or printable) form, it is not the job of a modern

editor to undertake this task for Shakespeare. It is not up to
a modern editor, for example, to make the lines scan by
piecing them out differently (a formidable task here), or to
distribute specific roles to the First, Second, Third, and
Fourth Lords, or to make other changes of an essentially
"improving" nature. I assume that the present-day reader
would like to have the play in a modernized form, but as
close as possible to the way Shakespeare left it. I have therefore made very few changes in the Folio text, even at the
expense of leaving loose ends or inconsistencies. (It would
be wonderfully satisfying to know whom Alcibiades is
pleading for in Act 3, Scene 5.)

Two matters of special interest are related to the nature of
the text: lineation and stage directions. In the text of *Timon*
there is either serious mislineation (the printing of blank
verse lines in some other form, either broken in two or run
together as prose), or a failure in a number of places to write
regular, five-beat, iambic lines. That is, either the compositor took wide liberties with the metrics, or the author himself made errors or allowed himself a great deal of freedom.
Considering the unrevised state of the text, one is forced to
conclude that the printed version is probably an accurate
rendering of the copy. "Mislineation" is, therefore, a mis-
leading term. I have generally followed the lineation of the
Folio, except where lines are obviously broken into two to
fill up the "cast off" space (that is, the amount of space estimated to be needed for a certain quantity of copy), or run
together as prose where not enough space was allowed. The
Folio lineation usually makes for good speech rhythm, with
important pauses at the ends of lines. To run these lines
through the blank verse meat grinder would distort their
quality as dramatic speech.

How one treats the Folio stage directions of *Timon* also
depends upon one's attitude to the text. The indications of
action in this play are of the permissive and literary sort
characteristic of an author's manuscript. For example, the
final part of the stage direction that opens Act 1, Scene 2,
reads: *"Then comes dropping after all, Apemantus, discontentedly, like himself."* This is a descriptive stage direction,
which would have been put into a more practical form in a
promptbook prepared by the stage manager. To change this

direction to *"Then enter Apemantus, alone and at a distance"* (as Sisson does in his fine text) is to throw away a significant Shakespearean line for the sake of some imagined modern production. In an unrevised play such as *Timon* there is a special sanction for retaining the obviously authorial stage directions of the Folio, which bring us closer to the original manuscript of the play than do the colorless, clarified directions of a modern editor. I have also avoided one other type of correction in the stage directions. When it is not clear who is being addressed, I have not seen fit to supply a name. In Act 5, Scene 1, for example, Timon is upbraiding Poet and Painter in turn, but the text never specifies which one. I have simply indicated *To one* and *To the other*, although in a production it would obviously have to be either to Poet or Painter. Perhaps these two characters are meant to have a Rosencrantz and Guildenstern interchangeability.

In the present text spelling has been modernized, except that certain older forms have been retained when they are essentially different from their modern counterparts, for example, "vild" (for "vile"), "huswife" (for "housewife"), "a th' " (for "o' th' "). The punctuation has been modernized within limits, but I have generally been wary of introducing changes where the Folio pointing makes good sense. Even editors scrupulous about the language of the Folio seem not to feel bound by the punctuation. Capitalization has been modernized, and contractions not affecting pronunciation have been eliminated (especially in the verb forms). For stylistic reasons, I have omitted many traditional exclamation marks. The speech prefixes have been expanded and somewhat clarified. The list of actors' names is taken from the Folio, where it is printed (with one name given twice, and with the names in a slightly different order) at the end of the play.

Typographical errors have been corrected, and some stage directions have been slightly moved. Many traditional stage directions, not in the Folio, have been supplied in square brackets. The traditional act and scene divisions and scene locations have been indicated for convenience, but the reader should recall that the action of the play was continuous and the scenes often unlocalized. The Folio indicates only "Actus Primus, Scaena Prima."

Other departures from the Folio are listed below. The reading of the present text is given first, in *italics*, and then the reading of the Folio (F) in roman.

1.1.s.d. *Enter Poet, Painter, Jeweler, Merchant* [F adds "and Mercer"] 21 *gum, which oozes* Gowne, which vses 87 *hands* hand 87 *slip* sit 166 *satiety* saciety 215 *cost* cast 280 *Come.* Comes 289 *I'll keep you company* [in F part of speech of Second Lord]

1.2.29 *ever* verie 115s.d. *Sound tucket* [F follows this with another s.d., "Enter the Maskers of Amazons, with Lutes in their hands, dauncing and playing," incorrectly anticipating the entry at line 132; the necessary part of this s.d. is therefore added to that of line 132] 127 *Th'ear* There 132 *First Lord* First Lord Luc. 154 *First Lady* I Lord

2.2.4 *resumes* resume 43 *of broken* of debt, broken 80 *mistress'* Masters 110 *mistress'* Masters 138 *proposed* propose 195 *Flaminius* Flauius 195s.d. *Enter Flaminius, Servilius, and Third Servant* Enter three Seruants

3.1.s.d. *with* with a

3.3.21 *and I* and

3.4.s.d *two Servants* man 50 *ate* eate 87 *Hortensius* 1. Var. 111 *Sempronius—all* Sempronius Vllorxa

3.5.17 *An* And 67 *'em* him

3.6.92 *with your* you with 116–17 [speech prefixes reversed]

4.1.13 *Son* Some 21 *let* yet

4.3.12 *pasture* Pastour 13 *lean* leaue 88 *tub-fast* fubfast 117 *window-bars* window Barne 122 *thy* the 157 *scolds* scold'st 255 *drudges* drugges 256 *command* command'st 272 *rogue* ragge 284 *my* thy 402 *them* then 501 *mild* wilde 518 *A usuring kindness, as* If not a Vsuring kindnesse, and as

5.1.5–6 *Phrynia and Timandra* Phrinica and Timandylo 72 *men* man 116s.d. *Beats ... cave* Exeunt 127 *chance* chanc'd 134 *cauterizing* Cantherizing 148 *sense* since 183 *reverend'st* reuerends

5.4.55 *Descend* Defend 64 s.d. *Soldier* Messenger

The Sources of
Timon of Athens

The chief source for Shakespeare's play is probably
Lucian's satiric dialogue, *Timon,* written in Greek in the
second century A.D. It is unlikely that Shakespeare read
Lucian in Greek, but the earliest English translation, by
Thomas Heywood, was not published until 1637. There
may, of course, have been an earlier English translation that
has not survived, but a more likely possibility is that Shakespeare used the French translation by Filbert Bretin in 1582
(as Honigmann argues). A number of Italian versions were
also available, as well as a Latin translation by Erasmus. The
verbal parallels between Shakespeare and Lucian are few,
but there is a striking similarity in style and tone. Common
sense insists that Lucian must be Shakespeare's ultimate
source, even though the exact stages of transmission are not
clear to us. We reprint below the lively modern translation
of Lucian by Lionel Casson.

The most direct and commonly agreed-on source for
Timon is Sir Thomas North's translation of Plutarch, *The
Lives of the Noble Grecians and Romans,* first published in
1579 (although Shakespeare probably used the 1595 edition). There is a brief digression in the "Life of Marcus
Antonius" which recounts how Antony, despondent after his
defeat at the battle of Actium, lived apart from men in a
house by the sea called Timoneon. Plutarch follows Strabo's
version of the story, which represents Antony as deliberately
imitating the example of Timon. In the section reprinted
below, Timon's career is briefly described to explain the
erratic conduct of Antony. Timon was apparently an actual
person who lived in Athens in the fifth century B.C., and
about whose misanthropy many legends arose. He was a
favorite butt of the Greek comic dramatists. There are a few
further references to Timon in Plutarch's "Life of Alcibi-

ades," which was the Greek life paired with that of the Roman Coriolanus. If *Timon* was written around the time of *Antony and Cleopatra* and *Coriolanus*, it is not surprising that all three plays should draw on North's Plutarch. It is likely that Shakespeare used Plutarch more extensively than the few selections printed below would indicate. Six names in *Timon*, for example, come from the "Life of Marcus Antonius," and the "Life of Lucullus" provides us with an excellent background for the character in Shakespeare's play.

The account of Timon in William Painter's *The Palace of Pleasure*, first published in 1566 (but Shakespeare probably used the 1575 edition), draws on Plutarch for its facts, but orders them with an eye to making a good story. There is perhaps one bit of evidence of Shakespeare's literal use of Painter. Timon's epitaphs in the play are taken over verbatim from North's Plutarch except for one change: Shakespeare uses Painter's phrase, "wicked caitiffs," in place of North's "wicked wretches." Since Shakespeare probably drew on Painter for *All's Well That Ends Well*, and possibly for *Romeo and Juliet*, it is reasonable to suppose that he also read the brief account of Timon. The version of the Timon story given in Sir Richard Barckley, *A Discourse of the Felicity of Man* (1598), is derived almost entirely from Painter.

The most controversial and puzzling source that has been claimed for Shakespeare's play is the anonymous *Timon*, which the Reverend Alexander Dyce in 1842 first published from a manuscript for the Shakespeare Society (now Dyce MS 52 in the Victoria and Albert Museum, London). This is an academic play, full of self-consciously learned allusions and quotations. It is based on Lucian, although on at least three occasions it introduces material not in Lucian and also used, in somewhat different form, by Shakespeare: 1) a mock-banquet scene in which Timon serves stones painted to look like artichokes; 2) the faithful Steward Laches, who follows his master in adversity; 3) the burial by Timon of his newly discovered gold. None of these is so distinctive that it can only be accounted for by direct borrowing, but the combination suggests that Shakespeare may have seen a performance of the play, read the manuscript, or heard about the play from someone who had seen or read it. Just how this could have occurred is entirely a matter of speculation.

The date of the "old" *Timon* play (as it is usually called) is very uncertain. It has generally been assigned to the last quarter of the sixteenth century, but recently some scholars have argued that it may just as easily follow Shakespeare's *Timon* as precede it. This late date offers a simple way to account for the similarities not in Lucian, but it seems unlikely to me. It is difficult to reconstruct how the academic author could have known a Shakespearean play that was presumably never acted, never completely finished, and not published until 1623. The records may, of course, be incomplete, but then the argument has to be founded on a series of negative probabilities. Proponents of a late date for the "old" *Timon* play have heard echoes in it of *King Lear* and *The Merchant of Venice,* but these are questionable. One other explanation for the similarity of *Timon of Athens* to the "old" *Timon* play is that they both drew on a common source now lost. This is a convenient postulate, but not very helpful in the present case, since nothing further is known about this common source.

Two other sources for which claims have been offered have generally been rejected by scholars: Boiardo's *Timone* (1494) and Lyly's *Campaspe* (1584). In the latter play, Diogenes is rather close to Shakespeare's Apemantus, but the malcontent railer was a familiar type, and Shakespeare had already created Jaques in *As You Like It* and Thersites in *Troilus and Cressida.*

There are many allusions to Timon in Renaissance English literature. He was a stock figure for the misanthrope, whose life was often described in animal analogies. Shakespeare refers to Timon in *Love's Labor's Lost,* when Berowne hypocritically berates his companions for being in love:

> O me, with what strict patience have I sat
> To see a king transformèd to a gnat!
> To see great Hercules whipping a gig,
> And profound Solomon to tune a jig,
> And Nestor play at push-pin with the boys,
> And critic Timon laugh at idle toys!   (4.3.165–70)

LUCIAN

Timon

Timon, Zeus, Hermes, Wealth, Poverty,
Gnathonides, Philiades, Demeas, Thrasycles

The scene is a remote spot on the border of Attica, the
district about Athens. The time is the second half of the fifth
century B.C.

Timon. O Zeus, god of friends, strangers, comrades, the hearth,
lightning, and oaths; gatherer of the clouds, thunderer—
and whatever else the wild-eyed poets call you (particularly when they're stumped by their meter—with all
your names strung out you're a big help to a verse that's
short; you plug the gaps in the rhythm). Well, Zeus,
where's your crashing lightning and rolling thunder and
blazing, flashing, terrifying thunderbolt now? It's become
painfully clear that this is all nonsense, just poetic hot
air—the only crash and roar is the sound of the words.
That far-famed, far-flying, ever-ready missile of yours has
somehow or other fizzled out; it's stone cold; it hasn't a
spark of wrath left in it to descend on the heads of wrong-

From *Selected Satires of Lucian*, translated and edited by Lionel Casson.
New York: Doubleday & Company, Inc. (Anchor Books). Copyright © 1962
by Lionel Casson. Reprinted by permission of Doubleday & Company, Inc.
The notes have been abridged.

doers. As a matter of fact, anyone out to try his hand at perjury would get more of a scare from an old candle stump than the flame of that all-consuming thunderbolt of yours. You look so much like a mere person just wagging a torch that sinners aren't the least bit afraid of the fire and smoke; the worst hurt they think they can get is a messy smudge of soot. That's why Salmoneus* had the nerve to set himself up as a rival thunderer—a perfectly logical thing to do, considering what a cocksure hothead he was and how slow-burning your anger is. Why shouldn't he have? You're as fast asleep as if you'd taken a narcotic; you don't hear the perjurers or notice the wrongdoers; your eyes are bleary and can't focus on what's going on; your ears are as deaf as any dotard's. When you were young and hot-tempered and in the bloom of your anger, you carried on against the wicked and the violent. You never gave them a moment's peace in those days: the thunderbolt was always in action and the aegis† in motion; the thunder rolled, and the lightning flashed so thick and fast it seemed to come in volleys. Quakes tossed the earth like a salad, to use the vernacular; snow came down in bucketfuls, and the hailstones were like rocks. The rain pelted fast and furious, each drop a river. Why, back when Deucalion‡ was alive, in the twinkling of an eye such a flood took place that everything was swamped and only one vessel, some sort of ark, barely came through; it grounded on a peak of Parnassus carrying human seed with its spark of life so that greater wickedness could be propagated on earth. Well, you're reaping the reward of your laziness: men don't sacrifice to you any longer or wear garlands in your honor—someone may do it as an afterthought during the Olympic games, but he hardly thinks of it as an obligation; he's just helping to keep an old tradition alive.

Little by little, my King of the Gods, they're making a second Cronus of you and shoving you off your throne. I won't bother mentioning how many times they've robbed

---

*Salmoneus, son of the god of the winds, imitated thunder (he rolled chariots over a bridge of brass) and insisted that men sacrifice to him as to Zeus.
†Zeus's shield, the sight of which inspired terror.
‡The Greek Noah.

your temple by now. But some have even laid hands on your very image at Olympia—and you, Almighty Thunderer, didn't have the energy to unleash the bloodhounds or call out your neighbors so they could help you catch the criminals while still packing up for the getaway. The noble Destroyer of the Giants and Master of the Titans sat still, his fifteen-foot thunderbolt motionless in his hand, while his golden locks were clipped from his head. Well, Your Highness, when are you going to stop being so careless and indifferent to all this? When are you going to punish such wrongdoing? How much fire and flood do you think you'll need to deal with this rampaging human insolence?

Let me stop talking in generalities and bring up my own case. I raised dozens of Athenians to the heights; I found them in poverty and made them rich. I lent a hand to everyone in need. Even more—I actually poured out my money in a flood to help my friends. But now that all this has left me a pauper, they don't know me any longer, they don't look in my direction—the same people who used to bow and scrape before me and hang on my every word. When I meet any of them on the street they go by me the way people go by some old tombstone overturned by time and lying on its back, without bothering to look at the epitaph. When they catch sight of me from far off they turn up another street—they feel it's a bad omen, it'll bring bad luck, to look at the man who, not so long ago, had been their savior and benefactor. Because of all these troubles I've exiled myself in this remote outpost, put on overalls, hired out as a farm hand for a dollar fifty a day, and deliver my philosophical pronouncements to the solitude and my mattock. I feel I've gained this much: I no longer have to lay eyes upon so much undeserved prosperity; of the two evils, that's by far the worse.

But when, O Lord of the World, will you shake off this deep, sound sleep—you've been at it longer than Epimenides*—, stoke the fire in the thunderbolt (or relight it from Etna), get a mighty blaze going, and show the anger that Zeus used to, in his younger days when he

*The Greek Rip Van Winkle.

was a real man. Or maybe the stories the Cretans tell about you and your grave there are true.

Zeus. Hermes, who's that shouting? Down there in the foothills of Mt. Hymettus in Attica. That man there in overalls, covered with grime and dirt. He's bent over; I think he's digging. Talkative fellow with plenty of nerve. Must be a philosopher—otherwise he wouldn't utter such blasphemy about us.

Hermes. Father, don't you recognize Echecratides' son Timon? He's the one who fed us so often with top-grade sacrificial offerings, that *nouveau riche* who served us whole hecatombs and threw such magnificent parties for us on your festival day.

Zeus. My, oh my, what a change! You mean the wealthy, fine-looking fellow who always had so many friends around? Why is he like this? Poor devil! It looks as if he's a workman, a farm hand. That's a mighty heavy mattock he's swinging!

Hermes. You *could* say it was his goodness and philanthropy and the way he took pity on everyone in need that ruined him. But the truth of the matter is, it was his senselessness, stupidity, and lack of judgment in choosing friends. The man never realized he was indulging a pack of crows and wolves. The poor devil imagined that all those vultures, who were tearing out his liver, were his bosom friends, who enjoyed eating his food because they liked him so much. When they had stripped his bones, gnawed them clean as a whistle, and carefully sucked out all the marrow inside, away they went, leaving him like a withered tree trunk lopped off at the roots. They don't know him any longer; they won't look at him—perish the thought!—and they're certainly not going to play savior or benefactor in their turn. That's why you see him now in overalls, swinging a mattock. He was ashamed to stay in the city, so he hired out as a farm hand. He's going mad brooding over his troubles, over the way people he made rich pass him by with their noses in the air and don't even remember whether or not his name is Timon.

Zeus. We simply cannot pass over this man or neglect him
any longer. Naturally he's angry at his bad luck. Why,
we'd be behaving just like those damned parasites of his
if we forgot about a man who's sacrificed so many fat
haunches of beef and goat on our altars. I can actually still
sniff the aroma in my nostrils. You see, I've been so busy
and there's been such a fuss kicked up by perjurers and
ruffians and bandits, and then there's the scare the temple
robbers have been giving me—there are so many of them
and they're so hard to keep track of, they don't let me
close my eyes for a second—that it's been ages since I last
looked in on Attica. Particularly ever since philosophers
and their debates became the rage there. They wrangle
with each other and shout so loud I can't even listen to
prayers; I either have to sit around with my ears plugged
up or let them be the death of me with their endless hol-
lering about "virtue," "incorporeal substances," and all
that drivel. That's how I came to neglect this fellow,
who's really not a bad sort. Hermes, go get Wealth and
rush right down to the man. Tell Wealth to bring Treasure
along, and tell them both to stick with Timon and not be
in such a hurry to leave him this time even if, with that
bigheartedness of his, he tries to chase them out of the
house again. As for those scroungers and the ingratitude
they showed him—I'll look into the matter again and
they'll pay for what they did as soon as my thunderbolt is
fixed. I broke the two biggest flashes and ruined their edge
yesterday: Professor Anaxagoras* was trying to convince
his students that we gods are just nobodies, and I threw it
too hard at him. I missed—Pericles had his hand over
him—and it bounced off the temple of Castor and Pollux
and started a fire; it almost broke into bits on the stone. In
the meantime it will be punishment enough for those parasites when they see Timon rolling in money.

Hermes (musing as he goes to fetch Wealth). That's what it
means to have the nerve to shout and make a nuisance of

---

*A celebrated philosopher who argued that not gods but an intelligent force
governed the world. He was brought up on charges of impiety and would have
been executed had not Pericles, the all-powerful political leader of Athens at
the time, intervened in his behalf.

yourself. Very useful. Not only in court but at prayers too.
See? Because he raised a holler, said what was on his
mind, and got Zeus's attention, overnight Timon will go
from rags to riches. If he had stayed bent over his mattock
and kept on digging without opening his mouth, he'd still
be digging and nobody would be paying him the slightest
attention. (*Gets Wealth and brings him before Zeus.*)

Wealth. Zeus, I won't go to him.

Zeus. My dear Wealth, why not? It's my orders, you know.

Wealth. So help me Zeus, that man insulted me. He squan-
dered me. He cut me up into little pieces—me, an old
friend of his father's. He practically booted me out of the
house; he got rid of me quicker than you'd drop a hot
potato. Go back there and be handed over again to a bunch
of parasites, bootlickers, and whores? No, Zeus. Send me
to people who'll appreciate the gift, people who'll treat
me with respect, who value me and are anxious to have
me. Let gulls like him stick with Poverty since they prefer
her to me. Let the poor devils take the overalls and mattock she'll give them and be content to pocket their dollar
and a half a day—since they so cavalierly toss away gifts
worth a hundred thousand.

Zeus. Timon won't behave that way with you any longer.
Unless that back of his is impervious to aches, the mattock's been a good schoolmaster and taught him that
you're preferable to Poverty. But what's the matter with
you, anyway? You sound to me like a born faultfinder.
Now you're blaming Timon because he opened the doors
wide to let you circulate freely and didn't guard you jeal-
ously under lock and key. Up to now you used to get angry
at the rich for doing the reverse—you complained they
locked you up so tightly with bolts, bars, and seals you
couldn't see a ray of light. You were always wailing about
it to me, how they were asphyxiating you in pitch-darkness.
It made you look pale and worried, your fingers were
cramped from counting money, and you were always
threatening to run away if you ever got the chance. All in
all, you felt it was a downright outrage to live a virgin's
existence in a bronze or iron chamber, like Danaë, under

the tutelage of those exacting and rascally schoolmasters, Interest and Bookkeeping. You kept telling me that what the rich do makes no sense; they love you madly yet, though they have every right to enjoy you, they never dare to; you're the object of their passion yet, though they have you in their power, they never lay a finger on you. They stay awake guarding you, staring at the seals and bolts without closing their eyes, thinking it enjoyment enough, not that they have the right to enjoy you, but that they have the right to exclude all others from any share, like the dog in the manger who wouldn't eat the hay himself but wouldn't let the hungry horse have any. What's more, you even used to laugh at the way they scrimp and save, at the incredible fact that they're jealous of themselves, at how it never enters their heads that some damned servant or slave driver of a steward is going to sneak in and have himself a gay party, without a thought for his miserable, despised master who's lying awake the livelong night figuring interest by the light of a dim and skimpy lamp with an oil-starved wick. These are the accusations you used to make. Now you're blaming Timon for just the opposite. I don't think that's fair.

Wealth. If you look into the truth of the matter, I think you'll find I make sense in both cases. On the one hand, Timon's squandering is, to all intents and purposes, thoughtless and not very considerate toward me. On the other hand, those who put me under lock and key and keep me in the dark, watching over me so I put on weight and become fat as a pig, never touching me or bringing me out to the light for fear someone might see me, those I've always considered not only boobs but criminals: although I've done them no harm, they let me rot in all those chains; they don't realize that, before very long, they'll pass on and leave me to some of the luckier ones in life.

No, I'm for neither type, neither these nor the ones who are so careless with me. I'm for the people who can set a limit in the situation, who neither hold on to everything nor throw everything away. That's the best system. In the name of Zeus, Zeus, tell me this. Suppose a man marries a young, beautiful woman and then doesn't keep an eye on her or act the least bit jealous. Day and night he lets her go wherever she wants and be with whomever she chooses—or, rather, actually leads her into adultery by throwing the doors open and inviting everyone in, like a pimp. Would you say that man loves her? No, you wouldn't, Zeus, and you've had plenty of experience with love. Now suppose, on the other hand, a man takes a respectable woman as his lawfully wedded wife to be the mother of his children and then, though she's a beautiful girl in the bloom of youth, he never lays a finger on her or lets another man see her but locks her up to drag out a virgin's existence, barren and childless. Let's say he even keeps telling the world he's in love with her—and he looks it, too, with his pale face, loss of weight, and sunken eyes. Wouldn't you say that such a man is mad? He ought to have children and enjoy matrimony, yet he lets a beautiful, alluring girl wither away by treating her, her whole life long, like a Vestal Virgin. Well, it's behavior like this that makes me angry—at some people because they have no respect for me and push me around or gorge on me or pour me out like water, and at others because they clap me in irons as if I were a runaway slave.

Zeus. Why be angry? Both types pay you a handsome penalty: the one, like Tantalus, goes without food or drink and, drooling at the mouth, just eyes his gold; the other, like Phineus, has the food snatched right out of his throat by Harpies. On your way now. You'll find Timon a much wiser man.

Wealth. Timon? He'll never stop acting as if he's in a leaky canoe: he'll bail me out as fast as he can, even before I finish running in; he'll try to beat the inflow so I don't flood in and swamp him. If you ask me, it'll be like filling the cask Danaë's daughters used. I'll be pouring in and getting nowhere since the thing won't hold water; what flows in will practically be out before it gets in. The outlet is so much bigger: it's a gaping hole; it's unpluggable.

Zeus. Well, if he doesn't plug that gaping hole and it stays open once and for all, it won't take you long to spill out, and he'll have no trouble finding his overalls and mattock at the bottom of the cask. But get going now, and make him rich. And, Hermes, remember on your way back to pick up the Cyclops* at Etna and bring them here so they can put my thunderbolt on the grindstone and fix it up. I'm going to need it good and sharp.

Hermes. Let's go, Wealth. What's this? Are you limping? My dear fellow, I had no idea you were lame as well as blind.

Wealth. Not always, Hermes. Only when I get orders from Zeus to go to someone. Then, somehow or other, I'm lame in both legs and walk so slowly I barely make it to my destination. Sometimes the person expecting me waits around till he's old and gray. But when I have to leave someone, then you see me on wings; I'm swifter than a dream. The starting signal sounds—and at that very moment you hear the announcement that I've won the race. I take the whole course in one jump. Sometimes the spectators don't even see me.

Hermes. That isn't true. I can give you lots of examples of people who yesterday didn't have a penny to buy a rope to hang themselves with and suddenly today they're rich, they're millionaires. Before they didn't even have a pack mule, and now they drive a team of thoroughbreds; they go around in silks and satins and their fingers are full of rings. If you ask me, they themselves find it hard to believe that all this wealth isn't a dream.

Wealth. That's different, Hermes. In those cases I don't travel on my own legs, and the orders come, not from Zeus, but Pluto. He's another one who likes to give away money and make handsome gifts. You can tell it from his name.† Whenever I have to move out of one house into another, people wrap me in a will, sign and seal me carefully, pick me up like a bundle, and transfer me. While the corpse lies in some dark corner of the house with an old sheet tossed over its knees and the cats scrapping over it,

*The one-eyed giants who, with Hephaestus as foreman, ran the celestial smithy in the fiery crater of Mt. Etna.

†*Plouton*, the name of the god of the underworld, is very much like the Greek word for wealth (*ploutos*).

the people who hope to get their hands on me hang around in the main square with mouth agape, like twittering swallow chicks waiting for their mother to fly home. The seal is removed, the ribbon cut, the will opened, and my new master announced—a relative, or a parasite, or some pervert of a slave boy who, through his abilities in bed, became the master's favorite and who still shaves to keep that boyish look; in return for the various and multitudinous favors which, even after he became too old for that sort of thing, he furnished the master, our hero now reaps a munificent reward. This unknown grabs me, will and all, quickly changes his name from Pyrrhias or Dromo or Tibius to Megacles, Megabyzus, or Protarchus,* and off he runs, leaving behind the disappointed hopefuls looking at each other and mourning—this time for real—because such a fine fish, after gulping down so much of their bait,† had slipped out of the bottom of the net. Well, my new owner—a thick-skinned vulgarian who still shudders when he hears the clank of chains, pricks up his ears if some passer-by happens to crack a whip, and genuflects before the treadmill as if it were a shrine—once he's landed on me with both feet, becomes insufferable to everyone he meets. Respectable people he insults, and the slaves he once worked with he has whipped just to prove to himself he can do that sort of thing. He ends up either falling into the clutches of some cheap whore, or going in for breeding race horses, or handing himself over to a bunch of bootlickers who swear he's handsomer than Nireus, comes from a better family than Cecrops or Codrus, has more brains than Odysseus, and is richer than a dozen Croesuses rolled into one. Once that happens, in no time at all the poor devil squanders what took years of lying, cheating, and robbery to scrape together.

Hermes. You're right. That's about the size of it. But tell me, when you walk on your own two feet, how does a blind man like you find your way? When Zeus decides certain

---

*Pyrrhias, Dromo, and Tibius were common names of slaves and Megacles, Megabyzus, and Protarchus common names in the best aristocratic families.
†I.e., the presents they had given the deceased in the hope of being remembered in the will.

people should be rich and sends you to them, how do you
recognize them?

Wealth. Do you think I actually track them down? God, no!
In that case I never would have passed up Aristides and
gone to Hipponicus and Callias and a lot of other Athenians who didn't deserve a cent.

Hermes. Well, when Zeus sends you down, what do you do?

Wealth. I walk up and down and wander around until I bunk
into someone. The first person who happens to meet me
takes me away with him—and offers up heartfelt thanks
to you, Hermes, for the unexpected windfall.

Hermes. But Zeus is under the impression you follow his
decisions and give money to the ones he thinks merit it.
You mean to say you're deceiving him?

Wealth. Of course—and he's getting what he deserves. He
knew I was blind and yet he kept sending me to look for
something that became extinct ages ago, something so
hard to track down, so small and dim that Lynceus himself would have trouble finding it. So, since there's just a
handful of good people while the cities are filled with
thousands of good-for-nothings, as I stumble around it's
much easier for me to run across that breed and land in
their clutches.

Hermes. But when you leave them, how is it you can get
away so easily if you can't see where you're going?

Wealth. Somehow, when it comes to making a getaway—
but only then—I become quick as a flash and my vision is
perfect.

Hermes. Now explain this one last thing to me. You're
blind—it's the truth, let's face it—lame in both legs, and
you have a bad complexion. Yet how do you have so
many lovers? Everyone has eyes only for you; if they win
you they think they're in heaven, and if they lose out they
can't bear to stay alive. In fact, I know of quite a few who
were so desperately in love with you they went off and
threw themselves into the "deep bosom of the sea" or off
the "sky-towering cliffs" simply because they got the

notion you were deliberately snubbing them when actually you had never even seen them. If you have any idea of what you look like, you'll admit, I'm sure, that they're out of their minds to go wild over an inamorata like you.

Wealth. Are you under the impression they see me as I really am? Lame, blind, and whatever else is wrong with me?

Hermes. They must—unless they're all blind themselves.

Wealth. My dear fellow, they're not blind. It's simply that Ignorance and Self-Deceit, two factors having the upper hand everywhere these days, dim their sight. What's more, I take steps on my own not to appear so completely ugly: when I meet them I'm dressed in embroideries and wear a lovely mask gilded and studded with jewels. They think they see my real face, fall in love with my beauty, and destroy themselves if they don't win me. Let someone strip me bare and expose me before them, and they'd kick themselves, no question about it, for being blear-eyed enough to fall in love with something so hideous.

Hermes. But, once they get rich, why do they put on a mask, too, and go on deceiving themselves? Why, if anyone were to try to take it off, they'd sooner lose their heads than that mask! Once they've seen everything underneath, you wouldn't expect them to shut their eyes to the fact that your beauty is just paint and powder.

Wealth. There are quite a few things helping me out on that score.

Hermes. Such as?

Wealth. Whenever someone meets me for the first time and throws open the door to receive me, as I enter, in sneak Delusion, Stupidity, Arrogance, Sloth, Insolence, Deceit, and a thousand others of the same ilk. And once all these take possession of his soul, he marvels at things that aren't the least bit marvelous, longs for what he should shrink from, and goggles adoringly at me—me who begat all these ills that have come over him, me the very captain of the whole band. He'll suffer anything sooner than put up with losing me.

Hermes. It's amazing how slippery-smooth you are. You're hard to hold and quick to get away. There's no way to get a good grip on you; somehow you slither through a man's fingers just like an eel or a snake. Poverty, on the other hand, is sticky and clings. She has thousands of hooks all over her body so that the minute people come near they get caught, and it's not easy to break loose. Oh, damn! During all this chatter we forgot something very important.

Wealth. What?

Hermes. We didn't bring Treasure, and we particularly need him.

Wealth. Don't worry about that. I always leave him below on earth when I go up to you people. I give him orders to stay inside with the door shut and, unless he hears my voice, not to open to a soul.

Hermes. In that case let's land now on Attica. Hold on to my coat and follow me; we're going to the frontier.

Wealth. Good idea, this leading me by the hand, Hermes. If you got separated from me, I might wander around and bunk into Hyperbolus or Cleon.* But what's that noise? Sounds like iron on rock.

Hermes. That's Timon digging up a little piece of rocky hillside nearby. Damn! There's Poverty with him. And Toil and Strength and Wisdom and Manliness—the whole gang that's under the command of Hunger. Much better than the ones in your band.

Wealth. Hermes, why don't we get out of here as fast as we can? We're not going to cover ourselves with glory against a man backed up by an army like that.

Hermes. Zeus has other ideas. So let's not be cowards.

Poverty. My dear Hermes, where are you taking that fellow you're leading by the hand?

Hermes. To Timon here. Zeus's orders.

*Notorious Athenian demagogues.

Poverty. So now Wealth comes to Timon, eh? After I picked him up suffering from a bad case of soft living, handed him over to Wisdom and Toil, and made him into a fine, worth-while man? Do I seem so contemptible, so easy to wrong, that, after giving him a complete course of training in virtue, I'm to be robbed of the only possession I have? Robbed so that Wealth can get him in his clutches again, turn him over to Insolence and Delusion, and hand him back to me just as he was at first, soft, spineless, stupid, a worn-out rag of a man?

Hermes. That's the way Zeus wants it.

Poverty. I'm leaving. Toil, Wisdom, and all the rest of you, follow me. Timon here will find out soon enough what his desertion means—that he loses a fine fellow worker and a teacher of the best things in life. So long as he was with me he was sound in body and sane in mind; he lived the way a man should; he looked to no one else for help, and his basic principle—a perfectly valid one—was that extravagance and plenty were not for him.

Hermes. They're leaving. Let's go up to him.

Timon. Who the hell are you? What do you mean by coming here and disturbing a workingman who has to earn a living? You're damned nuisances, both of you. You'll be sorry you came: in one minute I'll start heaving clods and stones and smash the both of you.

Hermes. No, Timon, please! Put those stones down. We're not men. I'm Hermes, and this fellow here is Wealth. Zeus heard your prayers and sent us. So, no more of this hard work, take your riches, and good luck to you.

Timon. Gods, are you? Well, even if you are, you're going to be sorry for this. I hate everybody, you hear, gods and men both. I don't know who that blind fellow is, but I've a good mind to bash his head in with this mattock.

Wealth. Hermes, in the name of Zeus, let's go now or I won't get away from here under my own power. If you ask me, the man's stark raving mad!

Hermes. Mind your manners, Timon, and stop acting like some country bumpkin. Stretch out your hands and take your good luck. Be rich again; be the top man in Athens. Thumb your nose at those ingrates, and keep your fortune to yourself.

Timon. I want nothing from either of you. Don't annoy me. This mattock is all the wealth I need. Besides, I'm the happiest man in the world so long as no one comes near me.

Hermes. My dear Timon, how inhuman!

> This I'm to bring back to Zeus? A rejoinder so brutal
> and savage?*

To be a man-hater is natural after all you've suffered at their hands, but to be a god-hater is certainly not—not after all they've done for you.

Timon. Many thanks, Hermes, to you and to Zeus for all you've done for me—but I cannot accept your friend Wealth here.

Hermes. Why not?

Timon. Because he's to blame for endless trouble I went through earlier. He handed me over to parasites, brought adventurers to my door, stirred up hatred against me, ruined me with soft living, made people envy me bitterly—and wound up by suddenly walking out on me like a traitor and a hypocrite. But this wonderful woman Poverty put me in condition with the kind of labor a man should do, spoke to me truthfully and frankly, and provided me with the necessities of life—so long as I worked for them; she taught me to scorn the plethora of luxuries I once had and to depend on my own self for all I hoped for out of life. She showed me what my true wealth was—something no sycophant's flattery or blackmailer's threats or mob's violence or voter's ballots or dictator's intrigues can ever take away from me. And so, toughened by my hardships, I now work this field—and like it. I see nothing of the wickedness of the city, and I get the bread I need, enough to keep me going, from this mattock. So, Hermes,

*Iliad 15.202, Iris' words to the angry Poseidon.

turn right around, go back to Zeus, and take Wealth with you. If I had my way, I'd be satisfied to make everyone on earth, young and old, howl with pain.

Hermes. My dear man, not that! They're not all suited for it. Now stop being so cantankerous and acting like a child and take Wealth here. Gifts from the gods aren't to be tossed away.

Wealth. Timon, may I submit the case for my defense to you? Or can't you bear hearing me talk?

Timon. Go ahead. But make it short. No long-winded introductions, like those damned public speakers. For Hermes' sake I'll put up with listening to a few remarks from you.

Wealth. Considering all the accusations you've made against me, I'd be better off being long-winded. No matter. Just consider whether I've really done you wrong as you claim. In the first place, it was I who was responsible for all the very pleasant things that happened to you: honor, public recognition, medals, and everything else that goes with high society; you were famous, a celebrity, a man sought after, and all because of me. In the second place, I'm not to blame for any harm those scroungers did you—in fact, you've wronged *me* by treating me so disrespectfully and putting me at the mercy of a filthy bunch of fawning double-crossers who plotted against me in every conceivable way. And now your last point, your claim that I treacherously deserted. On the contrary, I could bring that charge against you—you did everything you could to drive me away, you tossed me out of the house on my ear. Result: that lady you think so much of, Poverty, has stripped you of your fashionable clothes and wrapped you in these overalls. Hermes here can bear witness how I pleaded with Zeus not to make me go to you, not after the unfriendly way you behaved toward me. (*Timon shrugs helplessly.*)

Hermes. See how he's changed, Wealth? Don't you worry; start living with him. Timon, keep digging just the way you are. Wealth, make Treasure go under the mattock; he'll listen to you if you call him.

Timon. I suppose I have to obey and be rich again. What can a man do when the gods put pressure on him? Look what you're getting me involved in! Of all the rotten luck! Up to now I was leading the happiest possible existence, and all of a sudden, though I haven't harmed a soul, I'm to get all this gold and have all the worries that go with it.

Hermes. Put up with it, Timon, for my sake, even if it's hard and you can barely stand it, just to make those bootlickers die of envy. Well, I'm off; I'm flying back to heaven via Etna.

Wealth. I think he's gone; it feels that way from the beating of his wings. You stay here; I'll go and send Treasure to you. Wait—I've got a better idea. Keep digging. Treasure! Gold! I'm calling you! Listen to Timon here and let him catch you. Dig, Timon. Sink that mattock in. Well, I'll be off now.

Timon. Come on, mattock. Put some muscle into it now for my sake and don't weaken. Invite Treasure out of the depths into the light of day. O god of miracles! O god of hysterics! O Hermes, you god of windfalls! Where did so much gold come from? Is this a dream? I'm only afraid I'll wake up and find it's just a sack of coal—but no, it's genuine, solid, ruddy gold, the loveliest sight the eye can see:

> O gold! The fairest gift a man can get!*

A blaze of light both night and day, like gleaming fire.† Come to me, my sweetest beloved. Now I really believe Zeus once turned into a shower of gold—what girl wouldn't open her arms wide to receive such a handsome lover trickling through the roof? Midas, Croesus, treasures of Delphi—you're nothing compared to Timon and his wealth. Even the King of Persia can't match it. Mattock and overalls, my old friends, if you ask me, the best thing would be to dedicate you Pan here.‡ For myself I

---

*A line from a lost play of Euripides.
†A paraphrase of the beginning of Pindar's first Olympic ode.
‡As a farmer, Timon maintained a rude shrine to Pan, the farmers' god.

think I'll buy up this whole frontier region right away and put up a tower over my treasure just big enough to be my house while I live and my tomb when I die.

Resolved that the law of my land until my demise be as hereinafter set forth:

that Timon is to cut himself off from society, know nobody, and scorn everybody; that friendship, hospitality, comradeship, and the sacred obligations of pity are all a lot of nonsense;

that compassion for those in mourning and assistance to those in need are felonies as well as breaches of ethics;

that Timon is to live the life of a lone wolf and have one friend—Timon. All other people are enemies and traitors; to address a word to any shall be a crime and, if I even merely happen to see one of them, the whole day is to be officially declared a day of mourning. In a word, I am to consider them exactly as so many stone or bronze statues: I will accept no messages from them; I will make no truce with them; the desert is to be the boundary between us; "clansman," "kinsman," "fellow citizen," and "fatherland" are cold, useless terms, the prized possessions of the ignorant;

that Timon is to look down on everyone else, keep his money for himself, and live a life of luxury by and for himself, free from parasitism and vulgar flattery;

that, as his own neighbor and boundary sharer, living as far from all others as he can, Timon will conduct sacrifices and celebrate religious holidays all by himself.

Be it further resolved that, when the day comes for Timon to die, he will say good-by to himself and put the winding sheet on with his own hands. "Misanthrope" is to be the name that sounds sweetest in his ears, and his characteristic traits are to be grouchiness, roughness, meanness, temper, and unsociability. If I see someone burning to death and he begs me to put out the fire, I am to put it out—with pitch and oil. If a winter torrent sweeps someone off and he stretches out his hands and beseeches me to take hold, I am to push the victim under water head first to pre-

vent his ever coming up again. That's the way to give
them what they deserve.

The foregoing was moved by Timon, son of
Echecratides, and seconded by the aforesaid Timon. The
ayes have it. So ordered—and may I abide by the provisions like a man. And yet I'd give a good deal to have
people know I'm a millionaire; they'd be fit to be tied at
the news. Wait—what's this? Lord, how quick! They're
pouring in from all sides, out of breath and covered with
dust. Somehow or other they caught the scent of my
money. Now how about climbing this hill so I can drive
them away by laying down a barrage of stones? Or should
I break my own law code just to the extent of speaking to
them once, so I can show my contempt and make them
even madder? That's a better idea, I think. All right,
Timon, stand your ground and receive them. Let's see,
who's coming first? That scrounger Gnathonides,* the
one who told me to go hang myself when I asked for a loan
the other day. And he used to puke up whole barrels of my
wine at my house! I'm glad he's come—he'll be the first
to howl.

Gnathonides. Didn't I always say that heaven wouldn't
neglect a good man like Timon? Hail, Timon, the best-
looking, best-tempered, best all-around good fellow alive.

Timon. Hail, Gnathonides, the most greedy, most damnable
bloodsucker alive.

Gnathonides. Always had to have your little joke, didn't
you? Well, where's the party? I've got a new song to sing
for you. One of the latest hits.

Timon. Song? You'll be singing funeral dirges. And with
real pathos—this mattock will see to it.

Gnathonides. What's this? An attack! I'm calling witnesses. . . . Ow! I'll sue you for assault and battery.

*The sycophants are given common Greek names which Lucian has care-
fully chosen for their etymological associations: Gnathonides, "cheeky";
Philiades, "friendly"; Demeas, "public servant"; Thrasycles, "nervy"; Blepsias, "shark"; Laches, "share-seeker"; Gnipho, "skinflint."

Timon. Stick around a little longer—you'll be able to make the charge murder.

Gnathonides. I should say not! But at least heal my injuries, will you? Just sprinkle a little gold on them. That medicine has a marvelous way of stopping bleeding.

Timon. Still here, are you?

Gnathonides. No, no, I'm on my way. You're going to be sorry you turned into such a brute. You used to be a wonderful fellow.

Timon. Who's the bald pate coming up? Philiades—the most repulsive bootlicker of all. Once I sang a song and nobody applauded except him; he raved about it and swore my voice was sweeter than an angel's. I paid for this flattery with one whole farm plus sixty thousand dollars to provide a dowry for his daughter. Yet the other day, when I came to him for help and he saw I was sick, the noble soul gave me the back of his hand.

Philiades. Disgraceful! So you all recognize Timon now, do you? So Gnathonides is his bosom friend now, is he? The ingrate! He got just what was coming to him. Even though Timon and I are old, old friends—we went to school together and later were neighbors—I'm taking it easy—I don't want to look as if I'm being pushy. Hello, sir! I warn you to watch out for all these damned bootlickers. They're only mealtime friends; the rest of the time they behave like a flock of crows. You can't trust anybody nowadays; men are ungrateful good-for-nothings, every last one of them. Now *I* was about to bring you ten thousand dollars so you'd have a little something to cover pressing expenses. I was on my way and had almost gotten here when I heard the news that you were rich, a millionaire. I came anyway so I could give you my word of caution. But a smart man like you doesn't need any advice from me— you could tell even Nestor* what to do in a tight spot.

Timon. I'll take your advice, Philiades. But come over here; I want to greet you—with this mattock.

*An aged chieftain in the *Iliad*, the giver of counsel par excellence.

Philiades. Help! I give the man some good advice—and the ingrate bashes my head in!

Timon. Look, here comes a third one, Demeas the politician. He's carrying a copy of some resolution and telling everybody he's my cousin. In one day that man paid the government a fine of a hundred and fifty thousand dollars—with my money. He'd been tried and convicted and, since he couldn't pay, was thrown in jail. I took pity on him and bought him his release. Yet the other day, when it was his turn to issue free theater tickets to all the people in my neighborhood and I came up and asked for mine, he claimed he didn't know I was a citizen.

Demeas. Hail, Timon, benefactor of our people, guardian of Athens, bulwark of Greece! The House, Senate, and Cabinet are in session and they've been waiting for you for hours. But first listen to the resolution I'm going to present in your honor:

> Whereas Timon, son of Echecratides, is not only a gentleman and scholar but the wisest man in all Greece,
> and whereas he has devoted a lifetime bestowing benefactions on his country,
> and whereas in one day at the Olympic games he took first prize in boxing, wrestling, running, two chariot events—

Timon. But I've never even seen the Olympics.

Demeas. What's the difference? You will sometime. It sounds better when we tack on a lot of things like that.

> and whereas last year he distinguished himself for gallantry in action at Acharnae and cut down two regiments of Spartans—

Timon. How? I couldn't afford a suit of armor, so I wasn't even in the army.

Demeas. You're too modest. We'd be ingrates if we were to forget what you did.

> and whereas he rendered great service on behalf of his country as legislator, administrator, and military commander,

be it therefore resolved by House, Senate, Supreme
   Court, counties, and wards, both individually and col-
   lectively, that, in return for such services, there be set
   alongside the statue of Athena on the Acropolis a
   statue of Timon in gold bearing a thunderbolt in the
   right hand and a halo around the head,

and be it further resolved that he receive as award seven
   gold crowns of honor and that public announcement
   to this effect be made at the customary time, to wit,
   prior to the presentation of new plays at the Festival
   of Dionysus—and in his honor we're to shift the date
   of the festival to today.

Respectfully submitted by Demeas the public speaker,
   Timon's next of kin and his pupil as well, inasmuch
   as Timon is an expert in public speaking—and whatever else he cares to take up.

Well, that's my resolution in your behalf. I wanted to
bring my son to see you. I've named him Timon in your
honor.

Timon. Son? You're not even married as far as I know.

Demeas. But, god willing, I'll get married next year, have a
child, and, since it's to be a boy, I hereby name my
prospective son Timon.

Timon. Listen, you, I'm not so sure you'll be interested in
getting married—not after this lands on you.

Demeas. Ow! What's going on here? Trying to be a dictator,
are you? The son of a slave beating up free citizens, eh?
You'll pay for this, and soon. For burning down the
Acropolis too.

Timon. Damn you, the Acropolis hasn't burned down. So
it's clear—you're blackmailing me.

Demeas. Well, then, you got all this money by breaking into
the treasury.

Timon. No one's broken into the treasury—so you won't get
away with that either.

Demeas. Then you'll do it later. But you've already got
everything that was inside there.

Timon. For that you get another wallop.

Demeas. Oh, my back!

Timon. Stop your yelling or you'll get a third one. The man who, unarmed, cut down two regiments of Spartans not able to break the bones of one godforsaken runt? Ridiculous idea! Those Olympic championships in boxing and wrestling wouldn't mean a thing.

Now what's this? Isn't this Thrasycles the philosopher? Exactly who it is. Here he comes with that flowing beard, those eyebrows up in the air, and that pile of hair on his head, swaggering along, wrapped in his thoughts, and glaring like a Titan—the image of Boreas or Triton in one of Zeuxis' paintings. He dresses in perfect taste, wears a plain dark-colored coat, has a dignified walk, and, from the crack of dawn on, never stops extolling virtue—he's all for the simple life and against anyone who enjoys a bit of pleasure. But, as soon as he's had his bath and sat down to dinner and the waiter's handed him his drink—a double-sized one, the stiffer the better—you'd think he'd had a swig of Lethe's waters. He proceeds to demonstrate exactly the opposite of the morning's sermons. He swoops down on the dishes like a vulture, elbows his tablemate aside, spills gravy all over his beard, bolts his food like a dog, hunches over his plate as if he expected to find there that virtue he talks about, and wipes the bowls clean as a whistle with his finger so he won't lose a drop of sauce. He can get the whole of a cake or roast all to himself and still not be satisfied—the price a person pays for insatiable gluttony. He's a drunk, too, the kind that doesn't stop with singing and dancing but gets wild and calls people names. What's more, even in his cups he babbles on about temperance and good behavior—that's when he does most of his talking on the topic. He'll hold forth when he's already three sheets to the wind and has such trouble getting the words out it's ridiculous. After all this he'll throw up; they'll finally lift him off the floor and cart him away—and he'll make a grab with both hands for the girl playing the flute as he goes. But, drunk or sober, he yields the palm to no one in lying, nerve, or avarice. He's the king of sycophants, the man most ready to perjure himself; deceit walks before him and shamelessness by his side—in a word, the cleverest thing on two legs, not a flaw anywhere, letter-perfect in all sorts of roles. Well, we'll have some howls from this pattern of virtue in a few moments.

Thrasycles, what's the matter? Why so late in coming to see me?

Thrasycles. I haven't come for the same reasons as this mob here. They're entranced by your money; they've scurried here en masse, hoping for silver and gold and for fancy parties, prepared to put on a full show of flattery before a simple soul like yourself who's so ready to share everything he owns. But you know very well that a crust of bread is a whole dinner for me, that my favorite dish is a bit of thyme or cress or, when I feel like indulging myself, a pinch of salt. And for drink just cold water. This threadbare coat I prefer to any purple robes. In my opinion gold has no more value than the pebbles on a beach. I've come purely for your sake—to keep your wealth from destroying you. It's the world's worst possession, the one people scheme for most; it's been responsible for irremediable harm to thousands, thousands of times. Now, if you'll listen to me, you'll throw it all into the sea—a good man who can discern philosophy's treasures doesn't need it. But, my dear Timon, not where it's deep. Go into the water just up to your hips and toss it a little beyond the line of breakers—with only me watching. If you don't like this way, I have another, even better, way: hurry and bring the money out of your house—all of it; don't keep a penny for yourself—and distribute it among the needy, a few dollars to this one, a few hundred to that, a couple of thousand to a third. If there are any philosophers it's only fair they get a double or triple share. As for me, I ask nothing for myself but just some to hand out to my needy friends. If you'll fill this sack—it holds less than four bushels—that'll be quite enough. Philosophers should live simply and frugally—and give no thought to anything beyond what's in their sack.

Timon. I fully agree, Thrasycles. But, if you don't mind, before I fill your sack let me fill your head with fists—after I test its capacity with this mattock.

Thrasycles. What's happened to our laws? Where's our democracy? This is a free country and this damned rascal is beating me up!

Timon. My dear Thrasycles, why so angry? I didn't cheat you, did I? All right, here's half a bushel more for good measure.

    What's going on here? They're coming in droves! There's Blepsias and Laches and Gnipho—an army of potential howlers. Why don't I climb on this rock, give my mattock a rest—it's put in a hard day—lay in a supply of stones, and pelt them at long range?

Blepsias. Timon! Stop! We'll leave!

Timon. Not before I draw blood you won't!

PLUTARCH

From The Lives of the Noble Grecians and Romans

Antonius followeth the life and example of Timon Misanthropus, the Athenian.

Antonius, he forsook the city and company of his friends and built him a house in the sea, by the Isle of Pharos, upon certain forced mounts which he caused to be cast into the sea, and dwelt there, as a man that banished himself from all men's company: saying that he would lead Timon's life, because he had the like wrong offered him that was before offered unto Timon, and that for the unthankfulness of those he had done good unto and whom he took to be his friends, he was angry with all men and would trust no man. This Timon was a citizen of Athens that lived about the war of Peloponnesus, as appeareth by Plato and Aristophanes' comedies, in the which they mocked him, calling him a viper and malicious man unto mankind to shun all other men's companies but the company of young Alcibiades, a bold and insolent youth, whom he would greatly feast and make much of, and kissed him very gladly. Apemantus, wondering at it, asked him the cause what he meant to make so much of that young man alone and to hate all others. Timon answered him, "I do it," said he, "because I know that one day he shall do great mischief unto the Athenians." This Timon sometimes would have Apemantus in his company, because he was much like of his nature and conditions, and also followed him in manner of life. On a time when they solemnly celebrated the feasts called Choae at Athens (to wit, the

From *The Lives of the Noble Grecians and Romans,* translated by Sir Thomas North (1579).

feasts of the dead, where they make sprinklings and sacrifices for the dead), and that they two then feasted together by themselves, Apemantus said unto the other: "O, here is a trim banquet, Timon." Timon answered again, "Yea," said he, "so thou wert not here."

It is reported of him also that this Timon on a time (the people being assembled in the marketplace about dispatch of some affairs) got up into the pulpit for orations, where the orators commonly use to speak unto the people: and silence being made, every man listening to hear what he would say, because it was a wonder to see him in that place, at length he began to speak in this manner: "My Lords of Athens, I have a little yard in my house where there groweth a fig tree, on the which many citizens have hanged themselves: and, because I mean to make some building on the place, I thought good to let you all understand it, that, before the fig tree be cut down, if any of you be desperate, you may there in time go hang yourselves."

He died in the city of Hales and was buried upon the seaside. Now it chanced so, that the sea getting in, it compassed his tomb round about that no man could come to it, and upon the same was written this epitaph:

Here lies a wretched corse, of wretched soul bereft.
Seek not my name; a plague consume you wicked wretches left.

It is reported that Timon himself when he lived made this epitaph, for that which is commonly rehearsed was not his, but made by the poet Callimachus:

Here lie I, Timon, who alive all living men did hate.
Pass by and curse thy fill, but pass, and stay not here thy gait.

Many other things could we tell you of this Timon, but this little shall suffice at this present. [from *The Life of Marcus Antonius*]

And on a day as he [Alcibiades] came from the council and assembly of the city, where he had made an excellent oration to the great good liking and acceptation of all the hearers, and by means thereof had obtained the thing he desired, and was accompanied with a great train that followed him to his honor: Timon, surnamed Misanthropus (as who would say, Loup-garou, or the manhater), meeting Alcibiades thus accompanied, did not pass by him nor gave him way (as he was wont to do to all other men), but went straight to him, and took him by the hand and said: "O, thou dost well, my son, I can thee thank that thou goest on and climbest up still, for if ever thou be in authority, woe be unto those that follow thee, for they are utterly undone." When they had heard these words, those that stood by fell a-laughing. Other reviled Timon; other again marked well his words and thought of them many a time after, such sundry opinions they had of him for the unconstancy of his life and waywardness of his nature and conditions. [from *The Life of Alcibiades*]

WILLIAM PAINTER

From The Palace of Pleasure

Of the strange and beastly nature of Timon of Athens, enemy to mankind, with his death, burial, and epitaph. The xxviii Novel.

All the beasts of the world do apply themselves to other beasts of their kind, Timon of Athens only excepted, of whose strange nature Plutarch is astonied in the life of Marcus Antonius. Plato and Aristophanes do report his marvelous nature, because he was a man but by shape only; in qualities he was the capital enemy of mankind, which he confessed frankly, utterly to abhor and hate. He dwelt alone in a little cabin in the fields not far from Athens. Separated from all neighbors and company, he never went to the city or to any other habitable place except he were constrained. He could not abide any man's company and conversation. He was never seen to go to any man's house, ne yet would suffer them to come to him. At the same time there was in Athens another of like quality, called Apemantus, of the very same nature, different from the natural kind of man, and lodged likewise in the midst of the fields. On a day they two being alone together at dinner, Apemantus said unto him: "O Timon, what a pleasant feast is this, and what a merry company are we, being no more but thou and I." "Nay," quoth Timon, "it would be a merry banquet indeed if there were none here but myself."

Wherein he showed how like a beast indeed he was. For he could not abide any other man, being not able to suffer the company of him which was of like nature. And if by chance he happened to go to Athens, it was only to speak with Alcibiades, who then was an excellent captain there, whereat many did marvel. And therefore Apemantus demanded of

From *The Palace of Pleasure* (1566).

him why he spake to no man but to Alcibiades. "I speak to him sometimes," said Timon, "because I know that by his occasion the Athenians shall receive great hurt and trouble." Which words many times he told to Alcibiades himself.

He had a garden, adjoining to his house in the fields, wherein was a fig tree, whereupon many desperate men ordinarily did hang themselves. In place whereof he purposed to set up a house, and therefore was forced to cut it down, for which cause he went to Athens, and in the marketplace he called the people about him, saying that he had news to tell them. When the people understood that he was about to make a discourse unto them, which was wont to speak to no man, they marveled, and the citizens on every part of the city ran to hear him. To whom he said that he purposed to cut down his fig tree to build a house upon the place where it stood. "Wherefore," quoth he, "if there be any man amongst you all in this company that is disposed to hang himself, let him come betimes before it be cut down."

Having thus bestowed his charity amongst the people, he returned to his lodging, where he lived a certain time after without alteration of nature. And because that nature changed not in his lifetime, he would not suffer that death should alter or vary the same. For like as he lived a beastly and churlish life, even so he required to have his funeral done after that manner. By his last will, he ordained himself to be interred upon the seashore, that the waves and surges might beat and vex his dead carcass. Yea, and that if it were possible, his desire was to be buried in the depth of the sea; causing an epitaph to be made wherein was described the qualities of his brutish life. Plutarch also reporteth another to be made by Callimachus, much like to that which Timon made himself, whose own soundeth to this effect in English verse:

> My wretched caitiff days,
>   expired now and past.
> My carren corpse interred here
>   is fast in ground.
> In waltring waves of swel-
>   ling sea, by surges cast,
> My name if thou desire,
>   the gods thee do confound.

mined him to choose one method of making himself conspicuous rather than another? Why did he not seek the distinction conferred by the display of a military or of a
political character? Or why did he not aspire after pageantry
and parade, the pomp of public buildings, and the ostentation of wealth, unconnected with any kind of beneficence?

In general, our love of fame or distinction is directed and
influenced by some previous cast of temper or early tendency
of disposition. Moved by powers and dispositions leading us to
one kind of exertion rather than another, we attribute superior
excellence to such exertion. We transfer the same sentiment to
the rest of mankind. We fancy that no preeminence can be
attained but by such talents as we possess, and it requires an
effort of cool reflection before we can allow that there may be
excellence in those things which we cannot relish, or merit in
that conduct to which we are not inclined. Guided by early or
inherent predilection, men actuated by the love of distinction
seek the idol of their desires in various situations—in the bustle
of active life or in the shade of retirement. Take the following
examples. The son of Olorus was present, while yet a boy, at
the Olympic games. All Greece was assembled; many feats of
dexterity, no doubt, were exhibited, and every honor that
assembled Greece could bestow was conferred on the victors.
Moved by a spectacle so interesting and so inspiriting, the
Spartan, Theban, or Athenian youth, who were not yet of vigor
sufficient to strive for the wreath, longed, we may readily suppose, for maturer years and became, in their ardent imaginations, skilful wrestlers and charioteers. The son of Olorus, if we
may judge by the consequence, felt little emotion; no sympathetic longings; and no impatience to drive a chariot.—But
hearing Herodotus, on that occasion, reciting his history, he
felt other sensations: his heart throbbed, and the tears de-
scended. The venerable historian observed him weeping, and
comprehending his character, "I give thee joy," said he to his
father, "for the happy genius of thy son." Now, the son of
Olorus became a historian no less renowned than Herodotus—
for Herodotus and Thucydides are usually named together.
The celebrated Turenne, in his early days, was an admirer, no
less passionate, of Quintus Curtius, than the son of Olorus was
of Herodotus; and we are told by Ramsay, from D'Ablancourt,
that when not yet twelve years of age, he challenged an officer

who called his favorite history a romance. But this admiration was not so much for the graces of flowery composition which abound in the Roman historian as for the valiant actions of Alexander. These drew his attention and soon after, his imitation. Though his breast heaved and his eyes sparkled in the perusal of favorite passages, he was not led to write fine descriptions like Curtius, but to break horses like the son of Philip.

Now, since those that are actuated by the love of distinction are led, by early or inherent predilection, to one kind of action rather than another, we have no difficulty in allowing principles of goodness and humanity to have reigned early, or originally, in the breast of Timon. Nay, after losing their authority, they continued for some time to attend him and resided in that breast where they formerly reigned. They became like those eastern princes, or those early sovereigns of a neighboring country, who grew so indolent and passive that they lay immured in their apartments and left the management of the state to some active minister, an ambitious vizier, or mayor of the palace. Some of these ministers acted for a while under the banner of the sovereign's authority, but afterwards, having left him but the shadow of power, they promoted themselves, became supreme and despotic.

Here, however, we are led to inquire, how happens it that a principle inherent in the soul, and once an active principle, becomes passive, suffers others to operate in its stead; not only so, but to perform similar functions, assume corresponding appearances, and, in general, to be guided apparently to the same tenor of conduct? Did the energy of the inherent affection suffer abatement by frequent exercise? Or were there no kindred principles in the soul to support and confirm its authority? Could not reason, or the sense of duty, support, and the power of active habit confirm? How came the sultan to submit to the vizier?

In general, original principles and feelings become passive if they are not, in their first operation, confirmed by reason and convictions of duty, and if the passion which springs up in their place assumes their appearance and acts apparently as they would have done. Nothing is more imposing than this species of usurpation. It is not the open assault of a foe, but the guile of pretended friendship. Nothing contributes more to dangerous self-deception. Applying this remark to our present subject and following the lights of observation, we shall briefly illustrate how early or inherent goodness may be subverted by the love of distinction. A person of good dispositions, inclined by his temper and constitution to perform acts of beneficence, receives pleasure in the performance. He also receives applauses. He has done good and is told of it. Thus he receives pleasure, not only from having gratified a native impulse, but from the praise of mankind and the gratitude of those whom he may have served. The applauses he receives are more liberally bestowed by designing and undeserving persons than by the deserving and undesigning. The deserving depend too much on the permanency of the original principle, independent of encouragement and may therefore be too sparing in their approbation. Gustavus Adolphus used to say that valor needed encouragement and was therefore unreserved in his praises. The same may be said of every virtue. But designing or undeserving persons, transferring their own dispositions to other men, and of course apprehensive lest the wheels and springs of benevolence should contract rust, are oiling them forever with profuse adulation. Meantime, our man of liberality begins to be moved by other principles than fine feelings and constitutional impulse. The pleasure arising from such actions as these produce is too fine and too delicate compared with the joys conferred by loud and continued applauses. Thus his taste becomes vitiated; he not only acquires an undue relish for adulation, but is uneasy without it; he contracts a false appetite and solicits distinction, not so much for the pleasure it yields him, as to remove a disagreeable craving. Thus, such benevolent actions as formerly proceeded from constitutional goodness have now their origin in the love of praise and distinction. Goodness may remain in his breast a passive guest and having no other power than to give countenance to the prevailing principle. It may thus reign in his language and reveries, but the love of distinction directs his conduct. The superseded monarch enjoys the parade of state and annexes his signature and sanction to the deeds of his active minister.

Perhaps it may now seem probable that a man of constitutional goodness may perform beneficent actions not from principles of humanity, though these may actually reside in his breast, but from the desire of being distinguished as a generous person, and that in the meanwhile, not discerning his real motives, he shall imagine himself actuated by pure generosity. That such characters may exist is all that is hitherto asserted. That Shakespeare has exhibited an illustration, accurately defined and exquisitely featured, in his *Timon of Athens,* we will now endeavor to show. We will endeavor to ascertain and trace in the conduct of Timon the marks of that beneficence which proceeds from the love of distinction. We will, at the same time, endeavor to trace the causes of the strange alteration that took place in his temper, and delineate the operations of those circumstances that changed him from being apparently social, and full of affection, into an absolute misanthrope.

I. Real goodness is not ostentatious. Not so is the goodness of Timon. Observe him in the first scene of the tragedy: trumpets sound; Timon enters; he is surrounded with senators, poets, painters, and attendants, chooses that moment to display his beneficence, and accompanies his benefits with a comment on his own noble nature.

> I am not of that feather to shake off
> My friend when he most needs me.

II. He is impatient of admonition. Knowing that he was formerly influenced by sentiments of humanity, he supposes that their power is abiding and that as he continues to do good, his principles of action are still the same. He is exposed to this self-imposition not only by the tendency which all men have to deceive themselves, but by the flatteries and praises he is fond of receiving.— Of consequence, he would suffer pain by being undeceived: he would lose the pleasure of that distinction which he so earnestly pursues; the prevailing passion would be counteracted; thus, there is a disposition in his soul which leads him to be displeased with the truth, and who that is offended with the truth can endure admonition?

> Ap. Thou giv'st so long, Timon, I fear me, thou
> Wilt give away thyself in paper shortly:
> What need these feasts, pomps, and vain glories?
> Tim. Nay,
> If you begin to rail once on society,
> I am sworn not to give regard to you.
> Farewell, and come with better music.

Ap. So— —
Thou wilt not hear me now.
— — — —Oh, that men's ears should be
To counsel deaf, but not to flattery.

III. The same self-deceit which renders him deaf to counsel renders him solicitous and patient of excessive applause. He endures even the grossest adulation. Notwithstanding the covering which hides him from himself, he cannot be quite confident that his principles are just what he wishes and imagines them to be. The applauses he receives tend to obviate his uncertainty, and reconcile him to himself. Yet, it is not affirmed that the man of conscious merit is either insensible of fame or careless of reputation. He feels and enjoys them both, but having less need of external evidence to strengthen him in the belief of his own integrity, he is less voracious of praise and more acute in the discernment of flattery.

IV. The favors bestowed by Timon are not often of such a kind as to do real service to the persons who receive them. Wishing to be celebrated for his bounty, he is liberal in such a manner as shall be most likely to draw attention and particularly to provoke the ostentation of those, on account of his munificence, whom he is inclined to benefit. He is therefore more liberal in gratifying their passions, and particularly their vanity, than in relieving their wants, and of contributing more to flatter their imaginations than to promote their improvement. Though he performs some actions of real humanity, and even these he performs in a public manner, yet his munificence appears chiefly in his banquets and showy presents.

V. He acts in the same manner in the choice he makes of those whom he serves and on whom he confers his favors. He is not so solicitous of alleviating the distress of obscure affliction as of gratifying those who enjoy some degree of distinction or have it in their power to proclaim his praises. He is not represented as visiting the cottage of the fatherless and widow, but is wonderfully generous to men of high rank and character. He is desirous of encouraging merit, but the merit must be already known and acknowledged. Instead of drawing bashful worth from obscurity, he bestows costly baubles on those eminent or reputable persons who shall be attended to if they publish his praises. These are such displays of beneficence as a man of genuine goodness would be apt to avoid. Yet, the persons whom Timon honors and obliges are loquacious poets, flattering painters, great generals, and mighty elders.

> TIM. I take all, and your several visitations,
> So kind to heart, 'tis not enough to give;
> Methinks I could deal kingdoms to my friends,
> And ne'er be weary. Alcibiades,
> Thou art a soldier, therefore seldom rich;
> It comes in charity to thee; for all thy living
> Is 'mongst the dead; and all the lands thou hast
> Lie in a pitched field.— —

Yet, this seeming want of discernment in Timon is not to be considered as a proof of weak understanding. Our poet, who has omitted nothing to render the features of this character, though perhaps not obvious, yet so distinct, consistent, and perfectly united that there is scarcely a lineament too little or too much, has guarded him from this objection and represents him as a man of ability. When the state, and rulers of Athens, in the hour of extreme urgency and distress, are threatened with an assault by Alcibiades, whom they had treated with disrespect, they have recourse for advice and assistance to no other than Timon. They tell him in terms of humble entreaty:

> Therefore, so please thee to return with us,
> And of our Athens (thine and ours) to take
> The Captainship, thou shalt be met with thanks,
> Allow'd with absolute power, and thy good name
> Live with authority; so soon shall we drive back
> Of Alcibiades the approaches wild,
> Who, like a boar, too savage, doth root up
> His country's peace.— —

VI. Timon is not more ostentatious, impatient of admonition, desirous of applause, injudicious in his gifts, and undistinguishing in the choice of his friends than he is profuse. Desirous of superlative praises, he endeavors, by lavish beneficence, to have unbounded returns.

> — — — — —He outgoes
> The very heart of kindness— — —
> — — — —Plutus, the god of wealth,
> Is but his steward.

The poet, with judicious invention, deduces the chief incident in the play, namely the reverse of Timon's fortune, from this circumstance in his conduct. The vanity of Timon renders him profuse, and profusion renders him indigent.

VII. The character we are describing sets a greater value on the favors he confers than they really deserve. Of a mind undisciplined by reason and moved by a strong desire, he conceives the state of things to be exactly such as his present mood and desire represent them. Wishing to excite a high sense of favor, he believes he has done so and that the gratifications he bestows are much greater than what they are. He is the more liable to this self-imposition, that many of those he is inclined to gratify are no less lavish of their adulation than he is of his fortune. He does not perceive that the raptures they express are not for the benefit they have received, but for what they expect, and imagines that while his chambers

> Blaze with lights, and bray with minstrelsy;

while his cellars weep "with drunken spilth of wine;" while he is giving away horses, and precious stones; entertaining the rulers and chief men of Athens, he fondly fancies that he is kindling in their breasts a sense of friendship and obligation. He fondly fancies that in his utmost need, he will receive from them every sort of assistance, and without reserve or reluctance, lays immediate claim to their bounty.

> — — —You to Lord Lucius;
> To Lord Lucullus, you—You to Sempronius:
> Commend me to their loves—and I am proud, say,
> That my occasions have found time to use them
> Toward a supply of money: let the request
> Be fifty talents.— —
> Go you, Sir, to the senators,
> (Of whom, even to the state's best health, I have

> Deserved this hearing), bid them send on th' instant,
> A thousand talents to me.

VIII. Need we be surprised that Timon, and men of his character, should meet with disappointment? Howsoever they may impose upon themselves, and believe they are moved by real friendship, and believe that they are conferring real benefits, the rest of mankind discern, and disapprove of their conduct. Even those very persons who, by adulation and a mean acceptance of favors, have contributed to their delusion, feel, or conceive themselves, under no obligation. The benefits they received were unsolicited, or unimportant, and the friendship of their benefactor was not so genuine as he believed. Thus, then, Timon demands a requital of his good deeds—he meets with refusal; when he solicits the affections of his professing friends, he is answered with coldness.

> STR. Why, this is the world's sport;
> And just of the same piece is every flatt'rer's soul.
> —Timon has been this Lord's father—
> He ne'er drinks,
> But Timon's silver treads upon his lip;
> And yet, (O see the monstrousness of man,
> When he looks out in an ungrateful shape),
> He does deny him, in respect of his,
> What charitable men afford to beggars.

There is no one passage in the whole tragedy more happily conceived and expressed than the conduct of Timon's flatterers. Their various contrivances to avoid giving him assistance show diversity of character, and their behavior is well contrasted by the sincere sorrow and indignation of Timon's servants. They are held out to deserved scorn by their easy belief that the decay of their benefactor's fortunes was only pretended and by their consequent renewal of mean assiduities.

IX. It remains to be mentioned that such disappointment, in tempers like that of Timon, begets not only resentment at individuals, but aversion at all mankind.

Timon imposes on himself, and while he is really actuated by a selfish passion, fancies himself entirely disinterested.

Yet he has no select friends and no particular attachments. He receives equally the deserving and undeserving, the stranger and the familiar acquaintance. Of consequence, those persons with whom he seems intimate have no concern in his welfare; yet, vainly believing that he merits their affections, he solicits their assistance, and sustains disappointment. His resentment is roused, and he suffers as much pain, though perhaps of a different kind, as, in a similar situation, a person of true affection would suffer. But its object is materially different. For against whom is his anger excited? Not against one individual, for he had no individual attachment, but against all those who occasioned his disappointment—that is, against all those who were, or whom he desired should be, the objects of his beneficence; in other words, against all mankind. In such circumstances, the violence of resentment will be proportioned to original sensibility; and Shakespeare, accordingly, has represented the wrath of Timon as indulging itself in furious invective, till it grows into lasting aversion.

> TIM. Who dares, who dares,
> In purity of manhood stand upright,
> And say, this man's a flatterer? If one be,
> So are they all; for every greeze of fortune
> Is smother'd by that below: the learned pate
> Ducks to the golden fool: all is oblique—
> —— — Then be abhorr'd,
> All feasts, societies, and throngs of men!
> His semblable, yea himself, Timon disdains;
> Destruction phang mankind! Earth give me roots!
> Who seeks for better of thee, sauce his palate
> With thy most operant poison.

The symptoms already mentioned are numerous and indicate to the attentive observer that the state of Timon's mind is more distempered with a selfish passion than he believes; yet the poet, by a device suited to his own masterly invention, contrives an additional method of conveying a distinct and explicit view of the real design. Apemantus, a character well invented and well supported, has no other business in the play than to explain the principles of Timon's conduct. His cynic surliness, indeed, forms a striking contrast to the smoothness of Timon's flatterers, but he is chiefly considered as unveiling the principal character. His manners are fierce, but his intentions are friendly; his invectives are bitter, but his remarks are true. He tells the flattering poet, who had written a panegyric on Timon, that he was worthy of him and adds, even in Timon's presence, "He that loves to be flattered, is worthy of the flatterer." He tells Timon, inviting him to his banquet—"I scorn thy meat; 'twould choke me, for I should ne'er flatter thee." Elsewhere he gives him admonitions to the very same purpose, and finding his advice undervalued, he subjoins—"I will lock thy heaven from thee"—meaning, as a commentator has well explained it, the pleasure of being flattered. He afterwards tells him, having followed him, nevertheless, into his solitude, with intentions of rendering him some assistance:

> — — — — What, thinkest
> That the bleak air, thy boist'rous chamberlain,
> Will put thy shirt on warm? Will those moss'd trees,
> That have outliv'd the eagle, page thy heels,
> And skip when thou point'st out? Will the cold brook,
> Candied with ice, caudle thy morning taste,
> To cure thy o'er-night's surfeit? Call the creatures
> Whose naked natures live in all the spite
> Of wreckful heaven, whose bare unhoused trunks
> To the conflicting elements exposed,
> Answer mere nature—bid them flatter thee—
> O! thou shalt find— —

There are few instances of a dramatic character executed with such strict regard to unity of design as that of Timon. This is not all. It is not enough to say that all the parts of his conduct are consistent, or connected with one general principle. They have a union of a more intimate nature. All the qualities in his character and all the circumstances in his conduct lead to one final event. They all co-operate, directly or indirectly, in the accomplishment of one general purpose. It is as if the poet had proposed to demonstrate how persons of good temper and social dispositions may become misanthropical. He assumes the social dispositions to be constitutional and not confirmed by reason or by reflection. He then employs the love of distinction to bring about the conclusion. He shows its effects in superseding the influence of better principles, in assuming their appearance, and so, establishing self-deceit. He shows its effects in producing ostentation, injudicious profusion, and disappointment. And lastly, he shows how its effects contributed to excite and exasperate those bitter feelings which estranged Timon from all mankind. Timon, at the beginning of the drama, seems altogether humane and affectionate; at the end he is an absolute misanthrope. Such opposition indicates inconsistency of character, unless the change can be traced through its causes and progress. If it can be traced, and if the appearance shall seem natural, this aspect of the human mind affords a curious and very interesting spectacle. Observe, in an instance or two, the fine lineaments and delicate shadings of this singular character. The poet refuses admission even to those circumstances which may be suitable and consistent enough with the general principle, but which would rather *coincide* with the main design than *contribute* to its consummation. Timon is lavish, but he is neither dissolute nor intemperate. He is convivial, but he enjoys the banquet not in his own, but in the pleasure of his guests. Though he displays the pomp of a masquerade, Phrynia and Timandra are in the train not of Timon, but of Alcibiades. He tells us, alluding to the correctness of his deportment,

> No villainous bounty yet hath pass'd my heart;
> Unwisely, not ignobly, have I given.

We may observe, too, that he is not so desirous of being distinguished for mere external magnificence as of being distinguished for courteous and beneficent actions. He does some good, but it is to procure distinction; he solicits distinction, but it is by doing good.

Upon the whole, "Shakespeare, in his *Timon of Athens,* illustrates the consequences of that inconsiderate profusion which has the appearance of liberality, and is supposed by the inconsiderate person himself to proceed from a generous principle, but which, in reality, has its chief origin in the love of distinction."

ROY WALKER

From Unto Caesar: A Review of
Recent Productions

Major Shakespearian productions run from knight to
knight. The Old Vic 1956–7 season opened with a production by the theatre's director, Michael Benthall, which
brought back Sir Ralph Richardson to Shakespeare's stage
in *Timon of Athens*. The final production of the Stratford-
upon-Avon 1957 season restored Sir John Gielgud's Prospero (much changed since he was seen at the Old Vic in
1940) in a production of *The Tempest* by Peter Brook which
had Drury Lane stamped all over it and was to transfer to that
capacious cavern for what was once the pantomime season.
Sir Ralph's Timon and Sir John's Prospero were cousins
once removed. Richardson's misanthrope in the wilderness
was no vituperative, half-naked poor Tom. In his sheepskin
coat he was protected against rough weather if not from
man's ingratitude. His revulsion from human greed for gold
was a molten melancholy that seethed inside him, not a vol-
cano spitting scalding satire on all comers. Gielgud's Prospero came halfway back to meet him. Until the end this was
no rich-robed and short-tempered magician but an ascetic
hermit in brief tunic, burning with resentment of past
wrongs which threatened to overthrow his reason altogether.
These two performances, in fact, invited some reconsideration of the transition from one play to the other in Shakespeare's mind, the dive from the beached verge of the salt
flood and the not altogether sea-changed surfacing on the
shores of the enchanted isle. . . .
By cutting some 500 of its 2300 lines, Michael Benthall

From *Shakespeare Survey* 11 (1958), pp. 128–32. Reprinted by permission
of the author and of the Cambridge University Press.

ran through *Timon of Athens* in two hours, including a single interval of fifteen minutes. The deletions included what may be regarded as the definitive announcement of the theme of the play and a whole scene of some importance. Some minor characters were amalgamated and the ending of the play was boldly remodeled.

The first heavy stroke of the producer's pencil made Timon's entry cut short the opening dialogue of the Painter and Poet. There was no talk of artistic images of the fall of the truly great man when the mood of Fortune changes. It might be argued that modern audiences do not want the moral of a dramatic fable at the outset. But can any actor of Timon spare the tribute, spoken before he comes on (and not, therefore, in flattery), to "his good and gracious Nature"? And can any satisfactory production of the play dispense with the preliminary raising of the particular instance which we are to see into a general rule: " 'Tis common." The effect, if not also the intention, of omitting this choric opening dialogue is to slant the drama away from its theme of man's ingratitude towards the tragedy of a particular fault in the protagonist which invites a general censure. The producer's trimming of Timon's exchanges with Apemantus and excision of the dialogue of abuse between the two Lords and that churlish philosopher, which should close the first scene, does no such damage, except to deprive the scene of its deliberate final emphasis on Timon (who has left the stage and, again, is not being flattered): "The noblest mind he carries, That ever govern'd man."

In the banquet scene which follows, Apemantus' carbolic commentary was reduced, and Act 2 lost little by cutting out the dialogue in which Apemantus and the Fool are involved with the creditors. In fact the scene gained by leaving the crucial interview between Timon and his Steward uninterrupted. There is no dramatic difficulty in taking the Steward's proper presentation of his accounts for granted, and the sole function of the indifferent dialogue with the Fool seems to be to mark time while that statement of accounts is supposed to take place.

The action so far had been acceptably staged in the hall of Timon's house, on one side of which was placed a tall and somewhat awe-inspiring statue of a goddess, presumably a stand-in for Fortune. Now a drop curtain depicting the outer walls of the city was lowered and lighted, but no scene was played before it. After a few moments it rose to reveal a street scene of which the main feature was the central portal and steps of Timon's house. The range of three steps was the same as for the interior scene, and was not enough to allow any symbolic effect of moving down the steps as reverses of Fortune followed thick and fast. This open-air scene worked very well to give a free flow to the first five scenes of Act 3. Instead of three servants, this production entrusted all the begging to Timon's Steward, who was of course addressed as Flavius where the text names the others. A climax to the three dialogues in the street was provided by bringing on Sempronius in a palanquin where he was lounging with a paramour. No pause or scene change was necessary for the fourth scene, in which the creditors pounded upon Timon's door, with Flavius taking the lines of Servilius and Timon appearing in a plain gray robe which made an effective contrast with the rich crimson he wore in the earlier scenes. The dialogue between the Senators (accompanied by a bald, stripped, dark-skinned executioner who seemed to have wandered in from *Hassan*) and Alcibiades was also played in the street. The drop curtain was used as before, with no action in front of it, while the scene was shifted back to Timon's hall for the mock-banquet.

Timon, in red robes again, served not water but only clouds of steam; he overturned tables, pulled down curtains and set the house afire. As he finally advanced to the forestage the drop curtain was lowered once more, semi-transparent where it was lighted from behind, to produce a most effective stage picture. Through the walls of Athens, outside which Timon now stood, could be seen to one side the ruins of the banquet in the lurid light of flames flickering offstage. On the other side the enigmatic white goddess gazed inscrutably on the scene of destruction. Timon went straight on from his speech near the end of Act 3 to the denunciation that opens Act 4. Throwing aside his cloak only, he made his departure from this City of Destruction by descending into the pit at the front of the stage, and the curtain fell for the single long interval.

The producer's decision to give a clear visual contrast

between the city scenes of the first half and the wilderness scenes of the second half dictated the omission of 4.2, the scene in which the steward shares his own remaining coins among Timon's other former servants. Instead the curtain rose upon the wilderness, or as the stage direction has it "in the woods." As soon as this scene was revealed it became evident that the production had not only cut the lines but missed the poetic point about the hero who is spurned down the slope of Fortune's Hill and ignored by those who had previously been his beneficiaries. Timon in Athens was on the same level as his fellows throughout, but for the insignificant range of three or four steps. Timon in exile had the vantage of a central rocky mound, to the top of which he frequently resorted. If the intention had been to show that Timon's last state was, despite appearances, better than his first, the placing might have been justified. But if this was in the producer's mind it was hardly the impression Sir Ralph Richardson left on his audience. The general effect of the scene, which included a long brown fringe of what looked rather like seaweed hung up to dry, and of the actor's armless sheepskin coat and bare cross-gartered legs, was more reminiscent of Robinson Crusoe than of the naked outcast Timon.

Sir Ralph's delivery of Timon's long speeches and his judgments on those who came to visit him were spoken with a quiet irony more effective than the negligent extravagance of the first half. After the name-calling contest with Apemantus, which culminated in a vigorous exchange of stones, the churlish philosopher did not stay to bandy further insults. Instead, there was a brief blackout in which the festoon was raised and the rocky buttress was now seen against a cyclorama sky. This might or might not have been at the verge of the salt sea; there was neither sight nor sound of the ocean.

Timon had set up on his rocky stronghold a huge slab, like a tombstone, on which he was carving his epitaph as he spoke the lines up to "make thine Epitaph, That death in me, at others' lives may laugh." A cut of some twenty lines allowed the three Bandits to interrupt the speech at this point. Richardson's uncanny stillness as he sat looking down unseen upon them, listening to their avaricious interchanges, gave him a memorable moment of moral superiority, which the thieves sensed when they looked up and met his quietly accusing gaze.

In the next interview, the last long speech of the Steward was omitted, and there was a cut of some thirty lines early in the scene with the Poet and the Painter. The Steward and the Senators departed sadly on "Trouble him no further . . ." and Timon resumed his chiseling for his final speech, "Come not to me again . . . let my gravestone be your Oracle . . . Timon hath done his reign," in a last ray of the setting sun.

There was a blackout while the actor left the stage, and to preserve unity of place the short scene of the Senators' report back to Athens (5.2) was omitted. Only the first two lines of 5.3 were spoken by the Soldier, who was interrupted by the entry of Alcibiades and his forces, not before Athens but at the base of Timon's rocky retreat, where they were confronted by the frightened Senators and people who enter from the opposite side of the stage. Alcibiades rejected the Athenian pleas for mercy and ordered the assault; but at this moment the Soldier, who had climbed up to examine the inscription, called urgently to him and Alcibiades halted the attack to read the epitaph himself. It was this reminder of human mortality that melted the banished general to pity, a bold rehandling of the end of the play which at least tied the main and subplots together in a theatrically effective way.

In the text of the play as we have it, Alcibiades relents for no dramatically adequate reason, and Michael Benthall's solution therefore deserves serious consideration. But whether the change which makes Timon's death the cause of that change of heart is an acceptable image of the death of misanthropy bringing forth new mercy, or whether it is only a last irony that the man who willed the destruction of Athens should be the inadvertent means of saving the city, remains a dangerous dramatic ambiguity.

Whatever its intention, the impression made by this production on audiences who had small knowledge of the play was that Timon was entirely to blame. The early scenes suggested to them not the noble magnanimity of a largess universal like the sun, only a reckless extravagance. Yet it was presumably the poet's intention to show how selfish society drives out true generosity (and makes of it a judgment on itself); much as, in the preceding play, the mob drives out military heroism and discipline in Coriolanus, whose story is echoed (with a happier ending) in the Alcibiades subplot of *Timon of Athens*. Modern middle-class audiences have been indoctrinated with ideals of prudence and economy and are, moreover, suffering the effects of inflation and a credit squeeze! But something more might be done for Timon's credit by making the friendship of his beneficiaries seem plausible while they can still feed on Timon's means, so that we share some of his disillusionment at their unmasking.

Michael Benthall certainly avoided the gross mistake of Tyrone Guthrie's production at the Old Vic four years earlier, when the cultural *élite* of Athens was a pack of comic scarecrows. Nor was Richardson, as André Morell had been, like some devout peasant who had won a chariot-pool and set up as a one-man Athenian Arts Council, a fool and his money soon parted. But if the role of Timon calls for a display of active magnanimity, like Antony's, in the first part, and an active agony, like Philoctetes', in the second, Richardson remained too near the middle of the road throughout. His negligent prodigality at first and his half-amused irony later failed to scale the heights or reach the depths of the poetry, and his occasionally careless delivery, as well as that of a company far from strong even by recent Old Vic standards, came in for deserved censure from some critics. . . .

DAVID COOK

Timon of Athens

As is well known, there are certain major themes which Shakespeare handles again and again throughout his plays, ideas which form the framework of his thinking as it continually develops. One such concept is, of course, that of order: the elaborate consideration of social order in the history plays leads to an investigation of emotional and moral order, in *Measure for Measure* for instance, in *Lear,* and finally, with a different emphasis, in the last romances. I find another recurrent theme in the consideration of human pride, and the difficulty of distinguishing proper pride, which is essential to human dignity and which keeps a firm hold on certain fundamental values, from presumptuous, fiercely egotistical pride, which is a denial of human contact. This duality is particularly apparent in Shylock; Iago strikes a different balance. Othello is destroyed by positive pride, and so in his death positive values are more important than the wastage of life; Macbeth, in his negative pride, destroys himself and rejects humanity. Cordelia properly asserts human dignity, and so can serve as the instrument to winnow what is destructive from what is constructive in Lear's pride. *Timon of Athens, Coriolanus, Measure for Measure* and *All's Well That Ends Well* investigate more specifically the distinction, often a fine one, between negative and positive pride: in doing so they move towards the resolution of the human dilemma which Shakespeare offers as an alternative to tragedy in the final romances. Of these plays, *Timon of Athens* analyzes pride most objectively, and offers least resolution of the issues raised.

From *Shakespeare Survey* 16 (1963), pp. 83–94. Reprinted by permission of the author and of the Cambridge University Press.

It is the magnificent scale of Timon's presumption which determines his dramatic stature. But his extreme self-assertion is made possible only by an equal self-blindness which, unlike that of Coriolanus, is irremediable even in the last resort; thus it is impossible for Timon to pass beyond the limitations set by his pride and by his ignorance of himself; he can arrive at no fundamental self-knowledge nor meet any new dispensation in death, as do the greater tragic figures.

It will already be clear that I do not share the view of *Timon of Athens* which sees its "theme" as the depiction of "the ruin of a frank and generous soul by ingratitude, public and private."* The manner of the play is certainly homiletic and many of the minor characters are shown in a fiercely sardonic light. But homily is the coil rather than the core; if such simple moralizing were the main subject, then this would indeed be a naïve and uninteresting work. Incidentally, Shakespeare handles ingratitude far more powerfully in the persons of Regan and Goneril. But the whole concept of Timon as a saintly man who, being wronged, understandably comes to hate mankind, runs quite counter, I am sure, to the actual dramatic impact. In fact, Timon is pictured as flagrantly wrongheaded in both halves of the play. Our untrammeled reaction is surely to feel that at first he is a well-meaning fool, and that later his misanthropy, however provoked, is perverse. Even in the play's still unfinished form, we possess enough to see clearly that such are the effects which Shakespeare intends, and consequently there can be no solemn moralization running counter to this strong dramatic current. I am inclined to agree with J. C. Maxwell that seeing Timon as an embodiment of overtaxed virtue results from a "subservience to classification and theory—to the traditional classification of *Timon* as a tragedy, and to quasi-philosophical theories . . . of what tragedy should be."† The critics who were more concerned in attributing parts of

*T. M. Parrott, *The Problem of Timon of Athens* (Shakespeare Association Papers no. 10, 1923), p. 3.
†"Timon of Athens," *Scrutiny,* xv, 3 (1948), 196. In reading (and sometimes rereading) *Timon* criticism, I find that I have agreed fairly closely with J. C. Maxwell on a number of specific points; and elsewhere with O. J. Campbell and A. C. Collins.

the play to various playwrights of their own choice than in assessing it as a whole found a spur to their activities in the obvious absurdities and contradictions inherent in this conventional view.

As I see it, *Timon of Athens* is an investigation of aberrations from natural order in the individual promoted by subtle forms of pride, just as *Troilus and Cressida* concerns itself with similar aberrations in the state. The backbone of Shakespeare's public thinking is the medieval, neoclassical conception of a universal hierarchy, embodied in Ulysses' best-known speech (and perhaps most coherently propounded for later generations in Pope's *Essay on Man*). E.M.W. Tillyard, describing this interpretation of the cosmos in *Shakespeare's History Plays,** quotes a characteristic passage from I.K.'s 1598 translation of Hannibal Romei's *Courtier's Academy,†* which conveniently expounds that part of the theory which seems to me relevant to *Timon of Athens*:

> Creatures live after the laws of nature: man liveth by reason, prudence and art. Living creatures may live a solitary life: man alone, being himself insufficient and by nature an evil creature, without domestical and civil conversation cannot lead other than a miserable and discontented life. And therefore, as the philosopher saith very well, that man which cannot live in civil company either he is a god or a beast, seeing only God is sufficient of himself, and a solitary life best agreeth with a beast.

"This passage . . . ," comments Tillyard, "would have been accepted without question by every educated Elizabethan." This familiar concept is, I suggest, the framework for *Timon of Athens*. In the first half of the drama Timon plays the god, far above all other men, aloof and indiscriminately munificent; in the second half he becomes the animal, alone and rejecting all fellow contact. In neither case will Timon consider or accept man's real condition. As Alcibiades declares in his funeral speech for Timon:

*P. 14. I have adopted Tillyard's modernized spelling and punctuation, except for two commas.
†P. 247.

Thou abhorr'dst in us our human griefs.*

The burden of the play, positively expressed in Alcibiades, is
the need to accept and love man as he is, and to acknowledge
our human condition. Thus *Timon* is closely linked in theme
with *Measure for Measure,* in the demand that fallible man
shall, without being pandered to, nevertheless be loved and
forgiven, a train of thought which eventually leads to *The
Tempest.* In *Timon,* however, it is a secondary character who
embodies this positive idea, while the protagonist acts out its
obverse: Timon is negative. Macbeth too is negative, but
Macbeth is perhaps Shakespeare's only tragedy of waste (a
much abused term) and so the hero remains the controlling
figure in presenting the dramatic idea; whereas Timon, when
measured against the very different idea which is central to
his play, is found wanting. Did this subject, apparently so apt,
prove in fact to be too negative to match Shakespeare's dramatic thinking at this time? Was this the reason why his
impulse flagged so that he did not finish revising the play?
This can be no more than a conjecture.

In the closer analysis of the play which follows I shall not
normally distinguish between the polished and unpolished
parts of the text. I believe the play can be interpreted as a
whole. Those passages which are clearly only in draft form
may carry somewhat less weight critically, but they take
their place in the general pattern of the play.

As a result of naïve blandness rather than of deliberate
presumption, Timon has assumed a godlike status, a role
which is clearly reflected in the phrasing and imagery. The
poet announces

> I have in this rough work shap'd out a man,
> Whom this beneath world doth embrace and hug.

Timon is irresistible to all men:

> You see how all conditions, how all minds,
> As well of glib and slipp'ry creatures as
> Of grave and austere quality, tender down
> Their services to Lord Timon.

*Quotations are from *Timon of Athens,* ed. H. J. Oliver (Arden Shakespeare, 1959).

And it is by an act of grace that Timon is seen winning his opponents to join the throng of followers:

> Whose present grace to present slaves and servants
> Translates his rivals.

This line of imagery intensifies, till the sycophants whispering in Timon's ear breathe only by his allowance:

> Rain sacrificial whisperings in his ear,
> Make sacred even his stirrup, and through him
> Drink the free air.

True the painting carries a moral, the warning that pride goes before a fall, but significantly Timon does not consider this when he later receives the work. At the end of the scene the second lord declares that Pluto is merely Timon's steward. The masque symbolically sets Timon again above mere mankind who have to war with the human condition:

> The five best senses acknowledge thee their patron,
> and come freely to gratulate thy plenteous bosom.

The original stage direction tells us that the Lords "rise from the table, with much adoring of Timon." And the Steward's bitter regrets carry a double meaning:

> His promises fly so beyond his state.

And even in his long speech at the mock-banquet Timon still, by implication but unmistakably, draws a parallel between himself and the gods.

Timon is not discriminatingly or positively generous. The opening of the play presents a repulsive picture of the competing toadies who bask in Timon's favor. They are willing to travesty art to please him, and to fawn on others whom he approves. He is too beneficent to be in real contact with lesser mortals, whom he advances regardless of their worth or worthlessness. And we see him buying a jewel with the same casualness as that with which he relieves a friend. In short, he emulates the indiscriminate generosity of an abstract deity like Fortune. The real difference is that Timon proves to have feet of clay. As Lucius' servant dryly comments:

> You must consider that a prodigal course
> Is like the sun's,
> But not, like his, recoverable.

The only two figures at Timon's court who retain their self-respect are Apemantus, who refuses his gifts, and the Steward, who well earns his comparatively slight rewards.

Timon does not stop to consider the shallowness of the friendship which he virtually buys. Apemantus is unheeded:

> That there should be small love amongst these sweet knaves,
> And all this courtesy!

But Timon is pleasant enough in all his dealings for us to be both disappointed that he should allow himself to be so duped, and chagrined by his blindness. For, however sour his manner, we must surely second Apemantus in

> He that loves to be flattered is worthy o' th' flatterer.

If Timon is easily deceived, the audience is not, and is not meant to be. We mark the warnings that Timon wilfully ignores: "I take no heed of thee." He sweeps aside the reasonable consideration of his own affairs with an imperious and dramatic selflessness similar to Julius Caesar's:

> *Steward.*   . . . it does concern you near.
> *Timon.*   Near? Why, then, another time I'll hear thee.

Act 1, the act that sets out the situation, ends with an authoritative, impersonal rhymed couplet:

> O that men's ears should be
> To counsel deaf, but not to flattery.

Timon allows riches to isolate him in a privileged position, so he remains ignorant of the truth about men, and about himself. "Why," he vapidly laments, "I have often

wish'd myself poorer that I might come nearer to you." This
is an idle and complacent comment, proper only to hypocrisy
or extreme ingenuousness, the more so as the sentence is
rounded out with, "we are born to do benefits": Timon takes
it for granted that the traffic between himself and others is in
effect one-way. He pays lip service to community: "O what
a precious comfort 'tis to have so many like brothers commanding one another's fortunes"; but we do not have to
await the event to realize what simple self-delusion this is.
We can hardly admire a man who cultivates such "brothers,"
or who understands so little about men; nor feel unqualified
pity when his own conduct overtakes him and he stands
aghast in wide-eyed innocence.

The refusal of Ventidius' repayment finally drives home
a number of these points. This is an unconsidered demonstration of bounty, part of the culpable display of reckless-
ness that shocks his Steward:

> Takes no accompt
> How things go from him, nor resumes no care
> Of what is to continue.

He is not here doing Ventidius any particular kindness, since
we are to understand that Ventidius' father has left him an
ample fortune. On the contrary, he is withstanding the one
proffered *exchange* of friendship and mutual honorableness
which he talks so much of. This can be nothing but a gesture;
a view which is confirmed by Timon's readiness to talk of
things which should be unspoken:

> Nay, my lords, ceremony was but devis'd at first
> To set a gloss on faint deeds, hollow welcomes,
> Recanting goodness, sorry ere 'tis shown;
> But where there is true friendship, there needs none.

Timon clearly means well: but that is not enough. His well
meaning favors knaves, smothers real friendship, and ruins
his own estate, thus preventing the judicious and constructive generosity he could be offering.

What is the faithful Steward's view of this so-called
munificence?

> When all our offices have been oppress'd
> With riotous feeders, when our vaults have wept
> With drunken spilth of wine, when every room
> Hath blaz'd with lights and bray'd with minstrelsy,
> I have retir'd me to a wasteful cock
> And set mine eyes at flow.

The constant impression is that the result of Timon's ready dispensing of cash is drunkenness, debauchery, orgy and waste:

> No care, no stop; so senseless of expense,
> That he will neither know how to maintain it,
> Nor cease his flow of riot.

Timon squanders money to maintain his own conception of himself:

> You may take my word, my lord, I know no man
> Can justly praise but what he does affect.
> I weigh my friend's affection with mine own,
> I'll tell you true. I'll call to you.

This is the vanity of giving:

> I take all and your several visitations
> So kind to heart, 'tis not enough to give:
> Methinks I could deal kingdoms to my friends,
> And ne'er be weary.

Timon's bounty is seen as a "humor," a wilful obsession: "There's no crossing him in's humor" declares the Steward. And while Timon thinks himself loved for his generosity, he is despised and made fun of:

> If I want gold, steal but a beggar's dog
> And give it Timon—why, the dog coins gold.

It is impossible to exaggerate the importance of such a line as,

> Never mind
> Was to be so unwise, to be so kind.

The play thus embodies truisms familiar to the neoclassicist. J. C. Maxwell declares that of all Shakespeare's works *Timon* "falls most easily within the framework of an Aristotelian scheme, and Timon, both before and after his fall, is clearly an example of excess."*

> The liberal man [says Aristotle] will give to the right people, the right amounts, and at the right time. . . . Nor will he neglect his own property, since he wishes by means of this to help others. And he will refrain from giving to anybody and everybody, that he may have something to give to the right people, at the right time, and where it is noble to do so. . . . For as has been said, he is liberal who spends according to his substance and on the right objects; and he who exceeds is prodigal.†

Certainly there are important qualifications to be made in Timon's favor: within his own limited vision, he is sincere and constantly imagines himself to be acting idealistically. Shakespeare does not suggest that Timon is always wrong in giving. His brief replies to the Old Man whose daughter he marries to his servant show immediate right feeling. He does indeed in some sort display generous friendship, especially to Ventidius in need, and at an early stage one almost imagines he might be a benevolent despot. There is, again, a certain splendor in his high-minded view of man, even if it rests on a failure to consider the evidence, and on childlike vanity. As Peter Alexander says, he has "a godlike image of a man in his heart." His behavior may be culpable, but it is not despicable. He is an "honest fool."

And so Timon is, on the one hand, wholly admirable to men who know no intimate facts about him, the strangers; while, on the other, to his Steward, who knows the individual behind the godlike façade, he is truly lovable. If the Steward weeps over Timon's folly, he is weeping for one for whom he feels real affection. Yet the emphasis remains on Timon's lack of self-control. He is indiscriminate. He does good at random; and naïvely squanders more than he wisely

---

*"Timon of Athens," *Scrutiny*, xv, 3 (1948), 197.

†*Ethica Nicomachea*, IV, i, 1020ª, 24–1020ᵇ, 25, translated by W. D. Ross, *The Works of Aristotle* (Oxford, 1915), IX.

distributes. The scene at the end of Act 2 between steward and master is revealing. With the coming of disaster, Timon abandons all fulsomeness; his tone is now direct and honest; but he is altogether at a loss. He is here like a hurt child beside the sorrowing maturity of his own overseer.

But whatever Timon's limitations, his society has, of course, no justification for treating him as it does: society is, in fact, ruthlessly and painstakingly indicted in the first half of the play. However, in considering Timon himself we are bound to remember that these are the very men he has chosen and fostered with his superficial beneficence, uncontrolled by reason or prudence, blindly presuming beyond man's proper scope to play the role of all-dispensing Fortune. Thus, Timon has no cause to blame Fate or mankind in general for what he wilfully brings on himself: his reaction to adversity is unwarrantably negative, just as his reaction to prosperity has been dangerously irresponsible and presumptuous.

The most difficult role to assess in this first part of the play is Apemantus. He is crabbed and uncouth, but his sour comments come close to the mark. His jibing is sometimes faintly reminiscent of the searching, cross talk from the Fool in *Lear,* who in his asperity also dismisses cliché and conventional attitudinizing:

> *Timon.*   Good morrow to thee, gentle Apemantus.
> *Apemantus.* Till I be gentle, stay thou for thy good morrow,
>   When thou art Timon's dog, and these knaves
>   honest.

Fools in Shakespeare are constantly in league with truth; so that, though the scene is little more than a rough draft, it is not insignificant that Apemantus is on more friendly terms with the Fool when they are together than with any other character. At one point he praises a riposte from the Fool by claiming, "That answer might have become Apemantus"; and the Fool says immediately afterwards, "I do not always follow lover, elder brother and woman; sometime the philosopher."

Critics who have seen Timon himself as a monument of wronged virtue have had to play down the caustic accuracy of Apemantus' social observation; and since he is not a warm or directly likable character, they have been able to do so by emphasizing his harshness at the expense of his insight. Nevertheless, Apemantus seems to be cast in the philosophical tradition of a Diogenes; he serves as the relentless mentor in the play. He is neither taken in by the glitter of society, nor does he withdraw from it, but stays to warn and moralize. His view of his fellows, if sometimes almost as black as Timon's is at the last, remains philosophic rather than petulant or personal; and he is engaged throughout in moral and prophetic admonition, never in self-glorification or self-pity. Shakespeare, as so often, had set himself a nice problem: how to introduce the voice of reason into the play without hopelessly weakening the protagonist's dramatic status. I do not think he has solved the problem altogether, simply by giving sanity such a rugged exterior. The result is to confuse the issue (as it would have been confused in *Lear* if the king had ultimately resisted the rebukes of the Fool and Kent), since Timon is still necessarily left in a negative position; but by this device Shakespeare at least makes his play viable, however tenuously.

The dividing line between the positions of Timon and Apemantus in the second half of the play is a fine one, a distinction which is not always dramatically clear in detail, though in the main the two voices remain in subtle contrast, except in the apparently unrevised passage wherein Apemantus makes Timon confound himself: here Apemantus' role becomes blurred; but I shall return to this point. In the whole design one can perceive that Apemantus is cast as the homilist: often his words become so impersonal that he seems to speak for the play rather than for himself.

One of Shakespeare's many structural experiments in his later plays was to adopt a simple form divided into two clearly marked halves boldly and significantly contrasted against each other. This is perhaps most subtly effected in *Coriolanus*, and most daringly in *The Winter's Tale*, where the duality is pinpointed in the words

thou met'st with things dying, I with things new-born.

A similar division is also explicitly summarized in *Timon:*

One day he gives us diamonds, next day stones.

In his days of prosperity, instead of trying to understand men and work on them positively with his wealth, Timon has lived immoderately: now he flies to the opposite extreme. The malcontent was, of course, a fashionable stage figure at this time; as ever Shakespeare takes the popular fabric and cuts it to his own design.

That Timon's "love" is so soon converted into hate bespeaks the empty and pretentious nature of his "generosity." A truly benevolent man could never be brought deliberately to cry down such vengeance upon his race; anyone might come to say such things in a state of hysteria, but Timon maintains them steadily from now till his death:

> Slaves and fools,
> Pluck the grave wrinkled senate from the bench,
> And minister in their steads! To general filths
> Convert, o'th'instant, green virginity!
> Do't in your parents' eyes! Bankrupts, hold fast;
> Rather than render back, out with your knives,
> And cut your trusters' throats! Bound servants, steal!
> Large-handed robbers your grave masters are,
> And pill by law. Maid, to thy master's bed;
> Thy mistress is o'th'brothel! Son of sixteen,
> Pluck the lin'd crutch from thy old limping sire;
> With it beat out his brains!

The malcontent is also indicting himself—the very excess makes this apparent. There is no poetic conviction in this opening speech of Act 4: compare it with the more savage passages of *The Revenger's Tragedy*. Shakespeare does not seem really to have entered into this wild loathing of mankind. Whatever Timon's state, he has certainly no more grounds for such indiscriminate denunciation than he had for his equally indiscriminate generosity. To underline this fact we are introduced at once to the innocent and open-hearted victims of Timon's excesses—the Steward and his fellows. Timon's unbridled damning of man must include these patient followers. Their direct feeling and real, simple generosity discredit Timon's megalomaniac ravings. Those Timon has cause to hate, he himself has bred up to it; while he forgets those who patently deserve his consideration. The Steward can see Timon's career in clear perspective:

> Who would be so mock'd with glory, or to live
> But in a dream of friendship. . . ?

But he has no bitter word, only sympathy and affection:

> Poor honest lord, brought low by his own heart,
> Undone by goodness.

And he concludes, "I'll ever serve his mind, with my best will": here is an unassuming nobility to which Timon cannot aspire.

So when Timon cries:

> Who dares, who dares,
> In purity of manhood stand upright,
> And say this man's a flatterer? If one be,
> So are they all,

we are reminded that his cynicism is culled from narrow and self-induced experience; and when he complains that "the learned pate Ducks to the golden fool," we remember that such is the conduct Timon has courted. When he concludes,

> all's obliquy;
> There's nothing level in our cursed natures
> But direct villainy,

we ask, "What of the Steward, of Alcibiades, the Servants, the Strangers, and their like?" At last we see Timon's fury as a private jaundice resulting from his failure to buy love by means of lavish distribution of favors.

When Timon finds his new supply of gold, his condemnation of the malpractices it could foster is eloquent, but he conveniently overlooks the fact that his own abuse of wealth is to be included in the indictment. To hide the coin is moral escapism, not a solution. Can he conceive it doing no good, simply because it breeds nothing but selfish greed in flatterers? And so Apemantus appears, to shake Timon from his complacent world of private hatred.

The frequency of animal imagery in the play has often been noticed. It should be added that in the early acts it is used almost exclusively by or of Apemantus, his role being contrasted with Timon's superhuman elevation. It is immediately after this dialogue in 1.1,

> *Second Lord.* Away, unpeaceable dog, or I'll spurn thee hence!
> *Apemantus.*   I will fly, like a dog, the heels o'th'ass.
> *First Lord.*   He's opposite to humanity,

that Timon is again raised to godhead, the opposite extreme:

> He pours it out. Plutus the god of gold
> Is but his steward.

We are kept aware of the two states outside the human condition. But Timon, when forced to abandon the one, eagerly adopts the other:

> *Alcibiades.*   What art thou there? Speak.
> *Timon.*   A beast as thou art.

Timon turns away friend and enemy alike; and he himself is utterly ungrateful in his petulance, while in the very act of brooding upon the ingratitude of others:

> *Alcibiades.*   Here is some gold for thee.
> *Timon.*   Keep it, I cannot eat it.

The tables are turned: Timon is thankless and incapable of responding to the generosity of others. He has forgotten his own words earlier: "Oh what a precious comfort 'tis, to have so many like brothers commanding one another's fortunes."

Apemantus immediately attacks Timon as a fake cynic who has turned misanthrope in an enormous huff because his irrational dreams about human nature have proved false:

Men report thou dost affect my manners ... putting on the
cunning of a carper.... Thou wast told thus.... Do not
assume my likeness.

The argument which Apemantus here presents is often
misrepresented. He is not saying that Timon would re-
nounce poverty if he had the chance: we know that he has
already found a fresh supply of gold. Shakespeare is not
merely concerned to show that Apemantus does not know
what he is talking about; far from it. What he says is that
Timon, being an escapist from reality, always seeks an
extreme, where issues are simplified into being either rosy or
without hope:

> Thou'dst courtier be again
> Wert thou not beggar. Willing misery
> Outlives incertain pomp—

in short, in hoping for nothing and dismissing mankind,
Timon has found a much more secure retreat than in his previous dream of perfect living. When his glittering world
crashed about his ears, he was bound to be involved; when
his lonely indulgence in loathing is shown to be ill-founded,
he can, and does, shut his eyes, as we have seen. Thus, like
Richard II and Coriolanus, though for different reasons,
Timon cannot bear mediocrity: he must be all-significant or
a cipher; life must appear a utopia or a hell. Timon will not
accept the human condition with its confusions and compromises. He must be more, or less, than man. If he cannot be a
god, he will become a beast.

It is in Act 4 that the distinction between Apemantus and
Timon, the caustic, satirical philosopher and the spoilt child
sulking in the face of a fate he has brought on himself, is
most important, and also most difficult to make dramatically. Timon has been "a madman so long, and now a fool."
In his own defense he enters on a long speech of self-pity, to
which Apemantus trenchantly replies, "Art thou proud yet?"
Apemantus exposes the falsity of Timon's values which
have led him to confuse gratitude with love, and comes to
the heart of the whole play in the sentence, "The middle of
humanity thou never knewest, but the extremity of both

ends." Eventually Apemantus adopts some of Timon's own arguments and attitudes ("Give it to the beasts, to be rid of men," and so on): presumably he is drawing Timon on. Already in the first act Timon has been made to condemn his own future conduct in terms exactly appropriate to the play, when he berates Apemantus' churlishness:

> Fie, th'art a churl, y'have got a humor there
> Does not become a man.

Now, as Apemantus plays devil's advocate, Timon is again made to condemn his own imitation of bestial life in even rounder terms:

> What beast couldst thou be that were not subject to a beast?
> And what a beast art thou already, that seest not thy loss in transformation!

It may seem like special pleading to argue that Apemantus here changes sides to draw Timon out and make him condemn himself. But one should consider that it is in fact Timon who truly adopts the "solitary life" which "best agreeth with the beast": it is Apemantus who sought the interview, and it is Apemantus who returns to mankind, to live in society as its moral mentor. His final "Live and love thy misery" shows him as having accurately sized up Timon's whole situation.

For now Timon proceeds to the final rejection of man. He hates life: "I am sick of this false world." And he dedicates the globe to the beasts: "that beasts May have the world in empire." He reaches a new pitch of cynicism when he advises the Banditti not only to hate others but even to "love not yourselves." The climax of this sequence falls in the scene with the Steward. Against all the evidence Timon at first tries to cling to his total rejection of man:

> *Steward.*   An honest poor servant of yours.
> *Timon.*   Then I know thee not.
>   I never had honest man about me, I; all
>   I kept were knaves, to serve in meat to villains.

But the play pursues him and pins him down till he is forced to acknowledge "One honest man." Is this, we wonder, to be the beginning of a new vision for him? By no means, for it proves the nadir of his wilful introversion. Timon is no longer dealing with men whom he can convince himself are contemptible: but how does he reward this honest man? He offers him gold, the gold which Timon, however wrongheadedly, believes to be evil, and which, as employed in the play, has become the symbol of destructive materialism: he exhorts him to hatred:

> Hate all, curse all, show charity to none;

and ends the act with the ominous words:

> Ne'er see thou man, and let me ne'er see thee.

Shakespeare shows great technical daring in planning the construction of the second half of *Timon* as a series of duologues or interviews. These are not simply repetitive but pile one on top of another to build, as it were, a negative climax. The aim is to achieve a powerful austerity in contrast with the shifting effects of the first half of the play, but also parallel to the successive appeals to Timon's "friends" in Act 3. The manner is severe and classical; but its success is only partial.

There is an attempt to dramatize Timon's last denial of mankind differently and more fully in Act 5. This depends on the appeal to Timon by the city of Athens in time of crisis to come and save them, and Timon's refusal. Unfortunately, there is no previous evidence in terms of the play that Timon has ever been a crucial figure in the state. So that, unlike the decision which is forced on Coriolanus, with the whole dramatic weight of the play behind it, the situation in *Timon* appears contrived, and largely fails of its effect. But the dramatic intention is clear enough: Timon's position is now represented by the words "I care not." His abandonment of life is negative, the confirmation and consummation of all that has gone before. Timon the absolutist could find no place on earth. This absolutism was at first innocent, and remains sufficiently naïve for him to retain a certain nobility, though a barren and inhuman nobility. In order to strengthen the presentation of Timon's death, his epitaph is introduced twice, not altogether successfully in dramatic terms; but the pattern is now complete.

The action centered on Alcibiades is no mere irrelevant incident. I agree with Peter Alexander that 3.5 is central to the whole play, though I would interpret it rather differently. The Senate admit that Alcibiades' friend has been subjected to wrongs, but they smugly declare, "He's truly valiant that can wisely suffer," and they advocate the wearing of one's injuries "carelessly." Alcibiades then reasonably asks why, if they believe this, they should possess an army instead of being pacifists. The First Senator's reply, "Nothing emboldens sin so much as mercy," recalls the debate between Isabella and Angelo. This passage is highly relevant to the whole play. The issue is concentrated in Alcibiades' lines,

> To be in anger is impiety;
> But who is man that is not angry?
> Weigh but the crime with this.

In short, he insists that man's fallibility must be taken into account in balancing justice against mercy. Surely there is no doubt that Alcibiades has, and is meant to have, our sympathy in this scene. He is felt to be right because he accepts man as man, with all his limitations and weaknesses. Thus Timon is paralleled with the Senate: each demands or assumes an unattainable absolute standard of conduct. The self-protective canker in the state is legislation by fear; Timon's canker, that of the individual, is fear of living in actuality and facing the complexity of man's condition.

To say this is not to argue that the two plots have been neatly integrated. But it now becomes quite clear why Alcibiades' action is allowed to conclude the play. Alcibiades, like Timon, has been betrayed and has reacted violently, but, unlike Timon, he comes to terms with life. When forced in turn to make his moral choice, his decision is positive; he accepts man and his limitations; and in the light of this acceptance can exercise mercy. The line of argument on which Alcibiades yields is:

> We were not all unkind, nor all deserve
> The common stroke of war,

which forcefully reminds us how oversimplified was Timon's judgment in condemning all men alike by a rule of thumb. "All have not offended"; and, by corollary, if the state does not consist exclusively either of good or bad members, so the individual is neither perfect nor utterly vile. In burying his anger, Alcibiades acts like a wise, merciful, and humanly inconsistent being, not like a god or a beast. This emphasis on the need to accept, minister to, correct and forgive fallible human nature links *Timon* to a far greater work, *Measure for Measure,* and points the way once again towards the final romances.

So the idea is rounded out. It has been powerfully conceived, but not realized in fully developed dramatic terms. The suggestion, often made both on textual and critical grounds, that we have no more than an advanced draft of *Timon,* seems convincing. It is easy to see why Shakespeare might seize on the subject of Timon in a period of troubled thinking and warring moods, and might modify his material along the lines I have suggested. And it is, further, quite feasible that the reason he failed to finish the work was that, in the event, the hero proved too negative a vehicle for his thinking, and the whole fabric of the play too destructive at a time when his thoughts were slowly gestating the new positive ideas of the final group of plays. It is interesting that Shakespeare's only other fundamentally negative play, *Troilus and Cressida* (though in a much more advanced state of revision than *Timon* and altogether more effective and disturbing), also lacks finish. Perhaps not only the treatment but also the rejection of the Timon motif may contribute to our understanding of the whole body of Shakespeare's thought.

SUSAN HANDELMAN

Timon of Athens: The Rage of Disillusion

Shakespeare's characters frequently express an obsession with the problems of creation, illusion, boundaries, dreams. The anxiety that the symbolic world will break down, vanish and leave not a rack behind, is present in all the plays, and perhaps accounts for their obsessive self-reflexiveness— their constant reflection on their own origins, their own natures as plays. The anxiety of the artist's ego is another variant of the primal shock to our universal narcissism. But with those characters who insist on retaining and trying obstinately to recapture that original state, Shakespeare is often not kind.

The inability to accept loss may express itself in the creation of higher narcissistic illusions or heightened rage. In Lear, both reactions exist simultaneously—holding dead Cordelia in his arms, he cries, "Never, never, never," etc. etc., and yet looks for signs of breath on her lips—"The feather stirs; she lives! If it be so,/It is a chance which does redeem all sorrows/that ever I have felt" (5.3.264–68). *Timon of Athens* follows *Lear* and is a play so close and yet so far from *Lear* because it asks the question: How do we go on living *after* Cordelia is dead? In *Timon of Athens* disillusion is absolute, no substitute is acceptable, there are no rituals of atonement, no provisions for mourning. The play is less about the experience of loss itself than a demonstration of the rage which refuses to accept loss. Perhaps this is why it is generally considered to be a bad play—it does not do what we expect of art in general: help us to accept loss.

All the questions about its authorship, which stem from

From *American Imago* 36 (1979), 45–68. Reprinted by permission of the author and of *American Imago*. About half of the original essay is herewith reprinted.

the many confusions and disjunctions in the text, indicate an unfinished play which somewhere broke down, would not allow itself to be composed. But that indeed, I think, is itself what the play is about—a breakdown of all those ways in which rage, pain, and loss can somehow be accepted, made sense of, transformed into life-affirming energies. That transformation indeed requires a magic power, and the magic of art which is always engaged in denying loss by making something from nothing, making dead matter live, conjuring presences, thieving immortality from time, does not work in this play—both structurally and symbolically.

In *Timon*, Shakespeare does not believe in his own art, and that is why the play is unfinished. *Timon* tells us something that the artist himself cannot dwell on too long: that mourning is never finished, that we can't and don't really know how to accept or redeem loss, that we are always pained and enraged. Says Alcibiades, "To be in anger is impiety;/But who is man that is not angry?" (3.5.57–58). . . .

In the world of *Timon* nothing can redeem sorrow. Nothing can come of nothing. There are no acceptable substitutes; loss is irrevocable. Therefore, Timon does not mourn, he rages. In a world without Cordelia, without an embodied ideal of love, art, nature, man himself is not man, but a beast. What Apemantus says also applies to the modern city: "The commonwealth of Athens is become a forest of beasts." What Timon asks him is also the question of contemporary history: "What beast couldst thou be, that were not subject to a beast? And what beast art thou already, that sees not thy loss in transformation!" (4.3.345–53).

That the embodied principle of good is often an idealized woman in Shakespeare is significant. In *Timon*, there is neither good art nor good women. The play itself is in part about the cultural and individual disaster of execution of the female. A world without women is a world not only without art, but without order. In *Lear*, the good woman, the ideal of pure love, was exiled, but not murdered until the end of the play. In *Timon*, she never existed; there is no feminine representative of goodness and constancy. When woman as nourisher is perceived as devourer, and relation with her as feared dependency; when the wish for a gratifying union with her is seen as threatening destruction only; when she is not only banished, but hated and murdered, then there can be neither manhood nor brotherhood, neither human being nor society. That is the condition of the world in *Timon of Athens.*

Accepting woman, however, means accepting loss, accepting not only the gap between self and other, but also the gap between self and self—recognizing the illusion of narcissistic omnipotence, knowing that one is limited, imperfect, dependent and not projecting that part of one's nature onto a conveniently hated and abhorred weak, false female. The world cannot be split, as Timon originally splits it, into a male brotherly good and a female fatal bad. Woman herself cannot be split, as the cultural myth splits her, into the Sacred Virginal Good and Profane Prostitute Bad. Accepting woman means accepting art itself. The world which excludes woman splits itself apart; the man who denies the female divides his own self and like Timon becomes his opposite, Misanthropos, monster, and beast. In *Timon of Athens,* there is no way back to humanity.

Thus, the world of *Timon* is a world of negations, mutually destructive oppositions—male-female, good-bad, love-hate, man-beast, friend-enemy, forgiveness-revenge. Contraries do not mutually exist, differences and separations are not tolerated; the gap between self and other, presence and absence, ideal and real, loss and recovery, is unbridgeable. The adjoining "bonds" are broken. The structure of the play itself operates on the principle of splitting, of incorporation and expulsion, orally ambivalent perception. The first half of the play centers around Timon's communal feasts, the second half around his solitary exile; the imagery turns from the intake of nourishing food to the vomiting of poison and disease. In place of an internal principle of integration which Timon lacks and cannot find, he had depended on a false, external, reified, material means of mutuality: money. . . .

In *Timon,* money has replaced the mediating power of the idealized woman (Blake's Emanation which joins man to man, but for him ultimately hermaphroditic), but instead of providing a way for contraries to mutually exist, marry, mingle, and create, money destructively converts opposites into negations of each other and Timon becomes Misanthropos. Marx, like Shakespeare, perceives that money is a psychological structure of alienated exchanges. When economics is conceived in terms of man's relation to man, and society as a system of exchanges, Marx asks what motivates the buying and selling of private property and answers:

> Need and want. The other person is also a property owner, but of another object which I lack and which I neither can nor want to be without, an object which seems to be something *needed* for the reintegration of my existence and the realization of my nature. . . . For the need of an object is the most evident and irrefutable proof that the object belongs to my nature and that the existence of the object for me and its *property* are the property appropriate to my essence.*

The problem of loss is the problem of need and want, the problem of wholeness, an integrated and not split identity. Art, money, law, love, all bonds and means of exchange between men, civilization itself, are means to recover loss. Timon's primitive communism is a dream of restored communion, an attempt to defend against primal loss, to become both Self and Other, to be fed by his friends' flattery and feed them from the overflow of his bounty—to be simultaneously the passive nursing one, and the beneficent nourishing Mother. Yet he can only replace the flow of female milk with the rigid exchange of male money. Timon's attempted identification with the role of the Mother is a way to deny the loss of that primal one who gratified the infant's every wish, and to thereby be autonomous, not dependent on any female, not in need or vulnerable to any woman. But his primitive communism is, in fact, a feudal lordship, a narcissistic dream of adoration from his retainers under the guise of a Holy Brotherhood, one which admits no women. . . .

Loss can be denied by identification with the lost object and by attempted appropriation of female magic. For Shakespeare, Timon's magic, however, is impotent because it is narcissistic, substitutive, cannibalistic, and not transformative. Coins, jewels, food, are nonhuman, inert matter that cannot gratify the wish to be at one. The failure of all nar-

---

*Karl Marx, "Comments on James Mill, *Élémens d'économie politique,*" *Karl Marx/Frederick Engels Collected Works* (New York: International Publishers, 1975), III, 218.

cissistic substitutions leads to expulsion, spitting, and vomiting out all with which Timon had identified—women, friends, food, money, art:

> Therefore, be abhorred
> All feasts, societies, and throngs of men!
> His semblable, yea, himself, Timon disdains.
> Destruction fang mankind!   (4.3.20–24)

> *Alcibiades:*   Why, fare thee well:
> Here is some gold for thee.
> *Timon:*   Keep it, I cannot eat it.   (100–01)

Timon, who had the world as his "confectionary" (261), would change his feast of love to devouring hate: "Get thee gone./That the whole life of Athens were in this!/Thus would I eat it" (281–82), eating a root. (Root possibly as phallic power and genital organization as opposed to oral ambivalence.) That which is orally incorporated is both loved and hated, united with and destroyed. As Timon's servant tells him: "Feast won, fast-lost" (2.2.181).

The first scene of the play contains in miniature the critique of the impossible feast of civilization in its art, love, money and law. The poet in lines 5–7 exclaims, "See./Magic of bounty/All these spirits thy power/Hath conjured to attend." The poet, too, though, is in attendance not because of free love, nor is his art a free gift, but rather a counter to be exchanged for monetary recompense. The painter's art is described as a "pretty mocking of the life" (1.1.35). The mentality of art as imitation is the same mentality as literal, externalized substitution—as the mentality of money and the merchant. Art mocks nature by holding up the mirror, by copying and aping. In Renaissance thought, over against this kind of art, is the idealized power of Nature—the divinely created order of things, the procreative power which art might tutor or tame, but which art does not possess itself. To transfer the belief in that kind of natural transformative and freely creative power to Art, as we have done since the Romantics, and as Shakespeare plays with doing especially in the later works, signifies the loss of the divinely ordered scheme (and not incidentally the rise of bourgeois capitalism). . . .

The inability to accept change as the inability to accept dif-

ference is also the Shakespearian theme of loss as ingratitude—
of betrayal as lack of faith and constancy. Woman is the first
betrayer of constancy, not only because she is different, but
because she forces separation from her body, through birth
and weaning, and because she cannot be possessed by the
child as the father possesses her. Thus it is that the changes
and petulance of "Fortune" are personified, especially in the
Renaissance, as female. Fortune is a fickle and false lady; the
poet in the first scene of *Timon* likewise portrays Timon's
ascent and fall from Fortune as a climbing of a female body:
Fortune sits on a "mount," her followers "labour on her
bosom" "to propagate" their states. Timon, "bowing his head
against the steepy mount/To climb his happiness" (64–76) is
pursued by followers who "rain sacrificial whisperings in his
ear . . . Drink the free air." The images are oral and phallic,
having the sense of a small boy mounting and climbing a large
woman to drink and copulate, and being spurned.

Timon's own first word as he enters the play is "Imprison'd"
and, one might say, he is indeed imprisoned in his own narcissism, his desire to have the love of the whole world, to devour
and incorporate all into his own body. His first act in the play
is to "free" a friend from "debt." "Your lordship ever binds
him," says the messenger (104). Timon's acts of beneficence
bind other men to him, defend against separation, dissolve
boundaries, as Marx showed it was the particular property of
money to do. Timon's next act is to put up money for his servant to equally "weigh" with a woman of higher status, "For
'tis a bond in men" (144). Bounty, Boundary, and Bond are all
significantly related both in sound and sense. Timon wants the
binding power of his money to be magically omnipotent. . . .

I think it makes more sense in terms of the play itself to
see Timon's raging waste, communal feasts, oral ambivalence, in terms of the superfluous sacred rather than in terms
of Freud's conception that the totem feast is a response to a
primal murder of the father, a mutual sharing of guilt. And
the superfluous sacred means at-one-ment, diffuse union
with an original lost mother instead of guilt over the jealous
murder of the father. . . .

Timon's love gifts (and Shakespeare's as well perhaps)
are an attempt at orgiastic giving and a denial of the need to
receive, a fear of passive dependence and a desire for it, a

wish to dissolve the differences between self and other: "You mistake my love; I gave it freely ever; and there's none/Can truly say he gives if he receives (1.2.9–11) ... O, what a precious comfort 'tis to have so many, like brothers, commanding one another's fortunes" (104–06).

When Timon discovers that his idealized brotherly communion is a cannibalistic mutual devouring, his response is not guilt or shame as it would be in the case of Freud's totemistic brotherhood, but rage and primitive hatred (what in Freud would precede the murder of the father). This rage is directed against and placed in terms of women, not men; the breeding and feeding generosity of the mother must be accepted as beneficent bounty or it becomes detested as parasitic dependence. Before he can give his gift, Timon needs to learn how to accept and receive the gift of nature, love, grace; he must accept the power of women. Instead, he tries to omnipotently become the woman and nourisher himself. He refuses to accept generation from the female, and thus *all* generation, all creation of something from nothing, is detestable debt and abhorred birth ... including the breeding of capital:

> He pours it out: Plutus, the god of Gold,
> Is but his steward. No need but he repays
> Sevenfold above itself; no gift to him
> But *breeds* the giver a return exceeding
> All use of quittance.   (1.1.287–91)

> If I want gold, steal but a beggar's dog
> And give it Timon; why the dog coins gold   (2.1.5–6)

The birth of man is an excrescence: "If thou wilt curse, thy father, that poor rogue,/Must be thy subject, who in spite put stuff/To some she-beggar and compounded thee/Poor rogue hereditary" (4.3.272–75). Timon curses Mother Nature: "Ensear thy fertile and conceptious womb; Let it no more bring out ingrateful man!" (188–89). . . .

Outside of the two whores who appear briefly with Alcibiades in Act 4, the only women in the play are, significantly, Amazons in a masque—threatening, warlike women placed under formalized and ritual control through art (the same defensive strategy used in *The Tempest*). "They dance? They are

mad women," says Apemantus, "I should fear those that dance
before me now/would one day stomp upon me" (1.2.135–46).
Women, he says, "eat lords; so they come by great bellies"
(1.1.209). After he loses his money, devoured by his debts,
woman becomes also for Timon a ravenous destroyer:

> This fell whore of thine
> Hath in her more destruction than thy sword,
> For all her cherubin look.   (4.3.62–64)

> Strike me the counterfeit matron;
> It is her habit only that is honest, herself's a bawd.
> Let not the virgin's cheek
> Make soft thy trenchant sword; for those milk paps
> That through the window [bars] bore at men's eyes,
> Are not within the leaf of pity writ.
> But set them down horrible traitors.   (113–19)

The taking in of nourishing milk reverses to the vomiting of
poison; communion with the mother and the other is now
a source of corruption and syphillitic disintegration. But
Timon's hatred, while it is a schizophrenic reversal, is itself
still a refusal to accept loss, a refusal to reconstruct, and
recover new objects, to transform or metamorphose. He cannot
find a substitute ideal. His rage remains primitively narcissistic. His hatred is as orgasmic, diffuse, and undifferentiated
as his love. It contains both the desire to control and enclose the
whole world, and the desire passively to see oneself as a victim
of universal corruption. On the one hand, it represents an all-
or-nothing split between ideas of good and evil, pure and
impure, and the outward projection of the primitive hatred at
the recognition of the discrepancy between self and other into
the outside world. The original unity of love and hate in oral
ambivalence becomes undone and in place of incorporation is
expulsion. Yet Timon's curses all center around the confusion
of opposites and boundaries, the collapse of splitting divisions:

> To general filths
> Convert o' th' instant green virginity. . . .
> Instruction, manners, mysteries, and trades,
> Degrees, observances, customs, and laws,

> Decline to your confounding contraries,
> And let confusion live!   (4.1.6–21)

To convert everything into its opposite means to negate and destroy one term of the existing contraries; such was the original aim of Timon's love and his use of money. His hate has the same purpose of destroying difference, of denying mourning and recovery. His split ego, even in its construction of a nightmare world, is seeking still a way back to primal undifferentiated unity. . . .

Yet how is Timon to react to betrayal, ingratitude, inconstancy? In the Alcibiades sub-plot, the alternative to hatred and vengeance, which is mourning, is identified with unacceptable womanishness. The idealized chaste virtue of a good woman, one who like Cordelia suffers, yet forgives full of pity and love, does not exist in this play, and is excluded from the code the men live by, and by which they control the world. Alcibiades argues for the pity of the law to absolve a man who revenged himself according to the noble male political and civil code of honor; that is, who made good his loss by a compensatory act. Says the Senator,

> To revenge is no valor, but to bear.   (3.5.40)

> He's truly valiant that can wisely suffer
> The worst that man can breathe.   (31–32)

Alcibiades points out the contradiction of these words in one who dispenses retaliation under the words "Justice" and "War."

>   If there be
> Such valor in the bearing, what make we
> Abroad? Why then, women are more valiant
> That stay at home, if bearing carry it;
> And the ass more captain than the lion, the fellow
> Loaden with irons wiser than the judge,
> If wisdom be in suffering.   (46–52)

The Senator who calls for forbearance also stands for the law of capital retaliatory punishment: "Friend or brother/ He forfeits his own blood that spills another" (87–88). Justice in its abstract disguise as a noble civil order is at bottom bloody revenge—the *lex talionis*, the economics of exchange based on a false reduction of human value to market value, of human life to dead coin and literalism. This same law exalts murder in war as valorous; the boundaries which demarcate the acceptable place of hatred, vengeance, and murder are false and confused. The cultural sanction of retaliation leads finally only to self-devouring.

In the world of Timon, as in the world at large, the nobility which defines itself in terms of the frozen exchanges of retaliatory violence, of life for life, destroys itself in the end; the society which sanctions mercantile exchange as a model for law ends by confusing the boundaries between the pure and impure, the permissible and inviolate. Alcibiades' giving of himself in the noble, altruistic pursuit of war to destroy his society's enemies is at bottom the same kind of narcissistic love feast in which Timon devours his friends. As Timon says to him in 1.2.76, "You had rather be at a breakfast of enemies than a dinner of friends." Alcibiades: "So they were bleeding-new, my lord, there's no meat like'm/I could wish my best friend at such a feast" (78–80).

Love and war are not opposites; politics is erotic. Destruction seeks to unite with its object by devouring incorporation, to have and to be the other. One can escape only through positing the superfluous sacred value, the idealized object, above recompense, revenge, law. In Shakespeare, this idealized vision of the feminine virtues of pity and forgiveness means also a kind of sacrifice of male selfhood. When there is no acceptance of woman or what woman represents, there is also no mediation between men. The idealized value of woman as mercy and selfless love becomes the bond between men, the surplus which allows man to unite to man. In *Timon*, this surplus love is found in the faithful servant, who seeks Timon out despite his poverty and exile to serve him without price. Weeping in front of Timon, Timon can exempt him from the general hatred and curse because of the servant's tears: "What, dost thou weep? Come nearer. Then I love thee./Because thou art a woman and disclaim'st/Flinty mankind" (4.3.491–93). Yet this singular act of the one poor servant is not enough in this play. Isolated acts of forgiveness exist, but do not redeem the world from the general curse. . . .

MAURICE CHARNEY

Timon of Athens on Stage and Screen

There is no indication that *Timon* was acted during Shakespeare's lifetime; and if Shakespeare did not regard the play as finished, it is not surprising that it was not staged. The first recorded performance is of Thomas Shadwell's version, *The History of Timon of Athens, the Man-Hater*, at Dorset Garden in 1678. Thomas Betterton played Timon; new female characters, Evandra and Melissa, were played by Mrs. Betterton (Mary Sanderson) and Mrs. Shadwell (Anne Gibbs). This adaptation was extremely successful, continuing on into the late eighteenth century with minor modifications. Shadwell claimed that his play was a "Scion grafted upon Shakespeare's stock," which is flattering to Shakespeare, but *The Man-Hater* is essentially Shadwell's play modeled on *Timon of Athens* with occasional direct quotes from Shakespeare. In his dedication to the Duke of Buckingham, Shadwell says with some admiration that *The Man-Hater* "has the inimitable hand of Shakespeare in it, which never made more Masterly strokes than in this. Yet I can truly say, I have made it into a Play."

Aside from changing the names and social function of all of the Senators, Shadwell's major alteration was to introduce two women, Melissa and Evandra, who pursue Timon. Melissa is a Restoration flirt who connives with her maid Chloe for Timon's wealth and power: "I am always true/To interest and to myself." She deserts Timon in adversity, but Evandra, a faithful and true friend (like the steward Flavius in Shakespeare), offers Timon all her money. When he dies in the final scene, Evandra stabs herself and dies with him. Everything is smoothed out and refined from Shakespeare, and even Apemantus is more of a gentleman than Shakespeare's snarling character. The original production of *The*

Man-Hater in 1678 had music by Henry Purcell, which figured importantly in the performance, as well as dancing.

Shakespeare's text, heavily cut, returns with George Lamb's version presented at Drury Lane in 1816 with Edmund Kean as Timon. The cuts are chiefly those dictated by "refinement of manners." Alcibiades' whores, Phrynia and Timandra, who are not essential to the action, disappear, and so does Timon's withering sexual diatribe that shapes the last two acts. It is hard to see how Shakespeare's *Timon*, without severe distortion, could be made into a refined play. Audiences were fascinated by Edmund Kean's passionate acting, and we have Leigh Hunt's eyewitness account, but Hunt did not think that the role of Timon offered "sufficient variety and flexibility" for Kean's talents. It was an electrifying performance, but not as satisfying overall as Kean's Shylock, Hamlet, or Richard III. Hunt says that Kean as Timon often mistakes vehemence for intensity. Kean's biographer, F. W. Hawkins, affirms that his acting "throughout was deep in feeling, intense, varied, and powerful." This enabled him to make the second part of the play more fascinating than the first, a difficult feat for an actor. Hunt thought that the earlier part was presented with a stately languor rather than with the "ardent animal spirits" that Kean undoubtedly possessed.

Samuel Phelps's production in 1851 (thirty-one performances), revived in 1856 (ten performances), restored most of Shakespeare's text, with about 20 percent of the play (463 lines) cut. This is not a great deal of cutting even by modern standards. Victorian expurgation was still at work on Phrynia and Timandra, although they did appear onstage, and Timon's curses were severely modified. In the ending, Phelps tended to idealize Timon and to present Alcibiades as a redemptive, conquering hero, a tendency that is still at work in modern productions (as in that of Ron Daniels at The Other Place in Stratford in 1980). Phelps himself was a dignified actor, slow in speech and without the intensity of Kean. He played Timon as a misunderstood aristocrat, deeply hurt in adversity, and never really a hater of mankind and a committed misanthrope. The reviewer for the *Athenaeum* observed that in Phelps's performance the misanthropy seemed affected, "something alien to his disposition, the expression of which severely tasks his capacity and is but ill accomplished after all." It is difficult to conceive the play without an effective despair and hatred of mankind, but in this respect Phelps's performance seems to resemble that of Ralph Richardson's, discussed below.

I will skip the details of the many productions of *Timon* in the later nineteenth and earlier twentieth centuries and concentrate on ten productions after World War II: Tyrone Guthrie (1952), Michael Benthall (1956), Peter Coe and Michael Langham (1963), John Schlesinger (1965), Peter Brook (1974), Jonathan Miller (1981), Michael Langham (1991), Brian Kulick (1996), Michael Bogdanov (1997), and Gregory Doran (1999). There seems to be a remarkable revival of interest in *Timon* as a play for our time.

Tyrone Guthrie's *Timon* in 1952 at the Old Vic in London was a satire rather than a tragedy. With characteristic gusto, Guthrie offered us a diatribe against the absurdity of riches and materialism. There is no pity and fear in all of this, and the last two acts of the play lag, but the play was brilliantly staged by Tanya Moiseiwitsch. Guthrie "vitalised the play with his usual turbulence and comic invention," and the symbol of gold flooded our consciousness. André Morell as Timon was not an unmixed success, since critics thought he was not powerful enough to sustain the part. Roy Walker, in a review reprinted (in part) in this edition, describes him "like some devout peasant who had won a chariot-pool and set up as a one-man Athenian Arts Council, a fool and his money soon parted" (p. 344). Apemantus was memorably played by Leo McKern, who was vitriolic, proud, and spiky.

This production raises vividly the sense of *Timon* as a two-part play that needs a different sort of staging in each part. How can a director unify these two segments? Guthrie's satiric brilliance in the first part worked against him in the second, when tragic values are invoked. How can we sustain interest in the play as a whole without feeling an inevitable falling-off as Timon wallows and indulges himself in his adversity? The play does nothing to mitigate our sense of a radical split between prosperity and adversity, as if it were a moral fable. How are we, then, to deal with this difficulty onstage?

Michael Benthall's *Timon* at the Old Vic in 1956 was radically cut (about 500 lines) and rearranged. The strongly satirical elements were reduced in the part of Apemantus and the Poet and Painter, and much in the play was moralized and idealized, especially the ending. Alcibiades and his army are made to enter before Timon's very visible tomb with its prominent epitaph. At this moment, they meet the frightened, pleading senators and citizens of Athens who enter from the other side of the stage. Alcibiades orders the assault on Athens, but he is cut short when he reads Timon's epitaph, which impels him to take mercy on his native city. This sentimental, nineteenth-century ending moralizes the play and makes a mockery of Timon's monumental despair.

Ralph Richardson's playing of Timon was similarly mitigated, without the fierceness inherent in the role. Kenneth Tynan spoke mockingly of the performance as "the story of a scoutmaster betrayed by his troop," and Muriel St. Clare Byrne thought that Richardson did not believe in the last two acts, which are a meditation rather than a curse. "On his own view of life, generosity, tolerance, a sweet reasonableness, and a natural philanthropy will keep breaking in. . . ." As the London *Times* critic remarked, Richardson's Timon was "as gently intoxicated as Richard II." Critics seem to be in general agreement against Richardson's sweetening the part of Timon. As Roy Walker says about Richardson's representation of Timon in exile, the actor, in his "armless sheepskin coat and bare cross-gartered legs, was more reminiscent of Robinson Crusoe than of the naked outcast Timon." Unlike Timon, who never knew the middle of humanity, Richardson avoided the extremes of active magnanimity and active agony and chose to remain throughout the play in the middle range of emotional expression. In the second part, he replaced fury and despair with a quiet irony.

Peter Coe and Michael Langham's modern-dress *Timon* at the Stratford Shakespeare Festival in Canada in 1963 was an explosive satire on the contemporary implications of the play. *Timon* lends itself to modern-dress productions because of its emphasis on an affluent and decadent society, but there is a danger that the parallels will be pursued for their own sake. Howard Taubman, the theater critic of *The New York Times*, complained that this production called attention to its own cleverness rather than to Shakespeare. A lavish dinner party showed Timon dressed in a dinner jacket of red brocade, and Apemantus was represented as a newspaperman with a cigarette dangling from his lips and with a photographer constantly in tow. The music was composed by Duke Ellington, and a trumpeter serenaded the guests at Timon's dinner party. John Colicos played Timon and the veteran William Hutt played Alcibiades. At one point, Alcibiades fired a shot at Apemantus for annoying him. Modern dress, of course, facilitated the satirical attack on the corruption of society, but there is a problem in representing Timon's despair and misanthropy. This is hardly a matter of dress, modern or period, and this is precisely where this production broke down. If it is a morality play for our times, the wit and cleverness and the use of contemporary stereotypes of character and costume hardly contribute to the morality effect.

John Schlesinger's production of *Timon* for the Royal Shakespeare Company in 1965 starred Paul Scofield as Timon. This was a memorable performance, extending the range of Scofield's Lear for Peter Brook in 1962 and endowing the two parts of *Timon* with equal fervor. No one spoke of Scofield excelling in prosperity or adversity, and this is a measure of his power as an actor. The *Times* critic said: "His way of handling verse often suggests a man struggling to lift a heavy weight, or being carried along by its momentum; and this part gives stupendous exercise to his technique." Even more eloquently, Robert Speaight observes that in Scofield's playing of the later scenes, "the excess of his misanthropy was the measure of his growth." The tragic effects were achieved without any exaggerated satire or contemporaneity in a style reminiscent of Samuel Beckett. For the scenes in the wilderness, Timon's cave was located in a barren waste like the heath in *King Lear*, with a single gnarled tree that reminded audiences of *Waiting for Godot*. Ralph Koltai designed a striking set of tragic significance.

The most important production of *Timon* in our time is that of Peter Brook, a veteran director of the Royal Shakespeare Company, in the Bouffes du Nord Theater in Paris in 1974. This was a plush and gilt Victorian theater built in 1876, but out of use as a theater since 1950. It was abandoned in June 1952 because of a disastrous fire, but Brook in 1974 put it to use pretty much as it stood, with the stage burned out and with gaping holes and gashes in the plaster of the walls. It was located in the unfashionable 10th district near the Gare du Nord—all in all, as David Williams calls it, "a lost theater for a lost play." Brook's experience with the Bouffes du Nord was used in the Majestic Theater in Brooklyn, which he reopened for *The Mahabharata* and *The Cherry Orchard*. Pierre Schneider said of the Bouffes du Nord: "Every spectator at once knows that he is sitting inside a symbol of the decline of the West."

Timon was translated into French by Jean-Claude Carrière, in consultation with Brook and the cast. The translation simplifies and modernizes the play, making it immediately comprehensible to the audience. In producing *Timon*, Brook draws upon the collective experience of his international company, which he had assembled in 1970 at the Centre International de Recherche Théâtrale. The staging is very Brechtian: the play is given a storytelling aspect with special emphasis on the circle, as in Brecht's *The Caucasian Chalk Circle*. The costumes, designed by Michel Launay, are simple and naïve, but strikingly symbolic and vivid. Underneath and still visible, the actors wear their own clothes. The staging is intense and concentrated on a few simple points.

The young actor François Marthouret played Timon with radiance and excitement, his beautiful white suit in rags in the second part of the play. Most striking was the role of Apemantus, played by Malick Bagayogo, an African, as a choric fool of bitter cynicism. Dressed as a North African street beggar in an Army surplus overcoat and boots, he represented a Third World antitype to Timon. Alcibiades, played by Bruce Myers, was in military fancy dress like a Mediterranean general and adventurer in the style of Colonel Quadaffi of Libya. At the end of the play, Alcibiades cynically takes over the decayed society of Athens.

Jonathan Miller's version of *Timon* for the BBC-TV series in 1981 is not an impressive production, but it is widely available to students. Miller's introductory remarks are so apologetic and dismissive of the play that we are not surprised to find a fairly tepid and not clearly thought out production. I most objected to the toning down of Apemantus, played by Norman Rodway. He is now an acerbic courtier, who amuses his fellow aristocrats and rich hangers on with his witty remarks, but he is hardly a counterweight to Timon and a gruff and biting truth speaker. Timon is well played by Jonathan Pryce. At first he is naïve and idealistic, believing in some outmoded and ill-starred concept of friendship. In his adversity, he is excessively hysterical, but also very static, hardly moving from his sitting-up position in the right corner of the television screen. We feel that Timon's despair has been reduced to empty rhetoric.

The Poet, Painter, and Jeweler are rendered in a simplified, affected style, and their remarks (especially those of the Poet) fail to make a strong impression on our sense of the play. The costuming very artfully uses italianate ruffs and black doublets in the style of Veronese. It is interesting that Jonathan Miller in his introduction said that the play could be done effectively in modern dress. It's a pity that he didn't take up his own suggestion, which might have made this production more lively. One notable minor performance in this *Timon* was John Welsh's Flavius, an old man whose gravity and whose loyalty to Timon were impressive. There is a moving reunion with his master toward the end.

Michael Langham's later production of *Timon* for the Stratford Shakespeare Festival in Canada in 1991 corrected many of the mannered touches that disturbed critics of the earlier production in 1963. For this version Langham conceived the play in relation to Beckett's *Waiting for Godot* and its implications for the decline of a decadent capitalist society. As he says in the Stratford program, he sees Timon now as a man "possessed with a passionate vision." Langham uses again the jazz score composed by Duke Ellington in 1963, but now considerably expanded by Stanley Silverman. Both productions were set in Europe in the 1920s with the stock market crash of 1929 triggering the devastating Part Two of the play. The first part of the play emphasizes the decadent luxury of Timon's lifestyle. Cases of champagne are being delivered as well as a rug, a piece of modern sculpture, and a candelabra, while an enormous tapestry is being hung far upstage.

Brian Bedford was a marvelous Timon in both parts of the play. He enters in a dapper white suit that is sharply con-

trasted with the tramplike appearance of Apemantus, played
by John Franklyn-Robbins. Alcibiades, played by Juan
Chioran, is a dashing military figure looking like Castro,
who enters with what appears to be a band of terrorists. The
Masque of Amazons is presented as a lascivious, night club
entertainment, with a near-nude black woman (Ordena
Stephens), shaking her bananas in a dance inspired by
Josephine Baker.

Act 2, Scene 1 presents the stock market crash of 1929 as
a prelude to Timon's bankruptcy. Part 2 is elaborately staged
in a wartime setting, with the sound of bombers flying overhead. The small forked tree downstage with a broken branch
in its crotch forming the image of a cross has echoes of
Beckett. In the fifth act we hear the sound of bombs
exploding and see the stage fill with smoke to prepare for
Alcibiades' conquest of Athens. The staging uses cinematic
effects, including strobe lights.

Brian Kulick's production of *Timon* for the New York
Shakespeare Festival in 1996 also draws on Beckettian
alienation in a modern capitalist society foundering in greed.
The director does a lot of rewriting and repositioning to give
the play a more defined shape. The boldest reinterpretation
is of the role of Apemantus, played by Sam Tsoutsouvas. In
this production he is a sympathetic, possibly heroic character, who plays a fatherly role to Timon. Kulick softens his
satiric railing. Michael Cumpsty is a young and athletic
Timon. In the second part of the play, however, he represents Timon as infantile, crying uncontrollably and crawling
on all fours.

One of the most distinctive aspects of this production is
the set, designed by Mark Wendland. A large, steel-covered
box—forty feet long, ten feet high, and ten feet wide—is
placed on the bare stage. It has four heavy chrome doors and
looks like a giant meat locker. It is mounted on wheels and
it represents most of the locales in the play. It serves well to
emphasize the barren industrial landscape. Throughout, a
severe black-and-white imagery is used to define a corrupt
moneyed society. Alcibiades wears a white uniform covered
by a black coat as a character who mediates between the
classes. The Amazons are reduced to one woman, flamboy-

antly clad in a red satin gown with elbow-length red gloves to create a brothellike effect.

Michael Bogdanov's *Timon* for the Chicago Repertory Theater in 1997 also sets the play in a corrupt industrial-capitalist context. A good deal is done to integrate audience and actors, as if to make the audience complicit in the degraded society of the play. Before the play begins, tuxedoed waiters in the lobby offer hors d'oeuvres and men in business suits circulate with the arriving audience. The houselights remain on as the play begins. Timon, played by Larry Yando, is an elegant, authoritative figure in a white suit who resembles Jay Gatsby not only in his lavishness but also in his sense of being set apart from the sycophants he entertains. Apemantus, played by David Darlow, wheels an old bicycle and has a scruffy gray beard and ponytail. The house lights dim as he enters and a spotlight focuses on him as he begins his tirade of curses. The sound of a helicopter is used effectively. The Masque of the Amazons is performed by three strippers who are black, blond, and red and scantily clad in black lingerie and leather. Throughout the play women and gross sexuality represent the decadent values of this society. Alcibiades, played by Daniel Allar, is a huge man in a military uniform made to look like Fidel Castro.

The second part of the play, as brilliantly designed by Ralph Koltai, is a junkyard, the garbage heap of a spendthrift consumer society. Timon's cave is the burned-out shell of a car. Among the trash is an oil drum, a wrecked bicycle, a rusted trunk; a helicopter flies overhead. Timon digs in the oil drum for garbage to eat. This production emphasizes his powerful misanthropy. As David G. Brailow sums it up in his review: "Precisely because no excuses are made for Timon, because he is at the start a knowing member of a fundamentally shallow, inhumane society with which we are all too familiar, his misanthropy acquires a ferocious authority we cannot ignore."

Gregory Doran's production of *Timon* for the Royal Shakespeare Company at Stratford-upon-Avon in 1999 is much less ideological than the productions of Bogdanov and Kulick. It was the first presentation of *Timon* on the main stage at Stratford in thirty-four years. For the first half of the play, Doran uses Duke Ellington's music, originally composed for Langham's production at Stratford, Ontario, in 1963. Stephen Brimson Lewis is the designer, most notable for the colorful, flamboyant costumes, a mix of Renaissance and neo-Romantic styles. It is interesting that Doran creates a new character, Antiacus, as Alcibiades' unknown friend. This makes the court scene in 3.5 completely intelligible. The Masque of Amazons is staged in drag by men in mock war gear who are lowered onto the stage on trapezes as they shoot streamers from gold bows and arrows.

Michael Pennington plays Timon at the beginning in a witty, simpering style. Outside the walls of Athens, Timon, as Nick Walton notes in his review, "spoke his lines as if doing a vocal exercise, varying his delivery from staccato, half-spat profanation to near screeches of wild despair." In the second part, Timon from his pit onstage had an often amusing misanthropic discourse with the audience. Richard McCabe's Apemantus was dressed in a sun hat and sunglasses and carried a beach towel and suntan lotion. The wit combat between the two, by virtue of its comic absurdity, often induced laughter. The invasion of Athens by Alcibiades, played by Rupert Penry-Jones, was effectively done with planes flying overhead, red smoke, and flashing lights.

Shakespeare's *Timon of Athens* is a difficult play to stage, and it is not surprising that there should be so few successful productions of it. Of all those we have considered, only the presentations of John Schlesinger and Peter Brook seem to have aroused the full enthusiasm of critics. Margaret Webster, the American director, never mounted *Timon* herself, but her comments on the play in *Shakespeare Without Tears* are typical:

> Timon is a great operatic part; but the mind of the plain man recoils before the pitiless, raging bitterness of the play. It is surmised that Shakespeare, with all these "plays unpleasant," was going through some experience of extreme personal disillusionment and that with *Timon* he reached the breaking point. There can be very little doubt that he was in some way spiritually and intellectually rudderless when he wrote it; and this lack of mental stability deprived him of his sure dramatic sense. *Timon* is bad philosophy and bad theater, however brilliant the writing.

This was written in 1942, but since that time we have a different sense of *Timon*. The play, with its intense bitterness, disillusion, and despair, now seems more appropriate for our world, and we may look forward to more sympathetic and challenging productions in the future.

Bibliographic note: There is an excellent study of the stage history of this play by Gary Jay Williams in Rolf Soellner, *Timon of Athens: Shakespeare's Pessimistic Tragedy* (1979). A list of theater studies and reviews may be found in the bibliography by John J. Ruszkiewicz (1986), but the reader is warned that this bibliography has many errors. More specifically, the following material has been used in the preparation of this essay. On Shadwell: Hazelton Spencer, *Shakespeare Improved* (1927). On Kean: F. W. Hawkins, *The Life of Edmund Kean* (1869) and *Leigh Hunt's Dramatic Criticism 1808–1831*, ed. Lawrence H. and Carolyn W. Houtchens (1949). On Phelps: Shirley S. Allen, *Samuel Phelps and Sadler's Wells Theatre* (1971). On Guthrie: Kenneth Tynan, *Curtains* (1971) and Audrey Williamson, *Old Vic Drama 2, 1947–1957* (1957). On Benthall: Tynan, *Curtains*; Williamson, *Old Vic Drama 2*; Muriel St. Clare Byrne, "The Shakespeare Season at the Old Vic, 1956–1957 and Stratford-Upon-Avon, 1957," *Shakespeare Quarterly* 8 (1957), 461–92; and review in the London *Times*, September 6, 1956. On Langham: David E. Jones, "Shakespeare Festivals, 1963: Stratford, Ontario," *Drama Survey* 3 (1963), 301–4; Arnold Edinborough, "The Stratford Shakespearean Festival," *Shakespeare Quarterly* 14 (1963), 433–36; and review by Howard Taubman in *The New York Times,* July 31, 1963. On Schlesinger: Robert Speaight, *Shakespeare on the Stage* (1973); Robert Speaight, "Shakespeare in Britain," *Shakespeare Quarterly* 16 (1965), 313–24; and E. Martin Browne, "Theatre Abroad . . . ," *Drama Survey* 4 (1965), 272–76. On Brook: Articles by Marienstras and Banu (with many photographs) in *Les Voies de la Création Théâtrale* (1977); David Williams, " 'A Place Marked by Life': Brook at the Bouffes du Nord," *New Theatre Quarterly* 1 (1985), 39–74; Eric Shorter, " 'Timon of Paris,' " *Drama* 115 (1974), 21–27; and review by Mel

Gussow in *The New York Times*, August 10, 1973. On Langham: Royal Ward's review, *Shakespeare Bulletin* 9, 4 (1991), 28–30. On Kulick: Jane Collins' review, *Shakespeare Bulletin* 14, 4 (1996), 14, and the review of Margaret Loftus Ranald in the same issue, 15–l6. On Bogdanov: David G. Brailow's review, *Shakespeare Bulletin* 15, 3 (1997), 22–24. On Doran: reviews by Robert Smallwood in *Shakespeare Survey* 53 (2000), 249–52; by Russell Jackson in *Shakespeare Quarterly* 51 (2000), 222–23; and by Nick Walton in *Shakespeare Bulletin* 19, 1 (2001), 23–24.

Suggested References

The number of possible references is vast and grows alarmingly. (The *Shakespeare Quarterly* devotes one issue each year to a list of the previous year's work, and *Shakespeare Survey*—an annual publication—includes a substantial review of biographical, critical, and textual studies, as well as a survey of performances.) The vast bibliography is best approached through James Harner, *The World Shakespeare Bibliography on CD-Rom: 1900–Present*. The first release, in 1996, included more than 12,000 annotated items from 1990–93, plus references to several thousand book reviews, productions, films, and audio recordings. The plan is to update the publication annually, moving forward one year and backward three years. Thus, the second issue (1997), with 24,700 entries, and another 35,000 or so references to reviews, newspaper pieces, and so on, covered 1987–94.

For guidance to the immense amount that has been written, consult Larry S. Champion, *The Essential Shakespeare: An Annotated Bibliography of Major Modern Studies*, 2nd ed. (1993), which comments briefly on 1,800 publications.

Though no works are indispensable, those listed below have been found especially helpful. The arrangement is as follows:

1. Shakespeare's Times
2. Shakespeare's Life
3. Shakespeare's Theater
4. Shakespeare on Stage and Screen
5. Miscellaneous Reference Works
6. Shakespeare's Plays: General Studies
7. The Comedies
8. The Romances
9. The Tragedies
10. The Histories
11. *Titus Andronicus*
12. *Timon of Athens*

The titles in the first five sections are accompanied by brief explanatory annotations.

1. Shakespeare's Times

Andrews, John F., ed. *William Shakespeare: His World, His Work, His Influence,* 3 vols. (1985). Sixty articles, dealing not only with such subjects as "The State," "The Church," "Law," "Science, Magic, and Folklore," but also with the plays and poems themselves and Shakespeare's influence (e.g., translations, films, reputation).

Byrne, Muriel St. Clare. *Elizabethan Life in Town and Country* (8th ed., 1970). Chapters on manners, beliefs, education, etc., with illustrations.

Dollimore, John, and Alan Sinfield, eds. *Political Shakespeare: New Essays in Cultural Materialism* (1985). Essays on such topics as the subordination of women and colonialism, presented in connection with some of Shakespeare's plays.

Greenblatt, Stephen. *Representing the English Renaissance* (1988). New Historicist essays, especially on connections between political and aesthetic matters, statecraft and stagecraft.

Joseph, B. L. *Shakespeare's Eden: the Commonwealth of England 1558–1629* (1971). An account of the social, political, economic, and cultural life of England.

Kernan, Alvin. *Shakespeare, the King's Playwright: Theater in the Stuart Court 1603–1613* (1995). The social setting and the politics of the court of James I, in relation to *Hamlet, Measure for Measure, Macbeth, King Lear, Antony and Cleopatra, Coriolanus,* and *The Tempest.*

Montrose, Louis. *The Purpose of Playing: Shakespeare and the Cultural Politics of the Elizabethan Theatre* (1996). A poststructuralist view, discussing the professional theater "within the ideological and material frameworks of Elizabethan culture and society," with an extended analysis of *A Midsummer Night's Dream.*

Mullaney, Steven. *The Place of the Stage: License, Play, and Power in Renaissance England* (1988). New Historicist analysis, arguing that popular drama became a cultural institution "only by . . . taking up a place on the margins of society."

Schoenbaum, S. *Shakespeare: The Globe and the World*

(1979). A readable, abundantly illustrated introductory book on the world of the Elizabethans.

Shakespeare's England, 2 vols. (1916). A large collection of scholarly essays on a wide variety of topics, e.g., astrology, costume, gardening, horsemanship, with special attention to Shakespeare's references to these topics.

2. Shakespeare's Life

Andrews, John F., ed. *William Shakespeare: His World, His Work, His Influence,* 3 vols. (1985). See the description above.

Bentley, Gerald E. *Shakespeare: A Biographical Handbook* (1961). The facts about Shakespeare, with virtually no conjecture intermingled.

Chambers, E. K. *William Shakespeare: A Study of Facts and Problems,* 2 vols. (1930). The fullest collection of data.

Fraser, Russell. *Young Shakespeare* (1988). A highly readable account that simultaneously considers Shakespeare's life and Shakespeare's art.

— — —. *Shakespeare: The Later Years* (1992).

Schoenbaum, S. *Shakespeare's Lives* (1970). A review of the evidence and an examination of many biographies, including those of Baconians and other heretics.

— — —. *William Shakespeare: A Compact Documentary Life* (1977). An abbreviated version, in a smaller format, of the next title. The compact version reproduces some fifty documents in reduced form. A readable presentation of all that the documents tell us about Shakespeare.

— — —. *William Shakespeare: A Documentary Life* (1975). A large-format book setting forth the biography with facsimiles of more than two hundred documents, and with transcriptions and commentaries.

3. Shakespeare's Theater

Astington, John H., ed. *The Development of Shakespeare's Theater* (1992). Eight specialized essays on theatrical companies, playing spaces, and performance.

Beckerman, Bernard. *Shakespeare at the Globe, 1599–1609* (1962). On the playhouse and on Elizabethan dramaturgy, acting, and staging.

Bentley, Gerald E. *The Profession of Dramatist in Shakespeare's Time* (1971). An account of the dramatist's status in the Elizabethan period.

———. *The Profession of Player in Shakespeare's Time, 1590–1642* (1984). An account of the status of members of London companies (sharers, hired men, apprentices, managers) and a discussion of conditions when they toured.

Berry, Herbert. *Shakespeare's Playhouses* (1987). Usefully emphasizes how little we know about the construction of Elizabethan theaters.

Brown, John Russell. *Shakespeare's Plays in Performance* (1966). A speculative and practical analysis relevant to all of the plays, but with emphasis on *The Merchant of Venice*, *Richard II*, *Hamlet*, *Romeo and Juliet*, and *Twelfth Night*.

———. *William Shakespeare: Writing for Performance* (1996). A discussion aimed at helping readers to develop theatrically conscious habits of reading.

Chambers, E. K. *The Elizabethan Stage*, 4 vols. (1945). A major reference work on theaters, theatrical companies, and staging at court.

Cook, Ann Jennalie. *The Privileged Playgoers of Shakespeare's London, 1576–1642* (1981). Sees Shakespeare's audience as wealthier, more middle-class, and more intellectual than Harbage (below) does.

Dessen, Alan C. *Elizabethan Drama and the Viewer's Eye* (1977). On how certain scenes may have looked to spectators in an Elizabethan theater.

Gurr, Andrew. *Playgoing in Shakespeare's London* (1987). Something of a middle ground between Cook (above) and Harbage (below).

———. *The Shakespearean Stage, 1579–1642* (3rd ed., 1992). On the acting companies, the actors, the playhouses, the stages, and the audiences.

———, and Mariko Ichikawa. *Staging in Shakespeare's Theatres* (2000). Like Alan C. Dessen's book, cited above, a careful analysis of what the Elizabethans saw on the stage.

Harbage, Alfred. *Shakespeare's Audience* (1941). A study of the size and nature of the theatrical public, emphasizing the representativeness of its working class and middle-class audience.

Hodges, C. Walter. *The Globe Restored* (1968). A conjectural restoration, with lucid drawings.

Hosley, Richard. "The Playhouses," in *The Revels History of Drama in English*, vol. 3, general editors Clifford Leech and T. W. Craik (1975). An essay of a hundred pages on the physical aspects of the playhouses.

Howard, Jane E. "Crossdressing, the Theatre, and Gender Struggle in Early Modern England," *Shakespeare Quarterly* 39 (1988): 418–40. Judicious comments on the effects of boys playing female roles.

Orrell, John. *The Human Stage: English Theatre Design, 1567–1640* (1988). Argues that the public, private, and court playhouses are less indebted to popular structures (e.g., innyards and bear-baiting pits) than to banqueting halls and to Renaissance conceptions of Roman amphitheaters.

Slater, Ann Pasternak. *Shakespeare the Director* (1982). An analysis of theatrical effects (e.g., kissing, kneeling) in stage directions and dialogue.

Styan, J. L. *Shakespeare's Stagecraft* (1967). An introduction to Shakespeare's visual and aural stagecraft, with chapters on such topics as acting conventions, stage groupings, and speech.

Thompson, Peter. *Shakespeare's Professional Career* (1992). An examination of patronage and related theatrical conditions.

———. *Shakespeare's Theatre* (1983). A discussion of how plays were staged in Shakespeare's time.

4. Shakespeare on Stage and Screen

Bate, Jonathan, and Russell Jackson, eds. *Shakespeare: An Illustrated Stage History* (1996). Highly readable essays on stage productions from the Renaissance to the present.

Berry, Ralph. *Changing Styles in Shakespeare* (1981). Discusses productions of six plays (*Coriolanus*, *Hamlet*, *Henry V*, *Measure for Measure*, *The Tempest*, and *Twelfth Night*) on the English stage, chiefly 1950–1980.

———. *On Directing Shakespeare: Interviews with Contemporary Directors* (1989). An enlarged edition of a book first published in 1977, this version includes the seven interviews from the early 1970s and adds five interviews conducted in 1988.

Brockbank, Philip, ed. *Players of Shakespeare: Essays in Shakespearean Performance* (1985). Comments by twelve actors, reporting their experiences with roles. See also the entry for Russell Jackson (below).

Bulman, J. C., and H. R. Coursen, eds. *Shakespeare on Television* (1988). An anthology of general and theoretical essays, essays on individual productions, and shorter reviews, with a bibliography and a videography listing cassettes that may be rented.

Coursen, H. P. *Watching Shakespeare on Television* (1993). Analyses not only of TV versions but also of films and videotapes of stage presentations that are shown on television.

Davies, Anthony, and Stanley Wells, eds. *Shakespeare and the Moving Image: The Plays on Film and Television* (1994). General essays (e.g., on the comedies) as well as essays devoted entirely to *Hamlet*, *King Lear*, and *Macbeth*.

Dawson, Anthony B. *Watching Shakespeare: A Playgoer's Guide* (1988). About half of the plays are discussed, chiefly in terms of decisions that actors and directors make in putting the works onto the stage.

Dessen, Alan. *Elizabethan Stage Conventions and Modern Interpretations* (1984). On interpreting conventions such as the representation of light and darkness and stage violence (duels, battles).

Donaldson, Peter. *Shakespearean Films/Shakespearean Directors* (1990). Postmodernist analyses, drawing on Freudianism, Feminism, Deconstruction, and Queer Theory.

Jackson, Russell, and Robert Smallwood, eds. *Players of Shakespeare 2: Further Essays in Shakespearean Performance by Players with the Royal Shakespeare Company* (1988). Fourteen actors discuss their roles in productions between 1982 and 1987.

———. *Players of Shakespeare 3: Further Essays in Shakespearean Performance by Players with the Royal Shakespeare Company* (1993). Comments by thirteen performers.

Jorgens, Jack. *Shakespeare on Film* (1977). Fairly detailed studies of eighteen films, preceded by an introductory chapter addressing such issues as music, and whether to "open" the play by including scenes of landscape.

Kennedy, Dennis. *Looking at Shakespeare: A Visual History of Twentieth-Century Performance* (1993). Lucid descriptions (with 170 photographs) of European, British, and American performances.

Leiter, Samuel L. *Shakespeare Around the Globe: A Guide to Notable Postwar Revivals* (1986). For each play there are about two pages of introductory comments, then discussions (about five hundred words per production) of ten or so productions, and finally bibliographic references.

McMurty, Jo. *Shakespeare Films in the Classroom* (1994). Useful evaluations of the chief films most likely to be shown in undergraduate courses.

Rothwell, Kenneth, and Annabelle Henkin Melzer. *Shakespeare on Screen: An International Filmography and Videography* (1990). A reference guide to several hundred films and videos produced between 1899 and 1989, including spinoffs such as musicals and dance versions.

Smallwood, Robert. *Players of Shakespeare 4* (1998). Like the volumes by Brockbank and Jackson, listed above, contains remarks by contemporary performers.

Sprague, Arthur Colby. *Shakespeare and the Actors* (1944). Detailed discussions of stage business (gestures, etc.) over the years.

Willis, Susan. *The BBC Shakespeare Plays: Making the Televised Canon* (1991). A history of the series, with interviews and production diaries for some plays.

5. Miscellaneous Reference Works

Abbott, E. A. *A Shakespearean Grammar* (new edition, 1877). An examination of differences between Elizabethan and modern grammar.

Allen, Michael J. B., and Kenneth Muir, eds. *Shakespeare's Plays in Quarto* (1981). One volume containing facsimiles of the plays issued in small format before they were collected in the First Folio of 1623.

Blake, Norman. *Shakespeare's Language: An Introduction* (1983). On vocabulary, parts of speech, and word order.

Bullough, Geoffrey. *Narrative and Dramatic Sources of Shakespeare*, 8 vols. (1957–75). A collection of many of the books Shakespeare drew on, with judicious comments.

Campbell, Oscar James, and Edward G. Quinn, eds. *The Reader's Encyclopedia of Shakespeare* (1966). Old, and in some ways superseded by Michael Dobson's *Oxford Companion* (see below), but still highly valuable.

Cercignani, Fausto. *Shakespeare's Works and Elizabethan Pronunciation* (1981). Considered the best work on the topic, but remains controversial.

Champion, Larry S. *The Essential Shakespeare: An Annotated Bibliography of Major Modern Studies* (2nd ed., 1993). An invaluable guide to 1,800 writings about Shakespeare.

Dent, R. W. *Shakespeare's Proverbial Language: An Index* (1981). An index of proverbs, with an introduction concerning a form Shakespeare frequently drew on.

Dobson, Michael, ed. *The Oxford Companion to Shakespeare* (2001). Probably the single most useful reference work for information (arranged alphabetically) about Shakespeare and his works.

Greg, W. W. *The Shakespeare First Folio* (1955). A detailed yet readable history of the first collection (1623) of Shakespeare's plays.

Harner, James. *The World Shakespeare Bibliography*. See headnote to Suggested References.

Hosley, Richard. *Shakespeare's Holinshed* (1968). Valuable presentation of one of Shakespeare's major sources.

Kökeritz, Helge. *Shakespeare's Names* (1959). A guide to pronouncing some 1,800 names appearing in Shakespeare.

– – –. *Shakespeare's Pronunciation* (1953). Contains much information about puns and rhymes, but see Cercignani (above).

Muir, Kenneth. *The Sources of Shakespeare's Plays* (1978). An account of Shakespeare's use of his reading. It covers all the plays, in chronological order.

Miriam Joseph, Sister. *Shakespeare's Use of the Arts of Language* (1947). A study of Shakespeare's use of rhetorical devices, reprinted in part as *Rhetoric in Shakespeare's Time* (1962).

The Norton Facsimile: The First Folio of Shakespeare's Plays (1968). A handsome and accurate facsimile of the first collection (1623) of Shakespeare's plays, with a valuable introduction by Charlton Hinman.

Onions, C. T. *A Shakespeare Glossary*, rev. and enlarged by R. D. Eagleson (1986). Definitions of words (or senses of words) now obsolete.

Partridge, Eric. *Shakespeare's Bawdy*, rev. ed. (1955). Relatively brief dictionary of bawdy words; useful, but see Williams, below.

Shakespeare Quarterly. See headnote to Suggested References.

Shakespeare Survey. See headnote to Suggested References.

Spevack, Marvin. *The Harvard Concordance to Shakespeare* (1973). An index to Shakespeare's words.

Vickers, Brian. *Appropriating Shakespeare: Contemporary Critical Quarrels* (1993). A survey—chiefly hostile—of recent schools of criticism.

Wells, Stanley, ed. *Shakespeare: A Bibliographical Guide* (new edition, 1990). Nineteen chapters (some devoted to single plays, others devoted to groups of related plays) on recent scholarship on the life and all of the works.

Williams, Gordon. *A Dictionary of Sexual Language and Imagery in Shakespearean and Stuart Literature*, 3 vols. (1994). Extended discussions of words and passages; much fuller than Partridge, cited above.

6. Shakespeare's Plays: General Studies

Bamber, Linda. *Comic Women, Tragic Men: A Study of Gender and Genre in Shakespeare* (1982).

Barnet, Sylvan. *A Short Guide to Shakespeare* (1974).

Callaghan, Dympna, Lorraine Helms, and Jyotsna Singh. *The Weyward Sisters: Shakespeare and Feminist Politics* (1994).

Clemen, Wolfgang H. *The Development of Shakespeare's Imagery* (1951).

Cook, Ann Jennalie. *Making a Match: Courtship in Shakespeare and His Society* (1991).

Dollimore, Jonathan, and Alan Sinfield. *Political Shakespeare: New Essays in Cultural Materialism* (1985).

Dusinberre, Juliet. *Shakespeare and the Nature of Women* (1975).

Granville-Barker, Harley. *Prefaces to Shakespeare*, 2 vols. (1946–47; volume 1 contains essays on *Hamlet, King Lear, Merchant of Venice, Antony and Cleopatra,* and *Cymbeline*; volume 2 contains essays on *Othello, Coriolanus, Julius Caesar, Romeo and Juliet, Love's Labor's Lost*).

———. *More Prefaces to Shakespeare* (1974; essays on *Twelfth Night, A Midsummer Night's Dream, The Winter's Tale, Macbeth*).

Harbage, Alfred. *William Shakespeare: A Reader's Guide* (1963).

Howard, Jean E. *Shakespeare's Art of Orchestration: Stage Technique and Audience Response* (1984).

Jones, Emrys. *Scenic Form in Shakespeare* (1971).

Lenz, Carolyn Ruth Swift, Gayle Greene, and Carol Thomas Neely, eds. *The Woman's Part: Feminist Criticism of Shakespeare* (1980).

Novy, Marianne. *Love's Argument: Gender Relations in Shakespeare* (1984).

Rose, Mark. *Shakespearean Design* (1972).

Scragg, Leah. *Discovering Shakespeare's Meaning* (1994).

———. *Shakespeare's "Mouldy Tales": Recurrent Plot Motifs in Shakespearean Drama* (1992).

Traub, Valerie. *Desire and Anxiety: Circulations of Sexuality in Shakespearean Drama* (1992).

Traversi, D. A. *An Approach to Shakespeare,* 2 vols. (3rd rev. ed, 1968–69).

Vickers, Brian. *The Artistry of Shakespeare's Prose* (1968).

Wells, Stanley. *Shakespeare: A Dramatic Life* (1994).

Wright, George T. *Shakespeare's Metrical Art* (1988).

7. The Comedies

Barber, C. L. *Shakespeare's Festive Comedy* (1959; discusses *Love's Labor's Lost, A Midsummer Night's Dream, The Merchant of Venice, As You Like It, Twelfth Night*).

Barton, Anne. *The Names of Comedy* (1990).

Berry, Ralph. *Shakespeare's Comedy: Explorations in Form* (1972).

Bradbury, Malcolm, and David Palmer, eds. *Shakespearean Comedy* (1972).

Bryant, J. A., Jr. *Shakespeare and the Uses of Comedy* (1986).

Carroll, William. *The Metamorphoses of Shakespearean Comedy* (1985).

Champion, Larry S. *The Evolution of Shakespeare's Comedy* (1970).

Evans, Bertrand. *Shakespeare's Comedies* (1960).

Frye, Northrop. *Shakespearean Comedy and Romance* (1965).

Leggatt, Alexander. *Shakespeare's Comedy of Love* (1974).

Miola, Robert S. *Shakespeare and Classical Comedy: The Influence of Plautus and Terence* (1994).

Nevo, Ruth. *Comic Transformations in Shakespeare* (1980).

Ornstein, Robert. *Shakespeare's Comedies: From Roman Farce to Romantic Mystery* (1986).

Richman, David. *Laughter, Pain, and Wonder: Shakespeare's Comedies and the Audience in the Theater* (1990).

Salingar, Leo. *Shakespeare and the Traditions of Comedy* (1974).

Slights, Camille Wells. *Shakespeare's Comic Commonwealths* (1993).

Waller, Gary, ed. *Shakespeare's Comedies* (1991).

Westlund, Joseph. *Shakespeare's Reparative Comedies: A Psychoanalytic View of the Middle Plays* (1984).

Williamson, Marilyn. *The Patriarchy of Shakespeare's Comedies* (1986).

8. The Romances (*Pericles, Cymbeline, The Winter's Tale, The Tempest, The Two Noble Kinsmen*)

Adams, Robert M. *Shakespeare: The Four Romances* (1989).

Felperin, Howard. *Shakespearean Romance* (1972).

Frye, Northrop. *A Natural Perspective: The Development of Shakespearean Comedy and Romance* (1965).

Mowat, Barbara. *The Dramaturgy of Shakespeare's Romances* (1976).

Warren, Roger. *Staging Shakespeare's Late Plays* (1990).

Young, David. *The Heart's Forest: A Study of Shakespeare's Pastoral Plays* (1972).

9. The Tragedies

Bradley, A. C. *Shakespearean Tragedy* (1904).

Brooke, Nicholas. *Shakespeare's Early Tragedies* (1968).

Champion, Larry S. *Shakespeare's Tragic Perspective* (1976).

Drakakis, John, ed. *Shakespearean Tragedy* (1992).

Evans, Bertrand. *Shakespeare's Tragic Practice* (1979).

Everett, Barbara. *Young Hamlet: Essays on Shakespeare's Tragedies* (1989).

Foakes, R. A. *Hamlet versus Lear: Cultural Politics and Shakespeare's Art* (1993).

Frye, Northrop. *Fools of Time: Studies in Shakespearean Tragedy* (1967).

Harbage, Alfred, ed. *Shakespeare: The Tragedies* (1964).

Mack, Maynard. *Everybody's Shakespeare: Reflections Chiefly on the Tragedies* (1993).

McAlindon, T. *Shakespeare's Tragic Cosmos* (1991).

Miola, Robert S. *Shakespeare and Classical Tragedy: The Influence of Seneca* (1992).

———. *Shakespeare's Rome* (1983).

Nevo, Ruth. *Tragic Form in Shakespeare* (1972).

Rackin, Phyllis. *Shakespeare's Tragedies* (1978).

Rose, Mark, ed. *Shakespeare's Early Tragedies: A Collection of Critical Essays* (1995).

Rosen, William. *Shakespeare and the Craft of Tragedy* (1960).

Snyder, Susan. *The Comic Matrix of Shakespeare's Tragedies* (1979).

Wofford, Susanne. *Shakespeare's Late Tragedies: A Collection of Critical Essays* (1996).

Young, David. *The Action to the Word: Structure and Style in Shakespearean Tragedy* (1990).

———. *Shakespeare's Middle Tragedies: A Collection of Critical Essays* (1993).

10. The Histories

Blanpied, John W. *Time and the Artist in Shakespeare's English Histories* (1983).

Campbell, Lily B. *Shakespeare's "Histories": Mirrors of Elizabethan Policy* (1947).

Champion, Larry S. *Perspective in Shakespeare's English Histories* (1980).

Hodgdon, Barbara. *The End Crowns All: Closure and Contradiction in Shakespeare's History* (1991).

Holderness, Graham. *Shakespeare Recycled: The Making of Historical Drama* (1992).

———, ed. *Shakespeare's History Plays: "Richard II" to "Henry V"* (1992).

Leggatt, Alexander. *Shakespeare's Political Drama: The History Plays and the Roman Plays* (1988).

Levine, Nina S. *Women's Matters: Politics, Gender, and Nation in Shakespeare's Early History Plays* (1998).

Ornstein, Robert. *A Kingdom for a Stage: The Achievement of Shakespeare's History Plays* (1972).

Rackin, Phyllis. *Stages of History: Shakespeare's English Chronicles* (1990).

Saccio, Peter. *Shakespeare's English Kings* (2nd ed., 1999).

Spiekerman, Tim. *Shakespeare's Political Realism* (2001).

Tillyard, E.M.W. *Shakespeare's History Plays* (1944).

Velz, John W., ed. *Shakespeare's English Histories: A Quest for Form and Genre* (1996).

11. *Titus Andronicus*

Especially useful recent editions of *Titus Andronicus* have been prepared by Eugene M. Waith (1984), Alan Hughes (1994), and Jonathan Bate (1995).

For readings concerned with stage and television productions, see the Bibliographic Note above, following *Titus Andronicus* on Stage and Screen, and see the material, also above, in Section 4 (Shakespeare on Stage and Screen) of this list of Suggested References.

For the play in the context of Shakespeare's other tragedies, see above, Section 9.

For a collection of essays on the play, including many reviews of productions, see the title below by Philip C. Kolin. Many important essays, on all aspects of the play, are reprinted in volumes 4, 17, 27, 43, 62, and 73 of *Shakespearean Criticism*.

Barker, Francis. *The Culture of Violence* (1993).
Bartels, Emily C. "Making More of the Moor: Aaron, Othello, and Renaissance Refashionings of Race." *Shakespeare Quarterly* 41 (1990): 433–54.
Charney, Maurice. *Harvester New Critical Introductions to Shakespeare: Titus Andronicus* (1990).
Hamilton, A. C. "*Titus Andronicus:* The Form of Shakespearian Tragedy." *Shakespeare Quarterly* 14 (1963): 201–13.
Hunter, G. K. "Sources and Meanings in *Titus Andronicus*." In *The Mirror up to Nature*, ed. J. C. Gray (1983).
Kolin, Philip C., ed. Titus Andronicus: *Critical Essays* (1995).
Liebler, Naomi Conn. *Shakespeare's Festive Tragedy: The Ritual Foundations of Genre* (1995).
Metz, G. Harold. *Shakespeare's Earliest Tragedy: Studies in Titus Andronicus* (1996).
Miola, Robert S. *Shakespeare's Rome* (1983).
Neill, Michael. *Issues of Death: Mortality and Identity in English Renaissance Tragedy* (1997).
Rudd, Niall. "*Titus Andronicus:* The Classical Presence." *Shakespeare Quarterly* 55 (2002): 199–208.
Spivack, Bernard. *Shakespeare and the Allegory of Evil* (1958).
Vickers, Brian. *Shakespeare as Co-Author: A Historical Study of Five Collaborative Plays* (2002).

12. *Timon of Athens*

For readings concerned with stage and television productions, see the Bibliographic Note above, following *Timon of Athens* on Stage and Screen, and see the material, also above, in Section 4 (Shakespeare on Stage and Screen) of this list of Suggested References.

For the play in the context of Shakespeare's other tragedies, see above, Section 9.

Bradbrook, M. C. *Shakespeare the Craftsman* (1969).
Brill, Lesley W. "Truth and *Timon of Athens*." *Modern Language Quarterly* 40 (1979): 17–36.
Butler, Francelia. *The Strange Critical Fortunes of Shakespeare's "Timon of Athens"* (1966).
Campbell, Oscar James. *Shakespeare's Satire* (1963).
Collins, A. S. "*Timon of Athens:* A Reconsideration." *Review of English Studies* 22 (1946): 96–108.
Ellis-Fermor, Una. "*Timon of Athens*: An Unfinished Play." *Review of English Studies* 18 (1942): 270–83. Reprinted in her *Shakespeare the Dramatist,* ed. Kenneth Muir (1961).
Empson, William. *The Structure of Complex Words* (1951).
Farnham, Willard. *Shakespeare's Tragic Frontier* (1950).
Hazlitt, William. *Liber Amoris and Dramatic Criticisms* (1948). *The Characters of Shakespear's Plays* (1817).
Honigmann, E.A.J. "*Timon of Athens*." *Shakespeare Quarterly* 12 (1961): 3–20.
Jackson, Ken. " 'One Wish' or the Possibility of the Impossible: Derrida, the Gift, and God in *Timon of Athens*." *Shakespeare Quarterly* 52 (2001) 34–66.
Kahn, Coppélia. " 'Magic of bounty': *Timon of Athens,* Jacobean Patronage, and Maternal Power." *Shakespeare Quarterly* 38 (1987): 34–57.
Klein, Karl, ed. *Timon of Athens* (2001).
Knight, G. Wilson. *The Wheel of Fire* (1930).
Nuttall, A. D. *Timon of Athens* (1989).
Oliver, H. J., ed. *Timon of Athens* (1959).
Ruszkiewicz, John J. *"Timon of Athens": An Annotated Bibliography* (1986).
Slights, William W. E. "*Genera mixta* and *Timon of Athens*." *Studies in Philology* 74 (1977): 39–62.
Soellner, Rolf. *"Timon of Athens": Shakespeare's Pessimistic Tragedy* (1979). With a stage history by Gary Jay Williams.
Spencer, Terence. "Shakespeare Learns the Value of Money: The Dramatist at Work on *Timon of Athens*." *Shakespeare Survey* 6 (1953): 75–78.

Tambling, Jeremy. "Hating Man in *Timon of Athens*." *Essays in Criticism* 50 (2000): 145–68.

Williams, Stanley T. "Some Versions of *Timon of Athens* on the Stage." *Modern Philology* 18 (1920): 269–85.